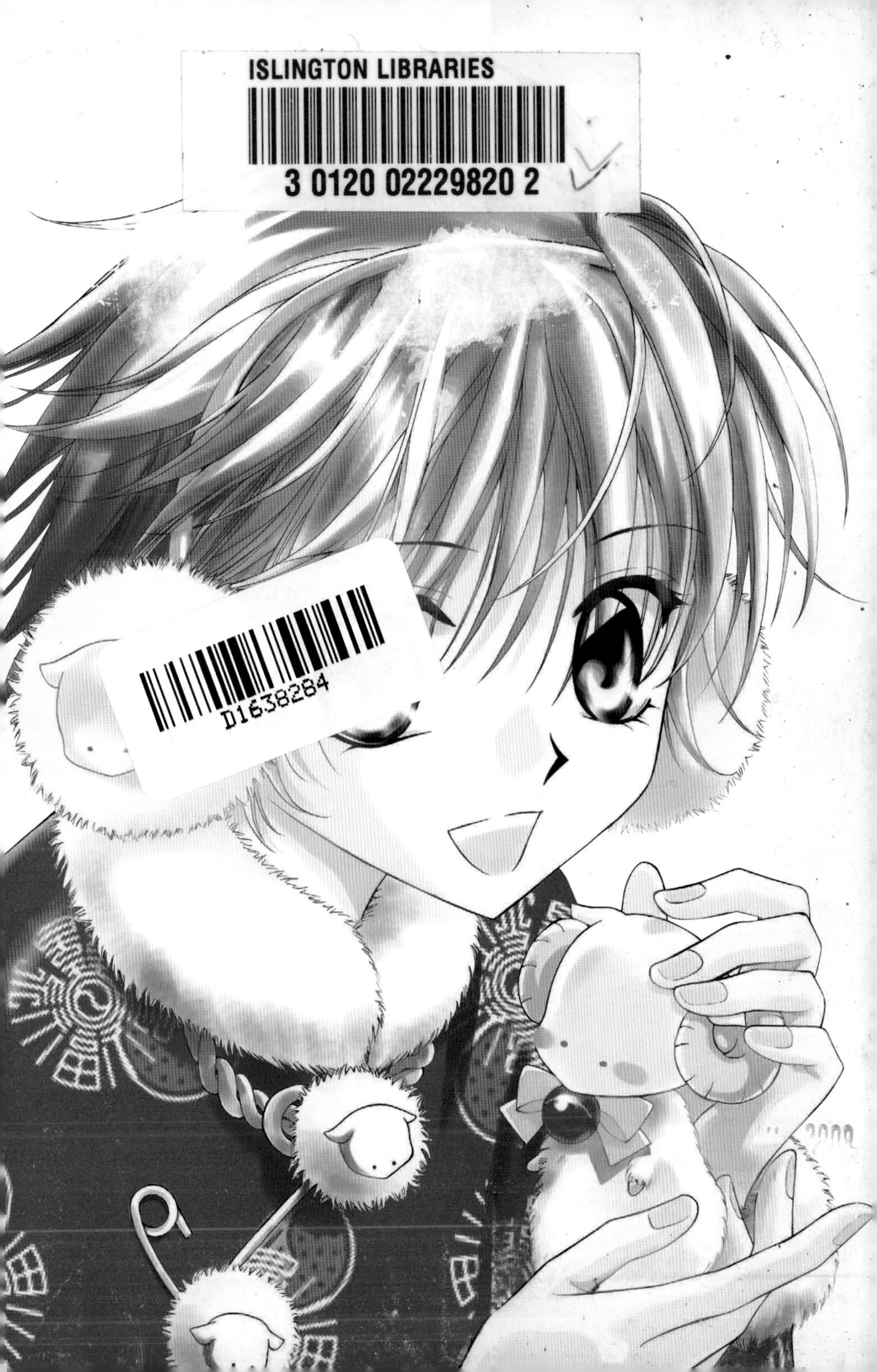

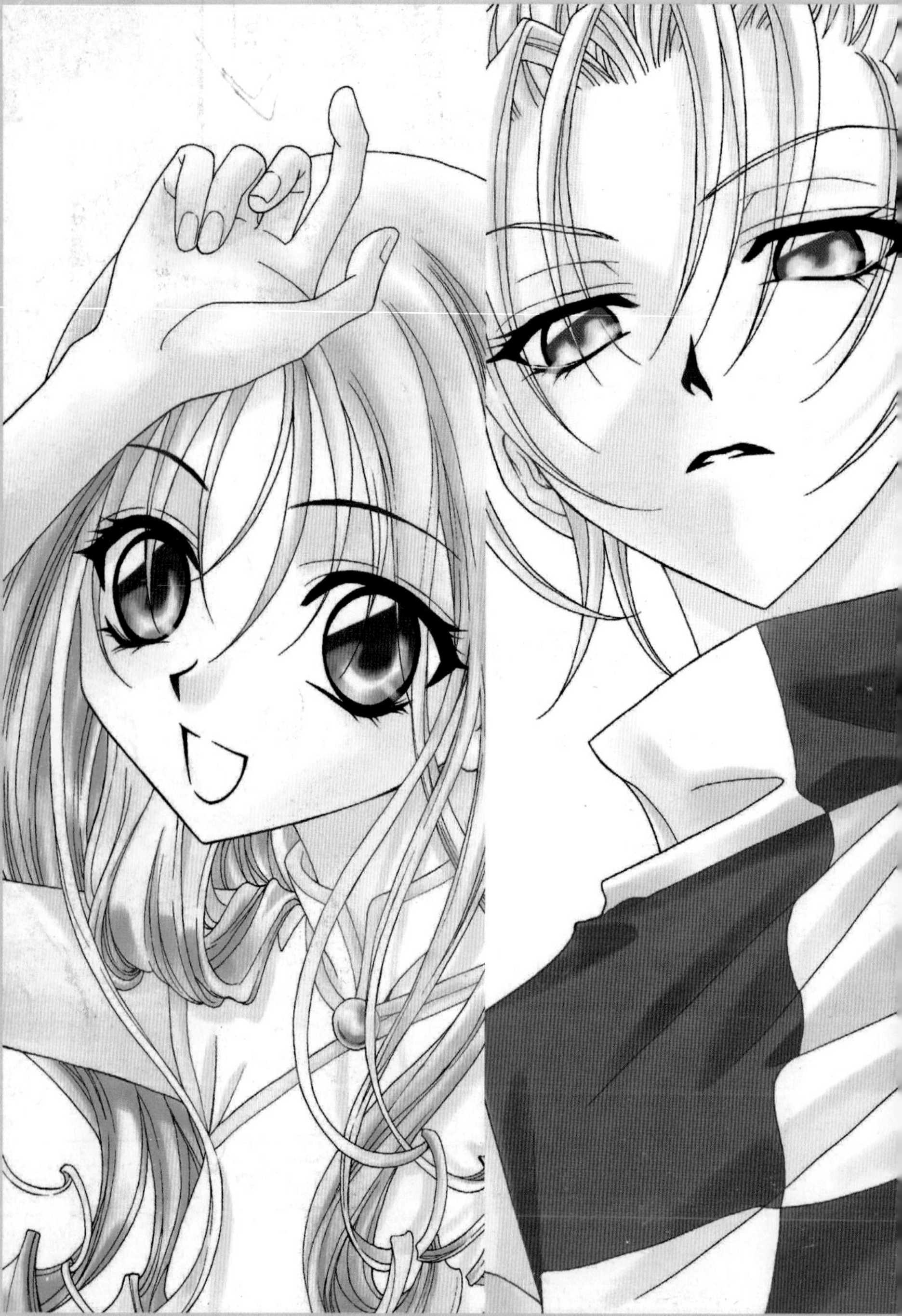

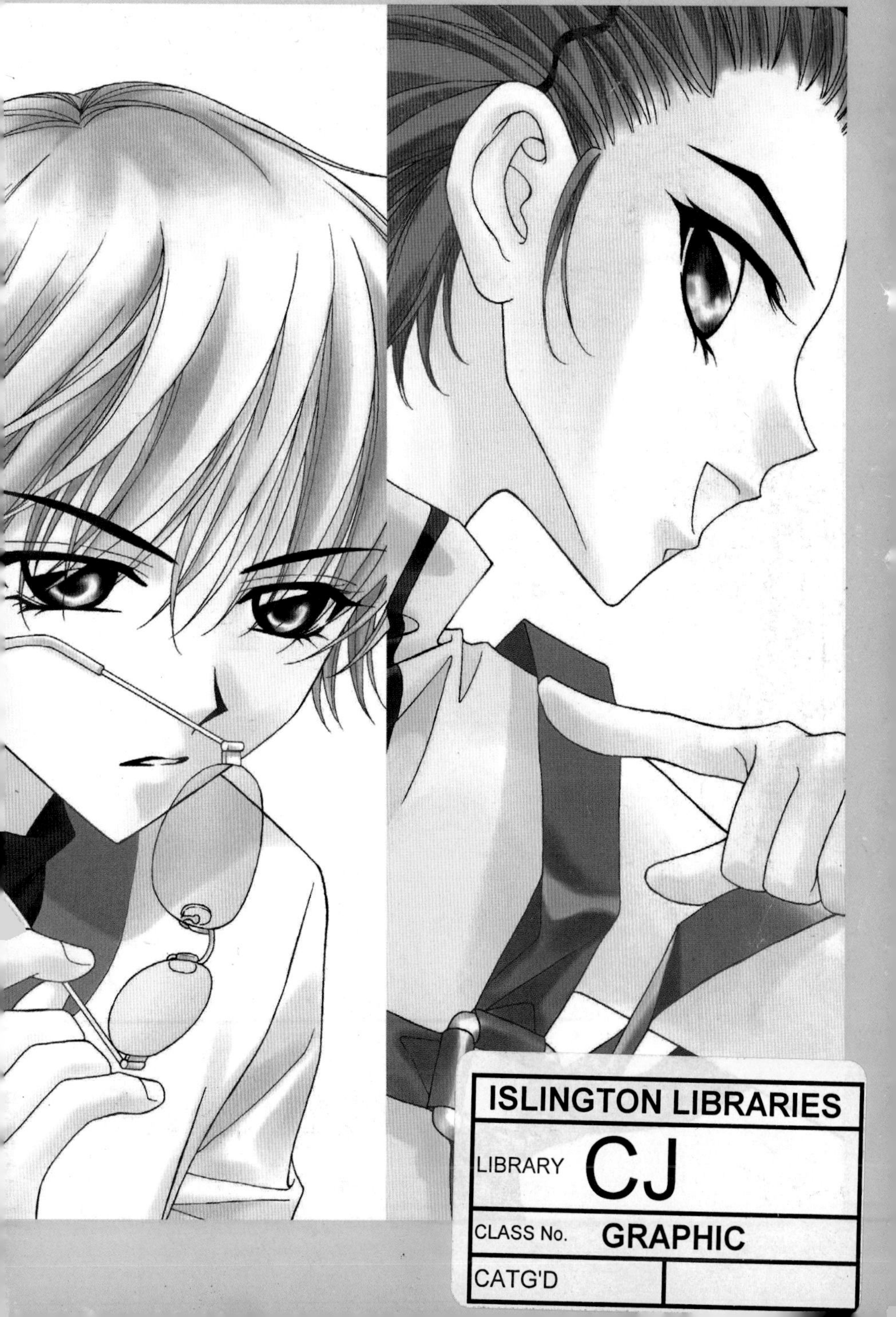

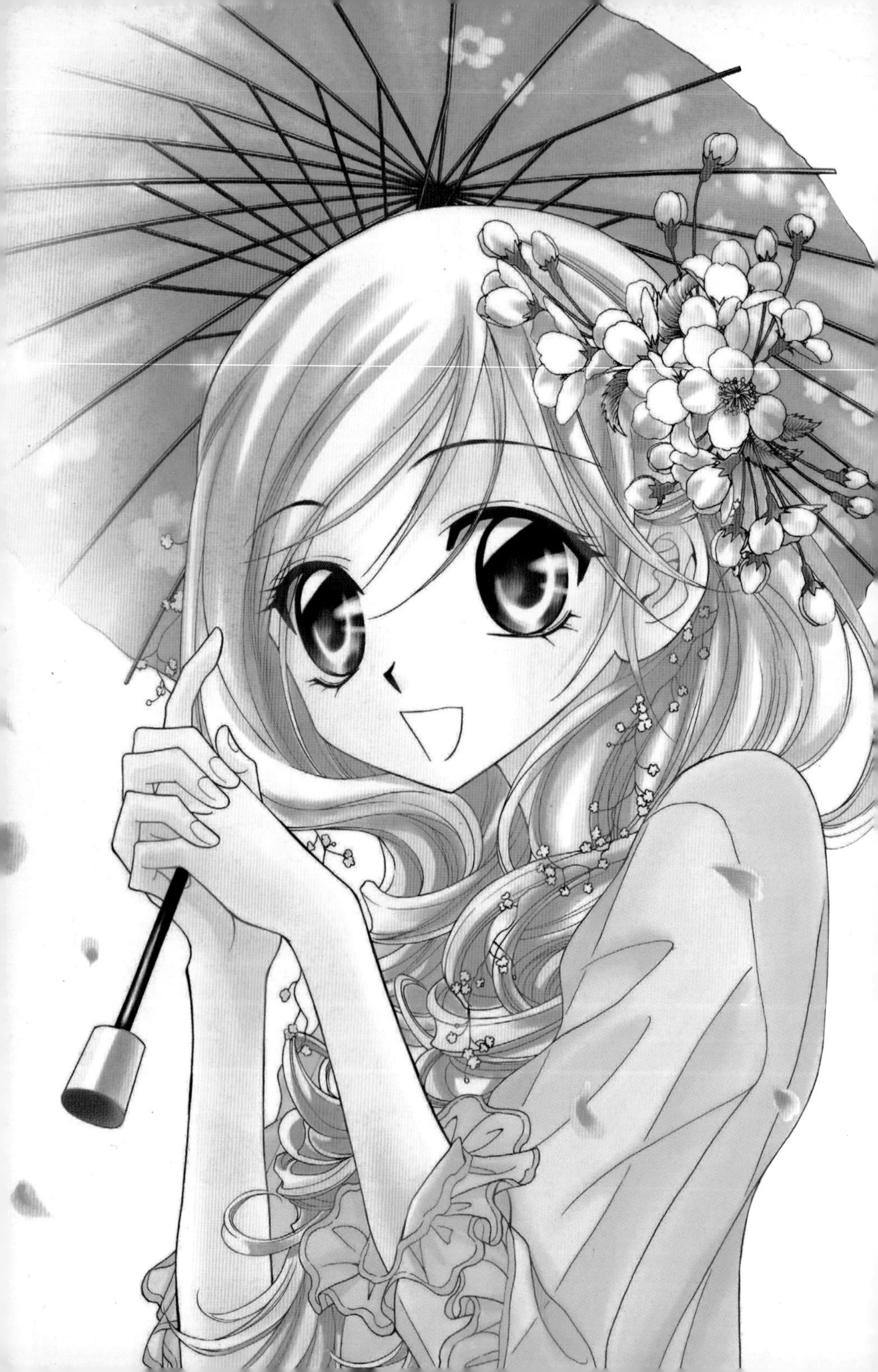

al · Danbi Original · Danbi Original · Danbi Original · Danbi Original · Danbi Original · D

Angel Diary

vol.3

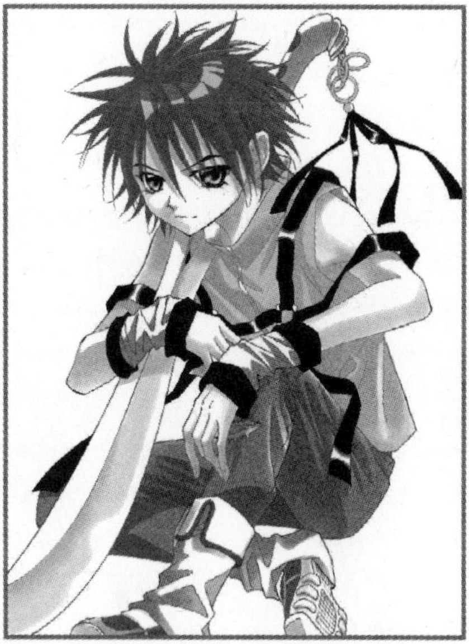

Kara · Lee YunHee

ice Kunion

WORDS FROM THE CREATORS

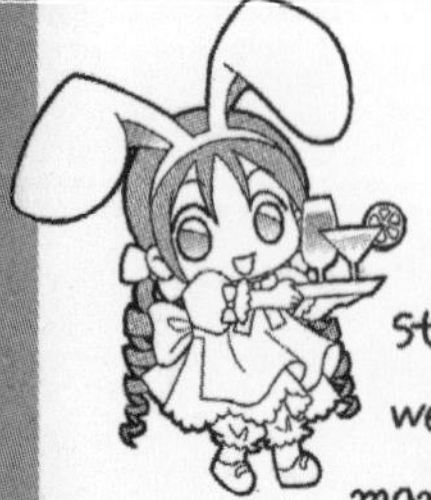

Even when 〈Devil Diary〉 started appearing in book stores and comic book rental places, we still felt like we had yet to accomplish what had been done by the manhwa creators we respected and wanted to emulate. We still don't feel like we're in the same league. Our dreams of becoming manhwa creators turned out to be 100% delusion; and we discovered that working on a title is 10% creativity and 90% hard work. 〈Angel Diary〉 started in the first issue of Bijou magazine. A month passes, then a couple of deadlines, followed by 3-4 more months to complete a book, and next thing you know a few years later and the whole series is completed. Before long several decades shall pass and a few manhwa series are under your belt. Here's hoping those books are republished to be read again and again over time. Be happy, dear readers!

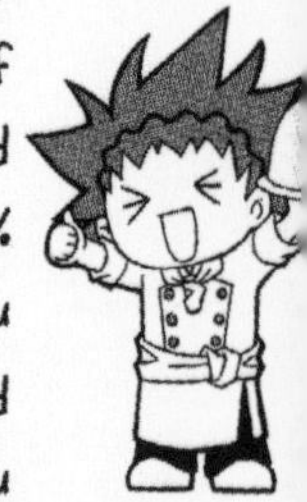

-Kara (Artists)

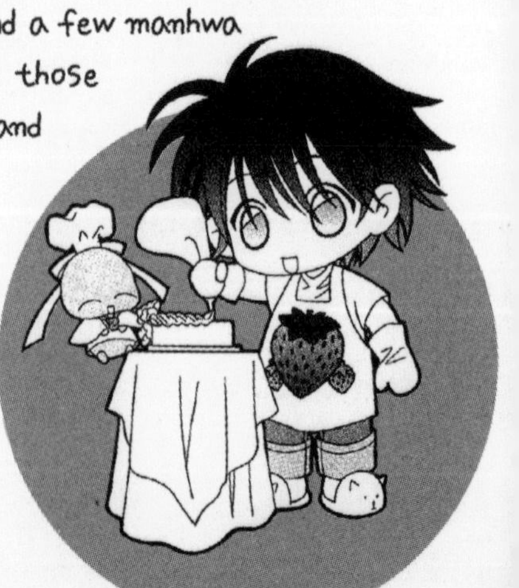

Volume 3 is here. I love the number 3. Number 2 feels short, number 4 feels unlucky and number 5 feels like too much. Number 3 feels stable and likable.

-Yun-Hee Lee(Writer)

Q&A

with Kara and Yun-Hee Lee
Pretty-Pretty-Pretty Boys!

❓ Can you describe your ideal pretty boy*?

Kara Pretty boy... should be average height and on the thin side, and has to have warm eyes. And the main point is that he should be in-between a boy and a man! Basically, he's young and not quite mature yet, but built more like a man than a boy! But the most important thing is that he must be pretty! (This is the rule of thumb!) Mind you, a man is not a man until he's in 30s... Right? (Whack!)

Yun-Hee Lee Height... he should at least be 180 cm on the average... and he should have smooth skin and white teeth when he smiles. His legs should be long and not bow-legged. As an added feature, he should have a beautiful behind (this is very important.) And he has to have a sweet voice... Gulp!

❓ What would you do if you could spend 24 hours with a pretty boy?

Kara If I could spend time with a pretty boy, I wouldn't need to do anything. I'd just sit beside him (but not too close) and enjoy the beauty(?).

Yun-Hee Lee Bwa-ha-ha-ha...

*Editor's note: "Pretty Boy" (or "Kot-Mi-Nam" in Korean) is the term used to describe a certain type of young male actor or singer with delicate, slight, and sometimes feminine features.

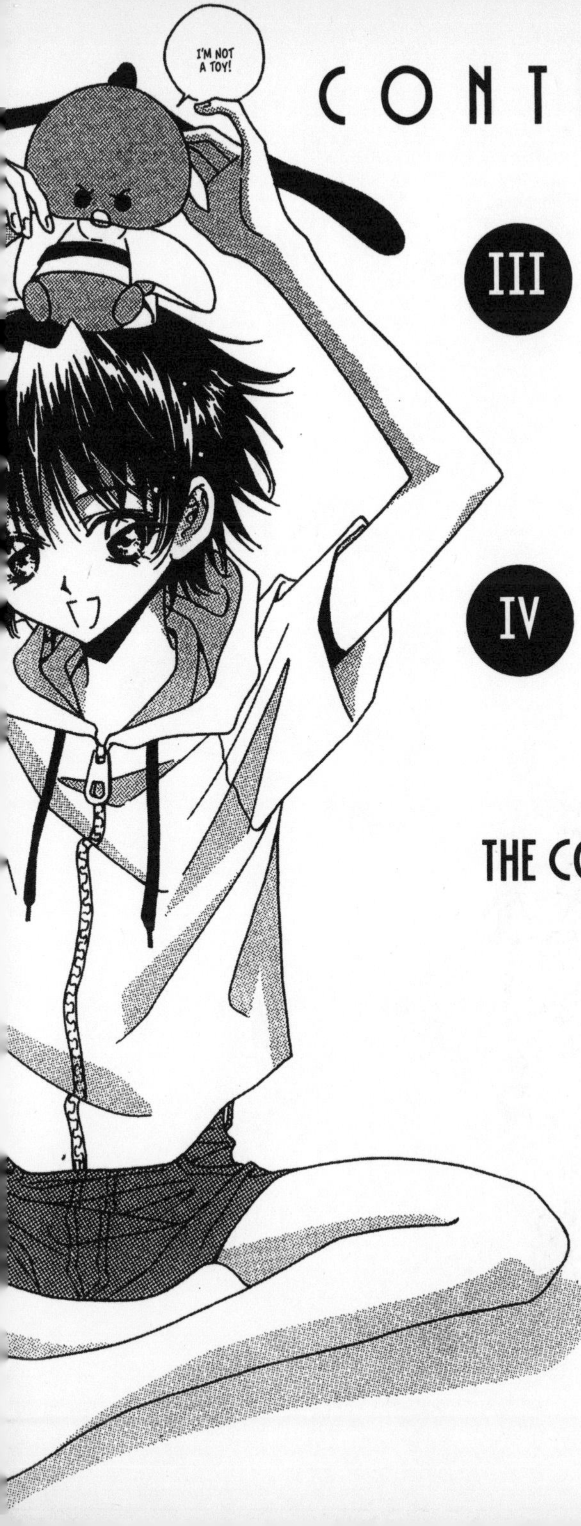
I'M NOT A TOY!

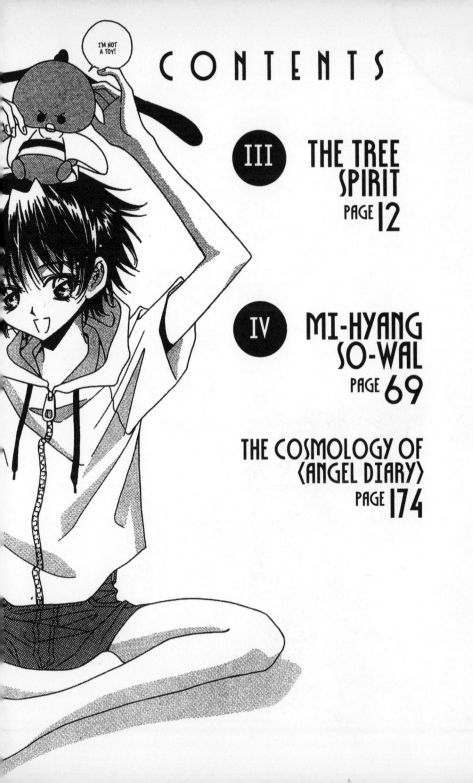

CONTENTS

III THE TREE SPIRIT

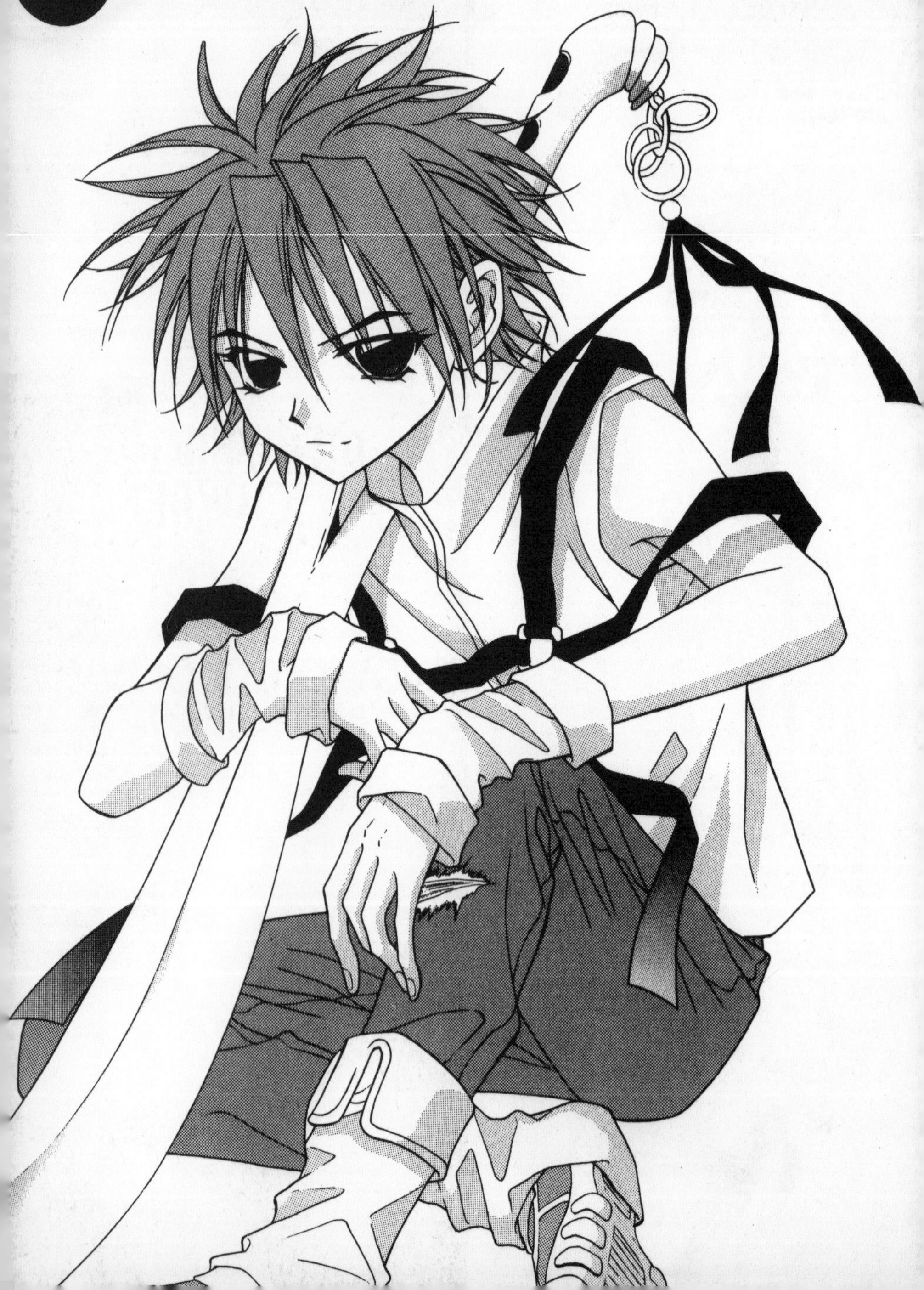

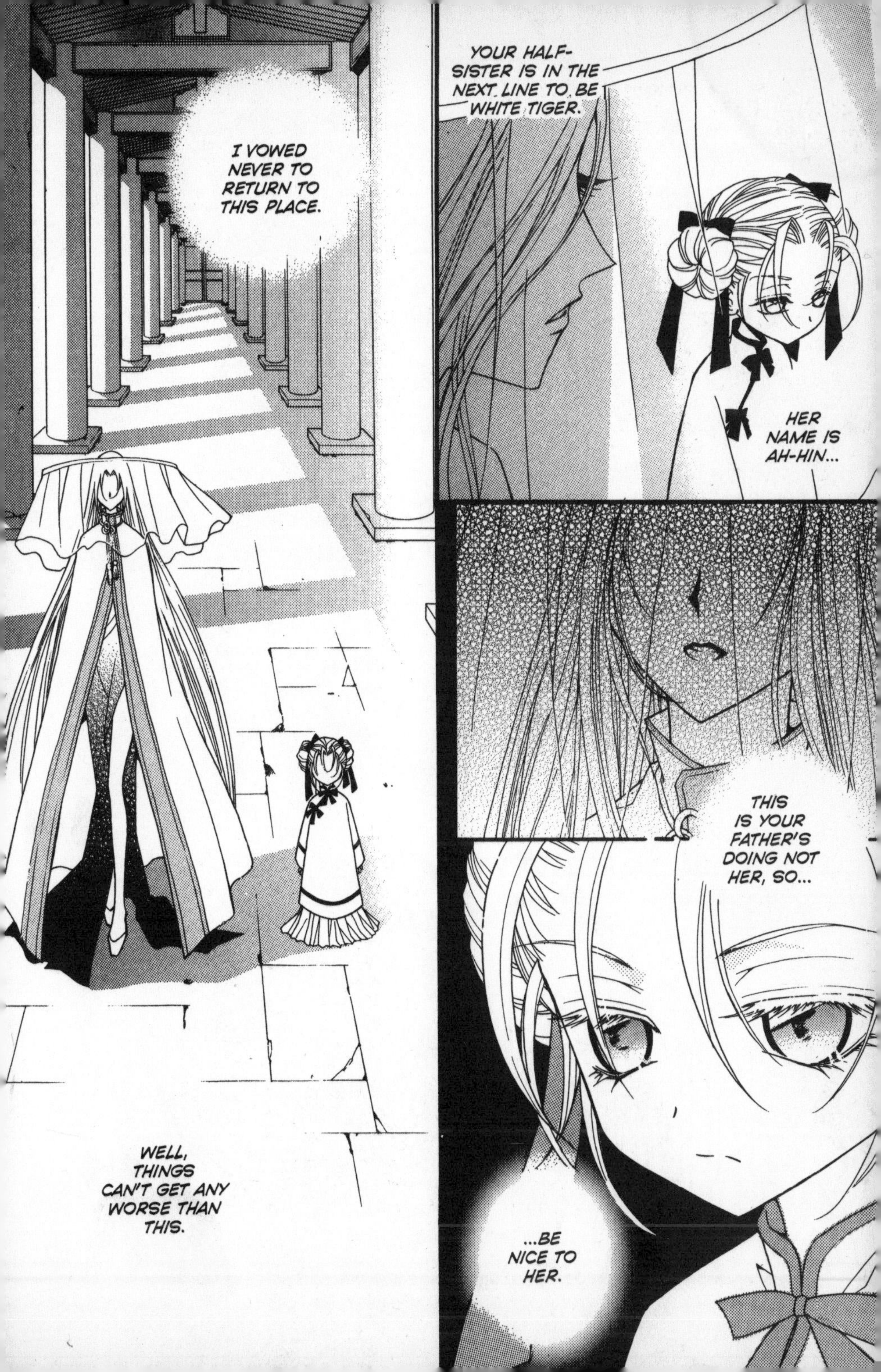
I VOWED NEVER TO RETURN TO THIS PLACE.
WELL, THINGS CAN'T GET ANY WORSE THAN THIS.
YOUR HALF-SISTER IS IN THE NEXT LINE TO BE WHITE TIGER.
HER NAME IS AH-HIN...
THIS IS YOUR FATHER'S DOING NOT HER, SO...
...BE NICE TO HER.

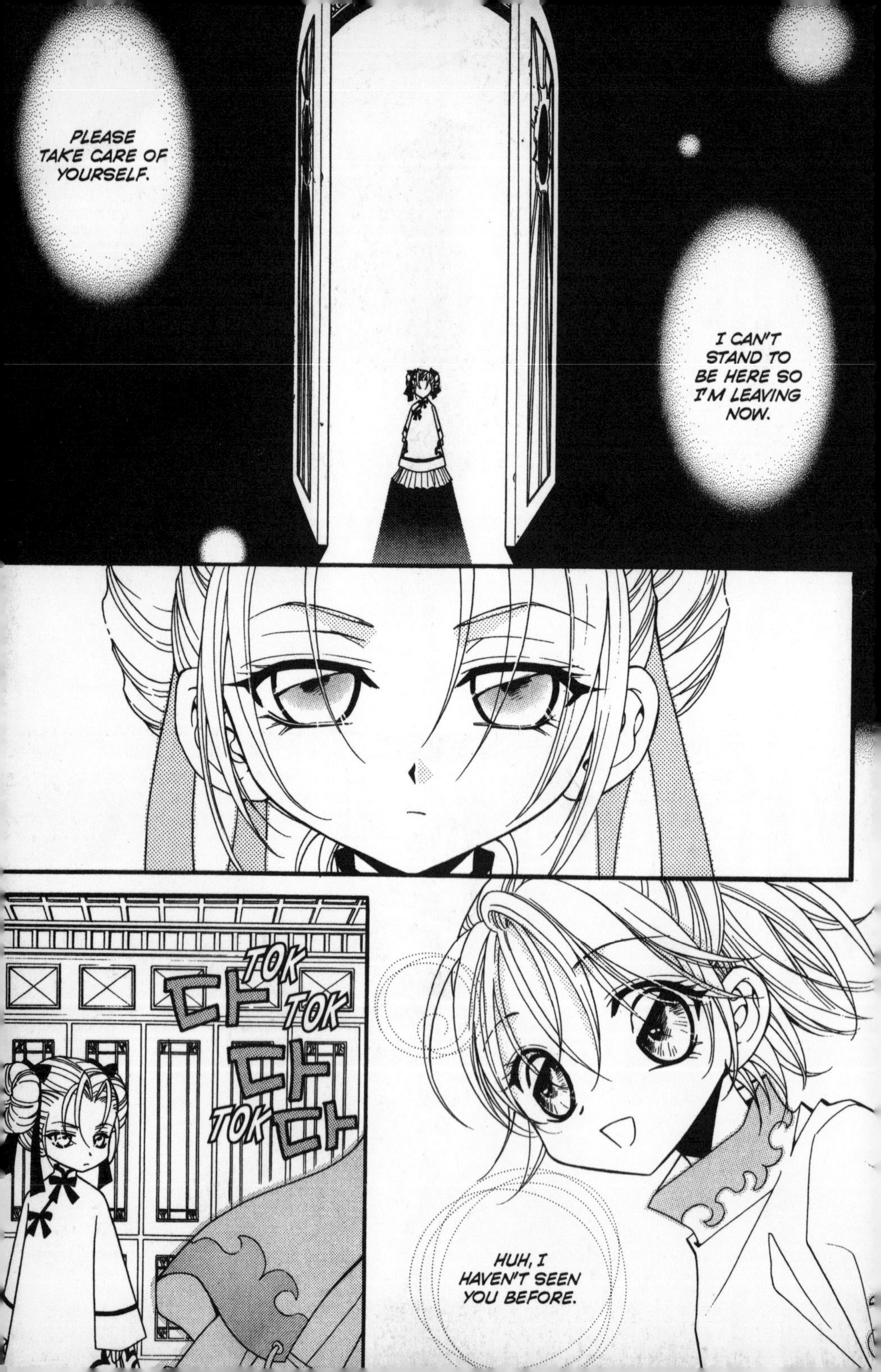
PLEASE TAKE CARE OF YOURSELF.
I CAN'T STAND TO BE HERE SO I'M LEAVING NOW.
다 TOK
다 TOK
다 TOK
HUH, I HAVEN'T SEEN YOU BEFORE.

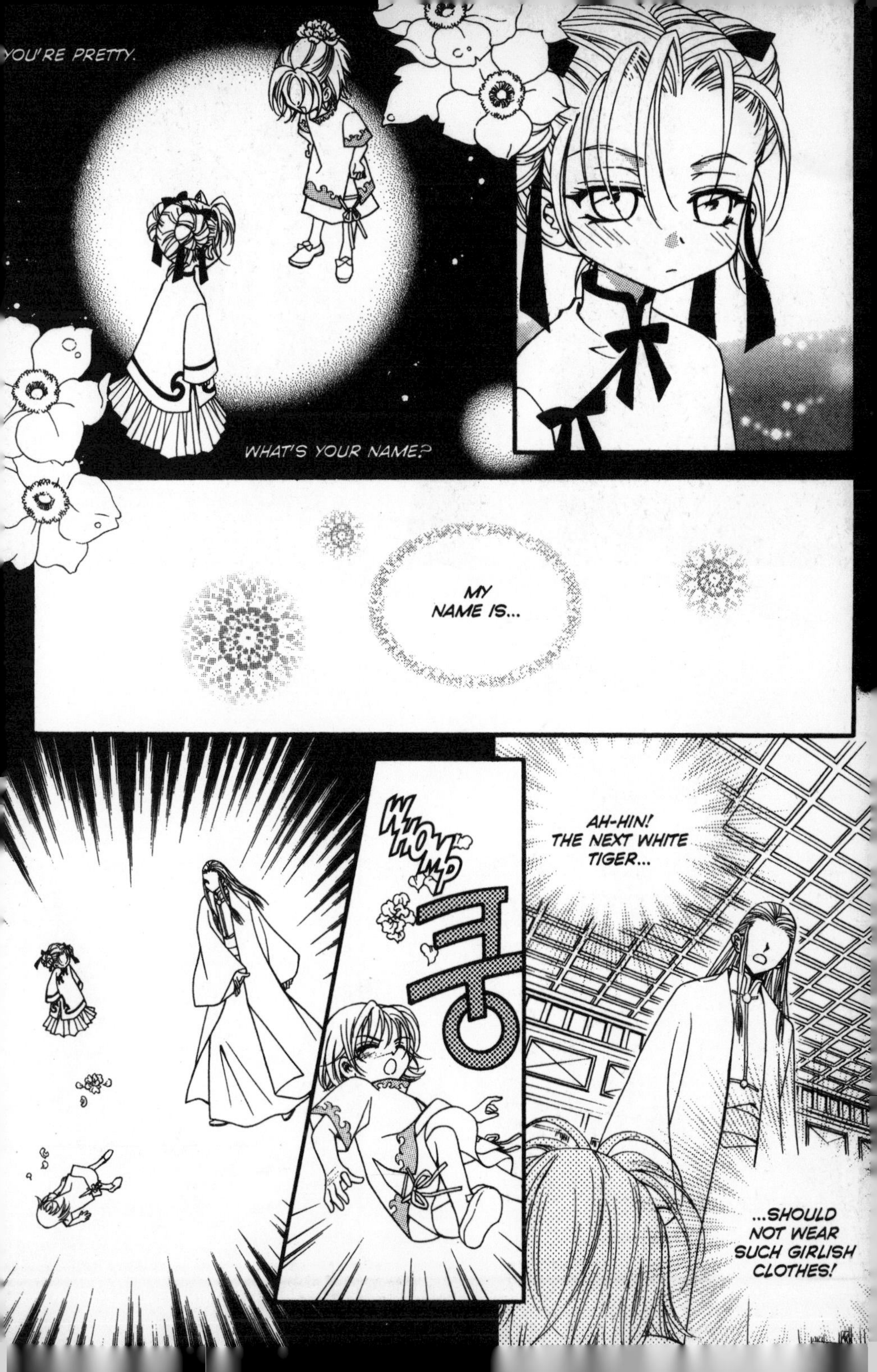
YOU'RE PRETTY.
WHAT'S YOUR NAME?
MY NAME IS...
WHOMP
AH-HIN! THE NEXT WHITE TIGER...
...SHOULD NOT WEAR SUCH GIRLISH CLOTHES!

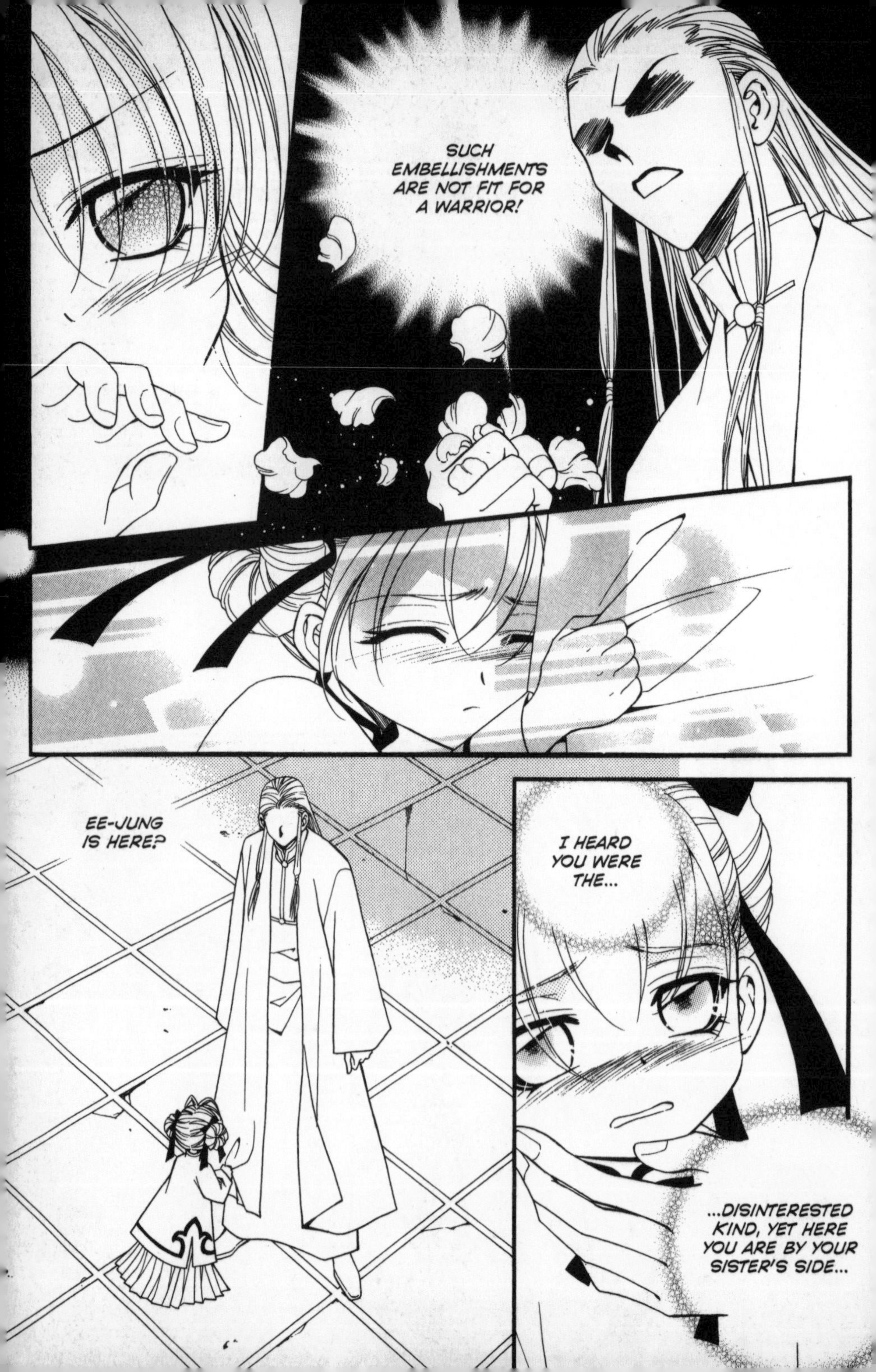
SUCH EMBELLISHMENTS ARE NOT FIT FOR A WARRIOR!
EE-JUNG IS HERE?
I HEARD YOU WERE THE...
...DISINTERESTED KIND, YET HERE YOU ARE BY YOUR SISTER'S SIDE...

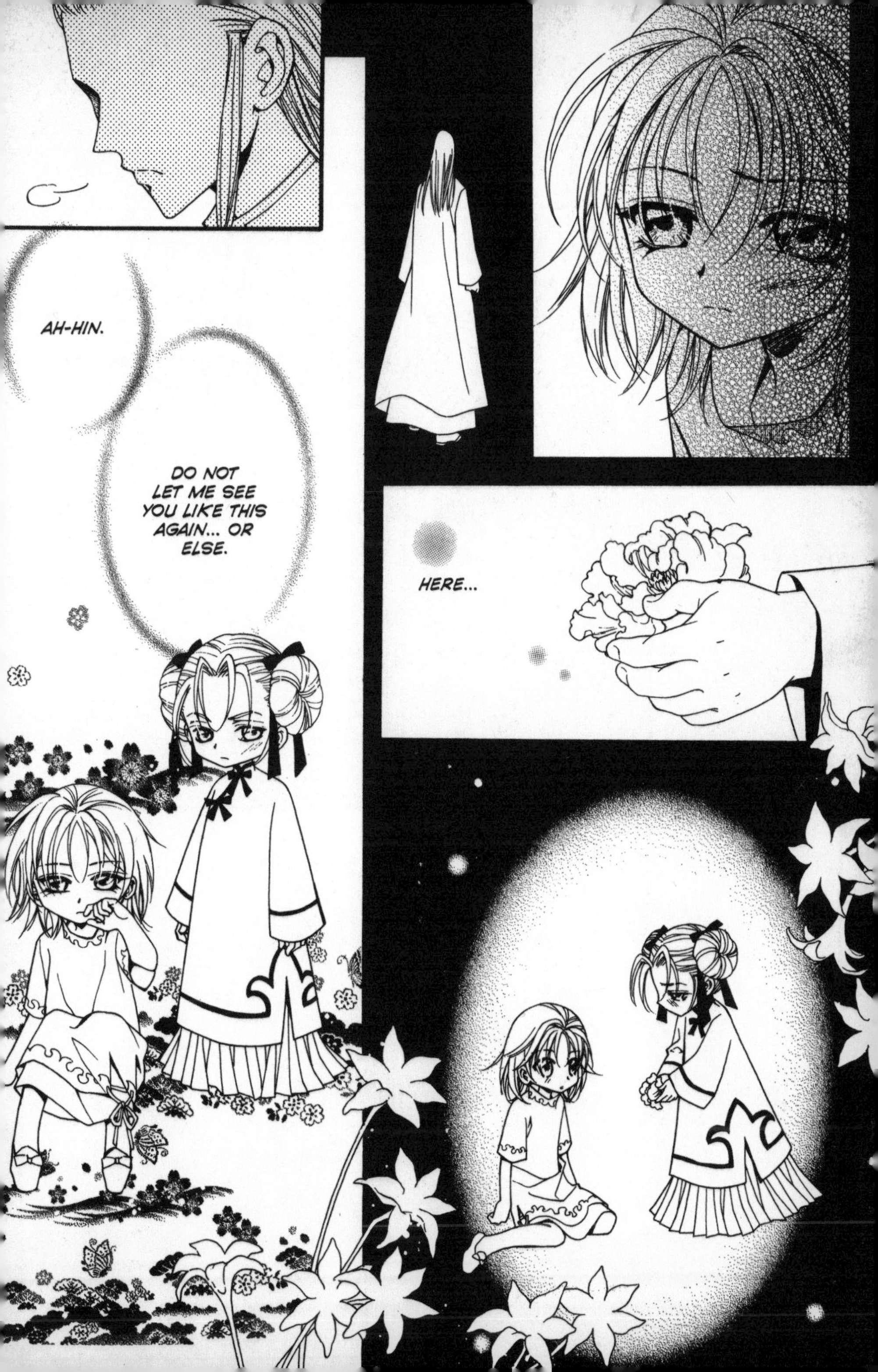
AH-HIN.
DO NOT LET ME SEE YOU LIKE THIS AGAIN... OR ELSE.
HERE...

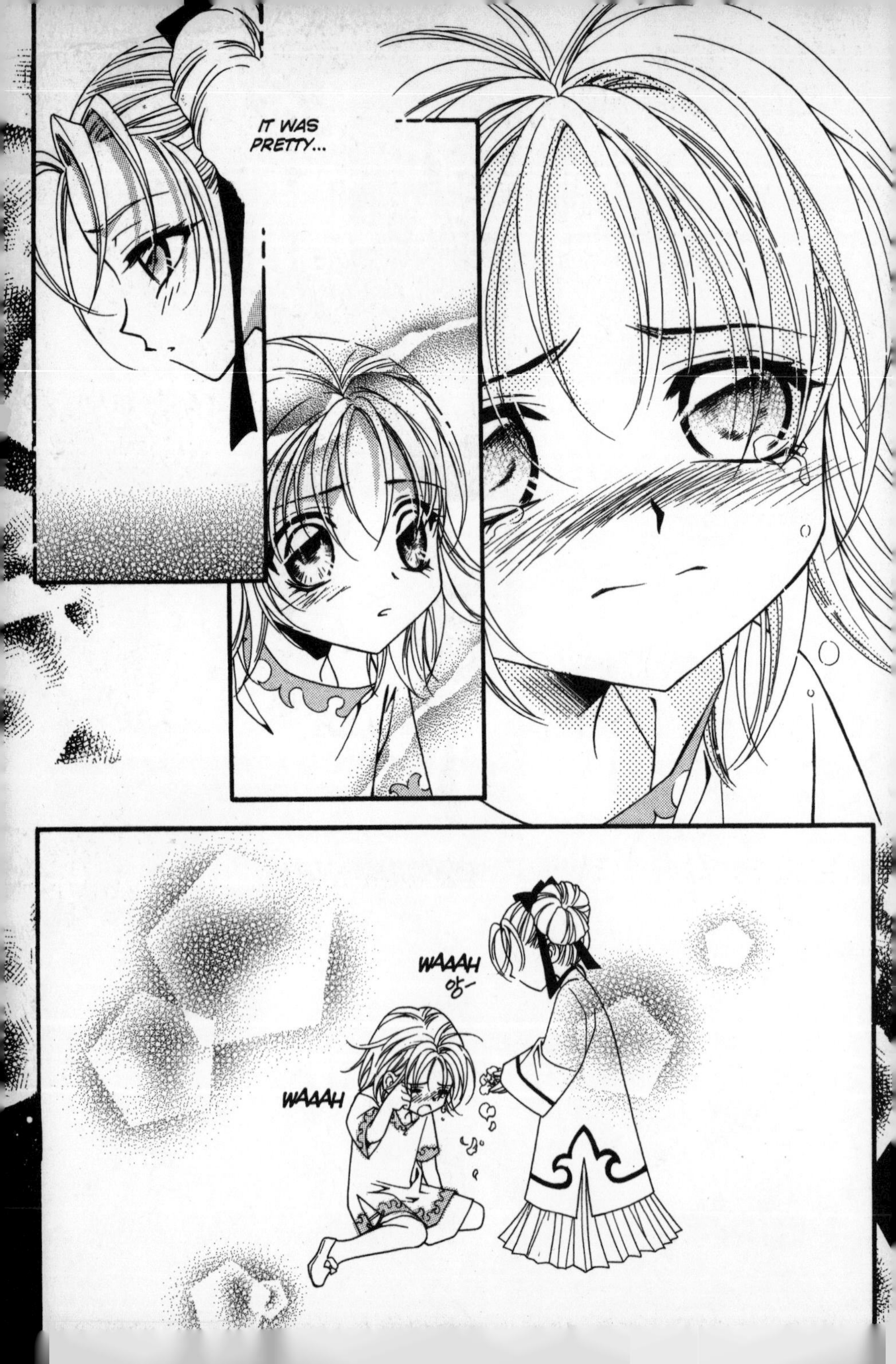
IT WAS PRETTY...
WAAAH
앙-
WAAAH

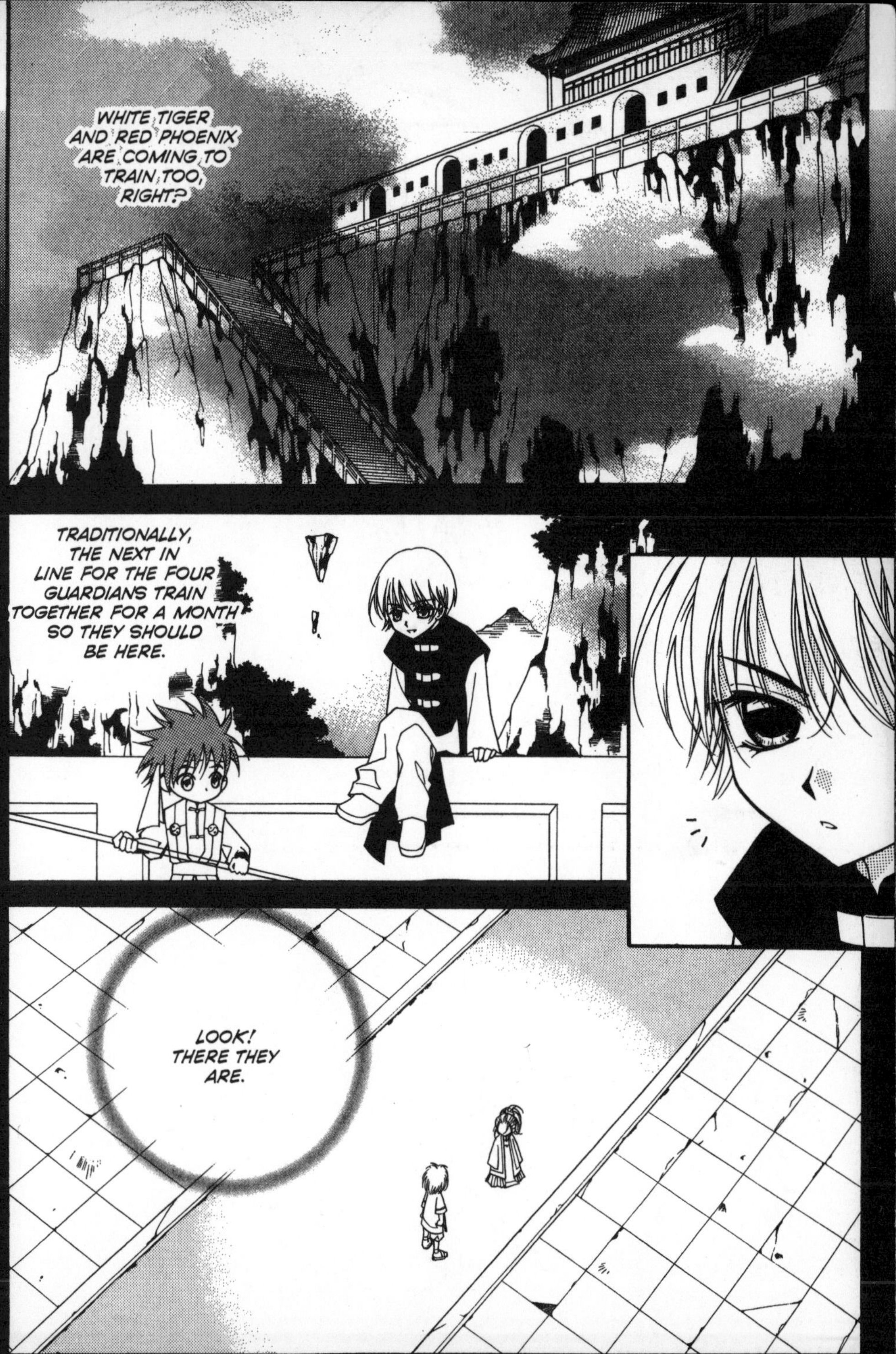
WHITE TIGER AND RED PHOENIX ARE COMING TO TRAIN TOO, RIGHT?
TRADITIONALLY, THE NEXT IN LINE FOR THE FOUR GUARDIANS TRAIN TOGETHER FOR A MONTH SO THEY SHOULD BE HERE.
LOOK! THERE THEY ARE.

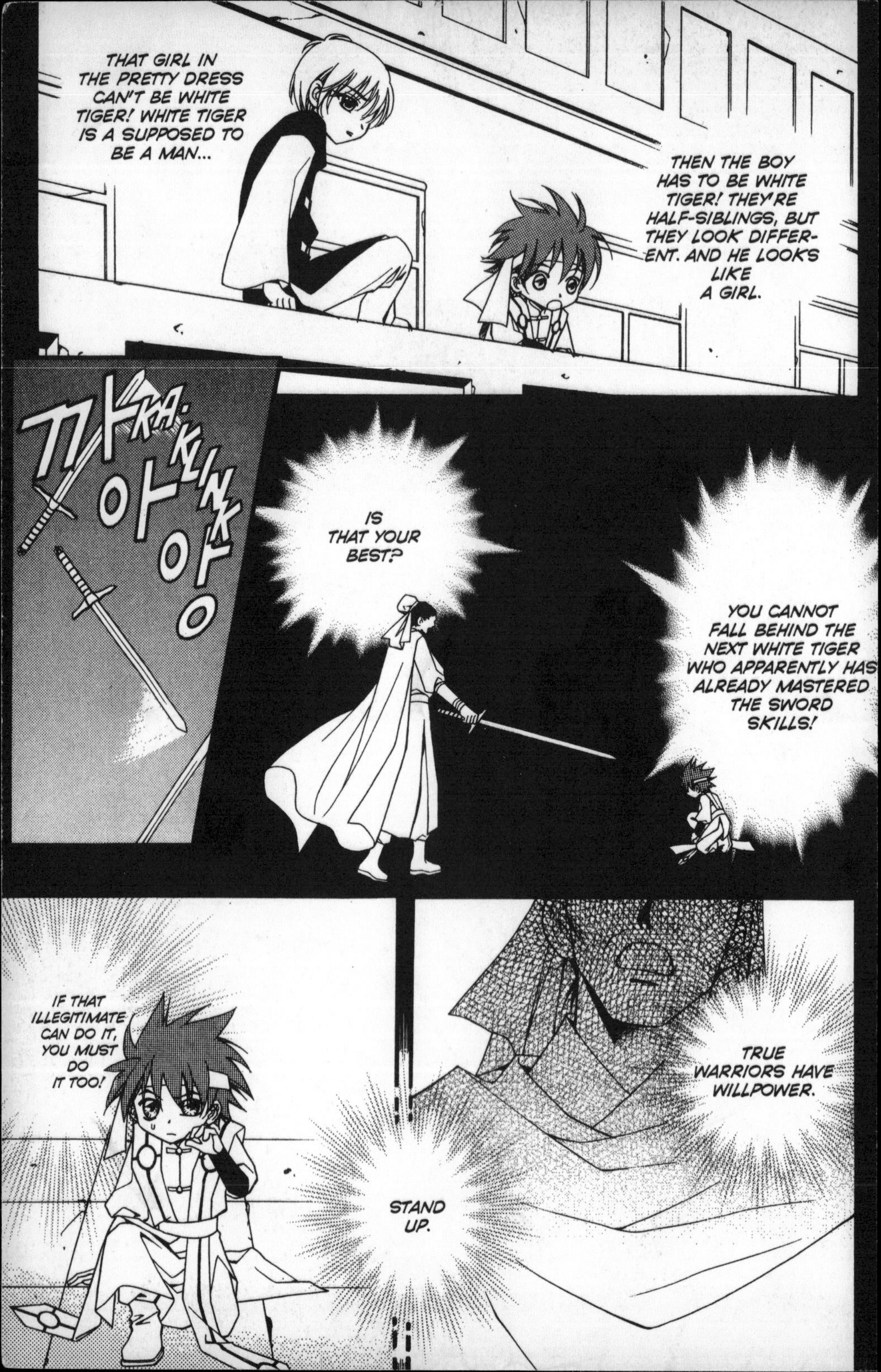
THAT GIRL IN THE PRETTY DRESS CAN'T BE WHITE TIGER! WHITE TIGER IS A SUPPOSED TO BE A MAN...
THEN THE BOY HAS TO BE WHITE TIGER! THEY'RE HALF-SIBLINGS, BUT THEY LOOK DIFFER-ENT. AND HE LOOKS LIKE A GIRL.
KA-KLINK
IS THAT YOUR BEST?
YOU CANNOT FALL BEHIND THE NEXT WHITE TIGER WHO APPARENTLY HAS ALREADY MASTERED THE SWORD SKILLS!
IF THAT ILLEGITIMATE CAN DO IT, YOU MUST DO IT TOO!
STAND UP.
TRUE WARRIORS HAVE WILLPOWER.

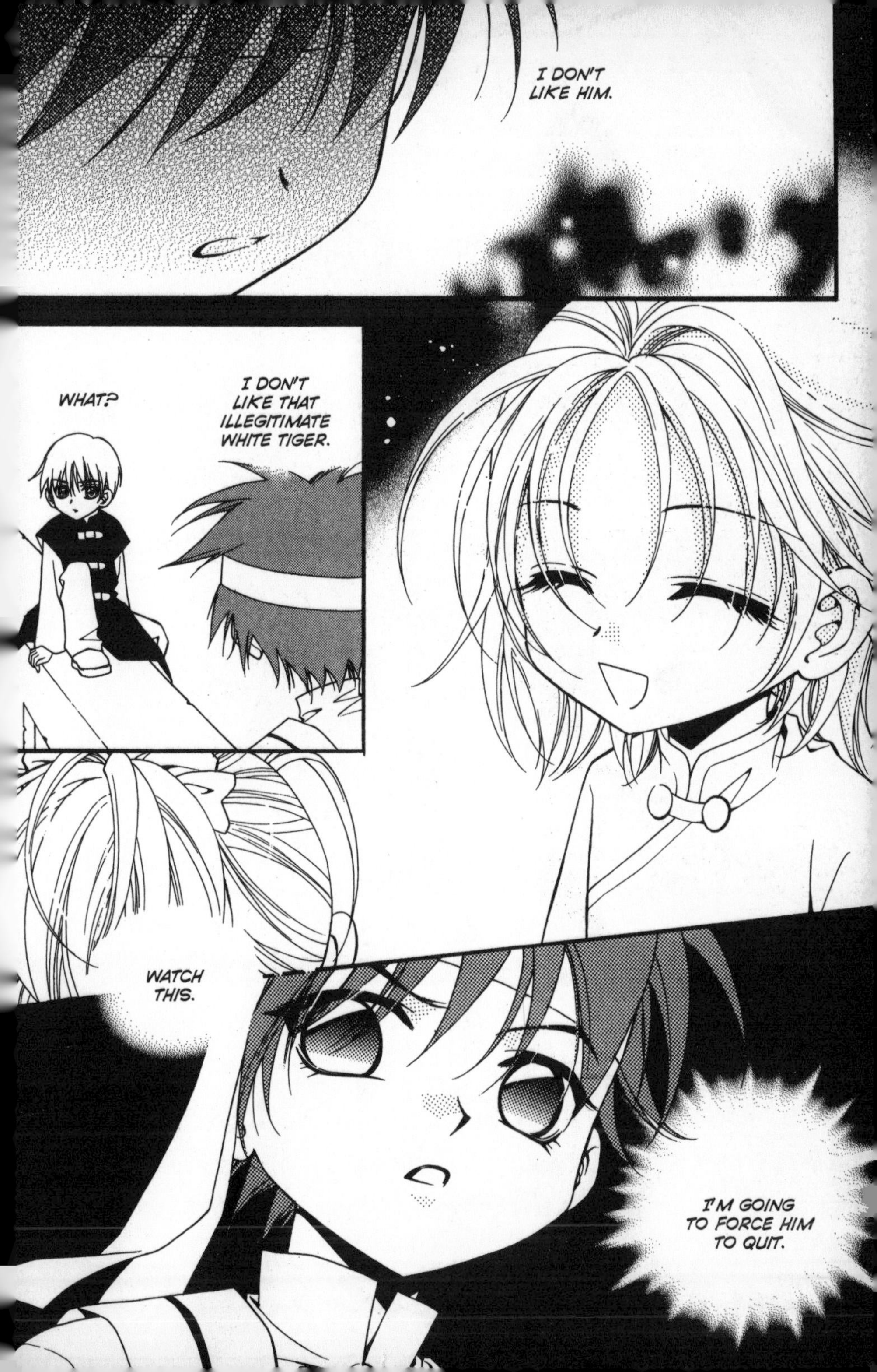
I DON'T LIKE HIM.
WHAT?
I DON'T LIKE THAT ILLEGITIMATE WHITE TIGER.
WATCH THIS.
I'M GOING TO FORCE HIM TO QUIT.

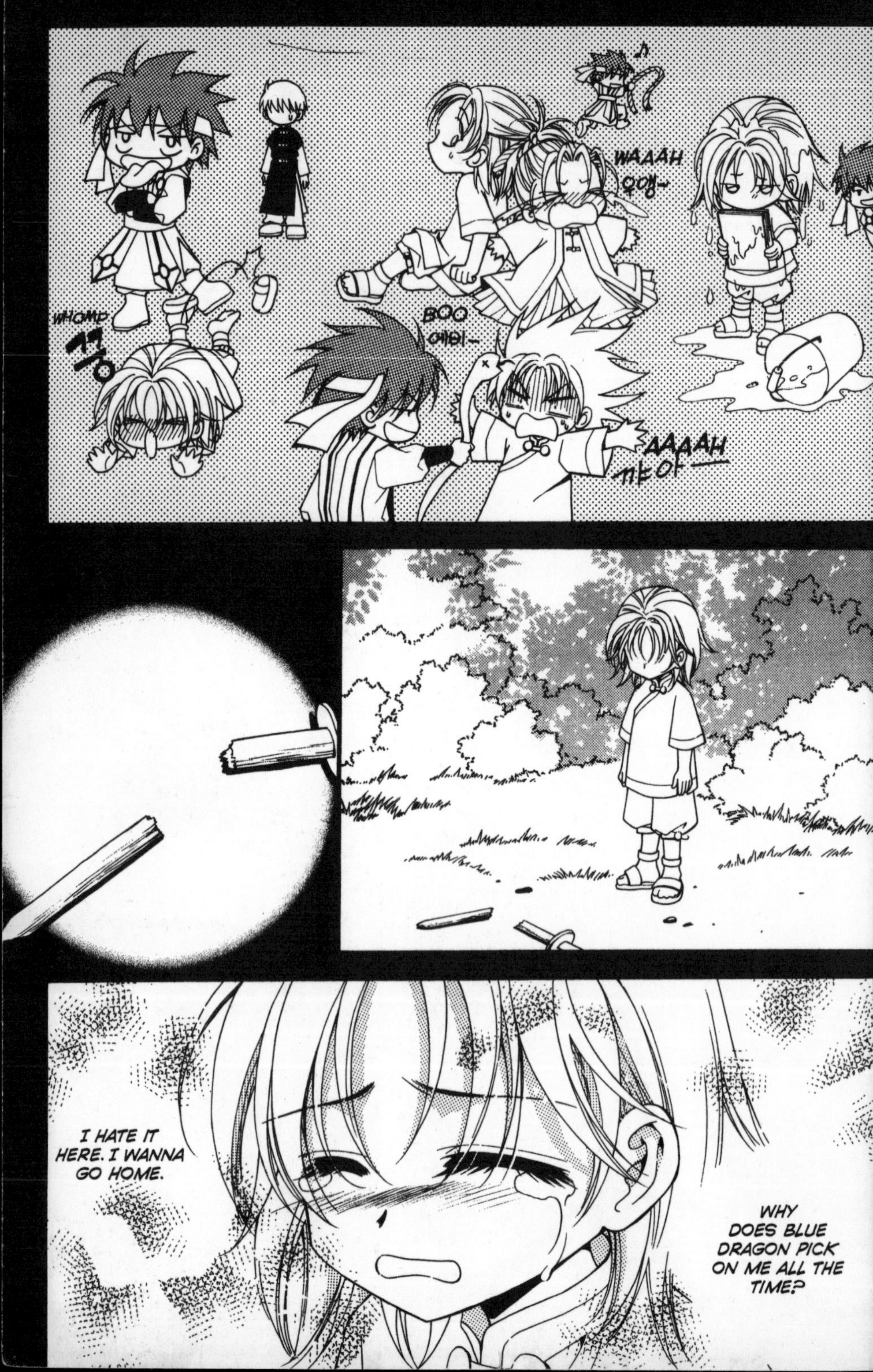
WAAAH
으앵~
WHOMP
쿵
BOO
에비~
AAAAH
까아—
I HATE IT HERE. I WANNA GO HOME.
WHY DOES BLUE DRAGON PICK ON ME ALL THE TIME?

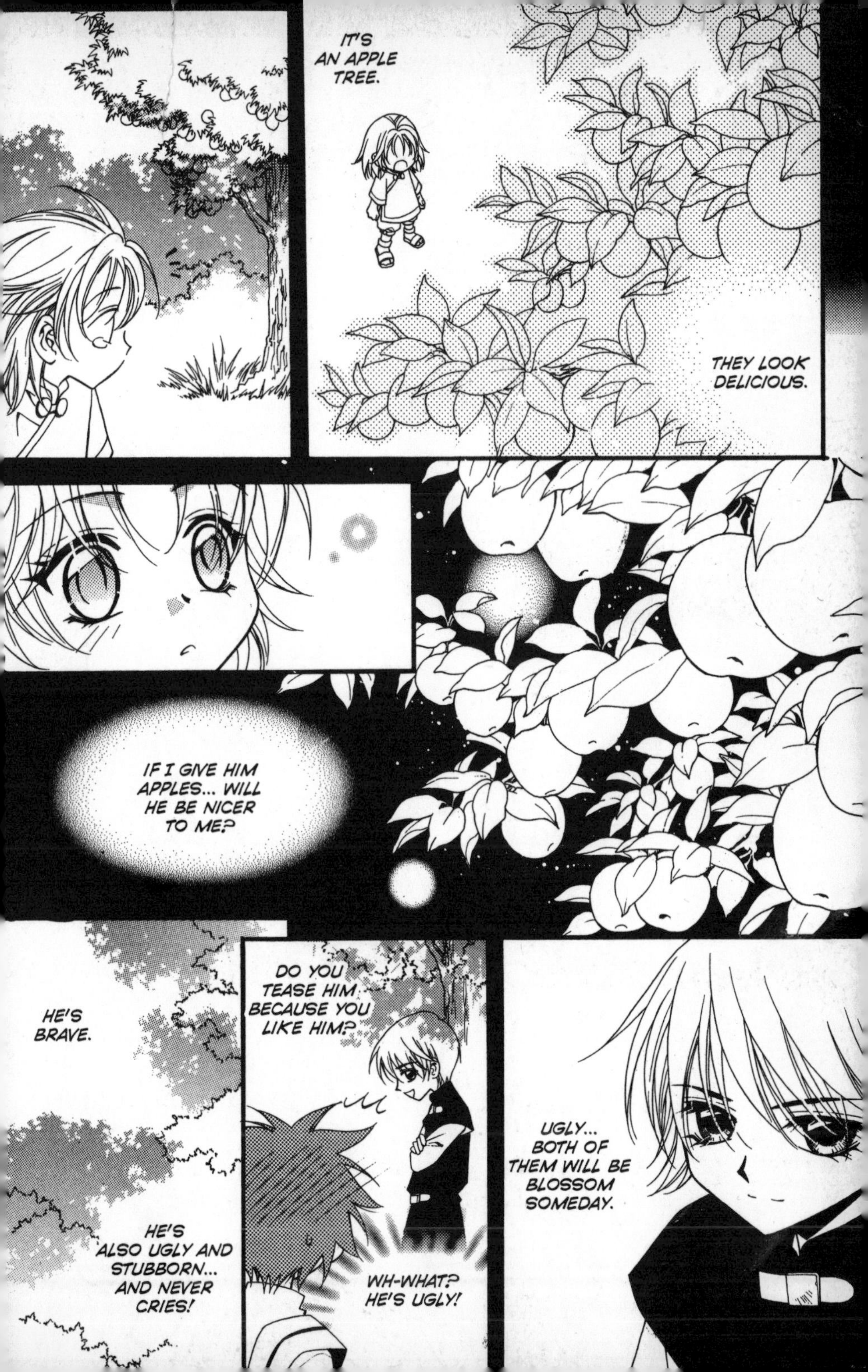
IT'S AN APPLE TREE.
THEY LOOK DELICIOUS.
IF I GIVE HIM APPLES... WILL HE BE NICER TO ME?
HE'S BRAVE.
HE'S ALSO UGLY AND STUBBORN... AND NEVER CRIES!
DO YOU TEASE HIM BECAUSE YOU LIKE HIM?
WH-WHAT? HE'S UGLY!
UGLY... BOTH OF THEM WILL BE BLOSSOM SOMEDAY.

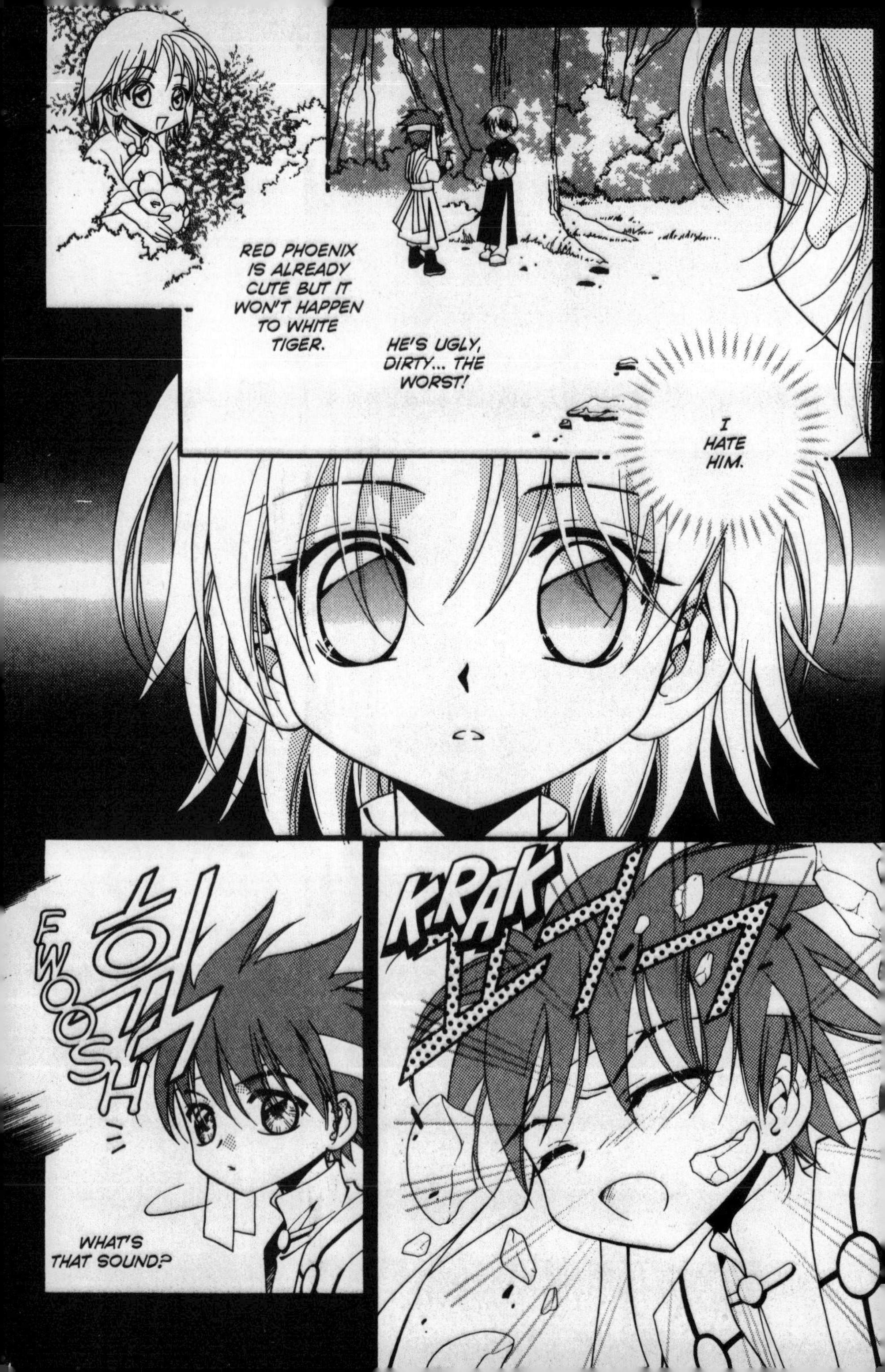
RED PHOENIX IS ALREADY CUTE BUT IT WON'T HAPPEN TO WHITE TIGER.
HE'S UGLY, DIRTY... THE WORST!
I HATE HIM.
FWOOSH
WHAT'S THAT SOUND?
KRAK

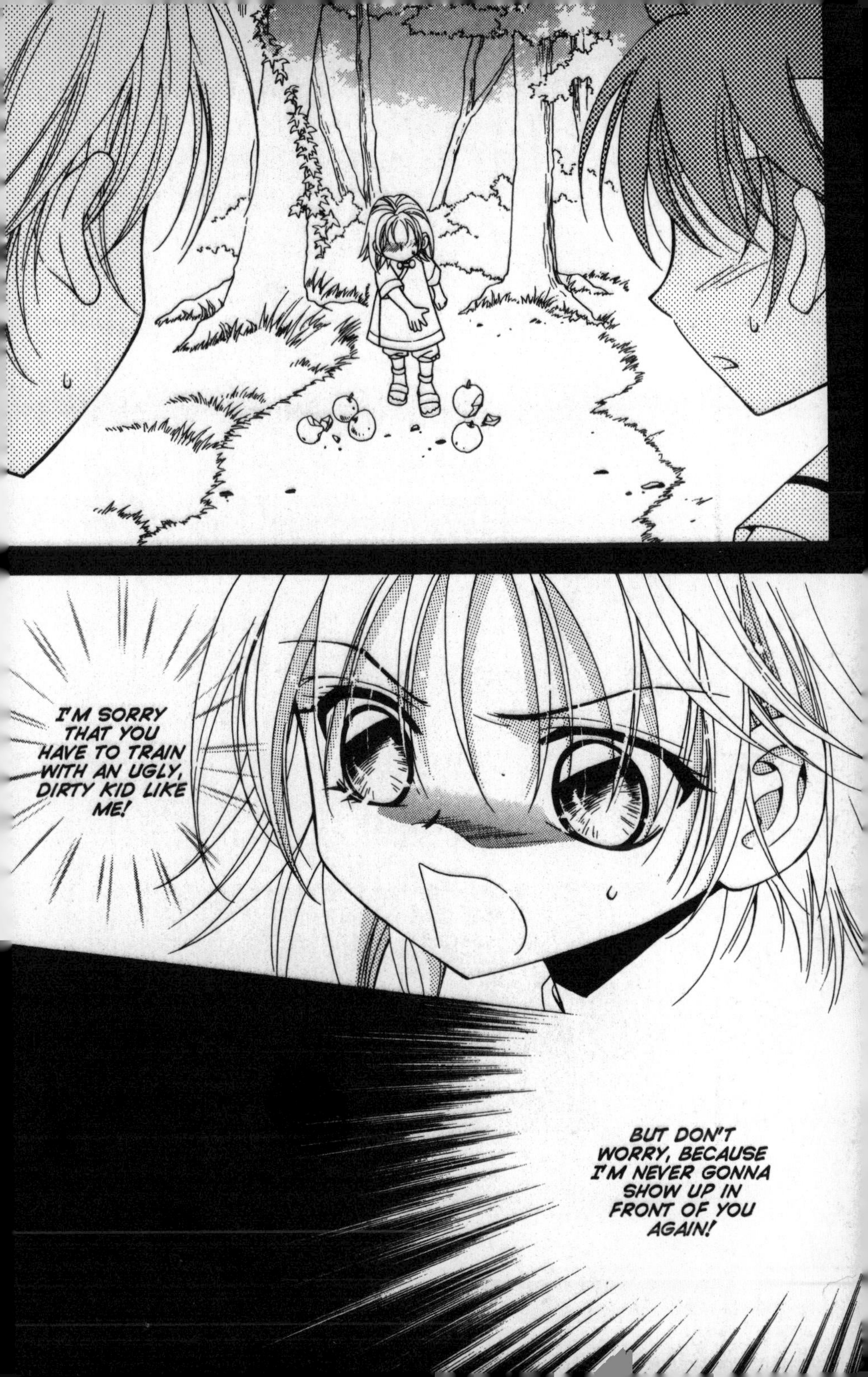
I'M SORRY THAT YOU HAVE TO TRAIN WITH AN UGLY, DIRTY KID LIKE ME!
BUT DON'T WORRY, BECAUSE I'M NEVER GONNA SHOW UP IN FRONT OF YOU AGAIN!

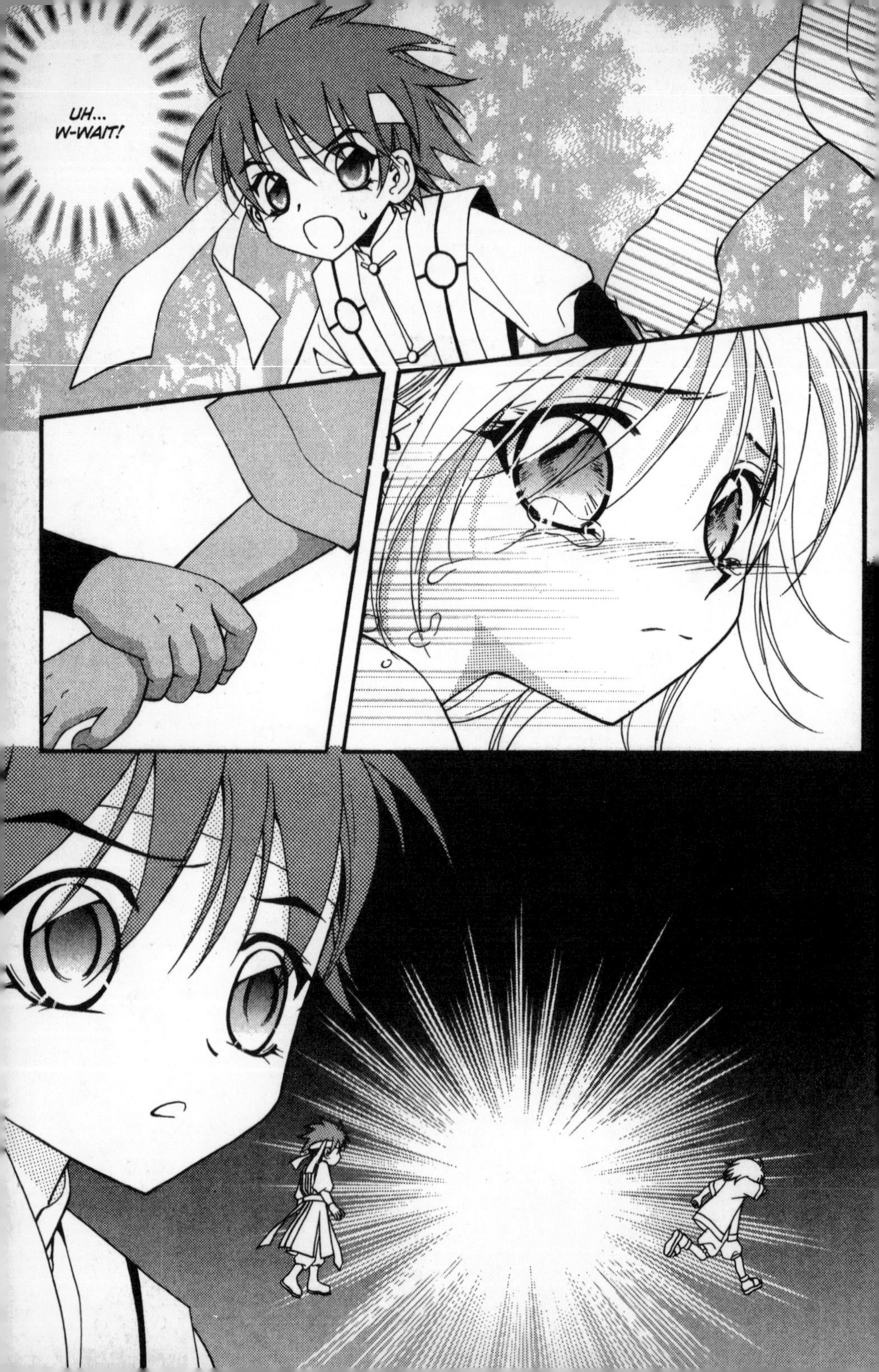
UH... W-WAIT!

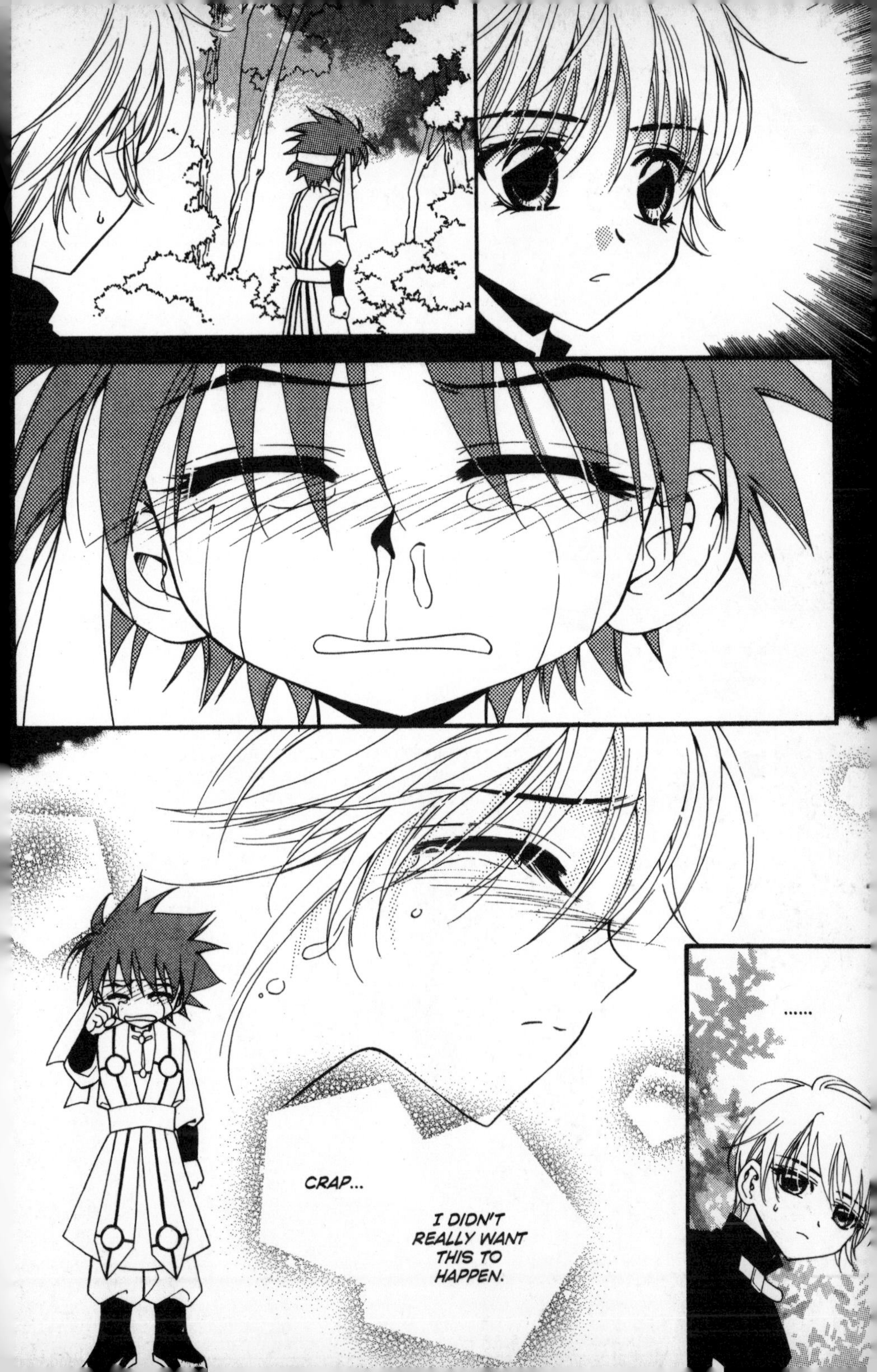
CRAP...
I DIDN'T REALLY WANT THIS TO HAPPEN.
......

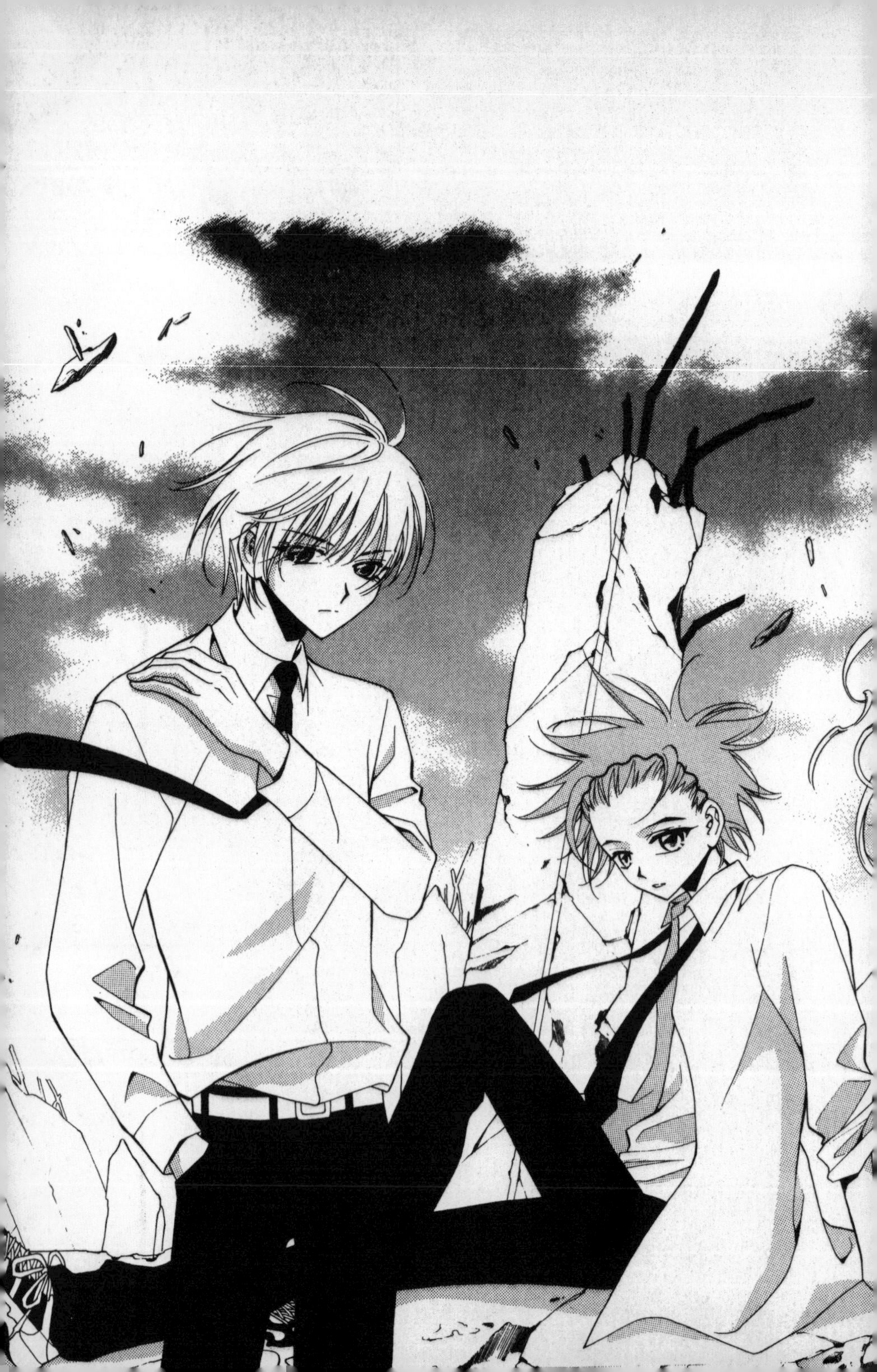

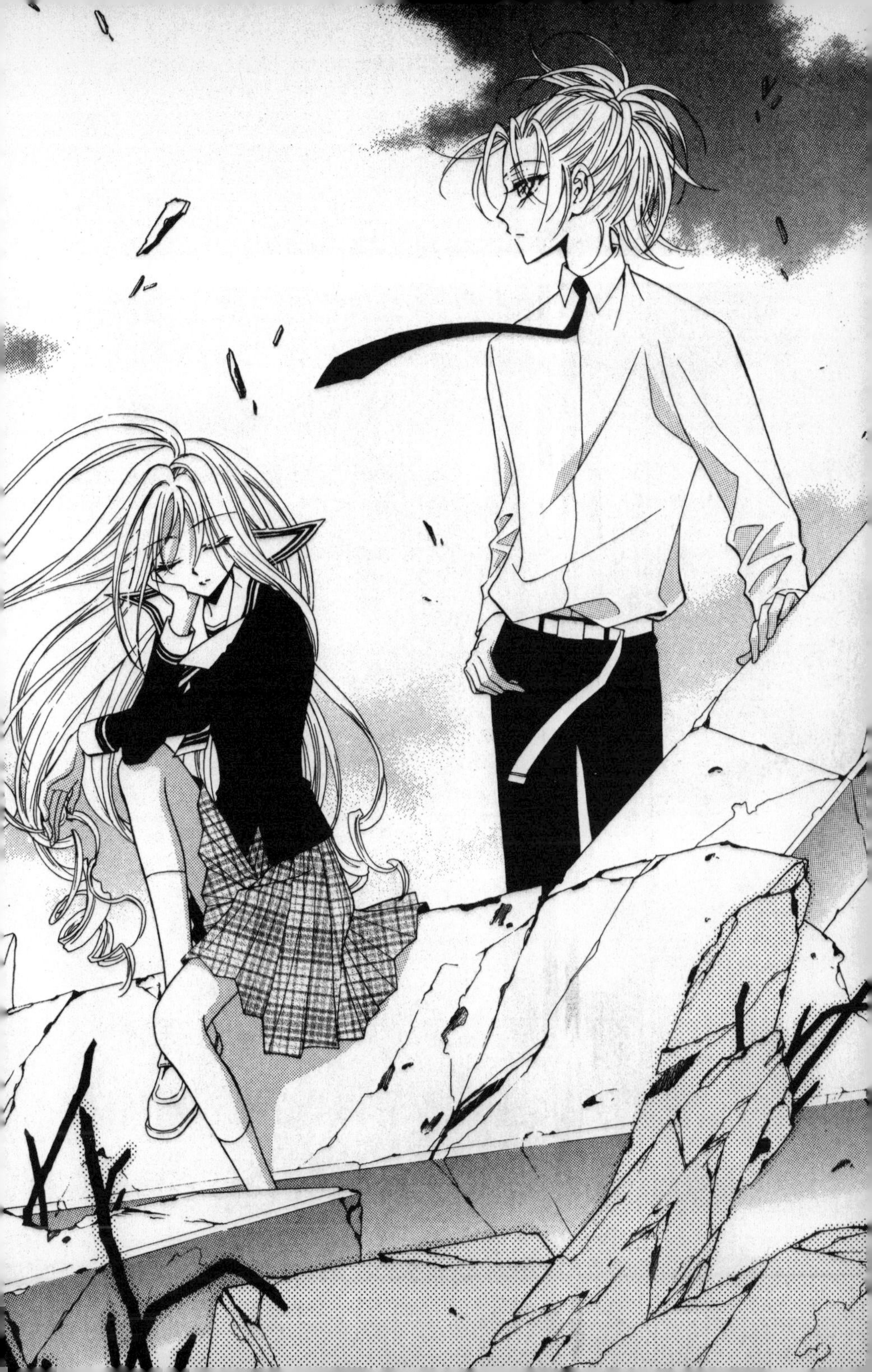

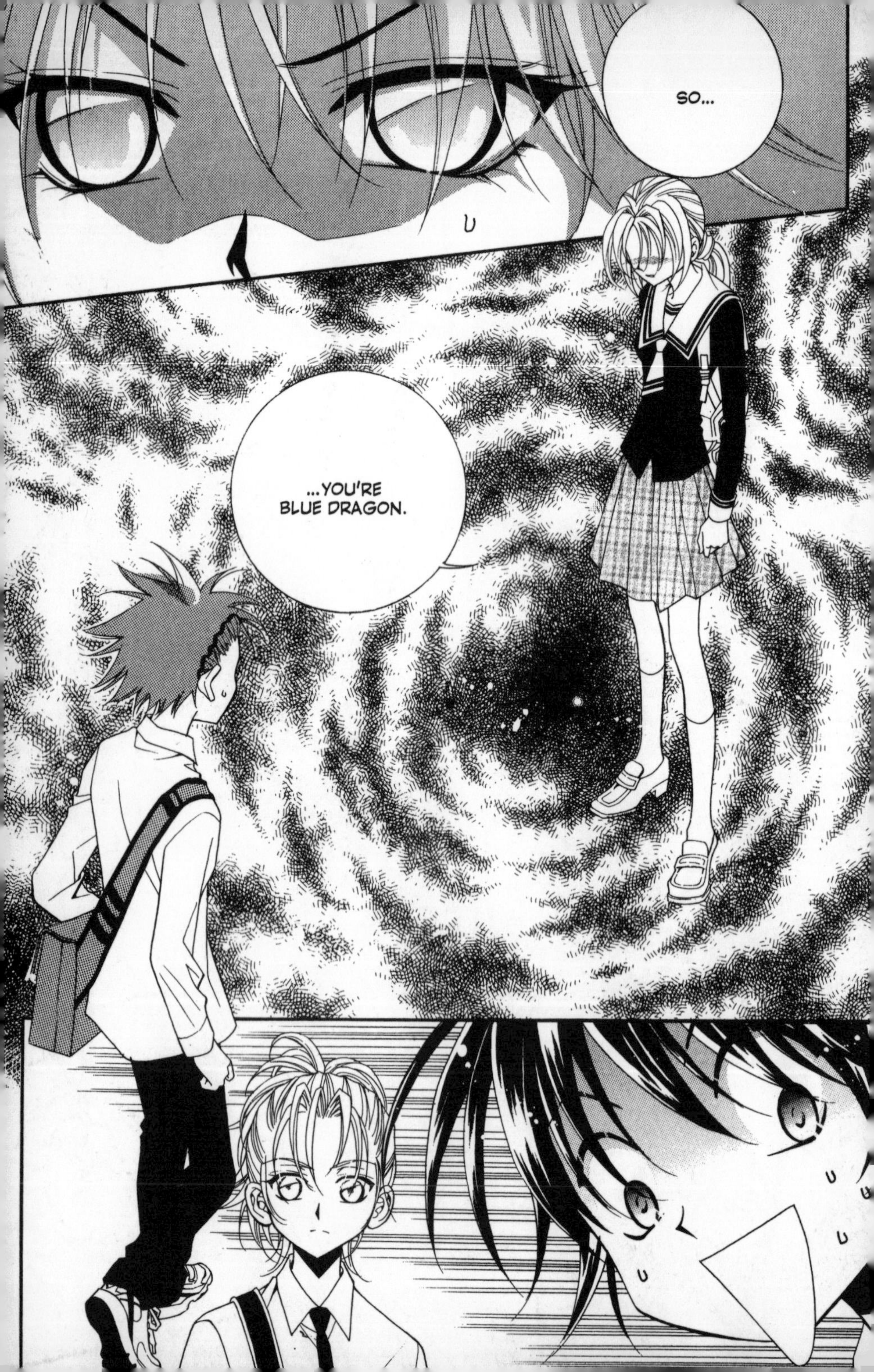
SO...
...YOU'RE BLUE DRAGON.

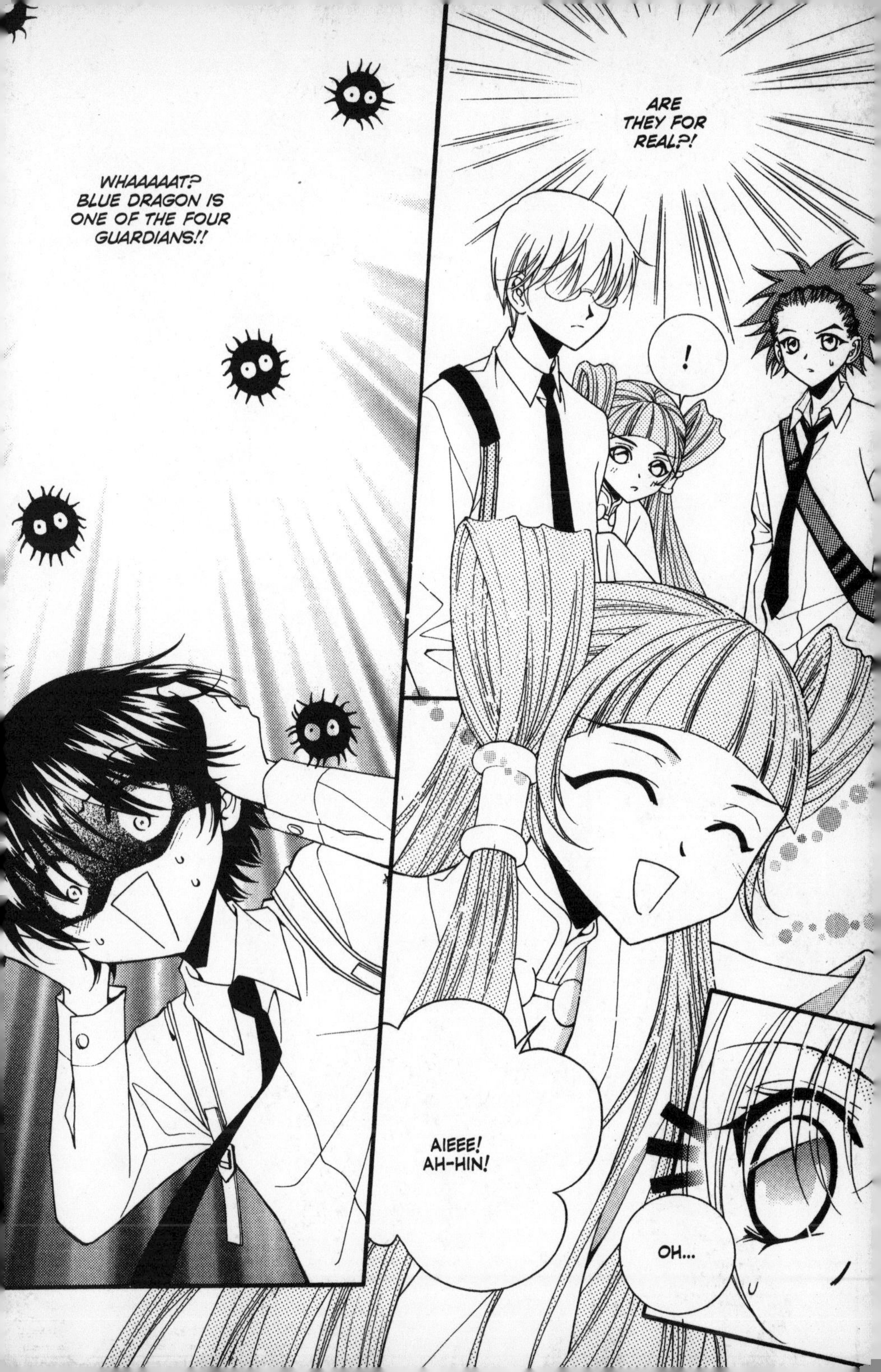
WHAAAAAT? BLUE DRAGON IS ONE OF THE FOUR GUARDIANS!!
ARE THEY FOR REAL?!
!
AIEEE! AH-HIN!
OH...

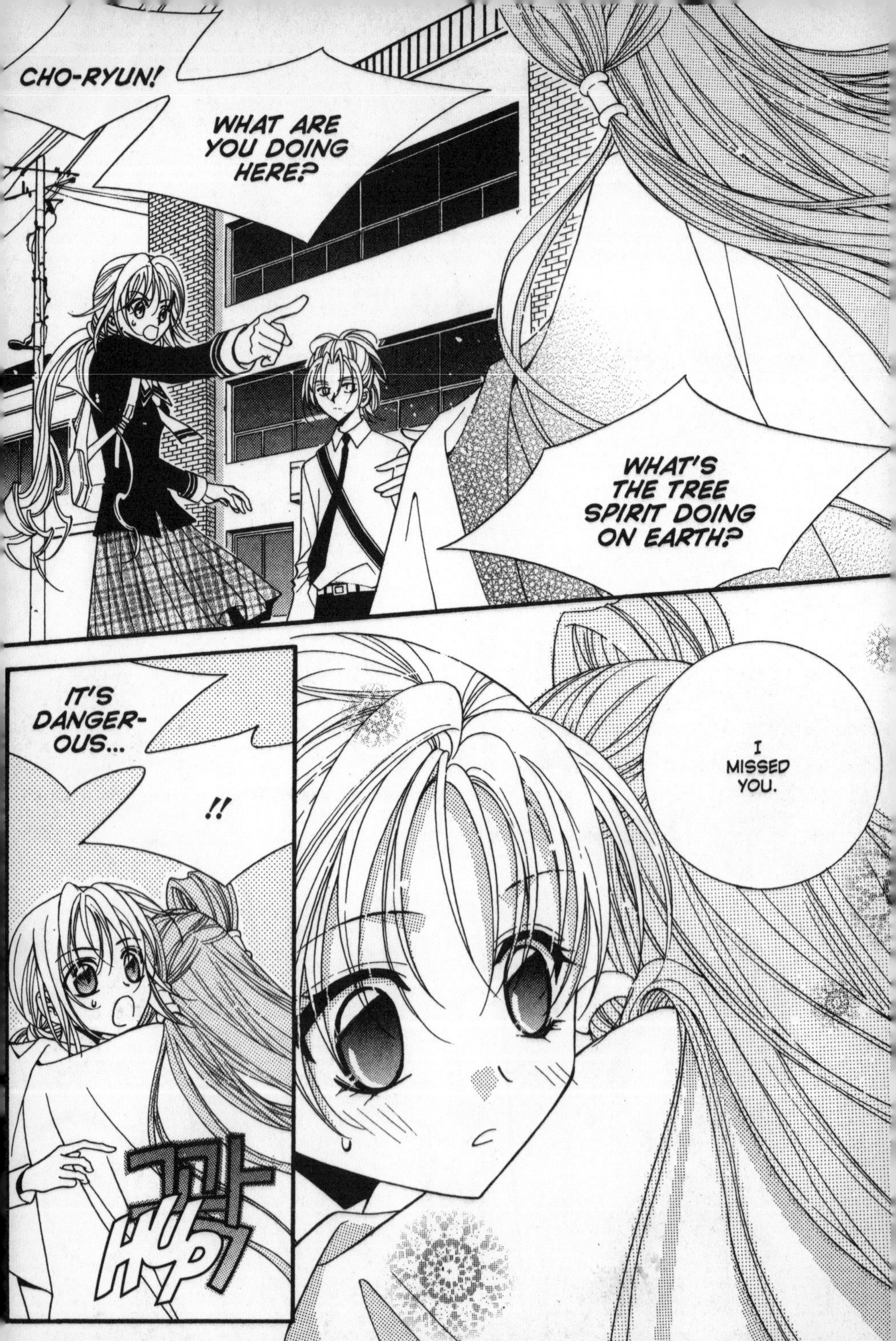
CHO-RYUN!
WHAT ARE YOU DOING HERE?
WHAT'S THE TREE SPIRIT DOING ON EARTH?
IT'S DANGER-OUS...
!!
HUP
I MISSED YOU.

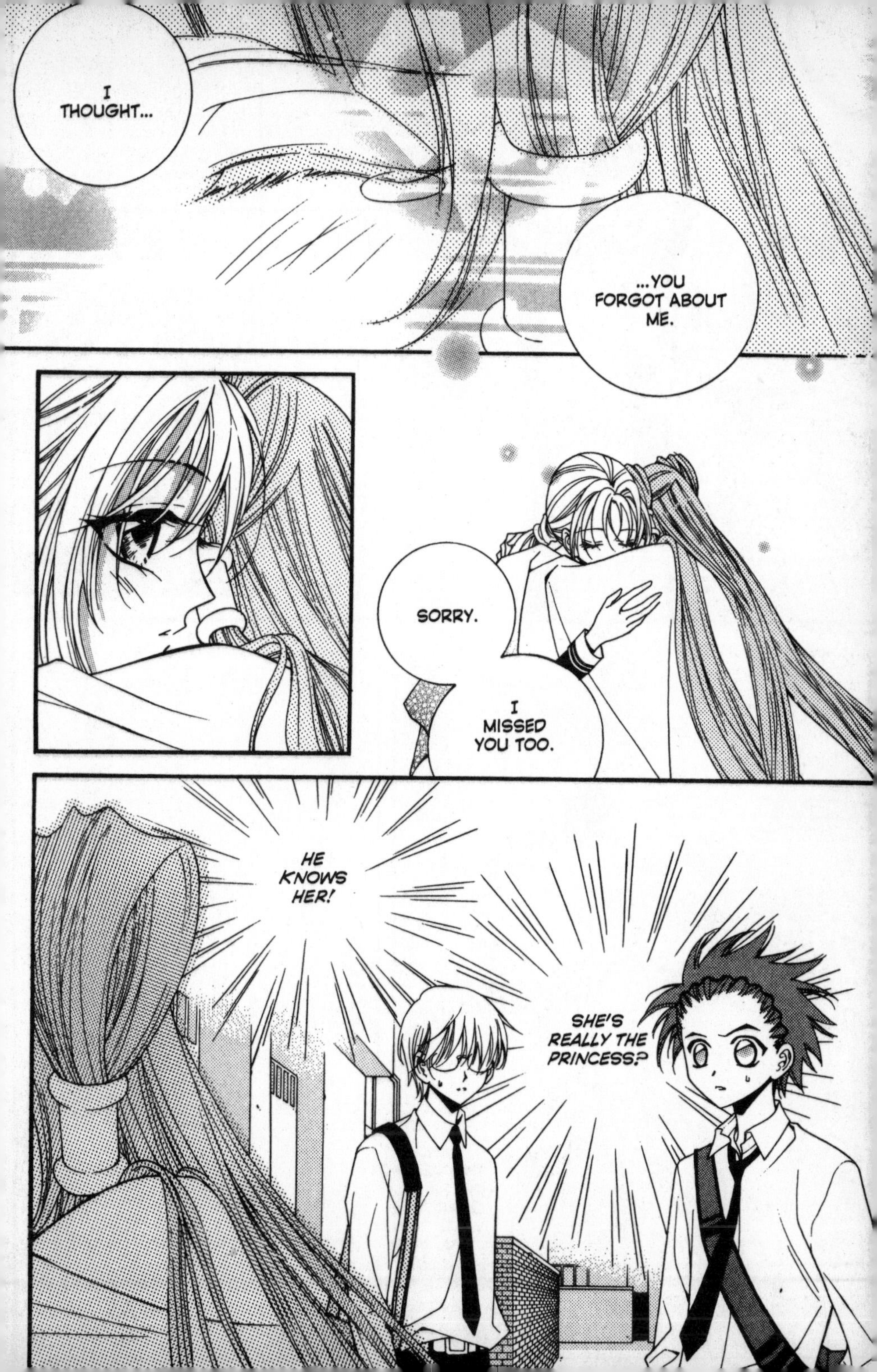
I THOUGHT...
...YOU FORGOT ABOUT ME.
SORRY.
I MISSED YOU TOO.
HE KNOWS HER!
SHE'S REALLY THE PRINCESS?

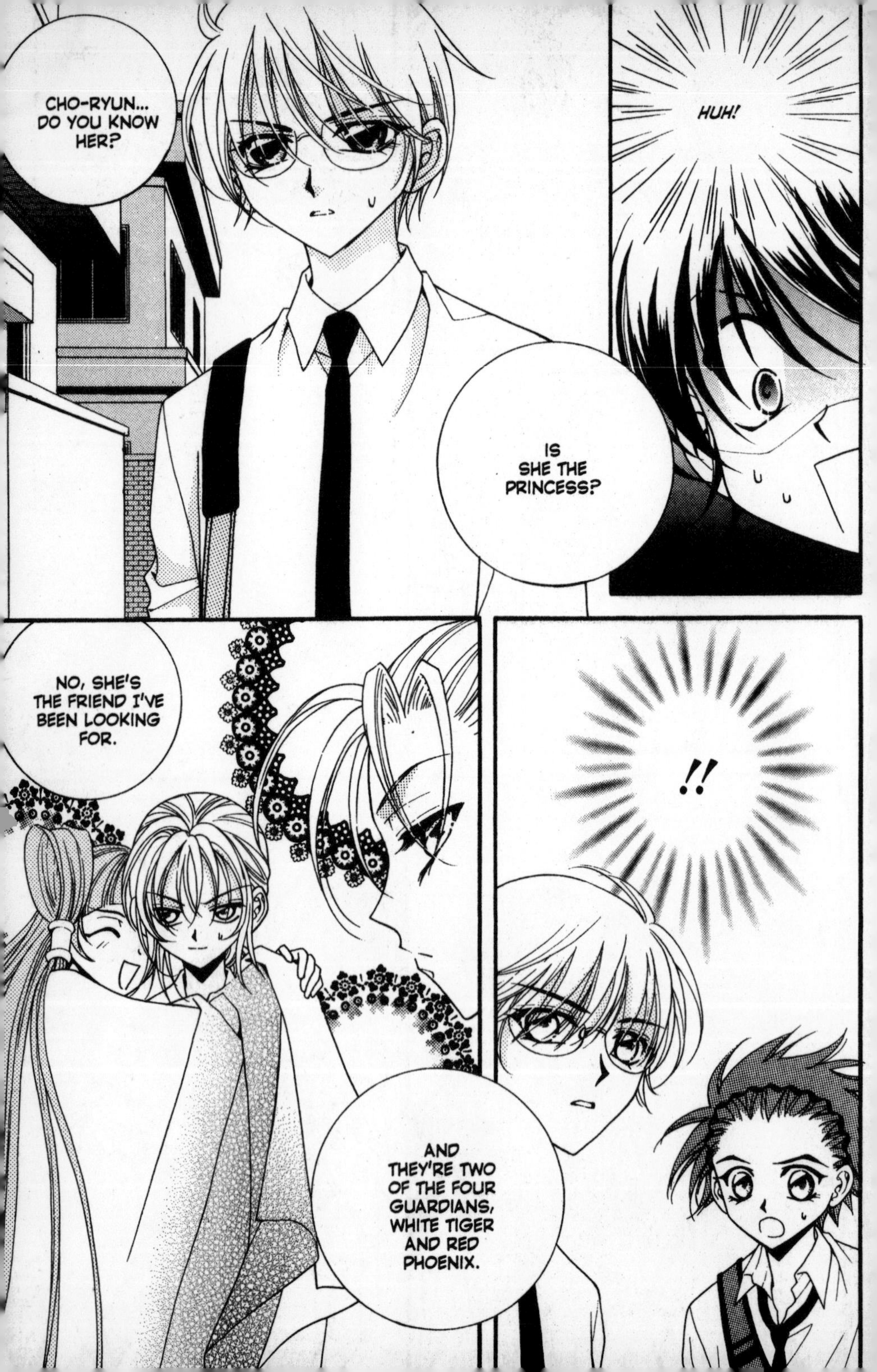
CHO-RYUN... DO YOU KNOW HER?
IS SHE THE PRINCESS?
HUH!
NO, SHE'S THE FRIEND I'VE BEEN LOOKING FOR.
!!
AND THEY'RE TWO OF THE FOUR GUARDIANS, WHITE TIGER AND RED PHOENIX.

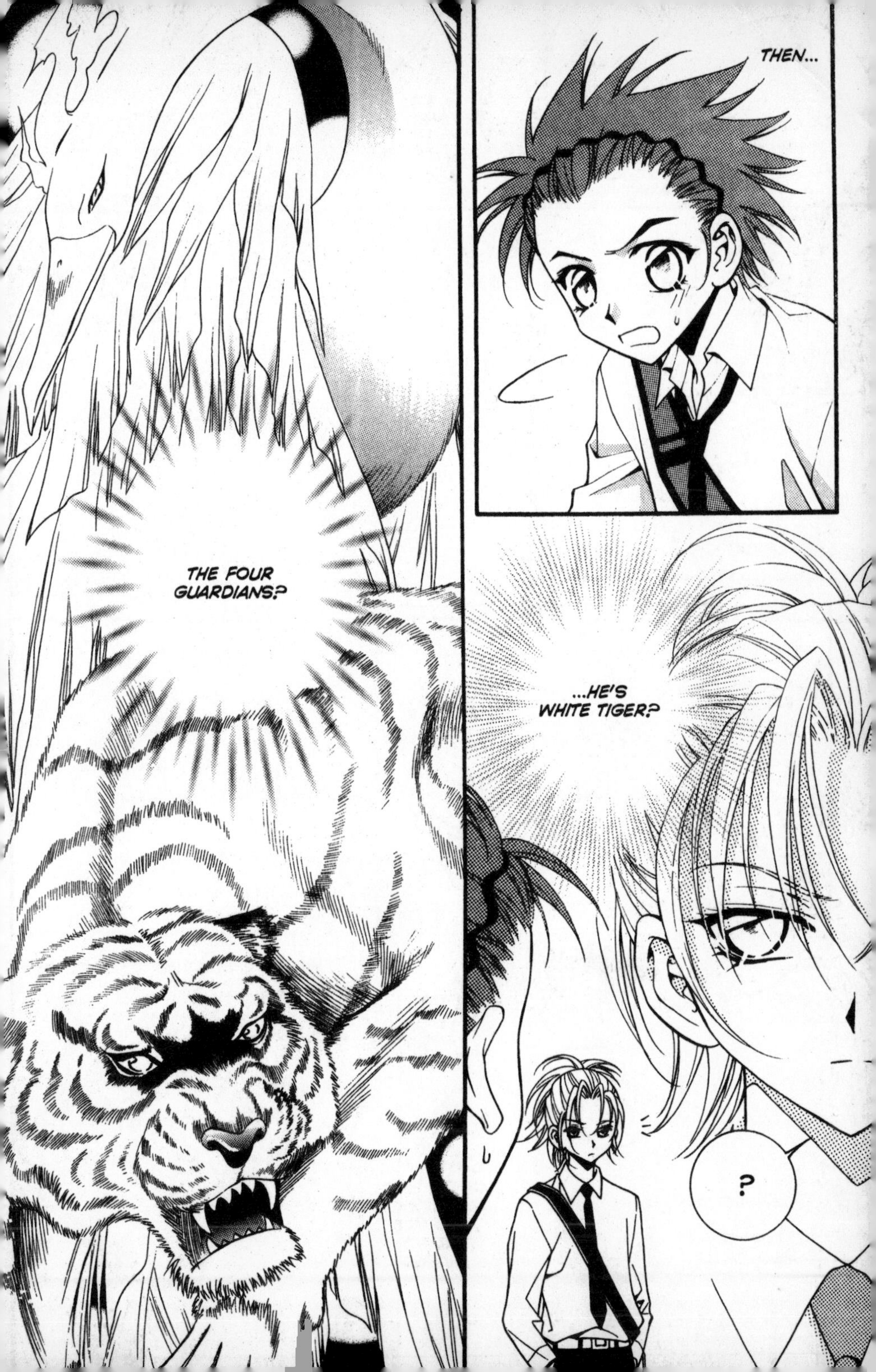
THE FOUR GUARDIANS?
THEN...
...HE'S WHITE TIGER?
?

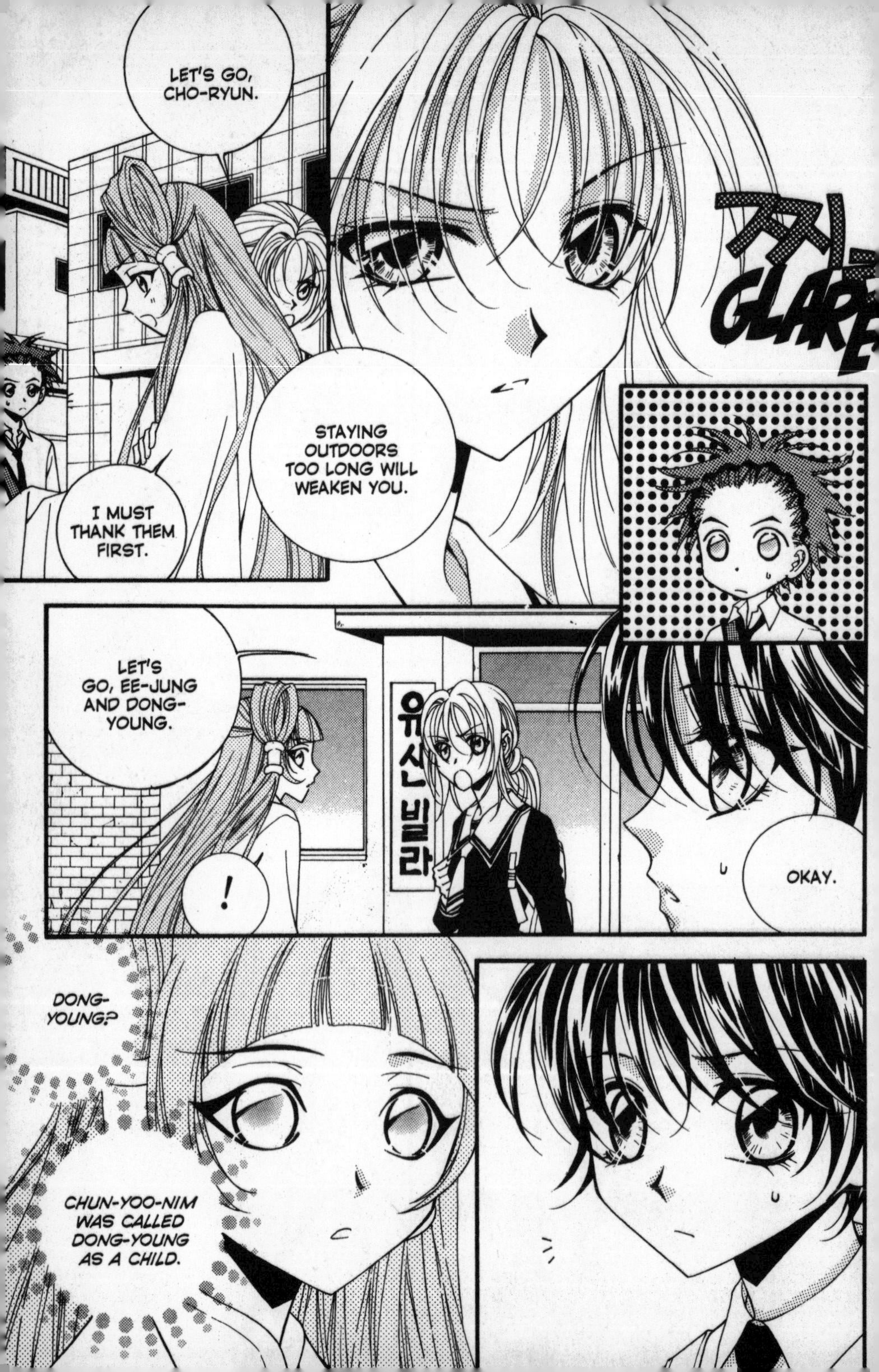
LET'S GO, CHO-RYUN.
I MUST THANK THEM FIRST.
STAYING OUTDOORS TOO LONG WILL WEAKEN YOU.
GLARE
LET'S GO, EE-JUNG AND DONG-YOUNG.
유신 빌라
!
OKAY.
DONG-YOUNG?
CHUN-YOO-NIM WAS CALLED DONG-YOUNG AS A CHILD.

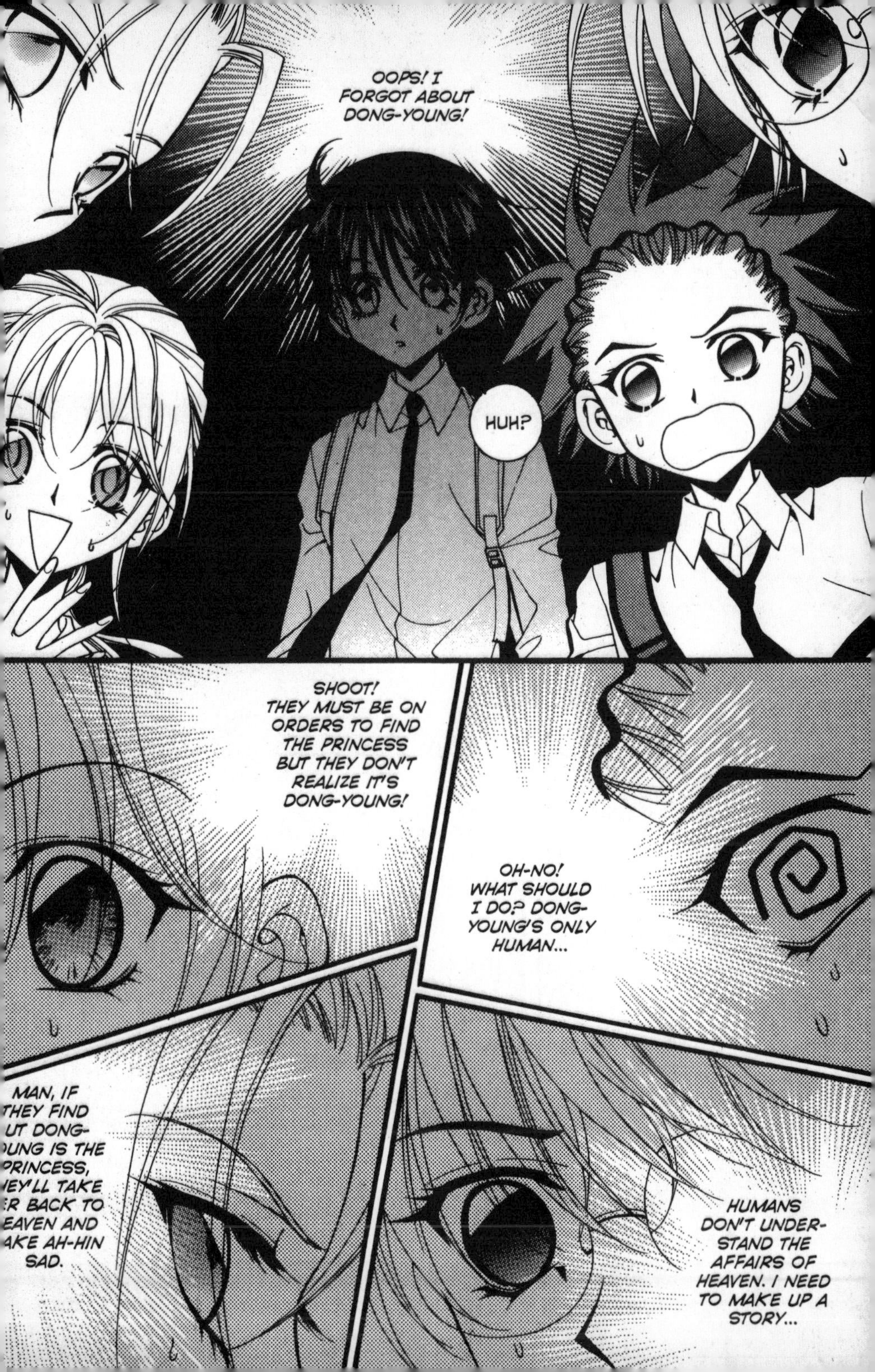
OOPS! I FORGOT ABOUT DONG-YOUNG!
HUH?
SHOOT! THEY MUST BE ON ORDERS TO FIND THE PRINCESS BUT THEY DON'T REALIZE IT'S DONG-YOUNG!
OH-NO! WHAT SHOULD I DO? DONG-YOUNG'S ONLY HUMAN...
MAN, IF HEY FIND UT DONG- OUNG IS THE PRINCESS, HEY'LL TAKE ER BACK TO EAVEN AND AKE AH-HIN SAD.
HUMANS DON'T UNDER-STAND THE AFFAIRS OF HEAVEN. I NEED TO MAKE UP A STORY...

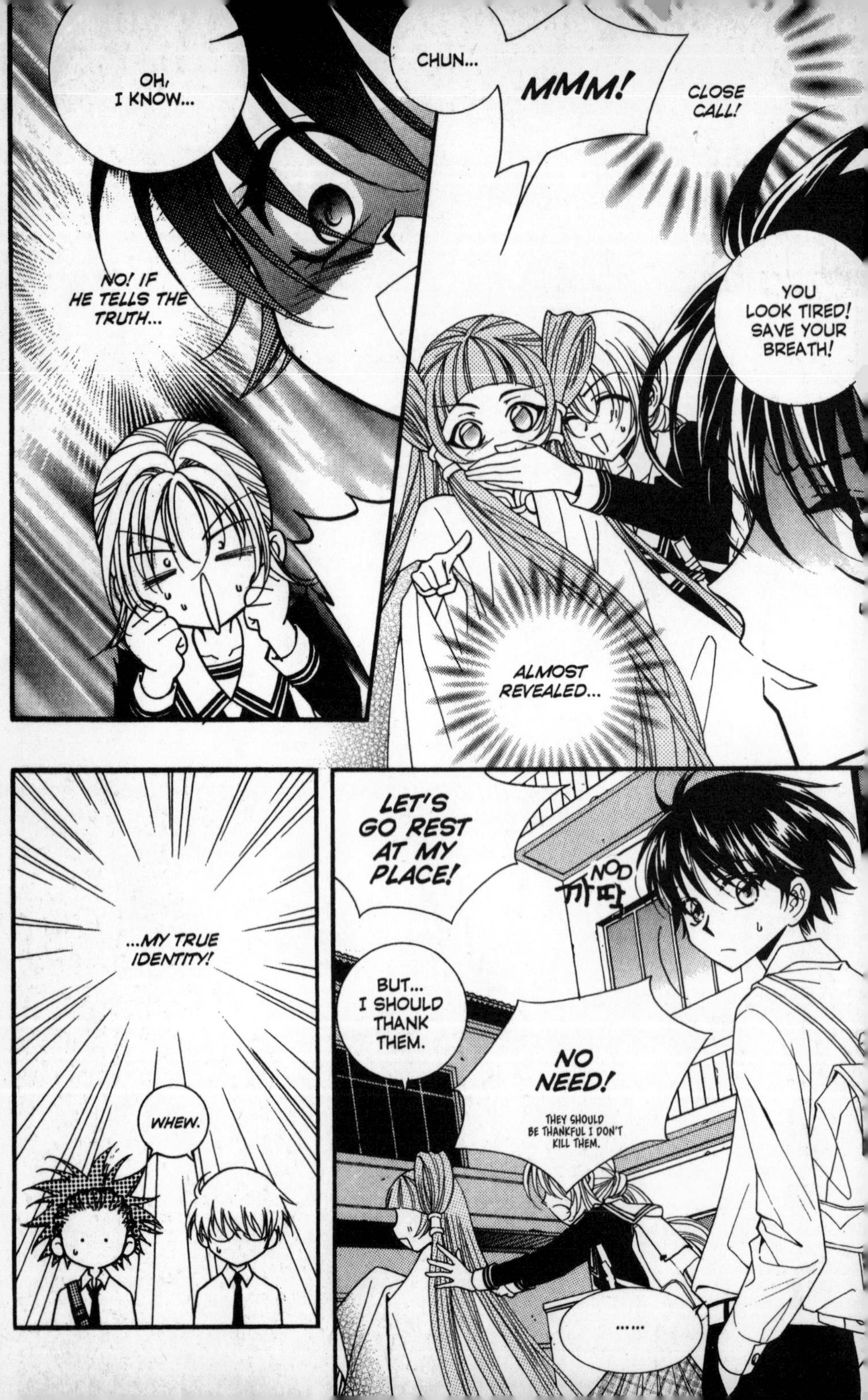
OH, I KNOW...
NO! IF HE TELLS THE TRUTH...
CHUN...
MMM!
CLOSE CALL!
YOU LOOK TIRED! SAVE YOUR BREATH!
ALMOST REVEALED...
...MY TRUE IDENTITY!
WHEW.
LET'S GO REST AT MY PLACE!
NOD
까딱
BUT... I SHOULD THANK THEM.
NO NEED!
THEY SHOULD BE THANKFUL I DON'T KILL THEM.
......

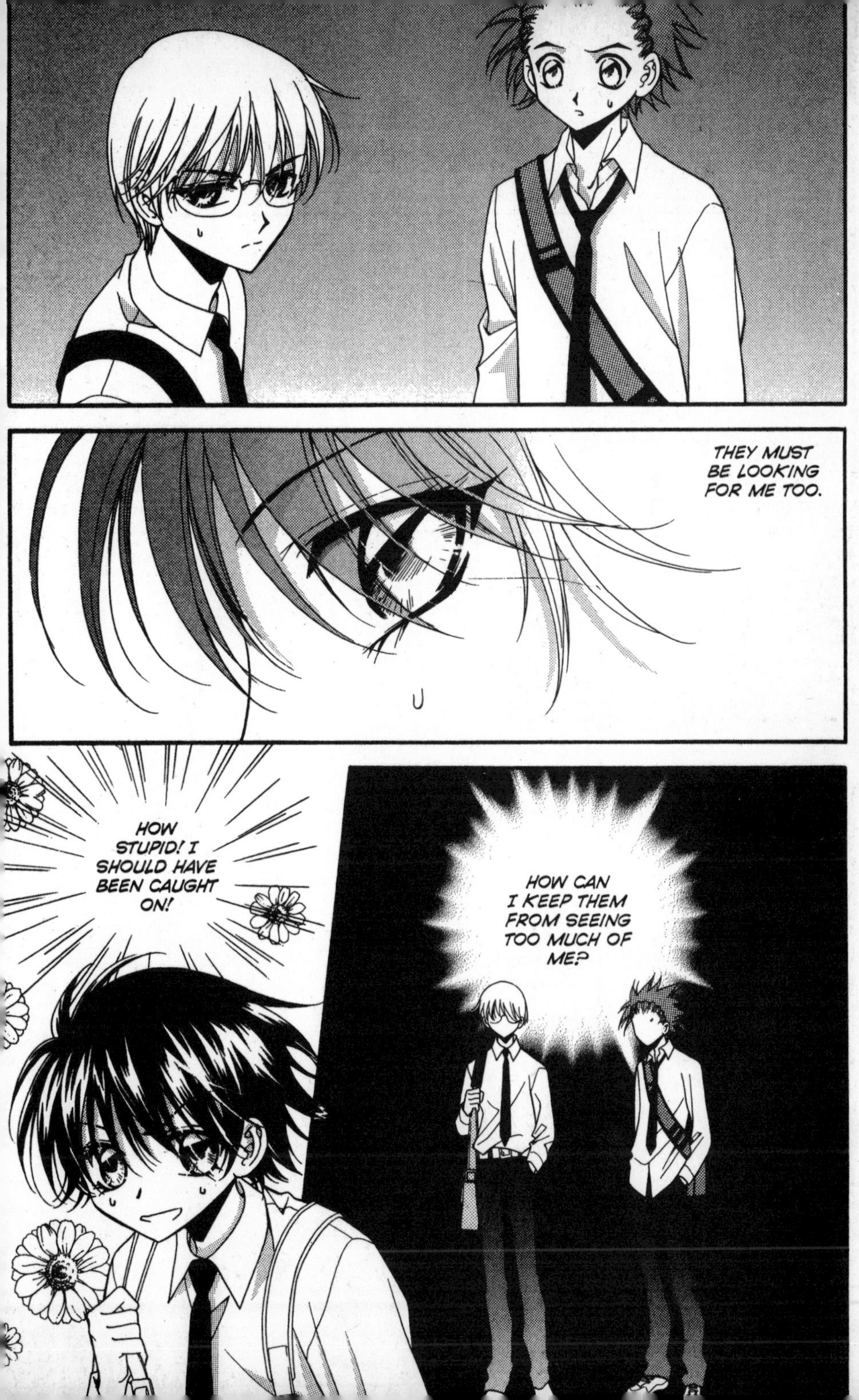
THEY MUST BE LOOKING FOR ME TOO.
HOW STUPID! I SHOULD HAVE BEEN CAUGHT ON!
HOW CAN I KEEP THEM FROM SEEING TOO MUCH OF ME?

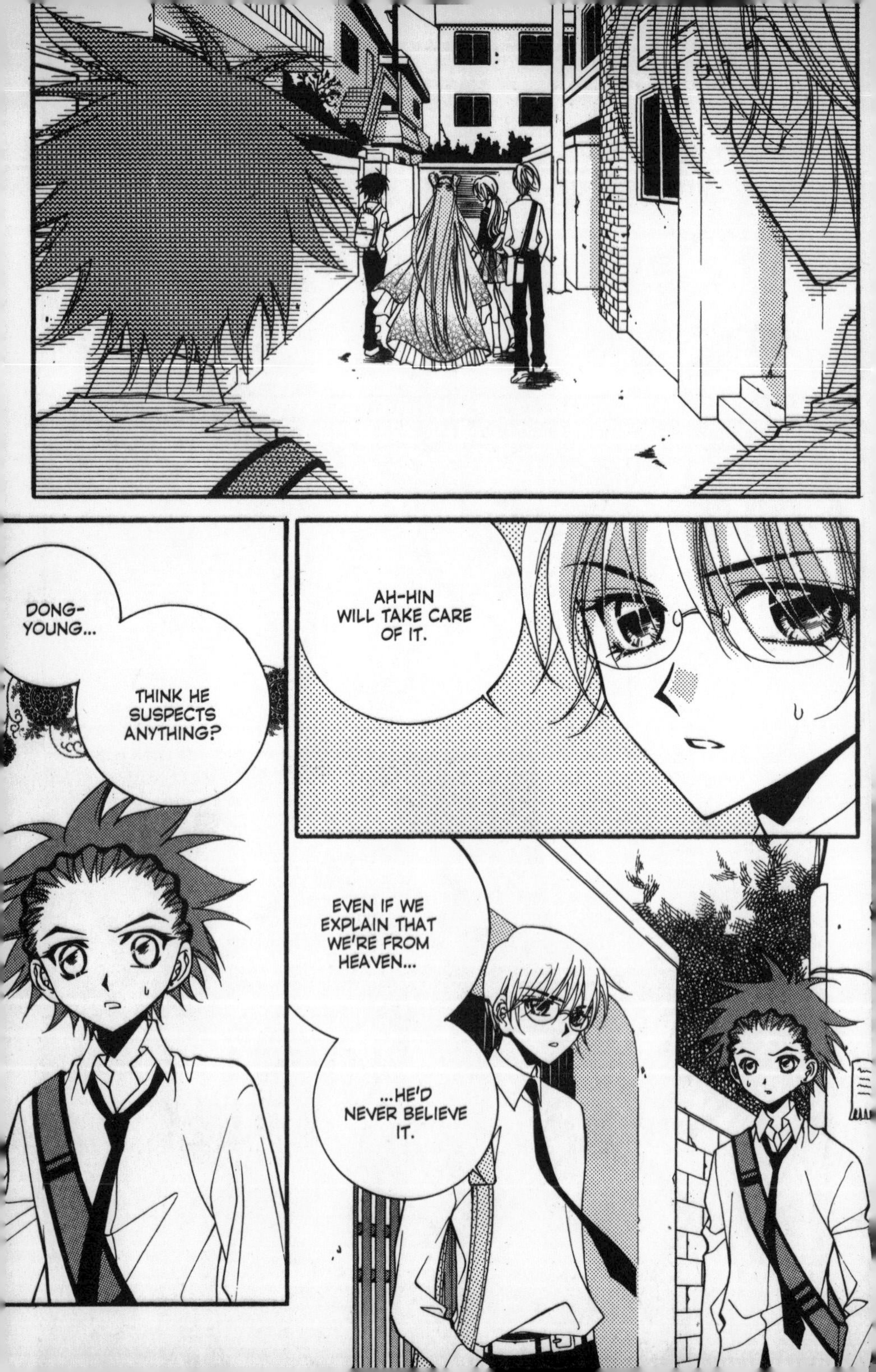
DONG-YOUNG...
THINK HE SUSPECTS ANYTHING?
AH-HIN WILL TAKE CARE OF IT.
EVEN IF WE EXPLAIN THAT WE'RE FROM HEAVEN...
...HE'D NEVER BELIEVE IT.

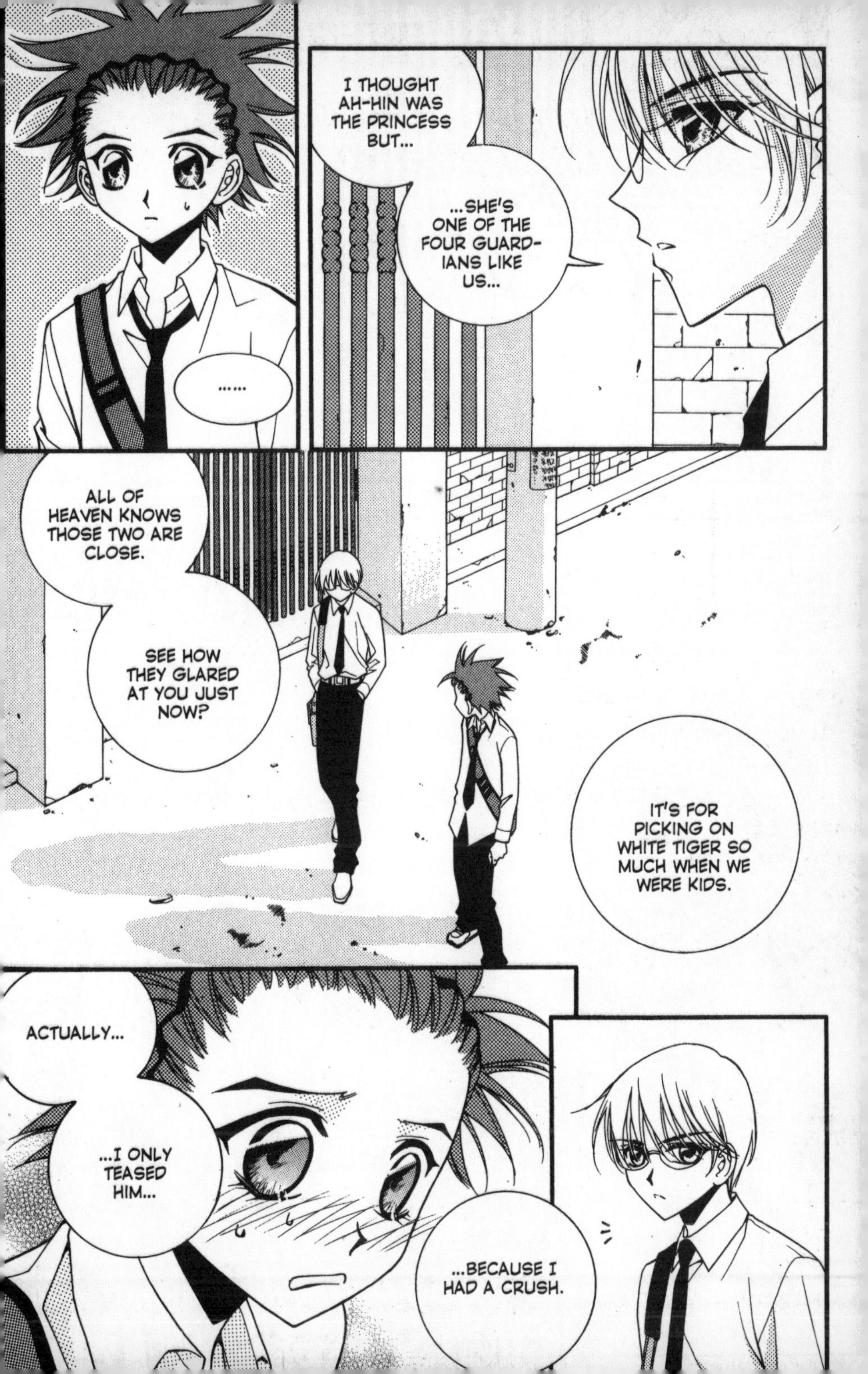

......
I THOUGHT AH-HIN WAS THE PRINCESS BUT...
...SHE'S ONE OF THE FOUR GUARD-IANS LIKE US...
ALL OF HEAVEN KNOWS THOSE TWO ARE CLOSE.
SEE HOW THEY GLARED AT YOU JUST NOW?
IT'S FOR PICKING ON WHITE TIGER SO MUCH WHEN WE WERE KIDS.
ACTUALLY...
...I ONLY TEASED HIM...
...BECAUSE I HAD A CRUSH.

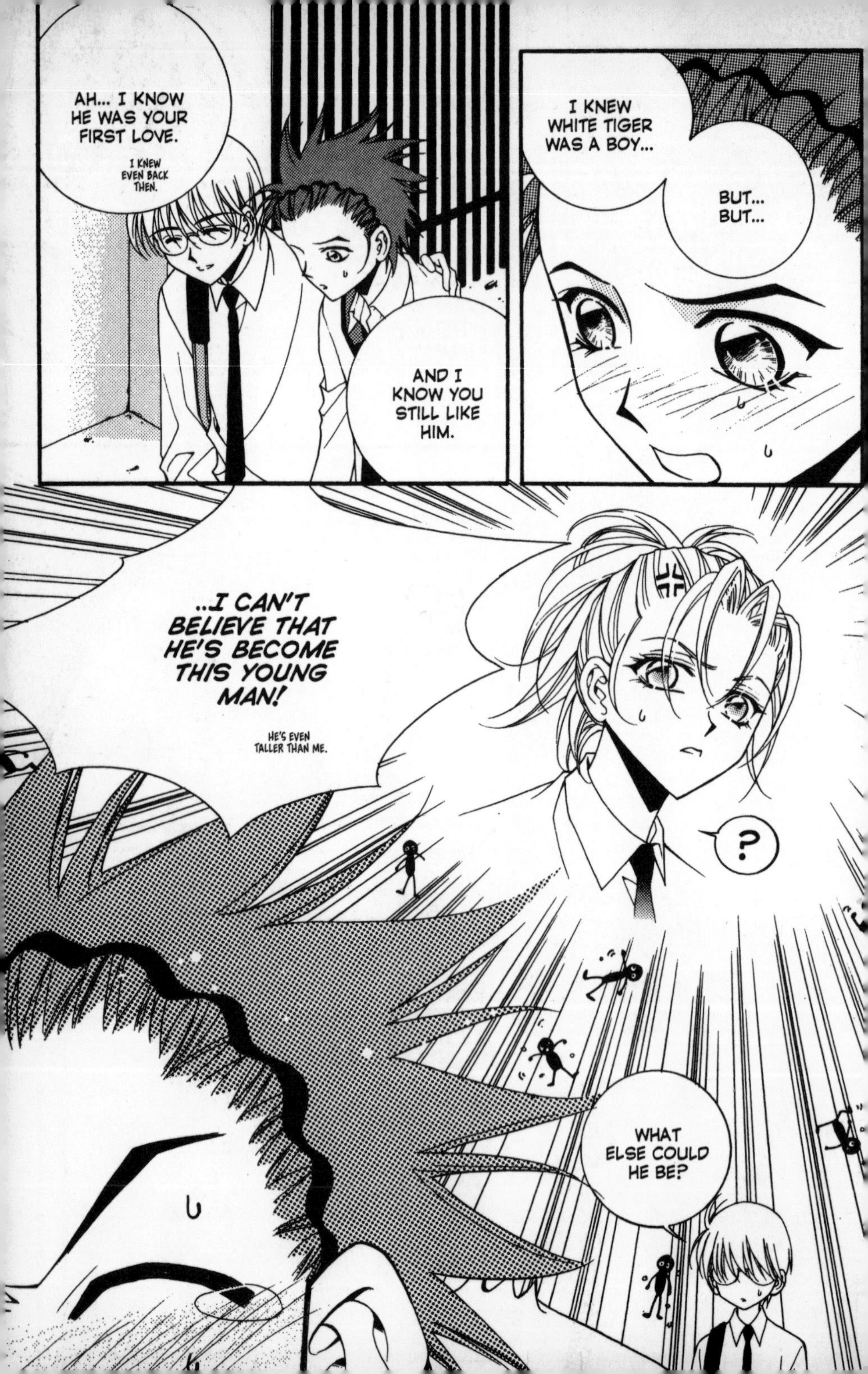
AH... I KNOW HE WAS YOUR FIRST LOVE.
I KNEW EVEN BACK THEN.
AND I KNOW YOU STILL LIKE HIM.
I KNEW WHITE TIGER WAS A BOY...
BUT... BUT...
...I CAN'T BELIEVE THAT HE'S BECOME THIS YOUNG MAN!
HE'S EVEN TALLER THAN ME.
?
WHAT ELSE COULD HE BE?

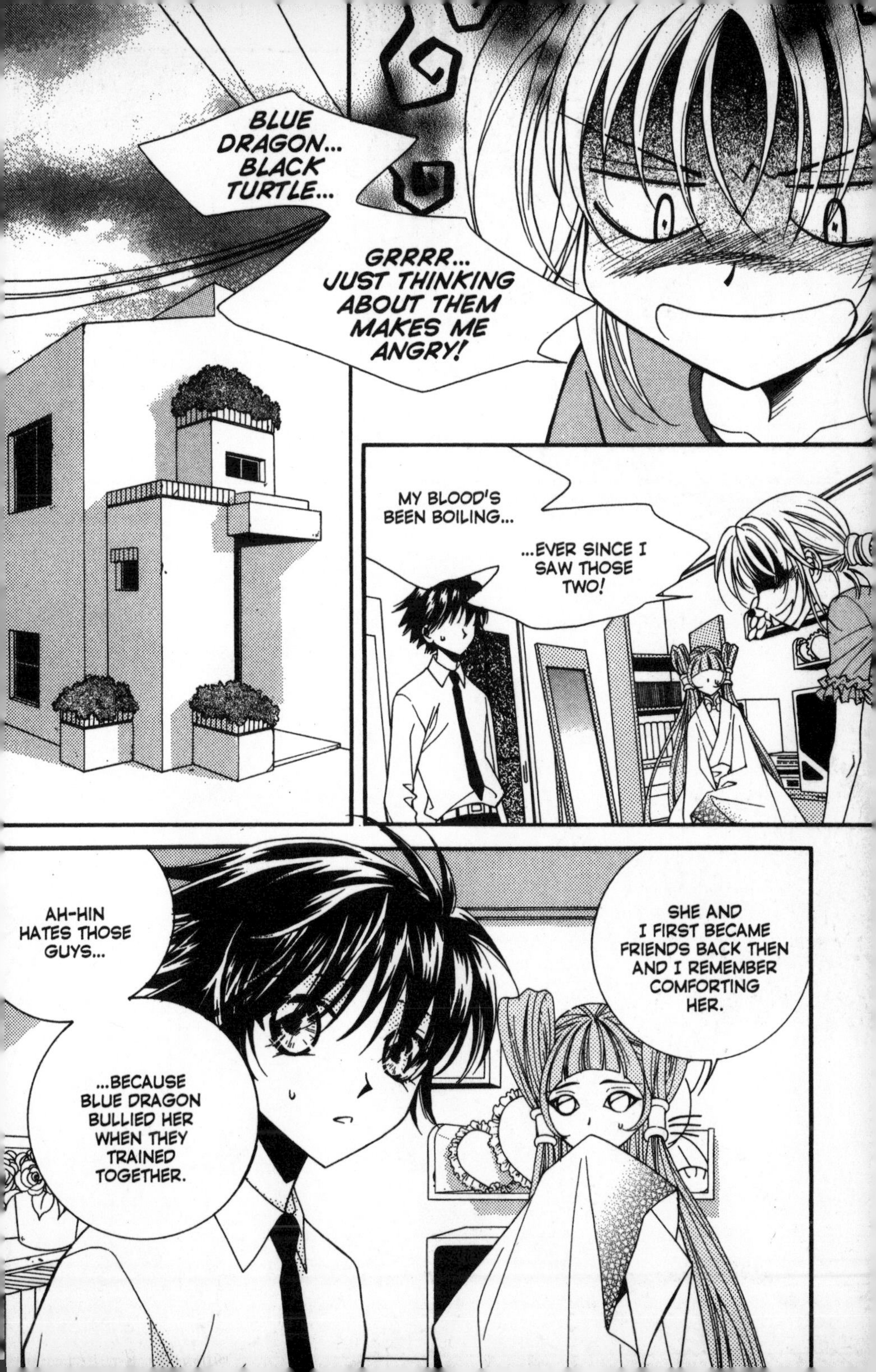
BLUE DRAGON... BLACK TURTLE...
GRRRR... JUST THINKING ABOUT THEM MAKES ME ANGRY!
MY BLOOD'S BEEN BOILING...
...EVER SINCE I SAW THOSE TWO!
AH-HIN HATES THOSE GUYS...
...BECAUSE BLUE DRAGON BULLIED HER WHEN THEY TRAINED TOGETHER.
SHE AND I FIRST BECAME FRIENDS BACK THEN AND I REMEMBER COMFORTING HER.

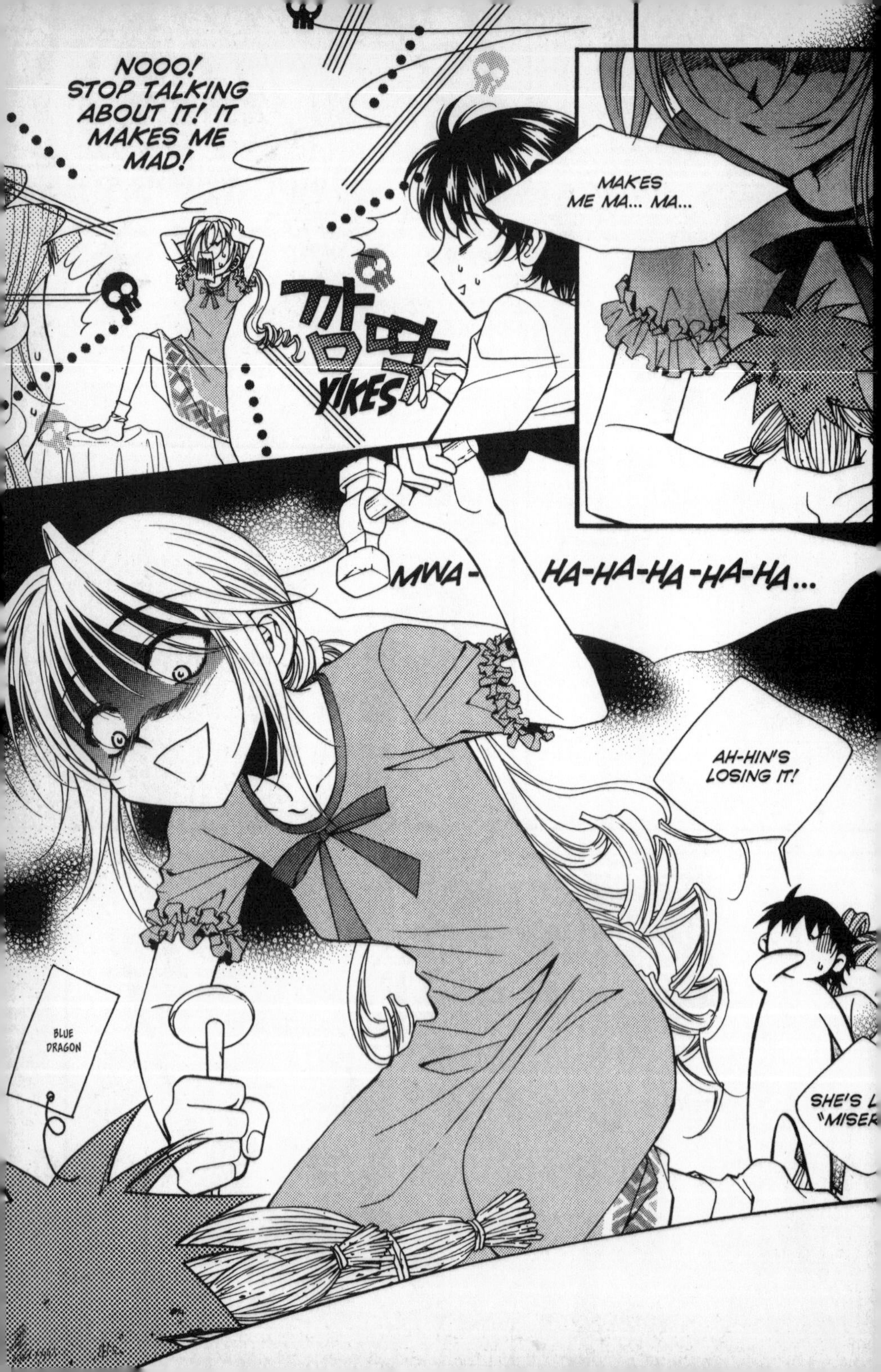

NOOO! STOP TALKING ABOUT IT! IT MAKES ME MAD!
YIKES
MAKES ME MA... MA...
MWA-HA-HA-HA-HA-HA...
AH-HIN'S LOSING IT!
BLUE DRAGON
SHE'S L
"MISER

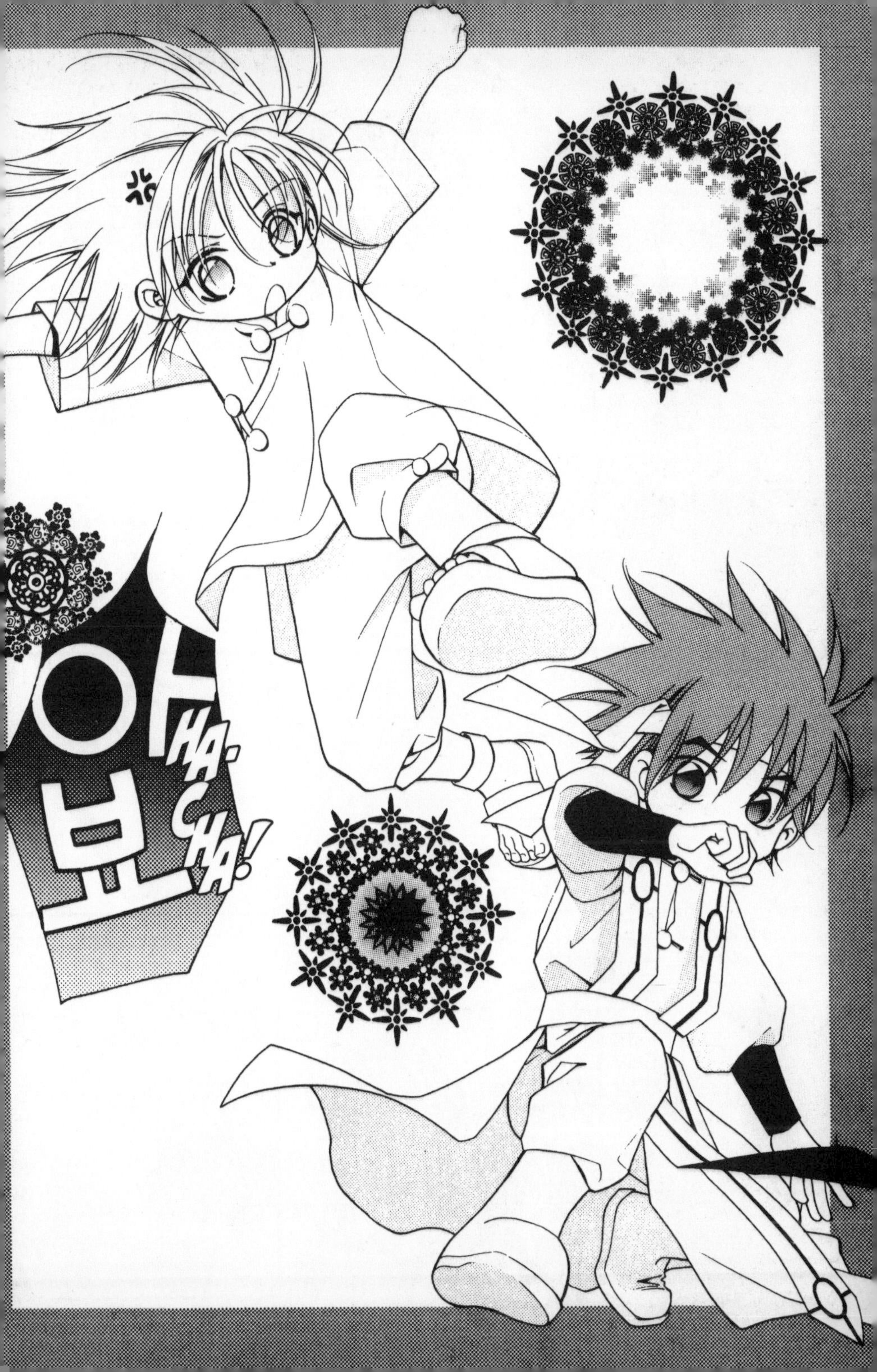
아뵤
HA-CHA-CHA!

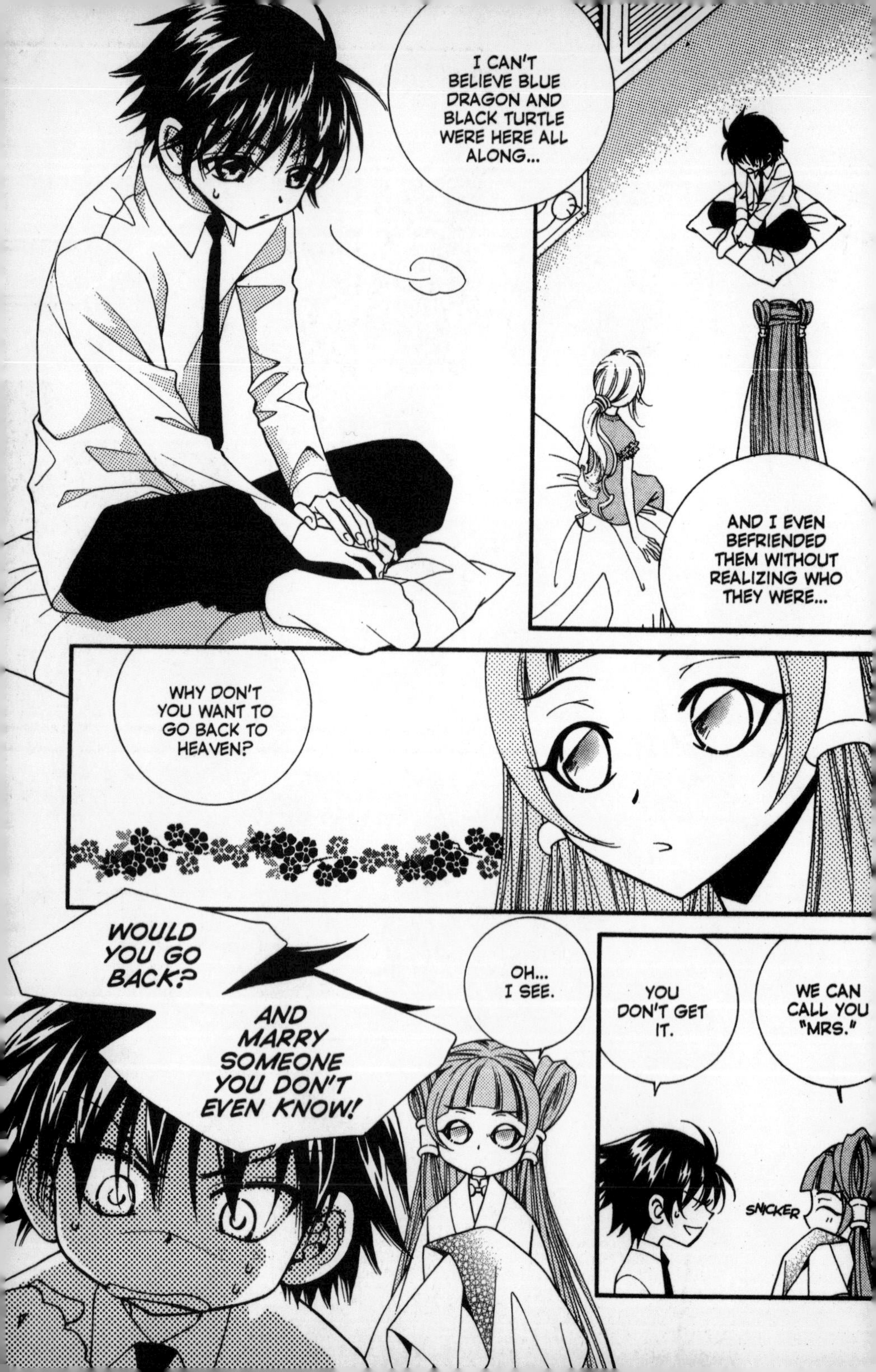
I CAN'T BELIEVE BLUE DRAGON AND BLACK TURTLE WERE HERE ALL ALONG...
AND I EVEN BEFRIENDED THEM WITHOUT REALIZING WHO THEY WERE...
WHY DON'T YOU WANT TO GO BACK TO HEAVEN?
WOULD YOU GO BACK?
AND MARRY SOMEONE YOU DON'T EVEN KNOW!
OH... I SEE.
YOU DON'T GET IT.
WE CAN CALL YOU "MRS."
SNICKER

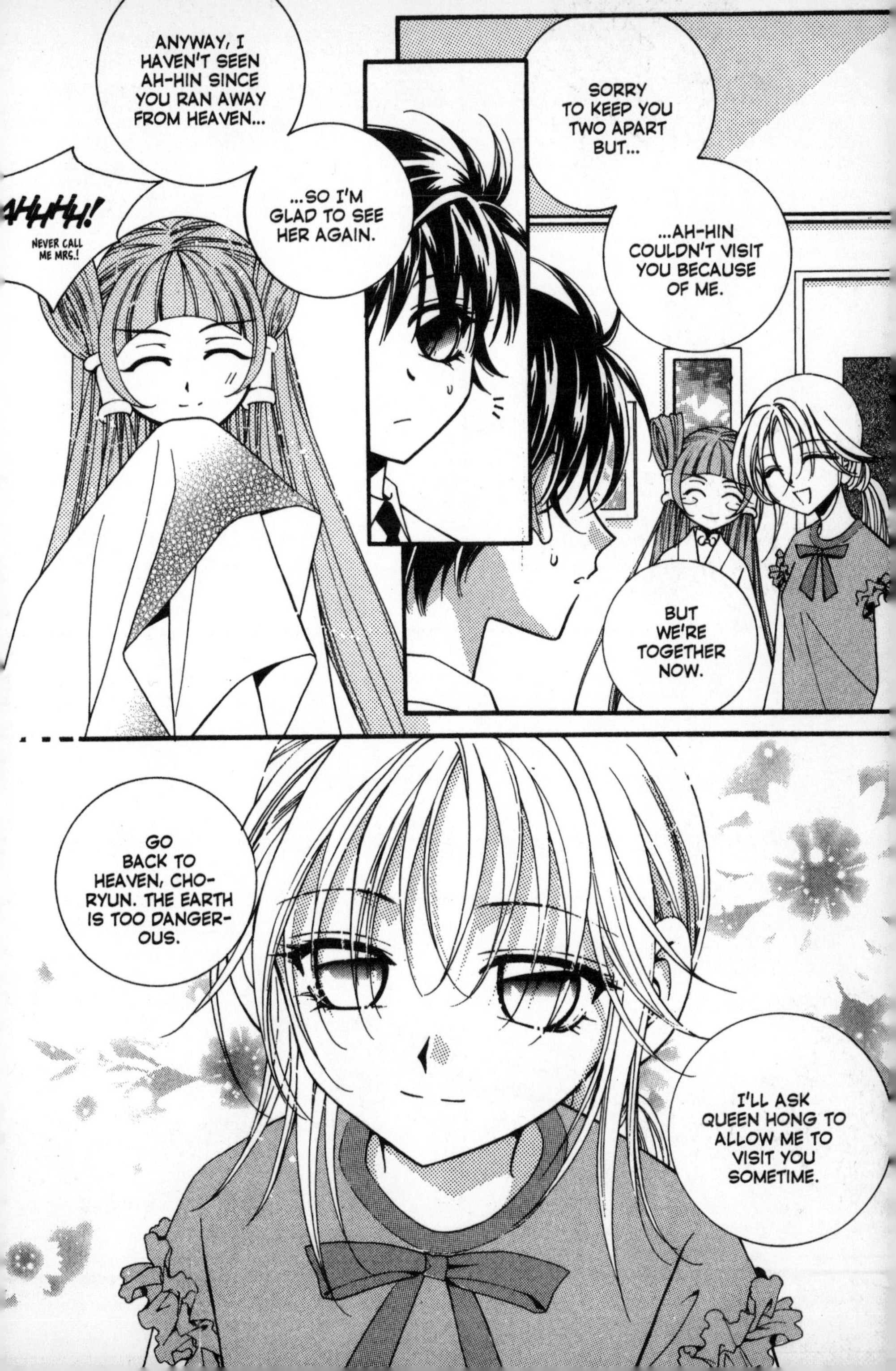
HHHH!
NEVER CALL ME MRS.!
ANYWAY, I HAVEN'T SEEN AH-HIN SINCE YOU RAN AWAY FROM HEAVEN...
...SO I'M GLAD TO SEE HER AGAIN.
SORRY TO KEEP YOU TWO APART BUT...
...AH-HIN COULDN'T VISIT YOU BECAUSE OF ME.
BUT WE'RE TOGETHER NOW.
GO BACK TO HEAVEN, CHO-RYUN. THE EARTH IS TOO DANGER-OUS.
I'LL ASK QUEEN HONG TO ALLOW ME TO VISIT YOU SOMETIME.

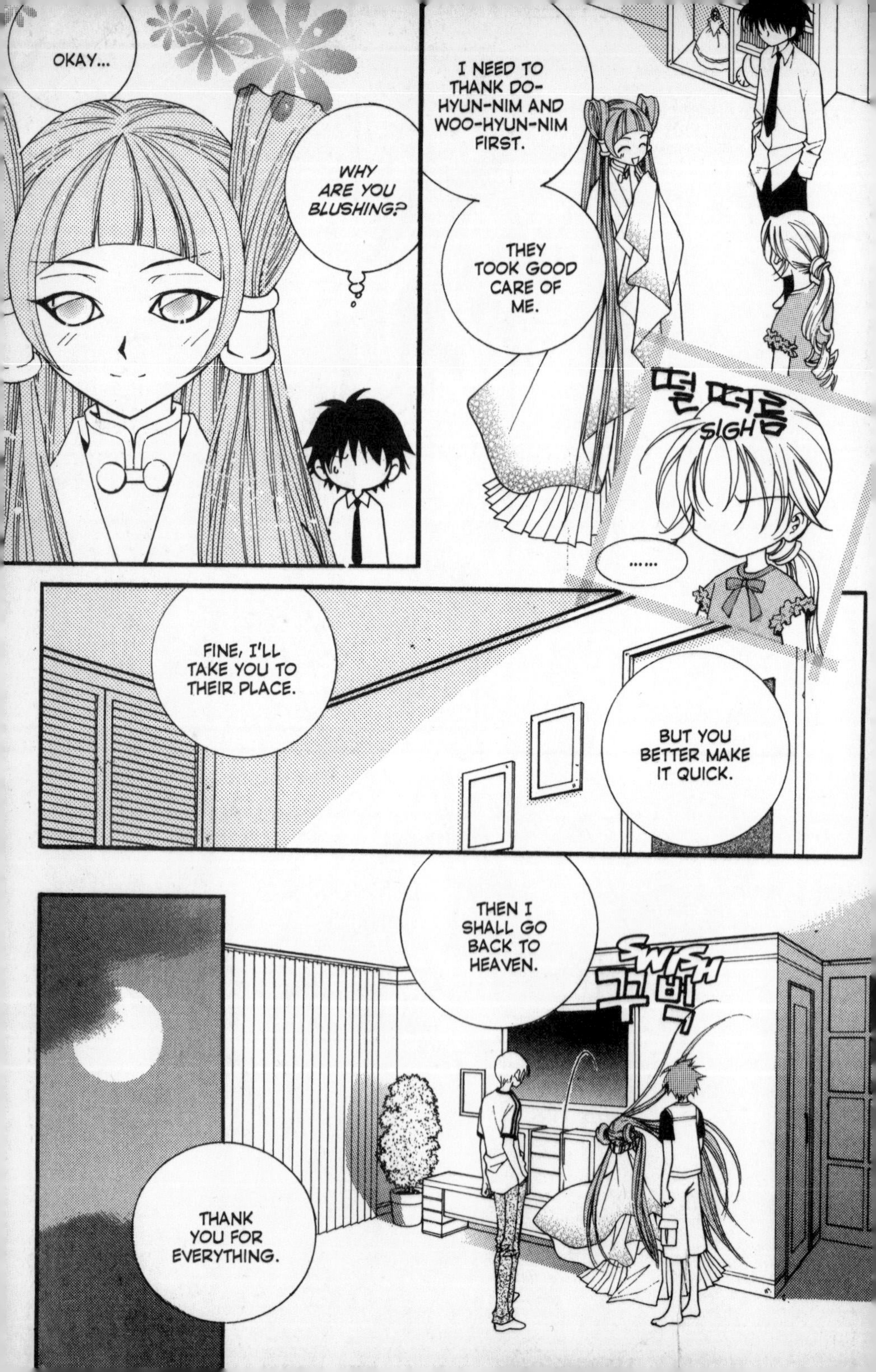
OKAY...
WHY ARE YOU BLUSHING?
I NEED TO THANK DO-HYUN-NIM AND WOO-HYUN-NIM FIRST.
THEY TOOK GOOD CARE OF ME.
떨떠름
SIGH
......
FINE, I'LL TAKE YOU TO THEIR PLACE.
BUT YOU BETTER MAKE IT QUICK.
THEN I SHALL GO BACK TO HEAVEN.
SWISH
꾸벅
THANK YOU FOR EVERYTHING.

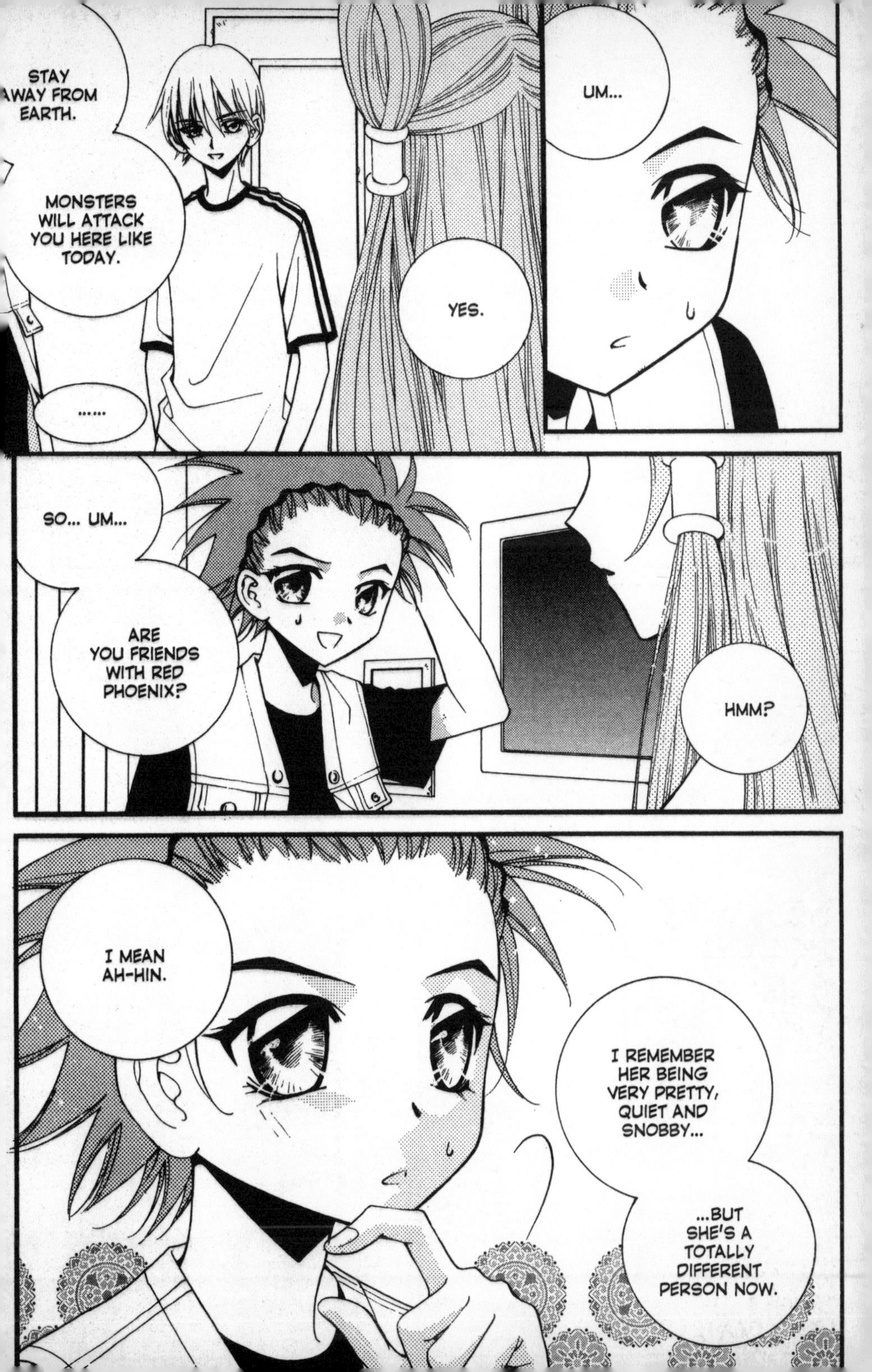
STAY AWAY FROM EARTH.
MONSTERS WILL ATTACK YOU HERE LIKE TODAY.
......
YES.
UM...
SO... UM...
ARE YOU FRIENDS WITH RED PHOENIX?
HMM?
I MEAN AH-HIN.
I REMEMBER HER BEING VERY PRETTY, QUIET AND SNOBBY...
...BUT SHE'S A TOTALLY DIFFERENT PERSON NOW.

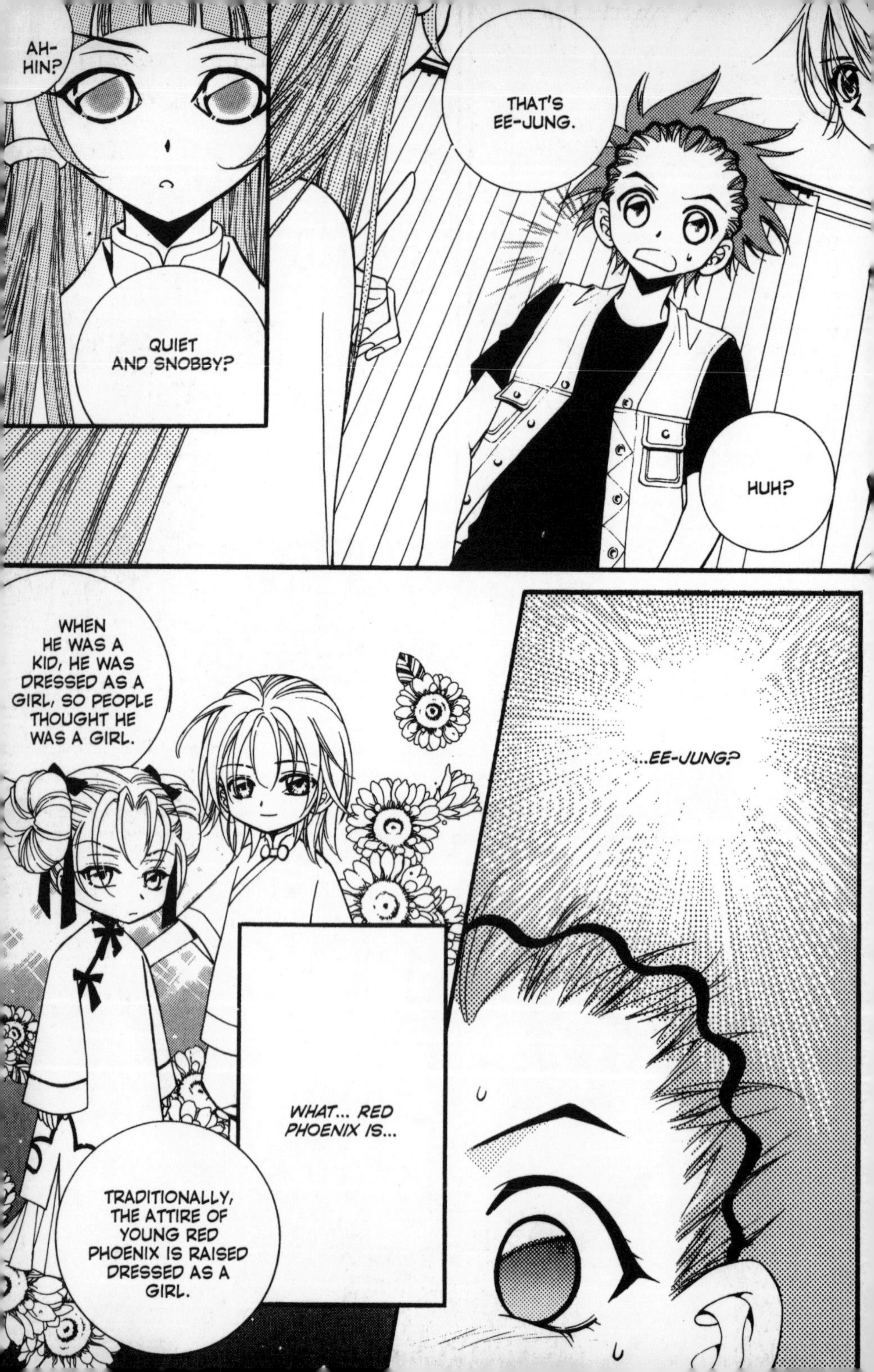
AH-HIN?
QUIET AND SNOBBY?
THAT'S EE-JUNG.
HUH?
WHEN HE WAS A KID, HE WAS DRESSED AS A GIRL, SO PEOPLE THOUGHT HE WAS A GIRL.
TRADITIONALLY, THE ATTIRE OF YOUNG RED PHOENIX IS RAISED DRESSED AS A GIRL.
WHAT... RED PHOENIX IS...
...EE-JUNG?

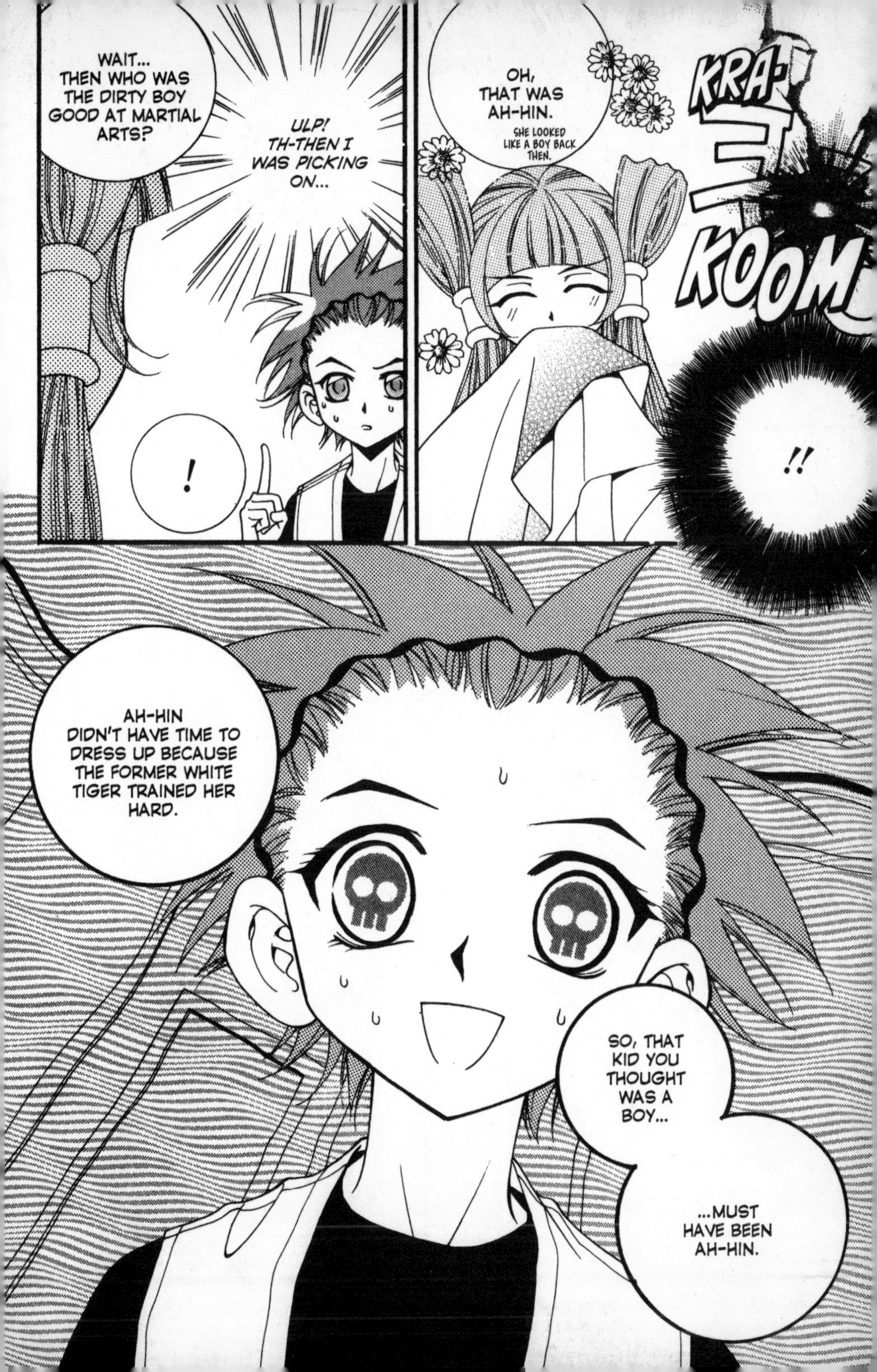
WAIT... THEN WHO WAS THE DIRTY BOY GOOD AT MARTIAL ARTS?
ULP! TH-THEN I WAS PICKING ON...
!
OH, THAT WAS AH-HIN.
SHE LOOKED LIKE A BOY BACK THEN.
KRA-
KOOM
!!
AH-HIN DIDN'T HAVE TIME TO DRESS UP BECAUSE THE FORMER WHITE TIGER TRAINED HER HARD.
SO, THAT KID YOU THOUGHT WAS A BOY...
...MUST HAVE BEEN AH-HIN.

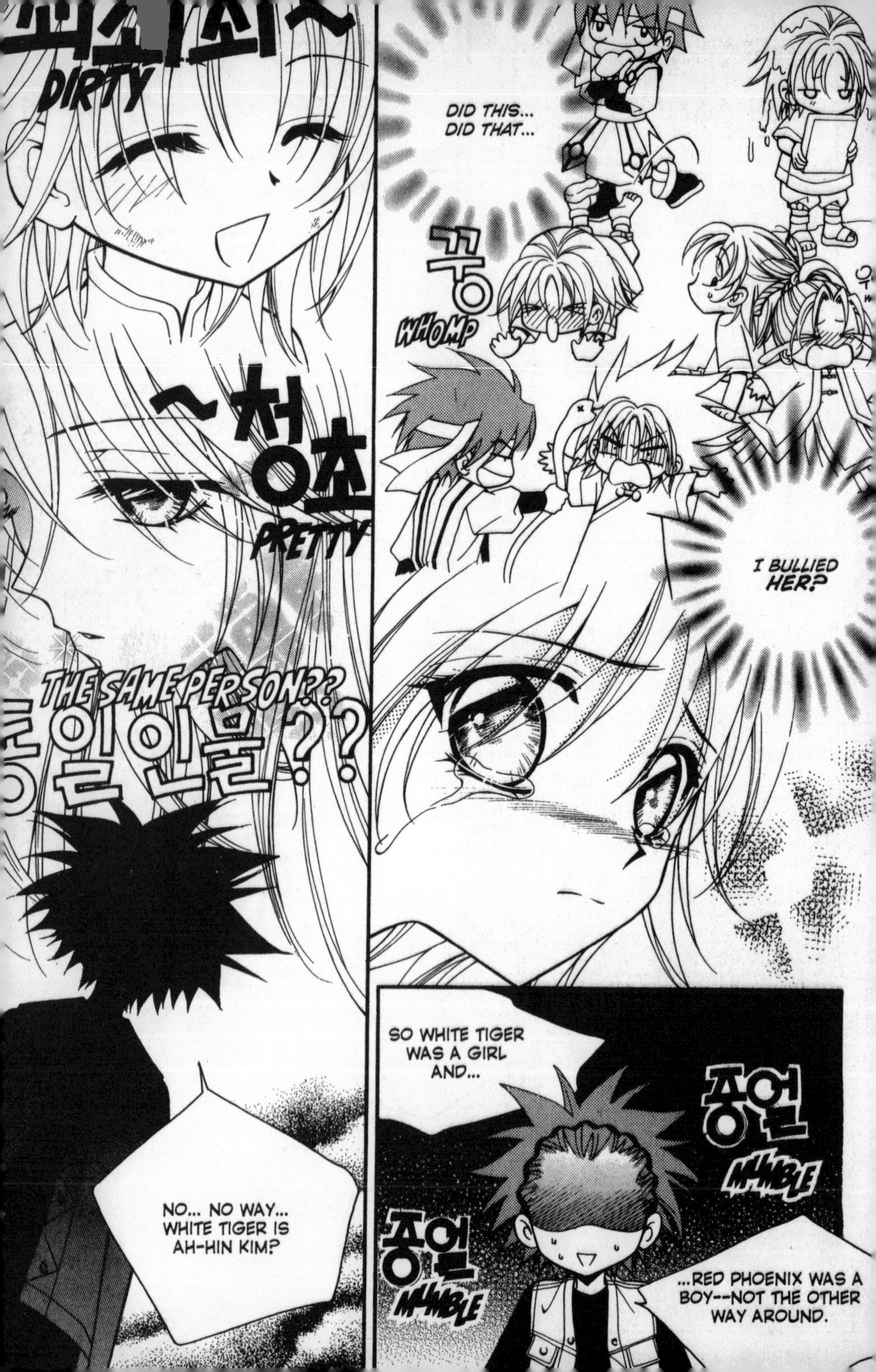

DIRTY
청초~
PRETTY
THE SAME PERSON??
NO... NO WAY... WHITE TIGER IS AH-HIN KIM?
DID THIS... DID THAT...
꽁
WHOMP
I BULLIED HER?
SO WHITE TIGER WAS A GIRL AND...
중얼
MUMBLE
중얼
MUMBLE
...RED PHOENIX WAS A BOY--NOT THE OTHER WAY AROUND.

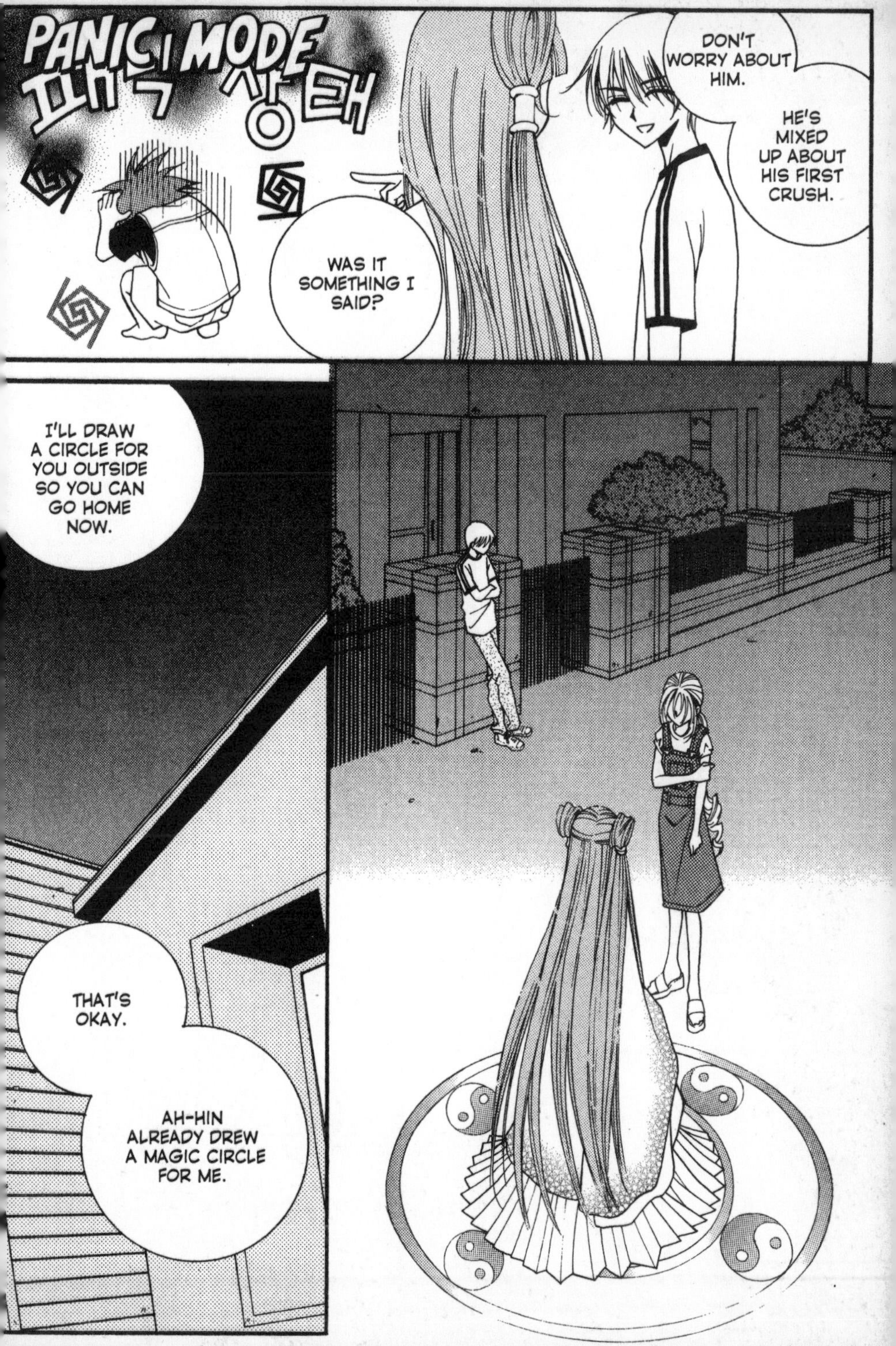
PANIC MODE
패닉 상태
WAS IT SOMETHING I SAID?
DON'T WORRY ABOUT HIM.
HE'S MIXED UP ABOUT HIS FIRST CRUSH.
I'LL DRAW A CIRCLE FOR YOU OUTSIDE SO YOU CAN GO HOME NOW.
THAT'S OKAY.
AH-HIN ALREADY DREW A MAGIC CIRCLE FOR ME.

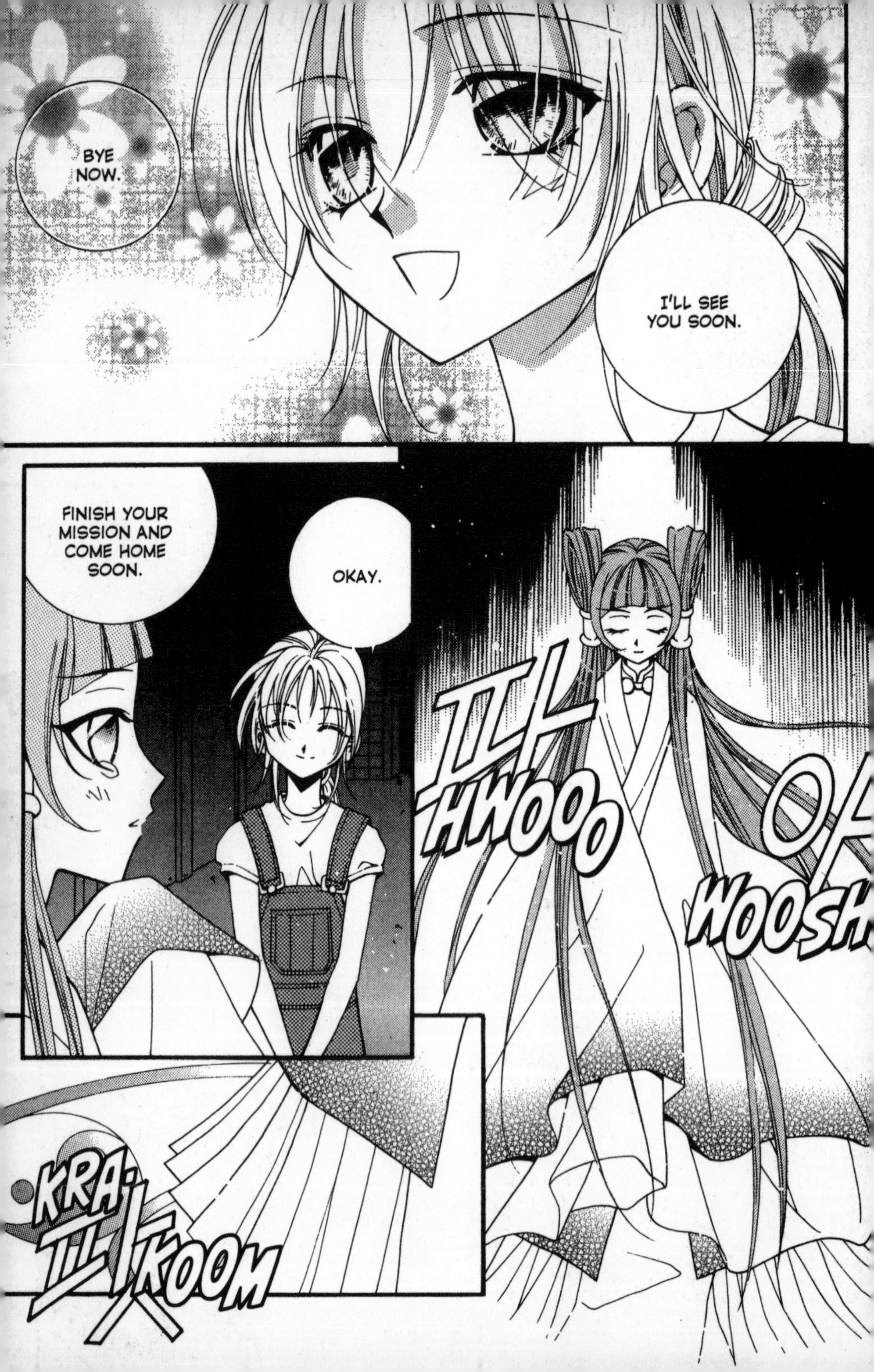
BYE NOW.
I'LL SEE YOU SOON.
FINISH YOUR MISSION AND COME HOME SOON.
OKAY.
HWOOO
WOOSH
KRA-
KOOM

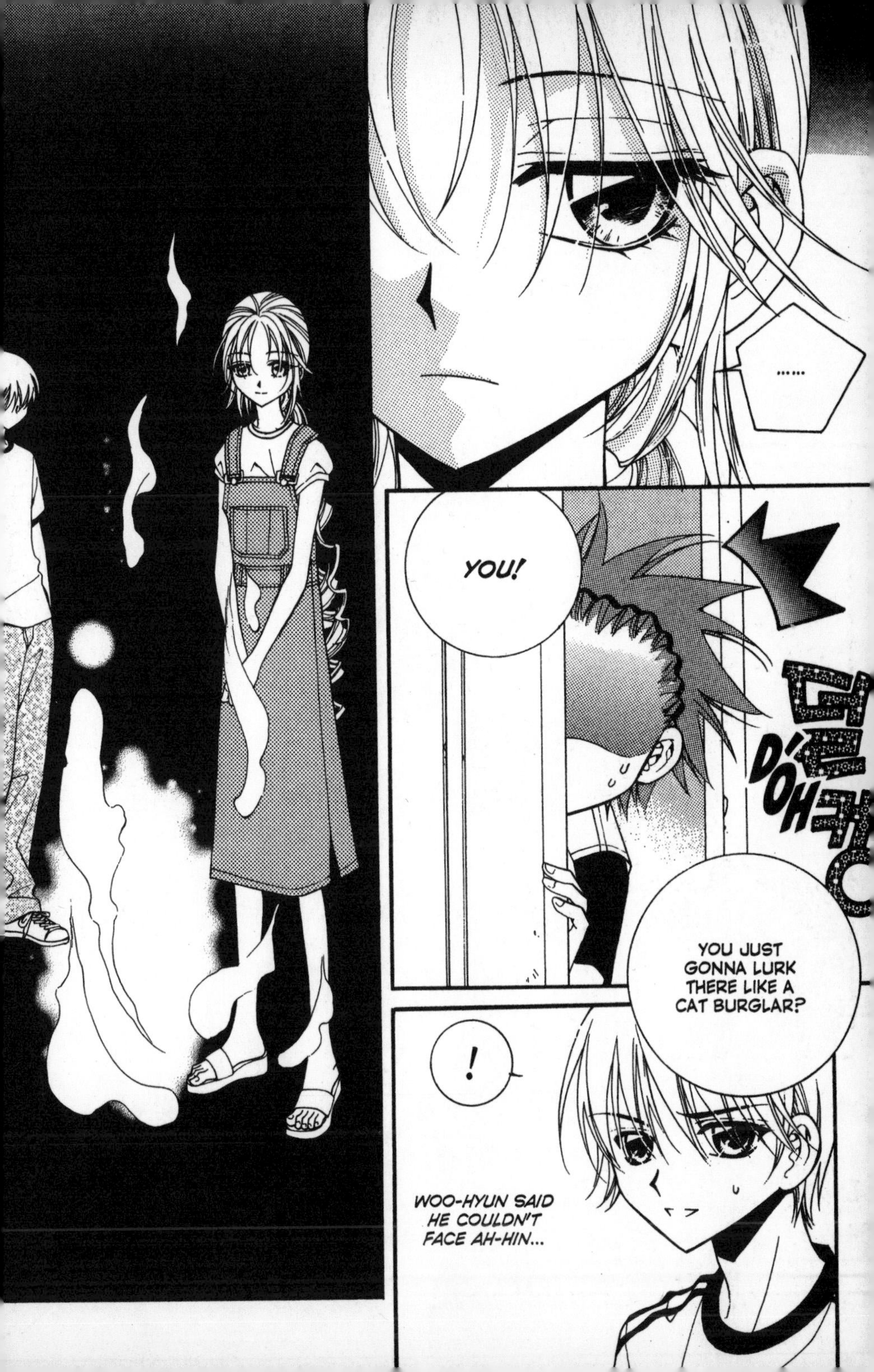
……
YOU!
덜컹
D'OH
YOU JUST GONNA LURK THERE LIKE A CAT BURGLAR?
!
WOO-HYUN SAID HE COULDN'T FACE AH-HIN...

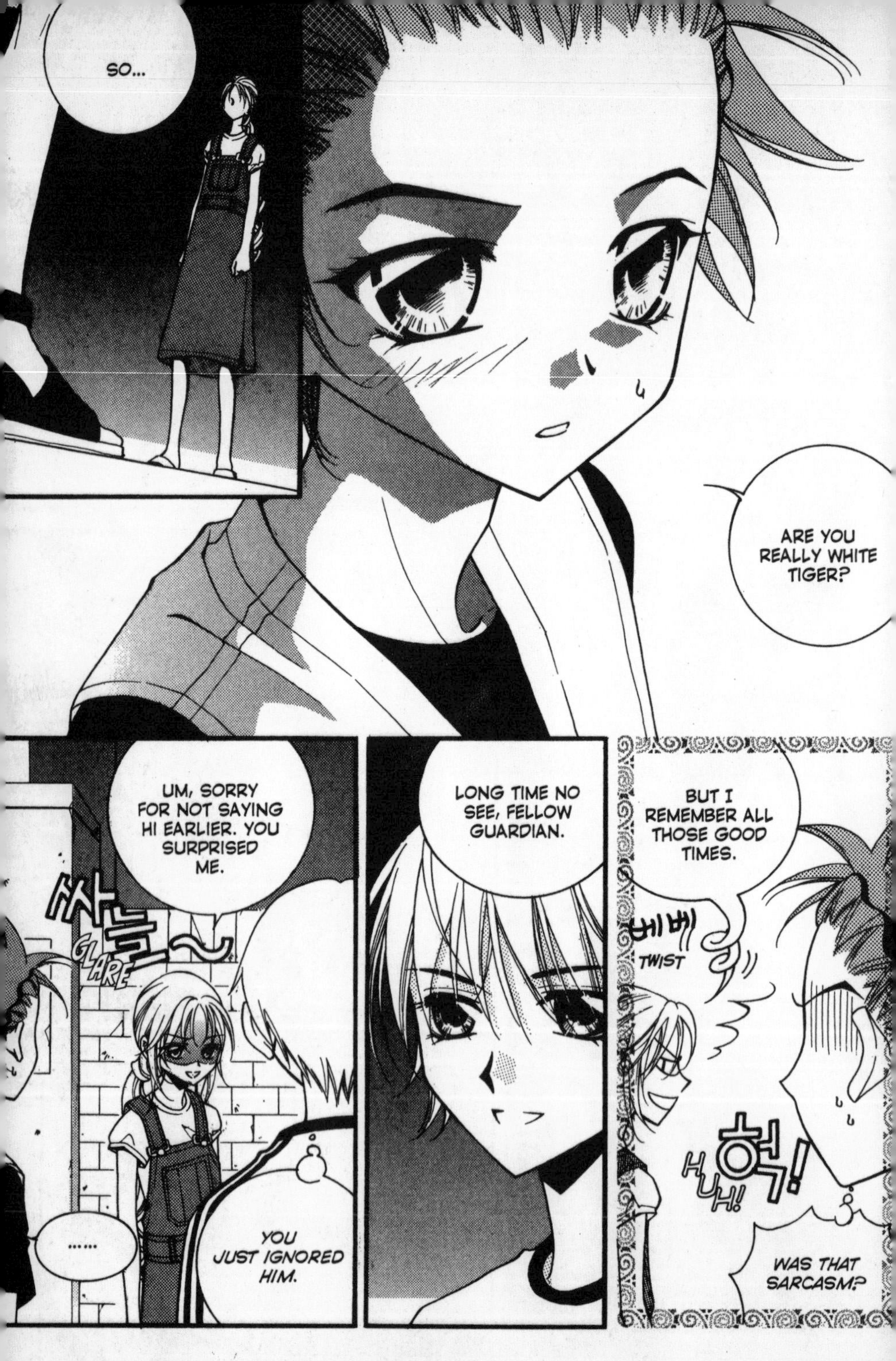
SO...
ARE YOU REALLY WHITE TIGER?
UM, SORRY FOR NOT SAYING HI EARLIER. YOU SURPRISED ME.
싸늘~
GLARE
......
YOU JUST IGNORED HIM.
LONG TIME NO SEE, FELLOW GUARDIAN.
BUT I REMEMBER ALL THOSE GOOD TIMES.
베베
TWIST
헉!
HUH!
WAS THAT SARCASM?

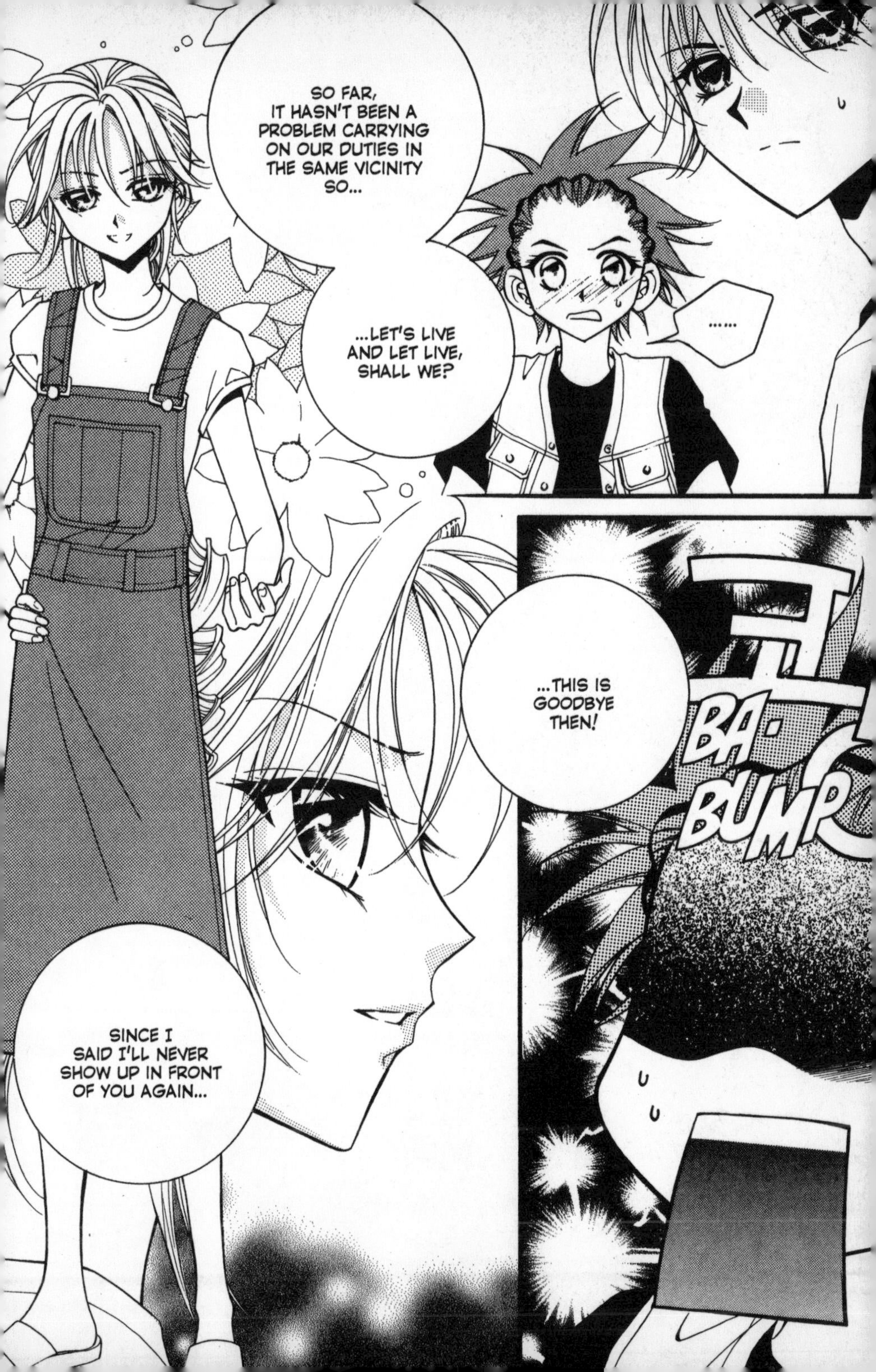
SO FAR, IT HASN'T BEEN A PROBLEM CARRYING ON OUR DUTIES IN THE SAME VICINITY SO...
...LET'S LIVE AND LET LIVE, SHALL WE?
……
SINCE I SAID I'LL NEVER SHOW UP IN FRONT OF YOU AGAIN...
...THIS IS GOODBYE THEN!
BA-BUMP

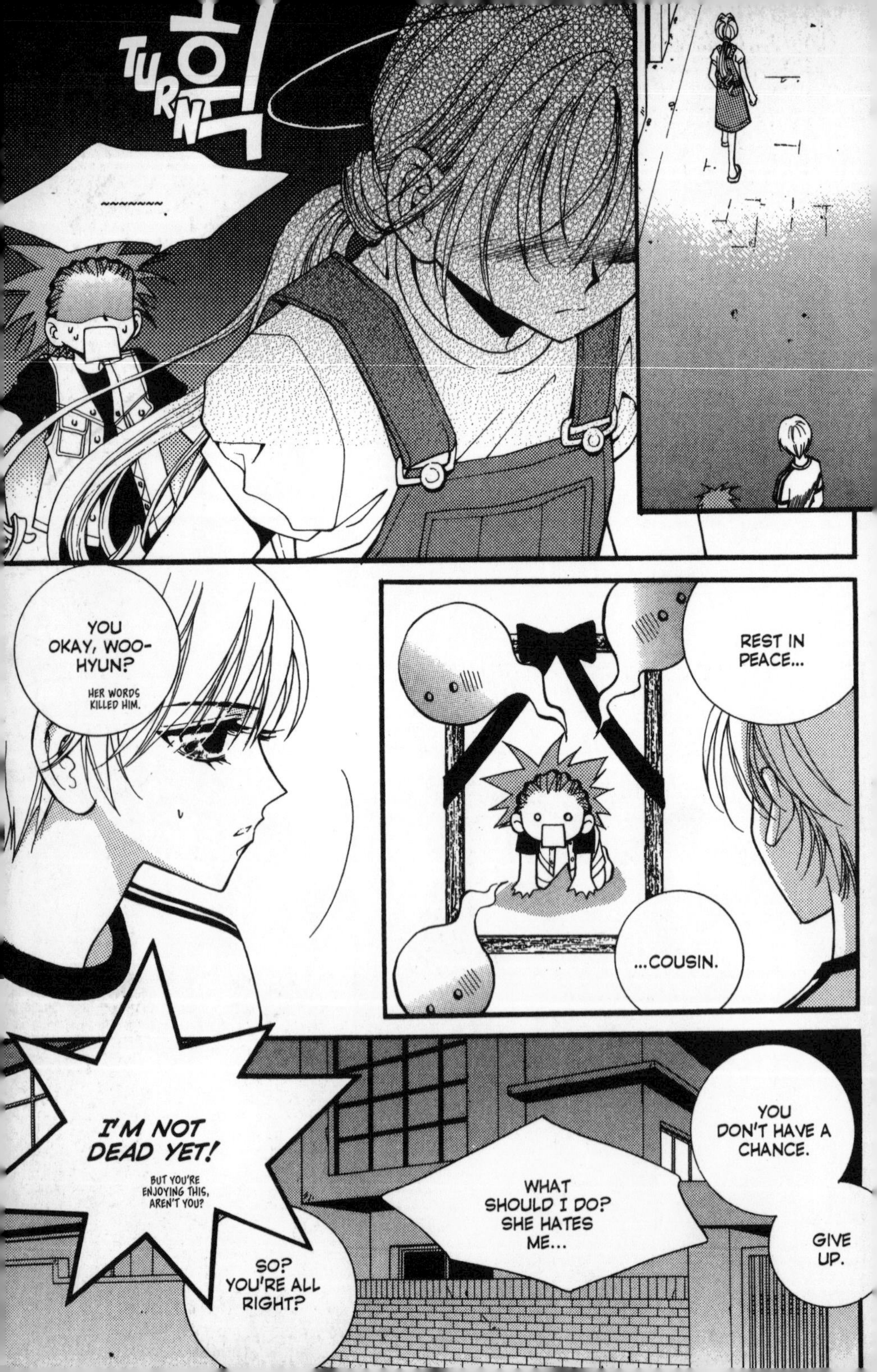
TURN
~~~~~~~
YOU OKAY, WOO-HYUN?
HER WORDS KILLED HIM.
REST IN PEACE...
...COUSIN.
I'M NOT DEAD YET!
BUT YOU'RE ENJOYING THIS, AREN'T YOU?
SO? YOU'RE ALL RIGHT?
WHAT SHOULD I DO? SHE HATES ME...
YOU DON'T HAVE A CHANCE.
GIVE UP.
~~~~~~~

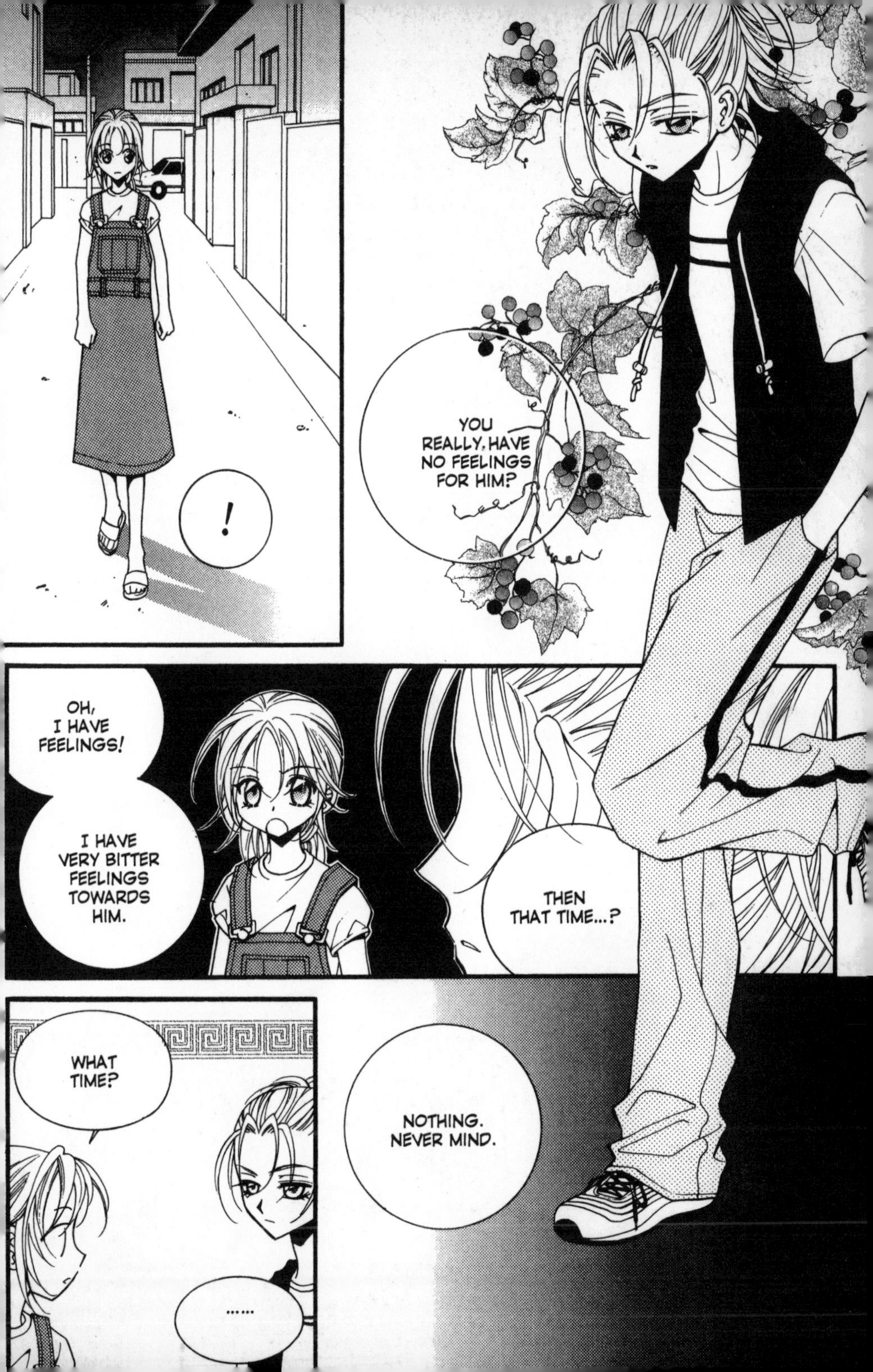
!
YOU REALLY, HAVE NO FEELINGS FOR HIM?
OH, I HAVE FEELINGS!
I HAVE VERY BITTER FEELINGS TOWARDS HIM.
THEN THAT TIME...?
WHAT TIME?
......
NOTHING. NEVER MIND.

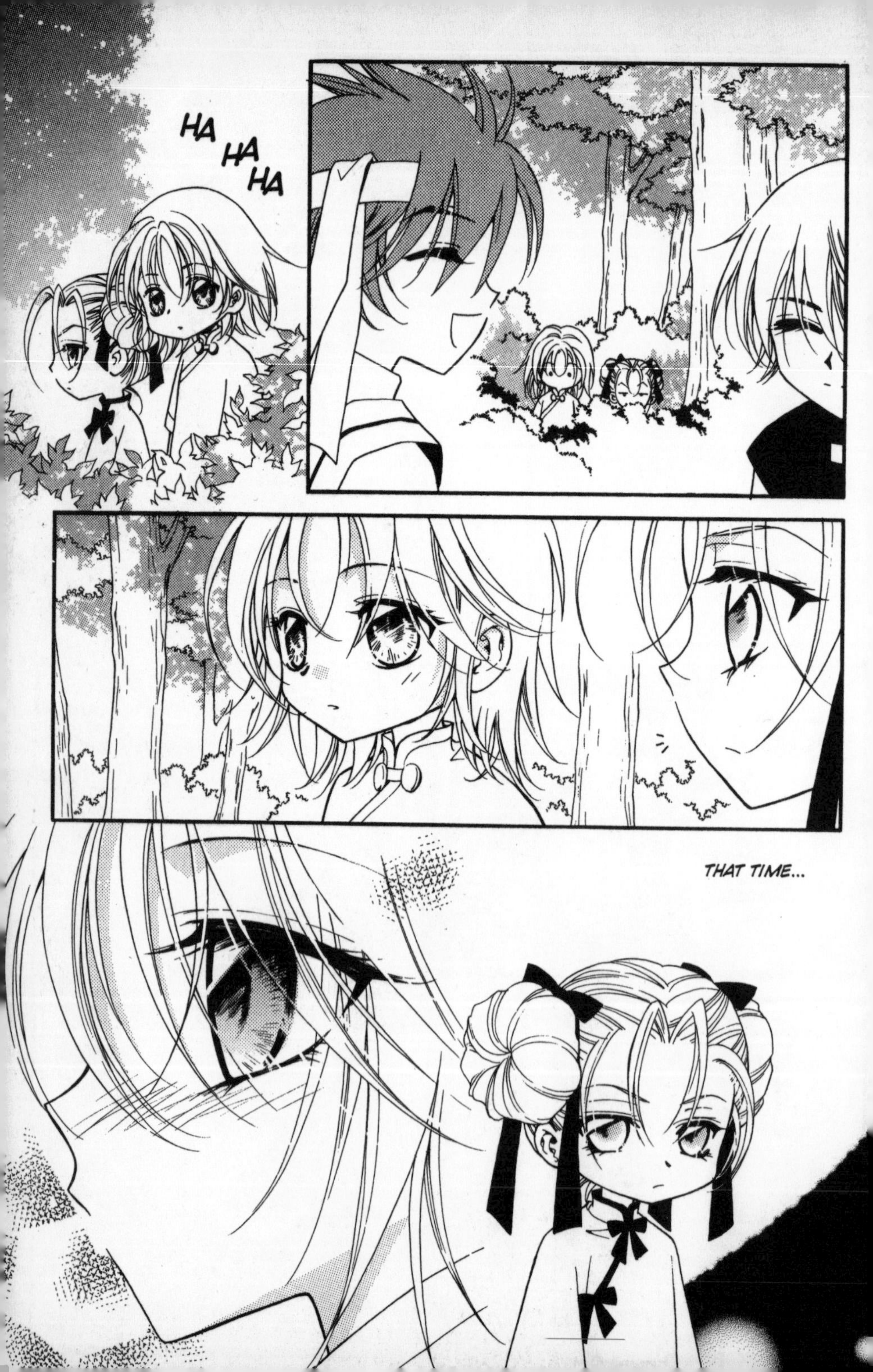
HA
HA
HA
THAT TIME...

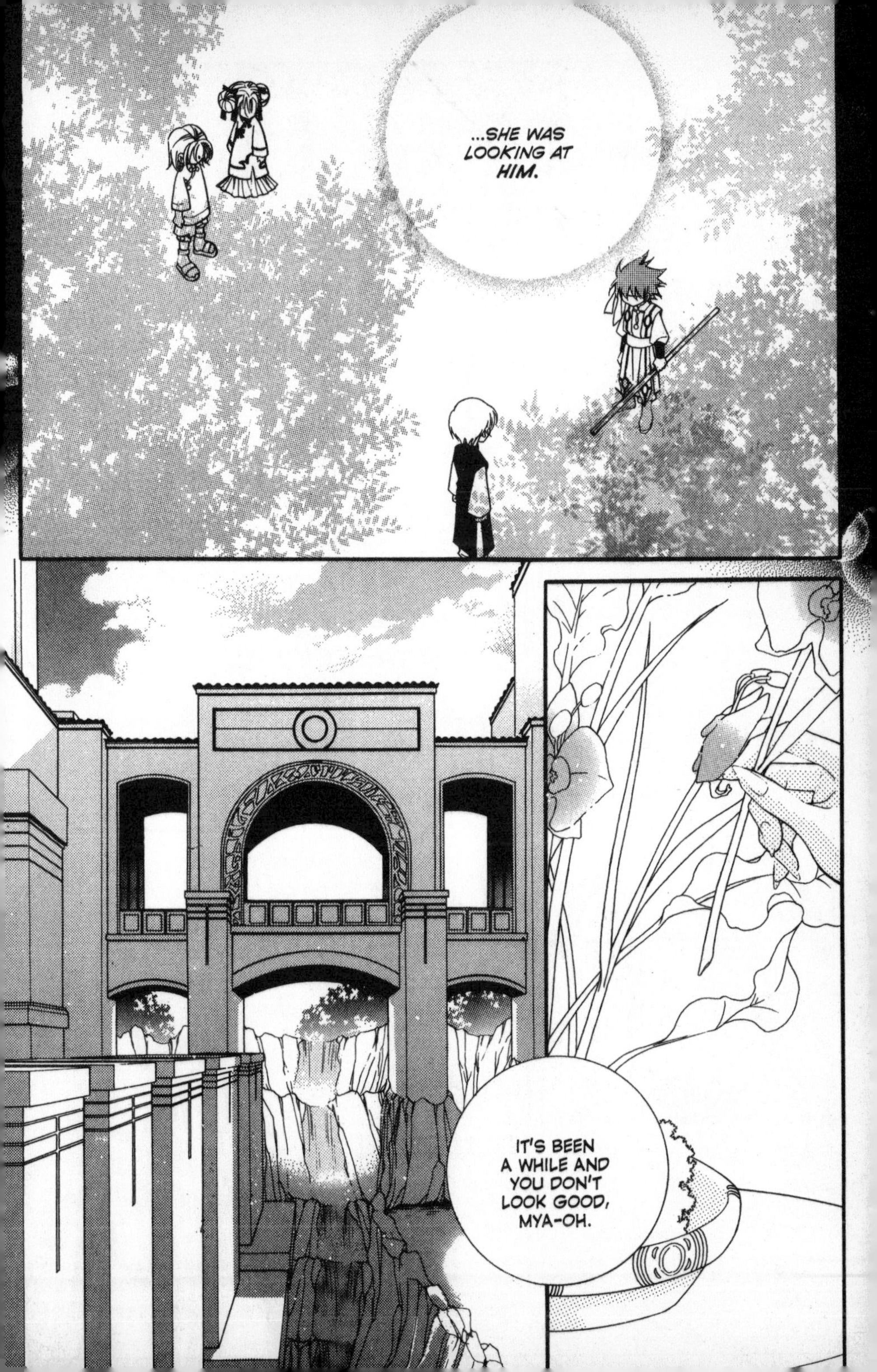
...SHE WAS LOOKING AT HIM.
IT'S BEEN A WHILE AND YOU DON'T LOOK GOOD, MYA-OH.

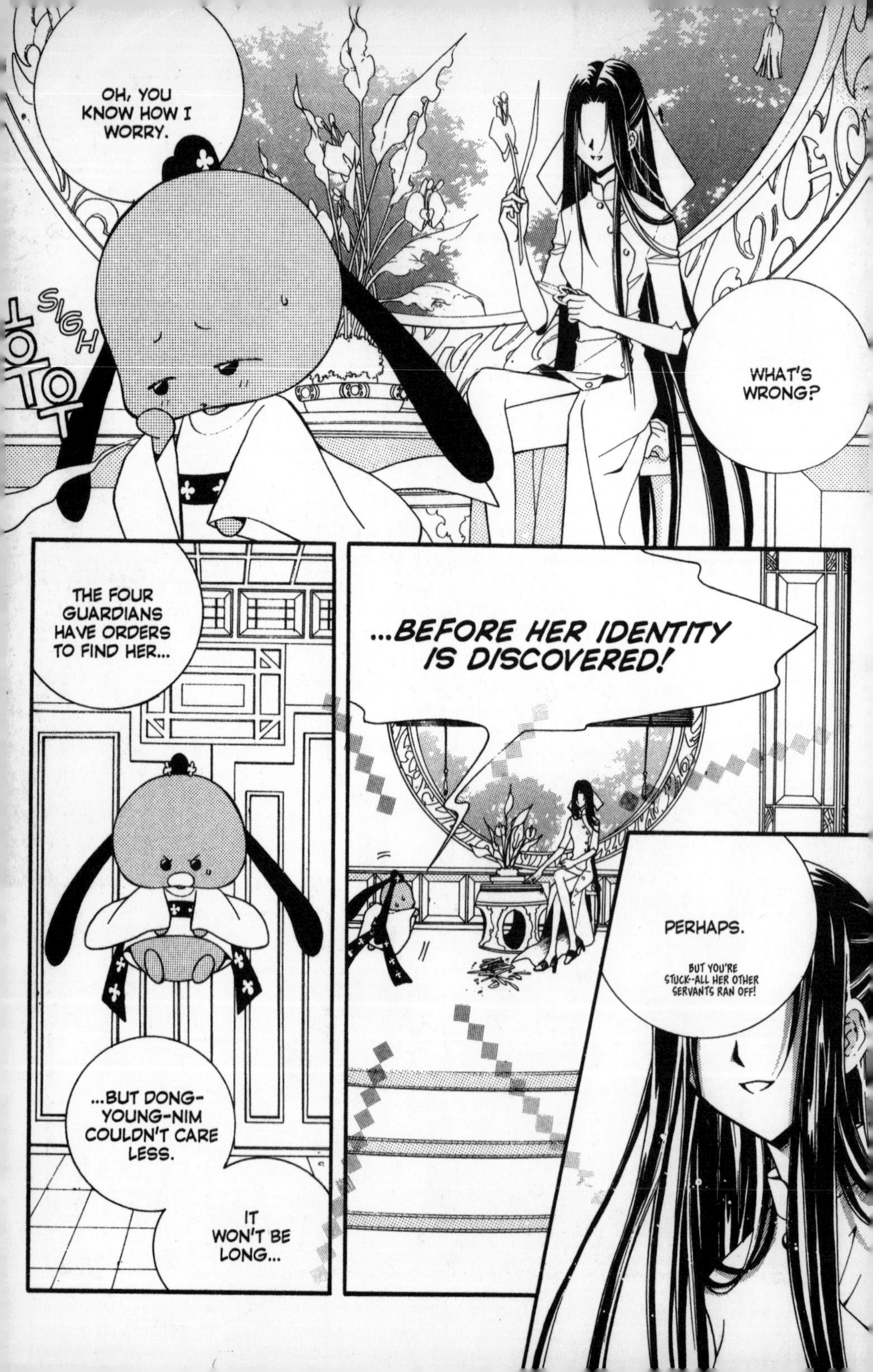
OH, YOU KNOW HOW I WORRY.
SIGH
WHAT'S WRONG?
THE FOUR GUARDIANS HAVE ORDERS TO FIND HER...
...BUT DONG-YOUNG-NIM COULDN'T CARE LESS.
IT WON'T BE LONG...
...BEFORE HER IDENTITY IS DISCOVERED!
PERHAPS.
BUT YOU'RE STUCK--ALL HER OTHER SERVANTS RAN OFF!

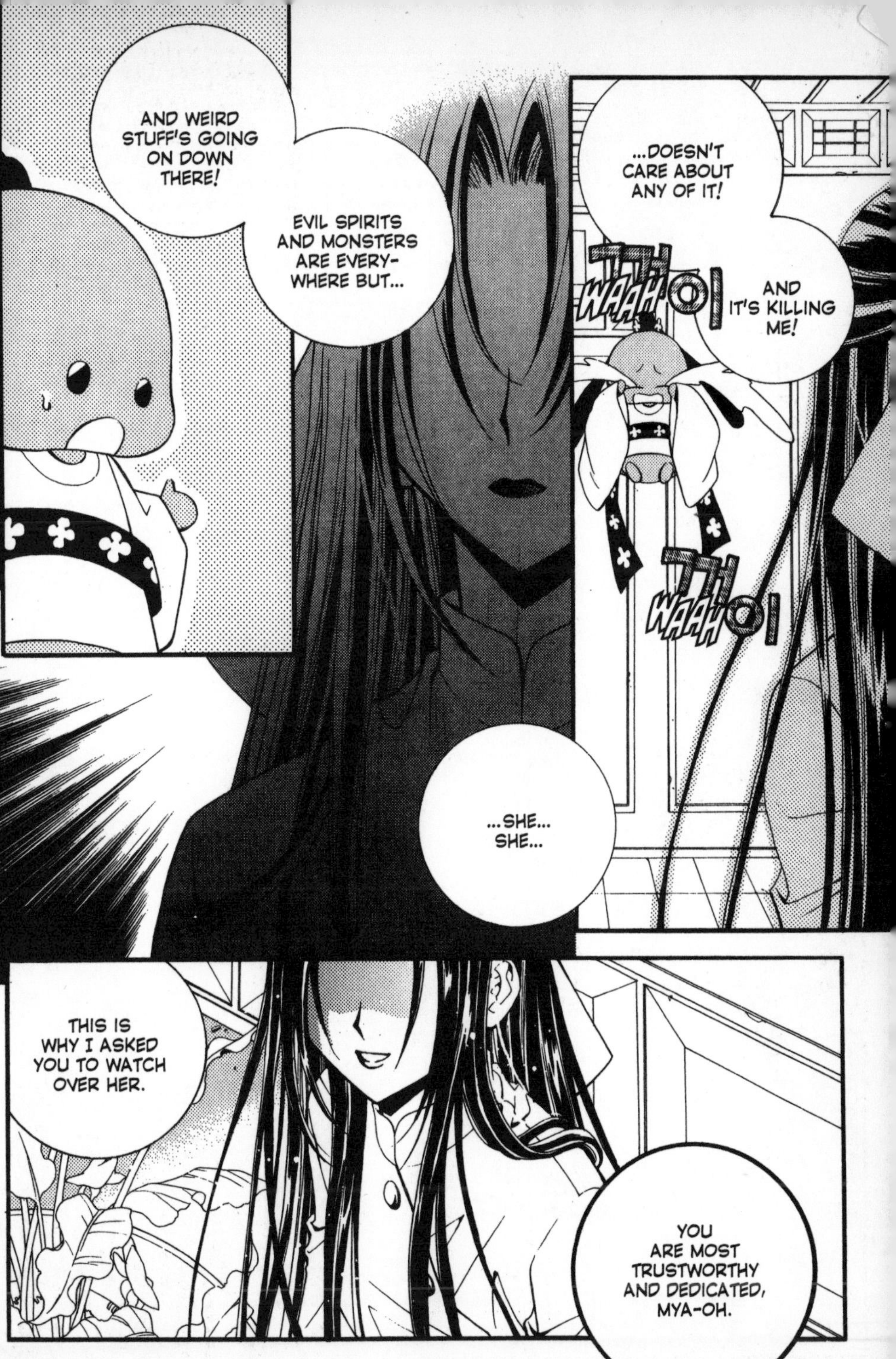
AND WEIRD STUFF'S GOING ON DOWN THERE!
EVIL SPIRITS AND MONSTERS ARE EVERY-WHERE BUT...
...SHE... SHE...
...DOESN'T CARE ABOUT ANY OF IT!
WAAH
AND IT'S KILLING ME!
WAAH
THIS IS WHY I ASKED YOU TO WATCH OVER HER.
YOU ARE MOST TRUSTWORTHY AND DEDICATED, MYA-OH.

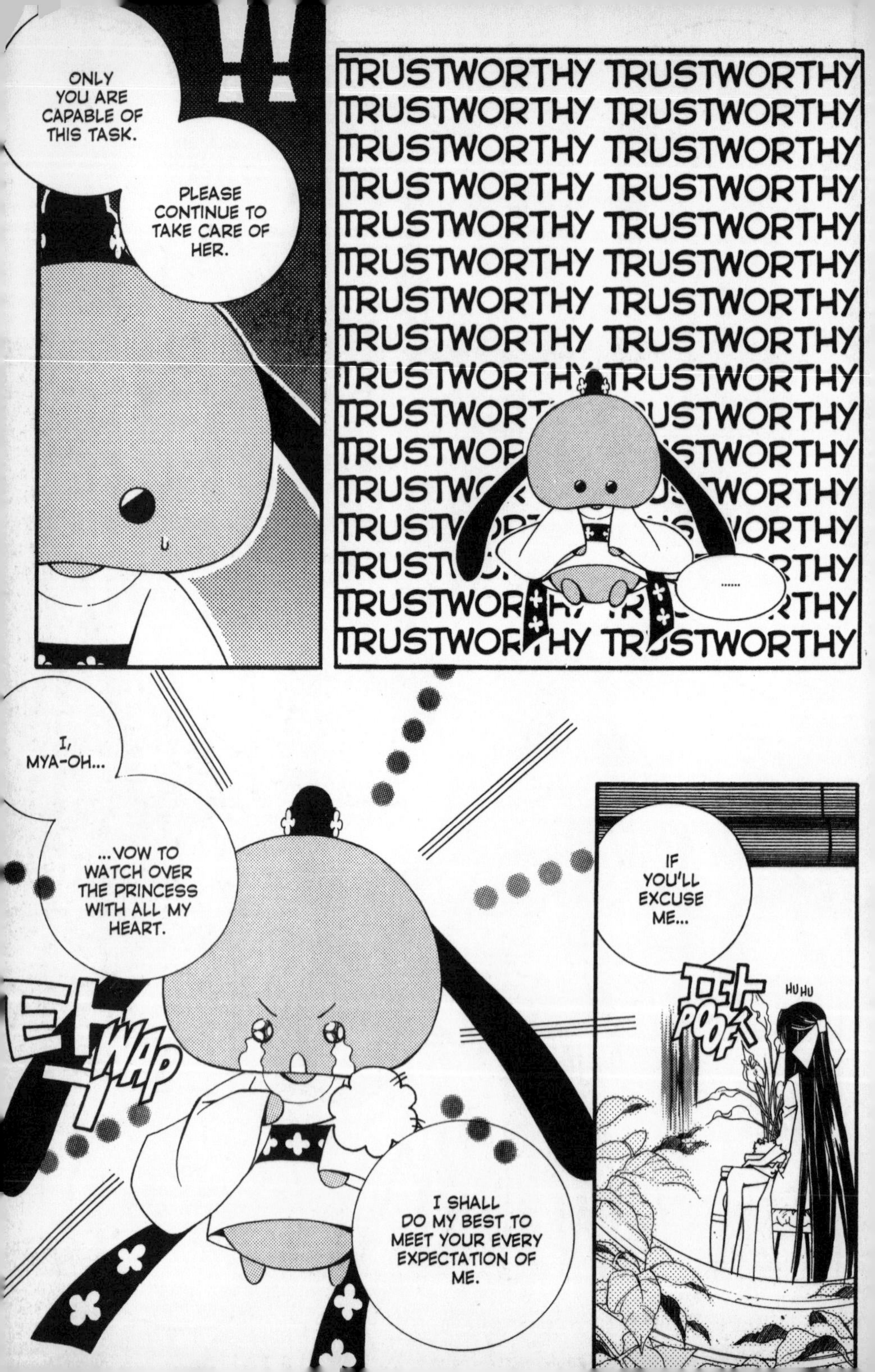
ONLY YOU ARE CAPABLE OF THIS TASK.
PLEASE CONTINUE TO TAKE CARE OF HER.
TRUSTWORTHY TRUSTWORTHY
TRUSTWORTHY TRUSTWORTHY
TRUSTWORTHY TRUSTWORTHY
TRUSTWORTHY TRUSTWORTHY
TRUSTWORTHY TRUSTWORTHY
TRUSTWORTHY TRUSTWORTHY
TRUSTWORTHY TRUSTWORTHY
TRUSTWORTHY TRUSTWORTHY
TRUSTWORTHY TRUSTWORTHY
......
I, MYA-OH...
...VOW TO WATCH OVER THE PRINCESS WITH ALL MY HEART.
WAP
I SHALL DO MY BEST TO MEET YOUR EVERY EXPECTATION OF ME.
IF YOU'LL EXCUSE ME...
POOF
HU HU

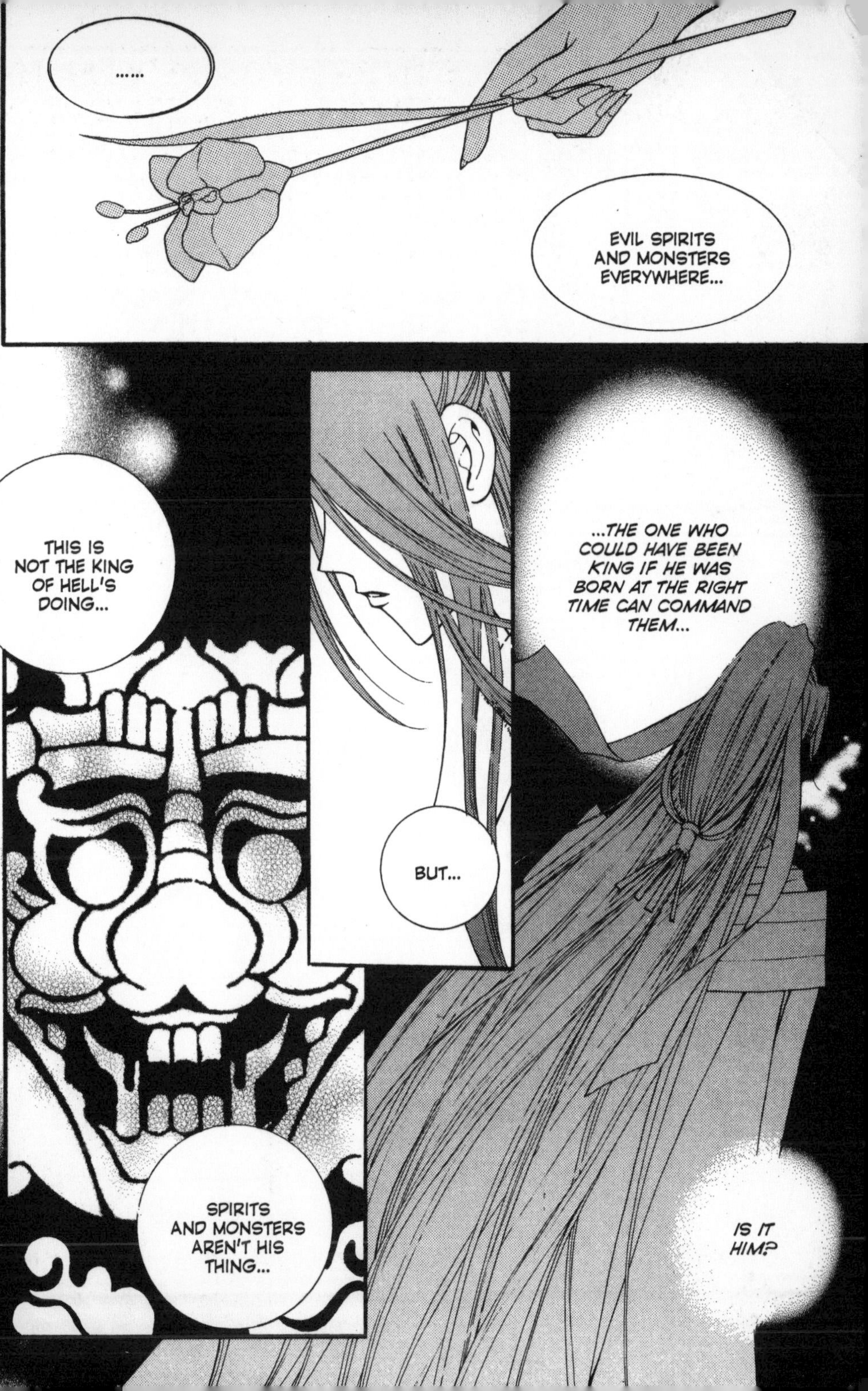
......
EVIL SPIRITS AND MONSTERS EVERYWHERE...
THIS IS NOT THE KING OF HELL'S DOING...
SPIRITS AND MONSTERS AREN'T HIS THING...
BUT...
...THE ONE WHO COULD HAVE BEEN KING IF HE WAS BORN AT THE RIGHT TIME CAN COMMAND THEM...
IS IT HIM?

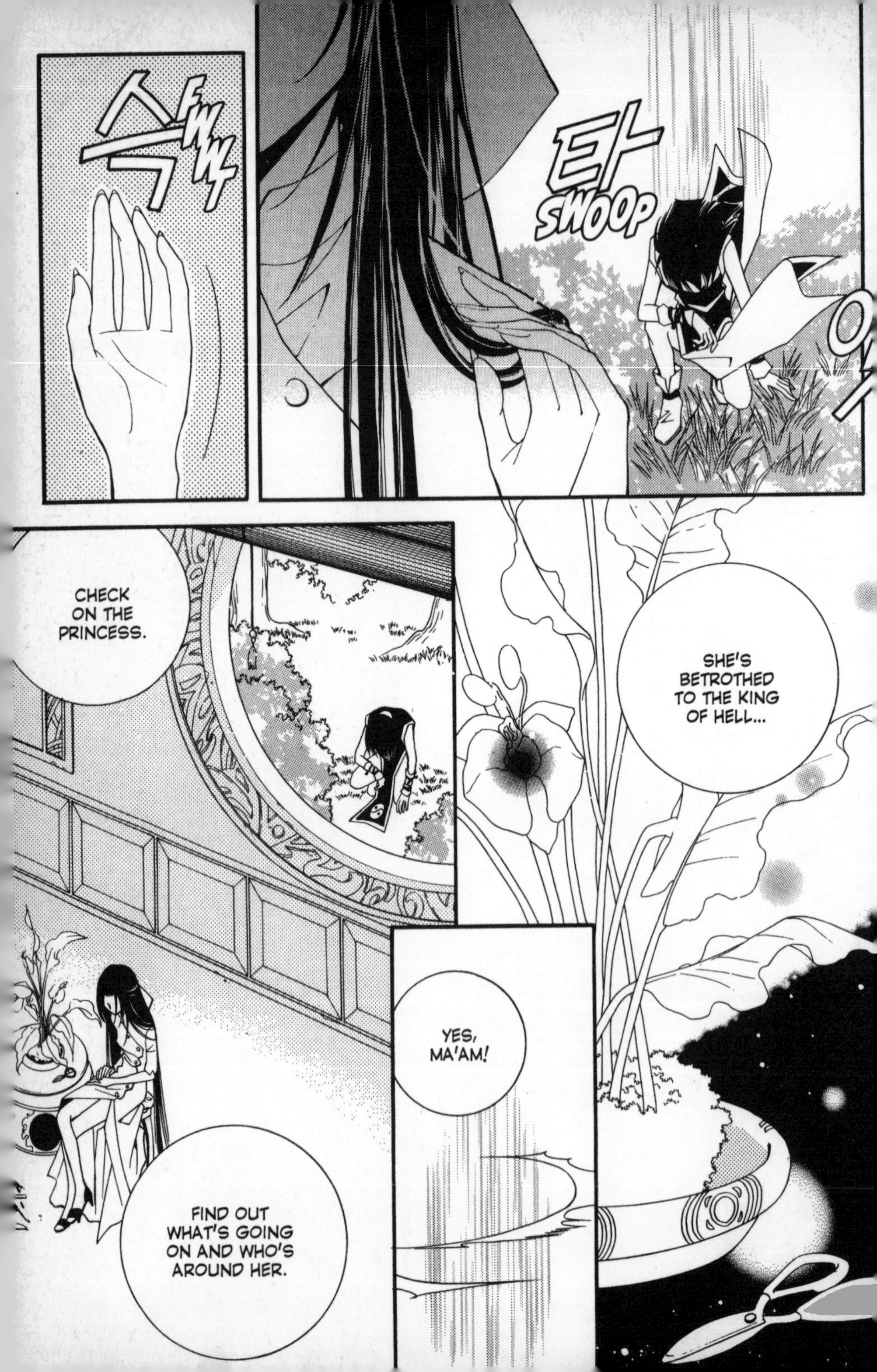
슥
FWWF
탁
SWOOP
CHECK ON THE PRINCESS.
FIND OUT WHAT'S GOING ON AND WHO'S AROUND HER.
SHE'S BETROTHED TO THE KING OF HELL...
YES, MA'AM!

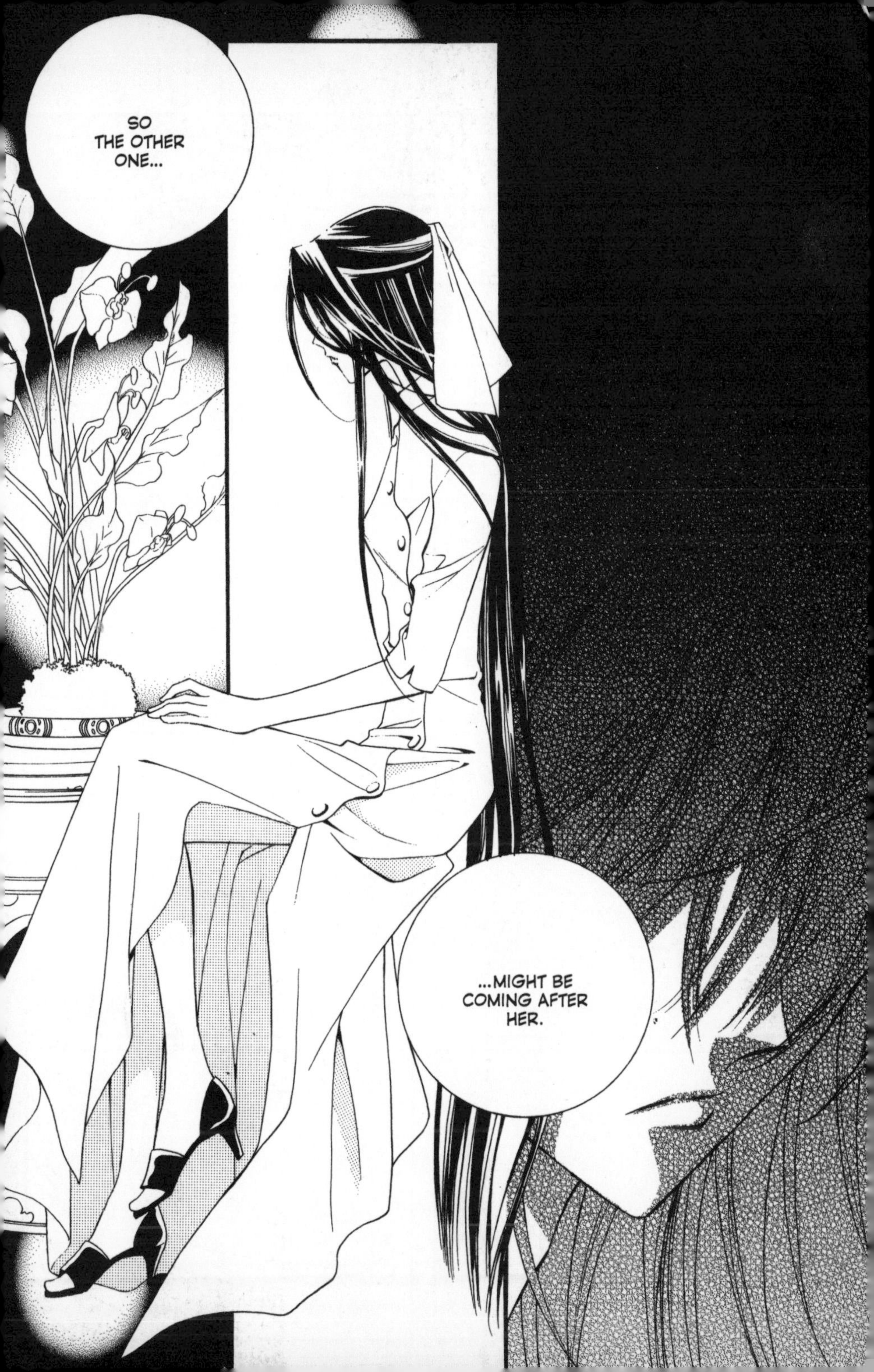
SO THE OTHER ONE...
...MIGHT BE COMING AFTER HER.

KARA'S CATS

1. WHEN WE CALL THEM...

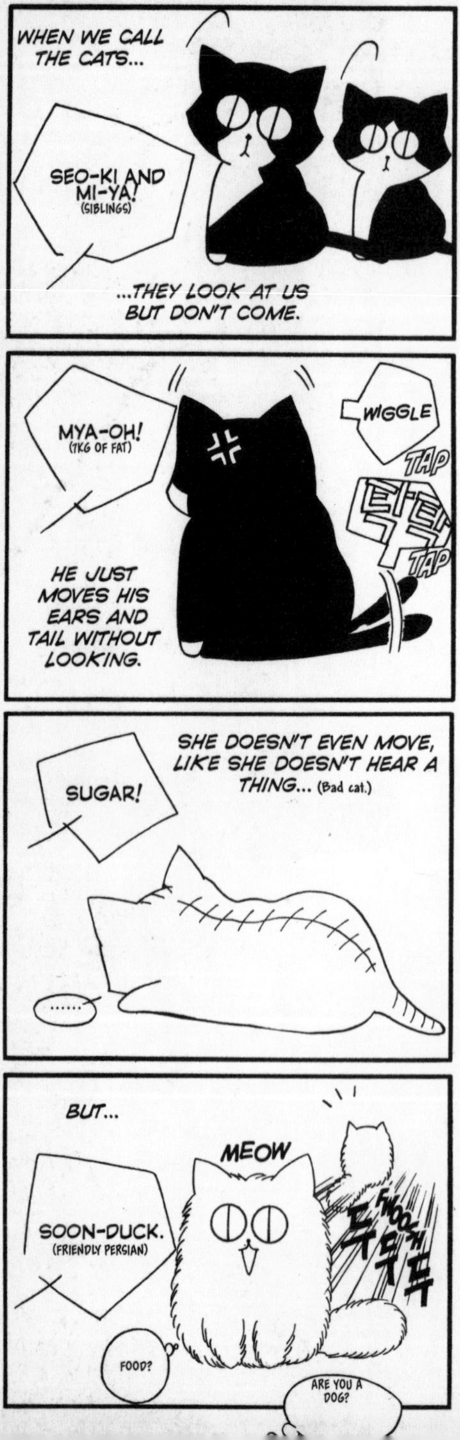
WHEN WE CALL THE CATS...
SEO-KI AND MI-YA!
(SIBLINGS)
...THEY LOOK AT US BUT DON'T COME.
MYA-OH!
(7KG OF FAT)
WIGGLE
TAP
TAP
HE JUST MOVES HIS EARS AND TAIL WITHOUT LOOKING.
SUGAR!
SHE DOESN'T EVEN MOVE, LIKE SHE DOESN'T HEAR A THING... (Bad cat.)
......
BUT...
SOON-DUCK.
(FRIENDLY PERSIAN)
MEOW
FWOOSH
FOOD?
ARE YOU A DOG?

2. CATS' TOYS

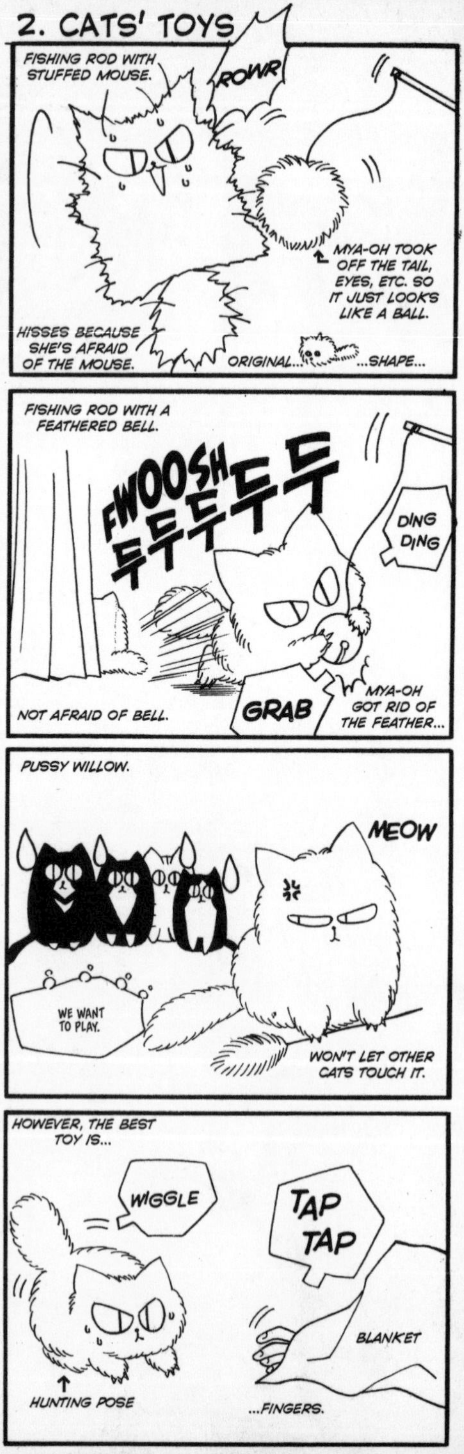
FISHING ROD WITH STUFFED MOUSE.
ROWR
MYA-OH TOOK OFF THE TAIL, EYES, ETC. SO IT JUST LOOKS LIKE A BALL.
HISSES BECAUSE SHE'S AFRAID OF THE MOUSE.
ORIGINAL...
...SHAPE...
FISHING ROD WITH A FEATHERED BELL.
FWOOSH
DING DING
NOT AFRAID OF BELL.
GRAB
MYA-OH GOT RID OF THE FEATHER...
PUSSY WILLOW.
MEOW
WE WANT TO PLAY.
WON'T LET OTHER CATS TOUCH IT.
HOWEVER, THE BEST TOY IS...
WIGGLE
TAP TAP
HUNTING POSE
BLANKET
...FINGERS.

IV MI-HYANG SO-WAL

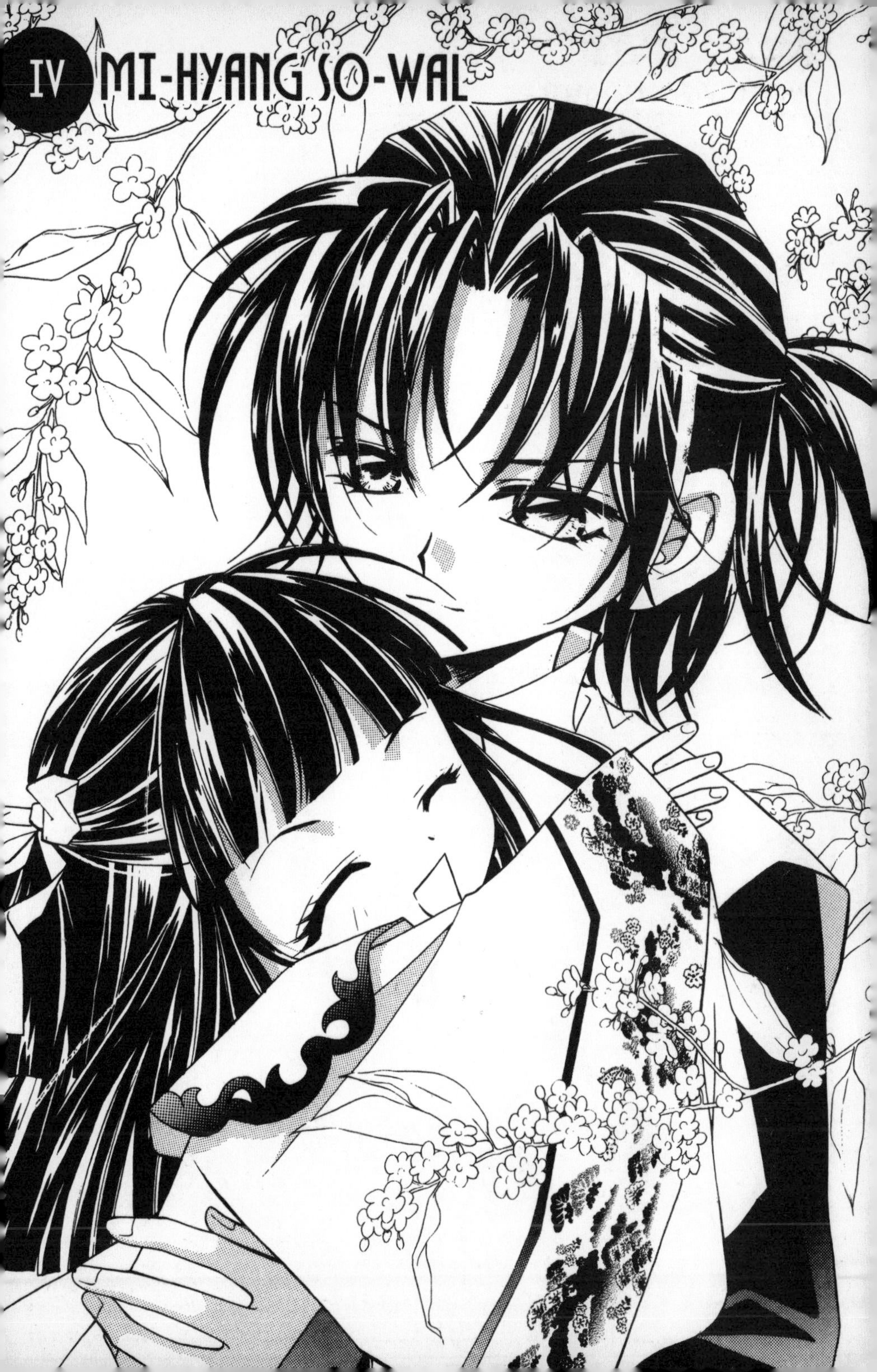

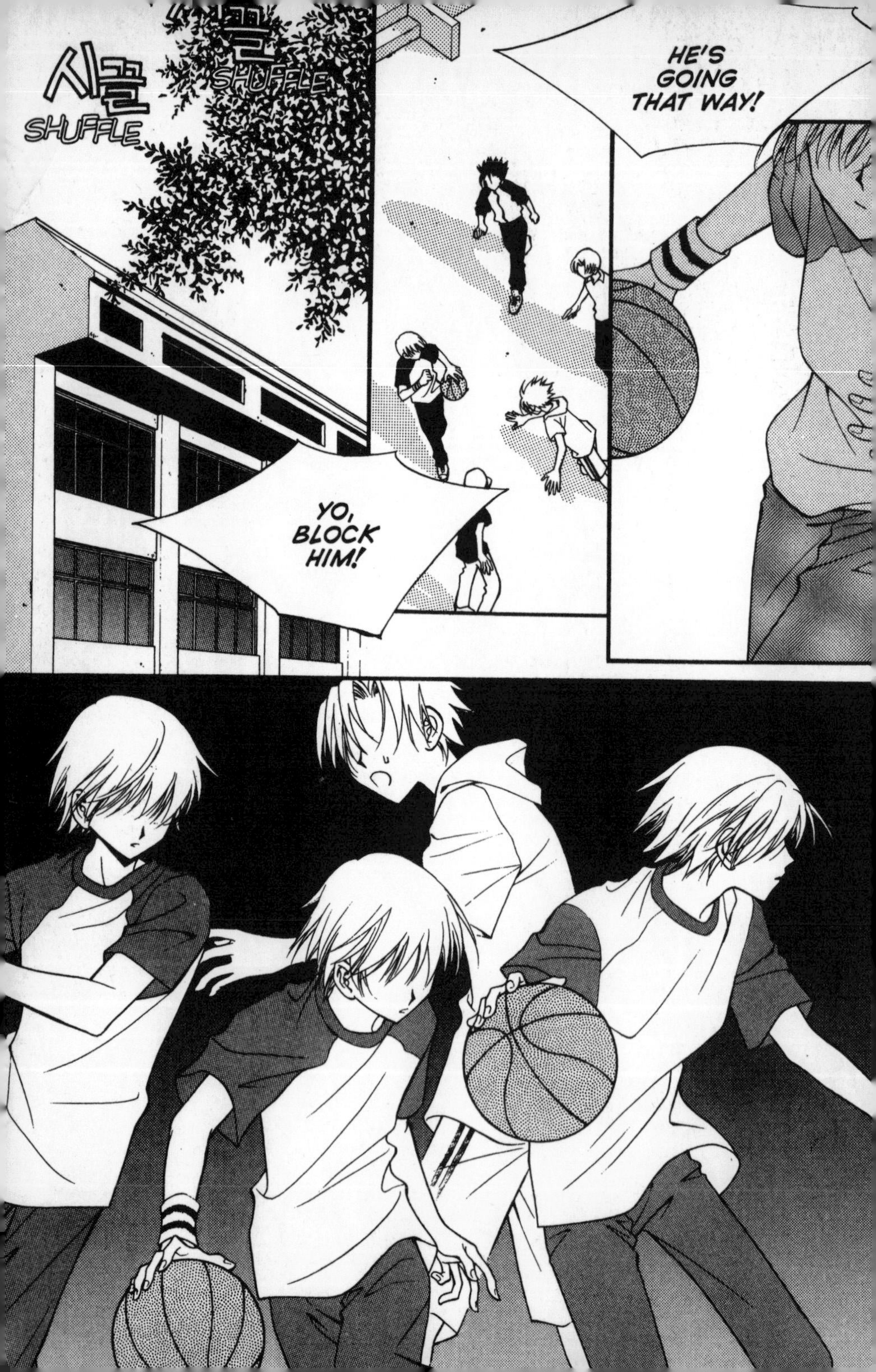
시끌
SHUFFLE
끌
SHUFFLE
YO, BLOCK HIM!
HE'S GOING THAT WAY!

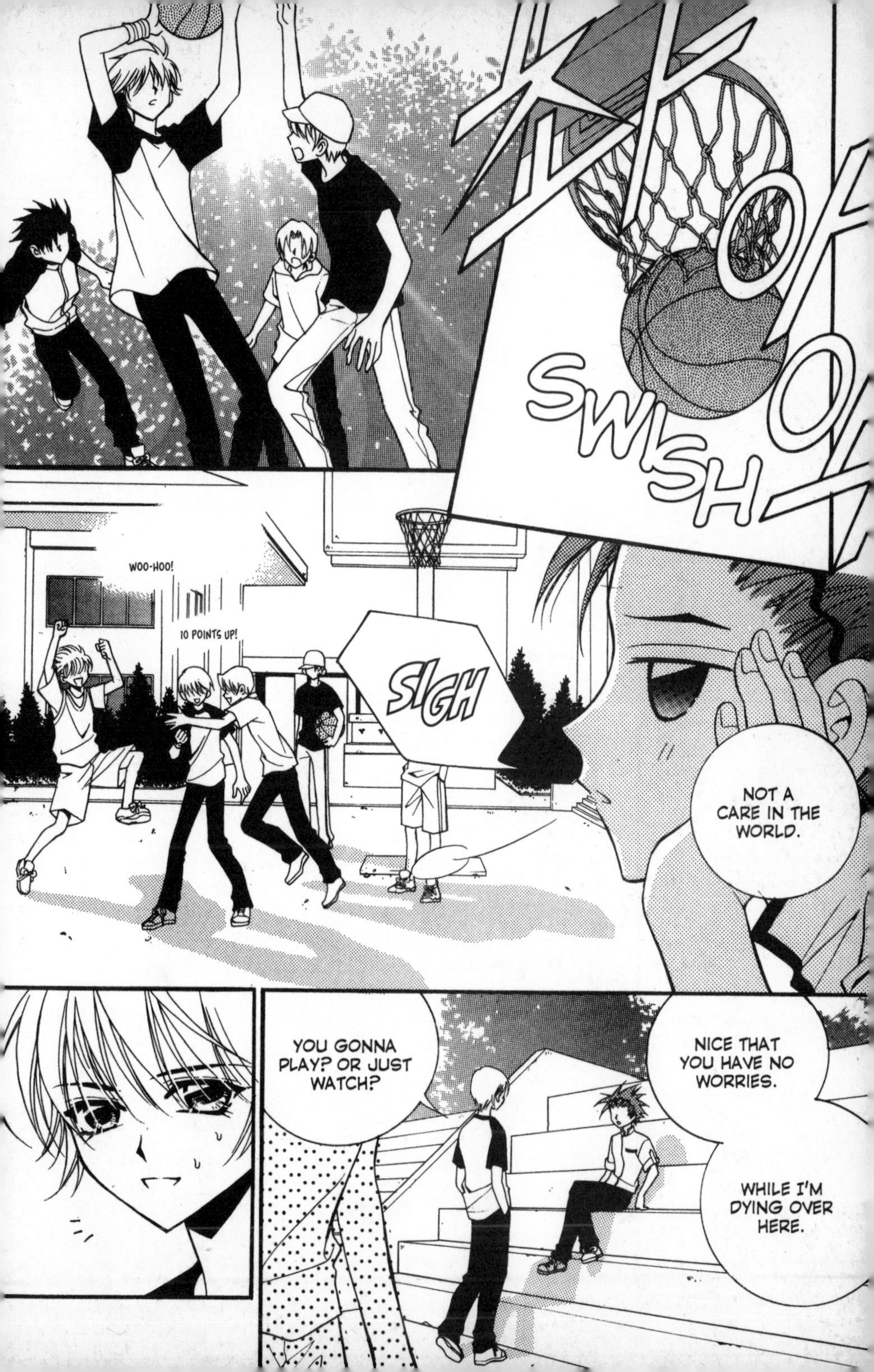
SWISH
WOO-HOO!
10 POINTS UP!
SIGH
NOT A CARE IN THE WORLD.
YOU GONNA PLAY? OR JUST WATCH?
NICE THAT YOU HAVE NO WORRIES.
WHILE I'M DYING OVER HERE.

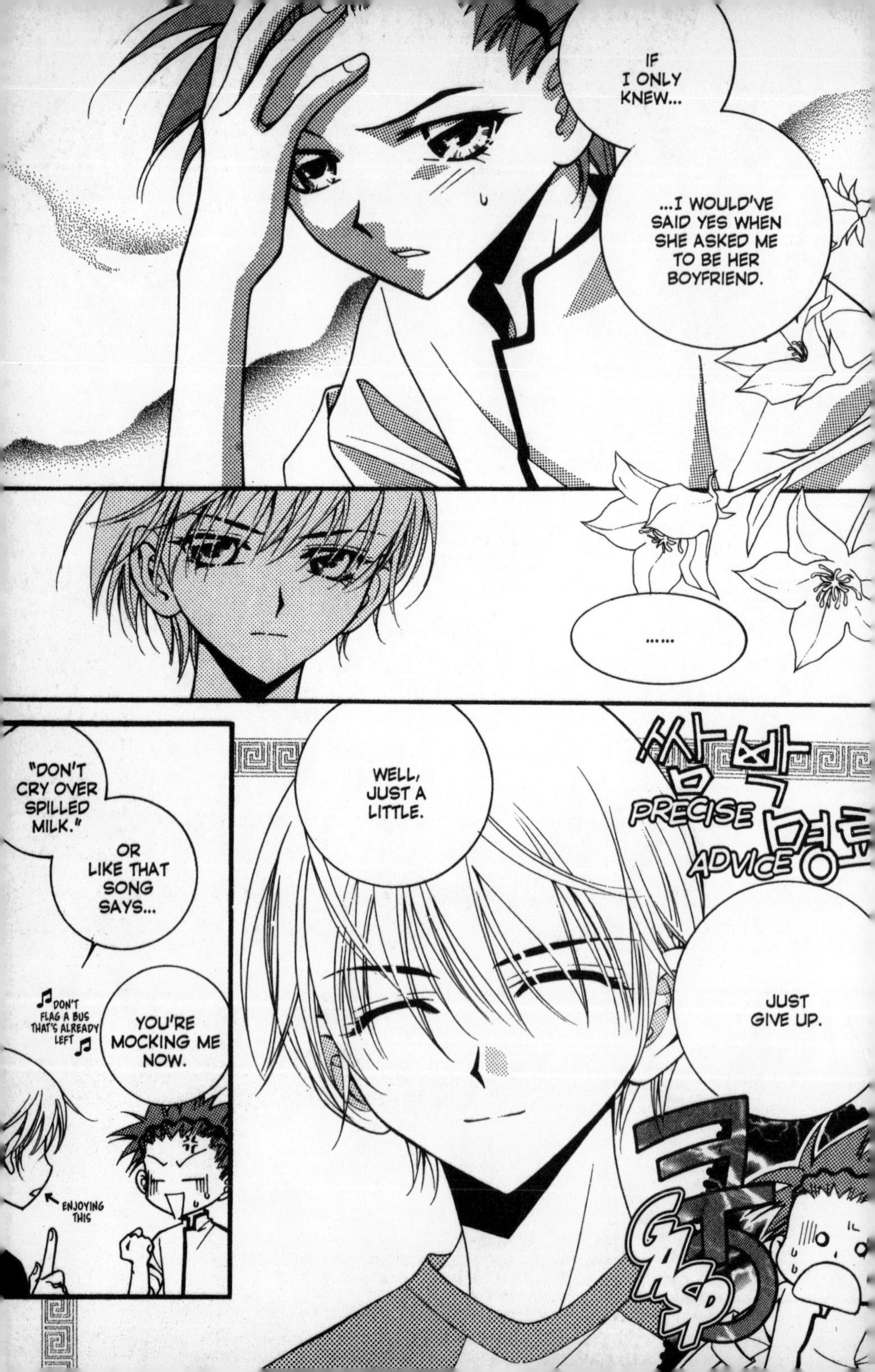
IF I ONLY KNEW...
...I WOULD'VE SAID YES WHEN SHE ASKED ME TO BE HER BOYFRIEND.
......
"DON'T CRY OVER SPILLED MILK."
OR LIKE THAT SONG SAYS...
♪DON'T FLAG A BUS THAT'S ALREADY LEFT♪
YOU'RE MOCKING ME NOW.
ENJOYING THIS
WELL, JUST A LITTLE.
쌈박 명료
PRECISE ADVICE
JUST GIVE UP.
GASP

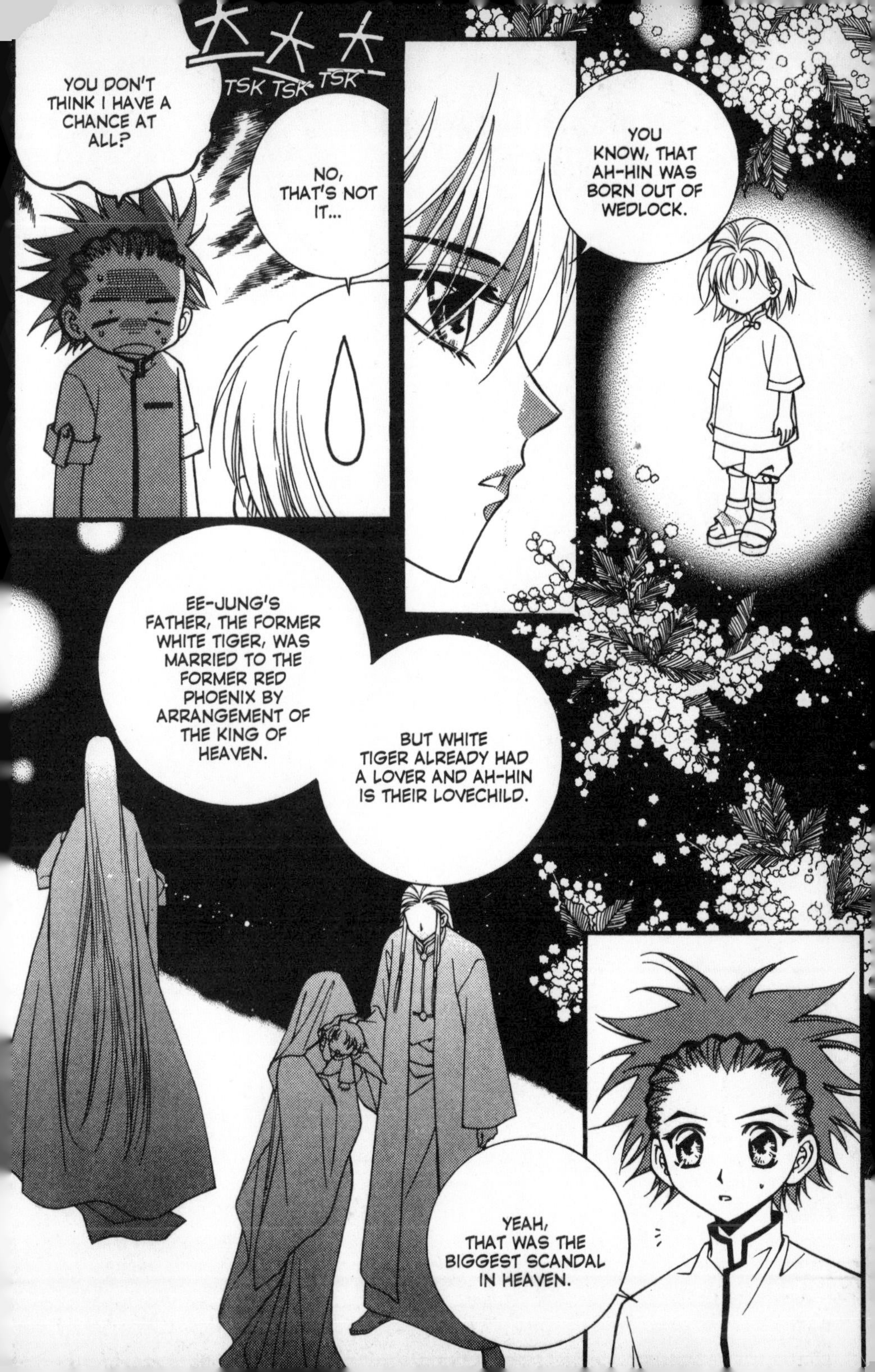
YOU DON'T THINK I HAVE A CHANCE AT ALL?
TSK TSK TSK
NO, THAT'S NOT IT...
YOU KNOW, THAT AH-HIN WAS BORN OUT OF WEDLOCK.
EE-JUNG'S FATHER, THE FORMER WHITE TIGER, WAS MARRIED TO THE FORMER RED PHOENIX BY ARRANGEMENT OF THE KING OF HEAVEN.
BUT WHITE TIGER ALREADY HAD A LOVER AND AH-HIN IS THEIR LOVECHILD.
YEAH, THAT WAS THE BIGGEST SCANDAL IN HEAVEN.

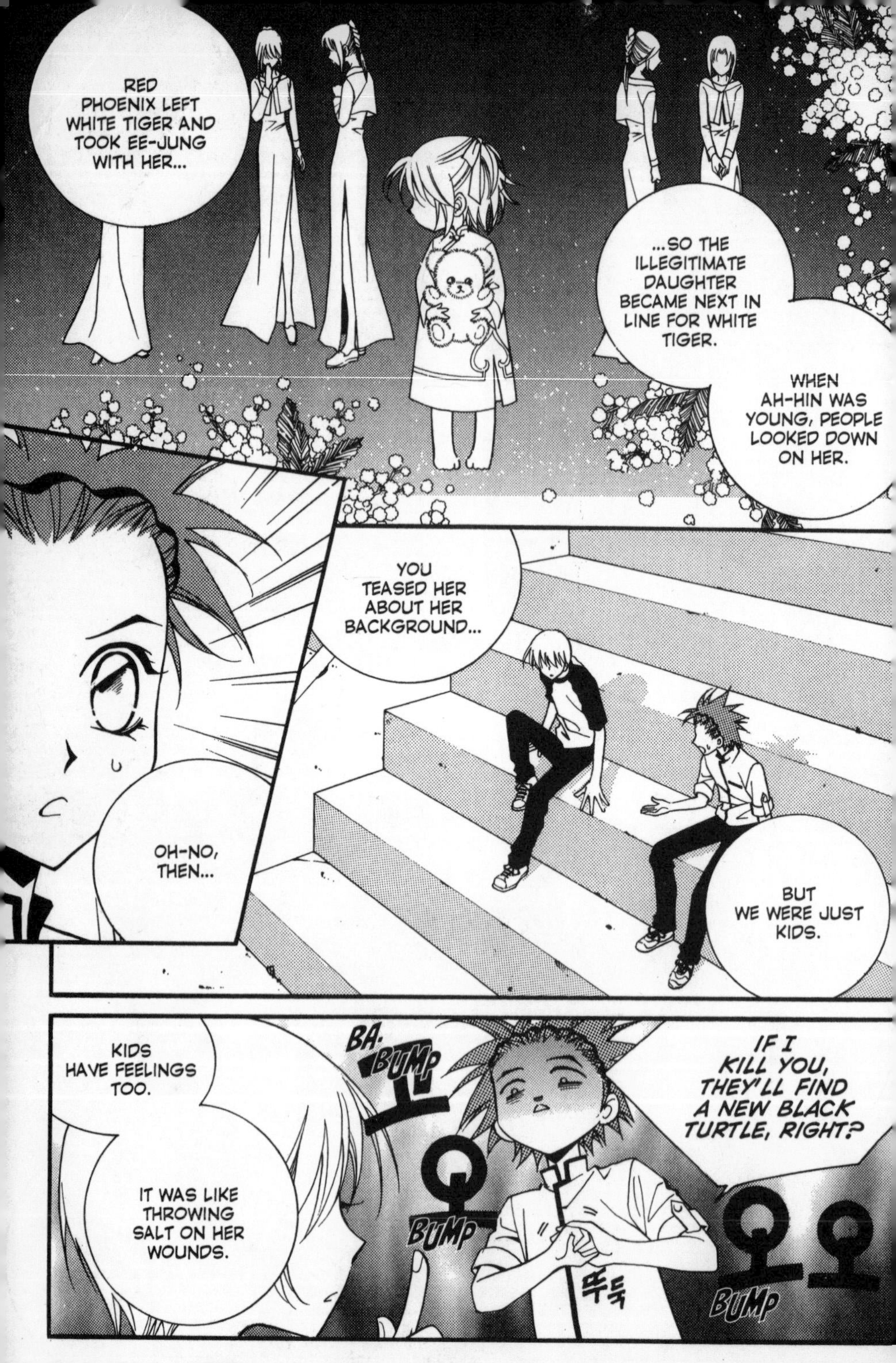
RED PHOENIX LEFT WHITE TIGER AND TOOK EE-JUNG WITH HER...
...SO THE ILLEGITIMATE DAUGHTER BECAME NEXT IN LINE FOR WHITE TIGER.
WHEN AH-HIN WAS YOUNG, PEOPLE LOOKED DOWN ON HER.
OH-NO, THEN...
YOU TEASED HER ABOUT HER BACKGROUND...
BUT WE WERE JUST KIDS.
KIDS HAVE FEELINGS TOO.
BA-BUMP
IT WAS LIKE THROWING SALT ON HER WOUNDS.
BUMP
IF I KILL YOU, THEY'LL FIND A NEW BLACK TURTLE, RIGHT?
BUMP

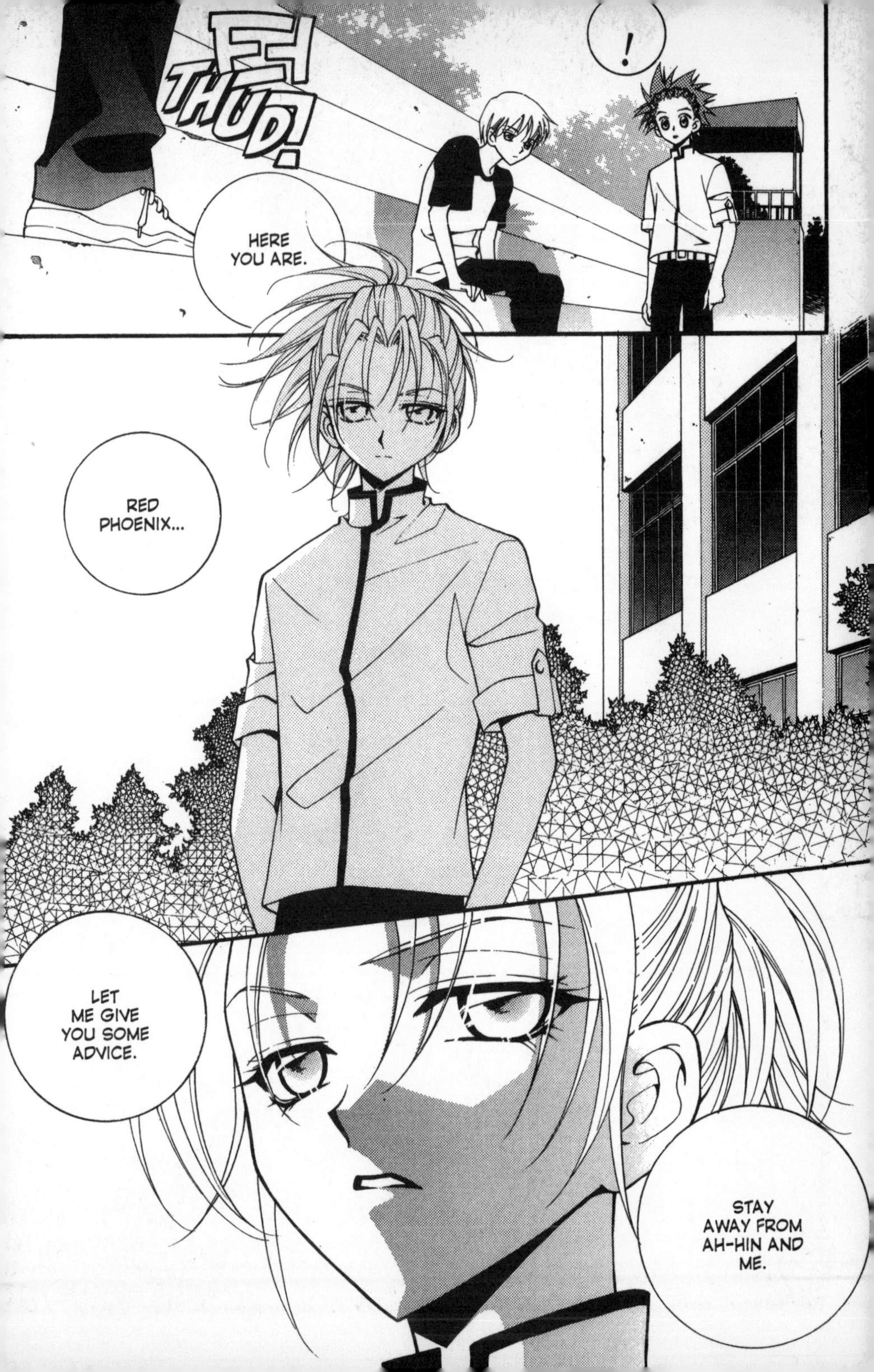
THUD!
!
HERE YOU ARE.
RED PHOENIX...
LET ME GIVE YOU SOME ADVICE.
STAY AWAY FROM AH-HIN AND ME.

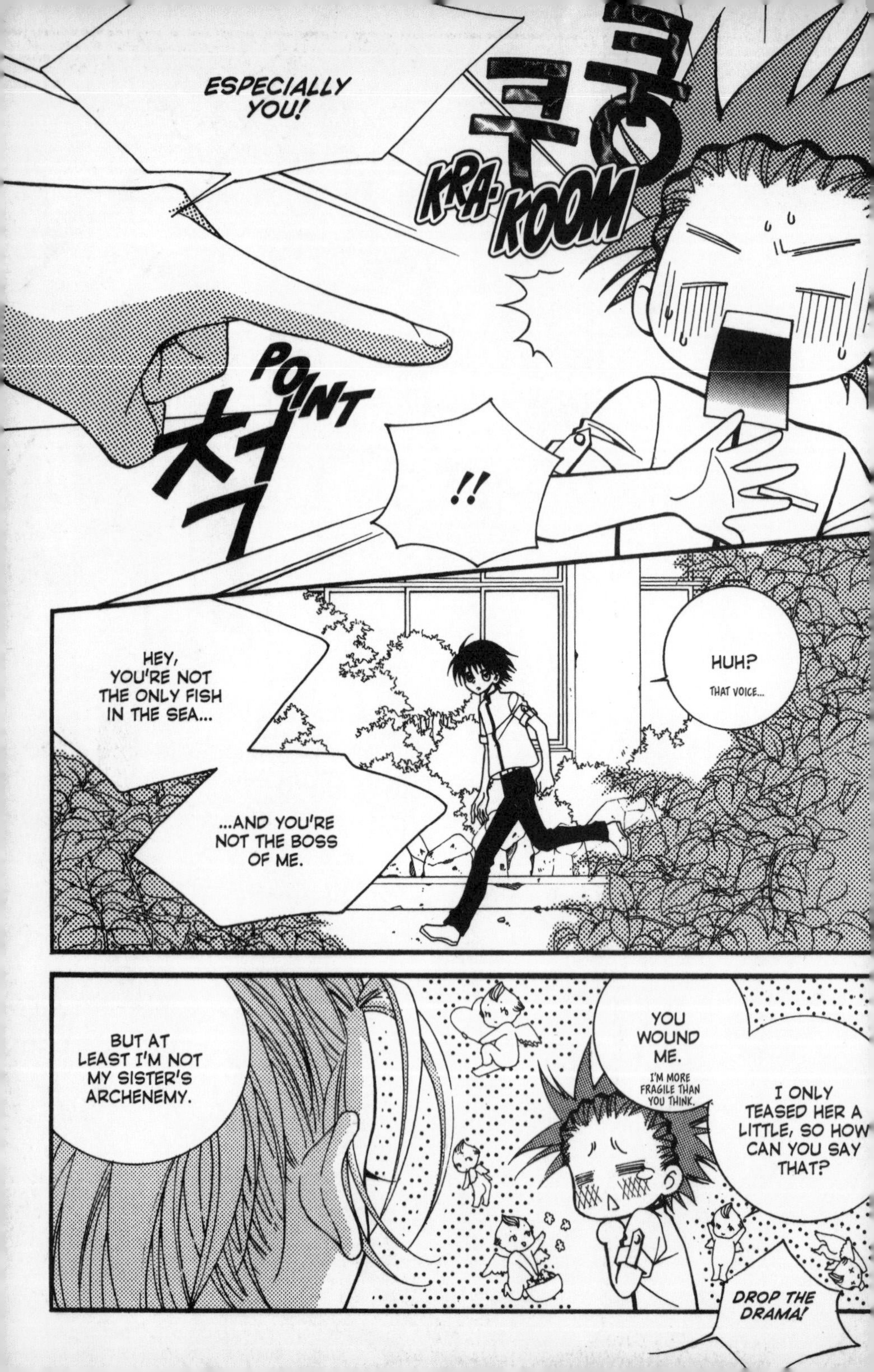
ESPECIALLY YOU!
쿠쿵
KRA-KOOM
POINT
척
!!
HEY, YOU'RE NOT THE ONLY FISH IN THE SEA...
...AND YOU'RE NOT THE BOSS OF ME.
HUH?
THAT VOICE...
BUT AT LEAST I'M NOT MY SISTER'S ARCHENEMY.
YOU WOUND ME.
I'M MORE FRAGILE THAN YOU THINK.
I ONLY TEASED HER A LITTLE, SO HOW CAN YOU SAY THAT?
DROP THE DRAMA!

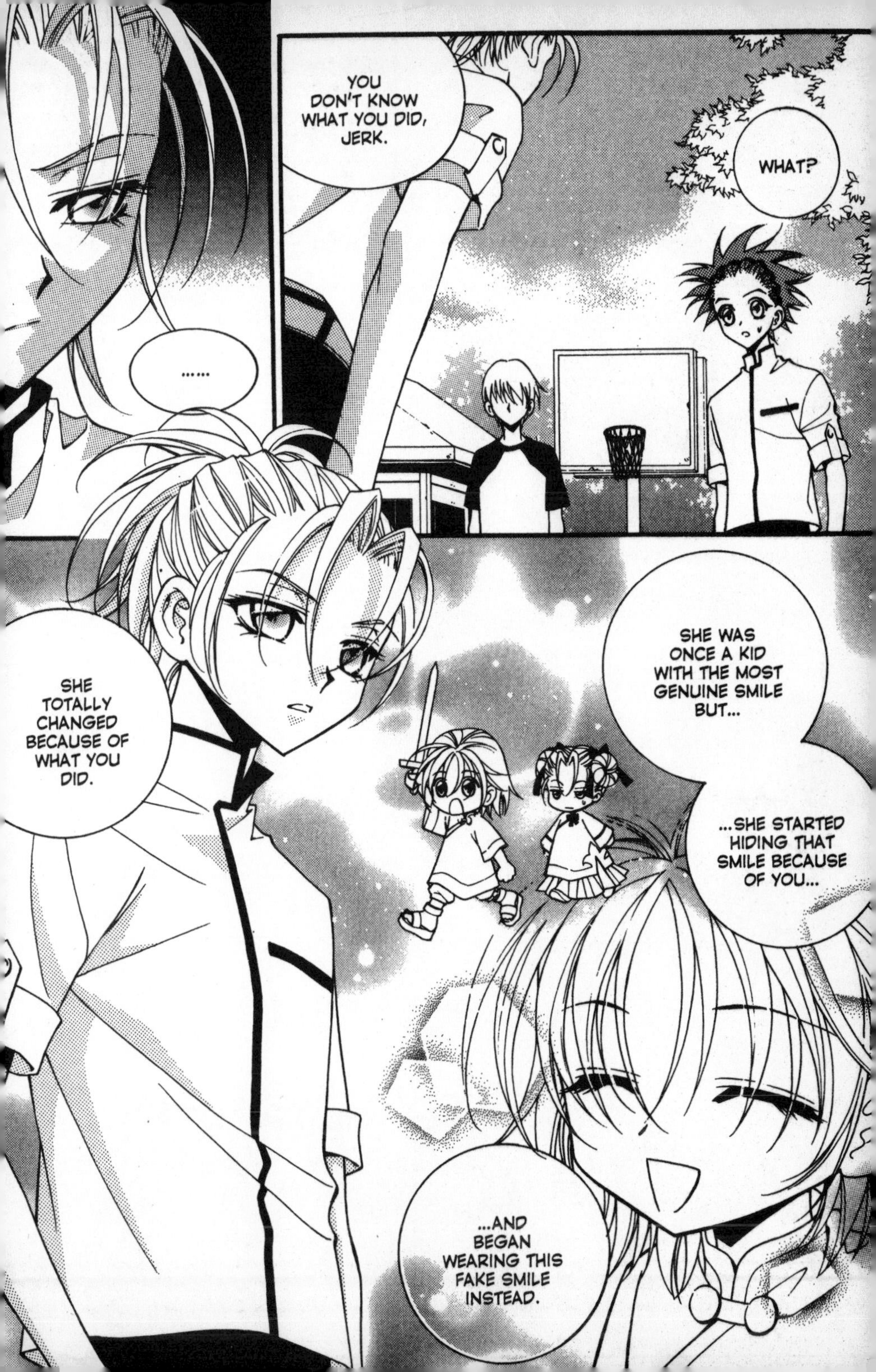
……
YOU DON'T KNOW WHAT YOU DID, JERK.
WHAT?
SHE TOTALLY CHANGED BECAUSE OF WHAT YOU DID.
SHE WAS ONCE A KID WITH THE MOST GENUINE SMILE BUT...
...SHE STARTED HIDING THAT SMILE BECAUSE OF YOU...
...AND BEGAN WEARING THIS FAKE SMILE INSTEAD.

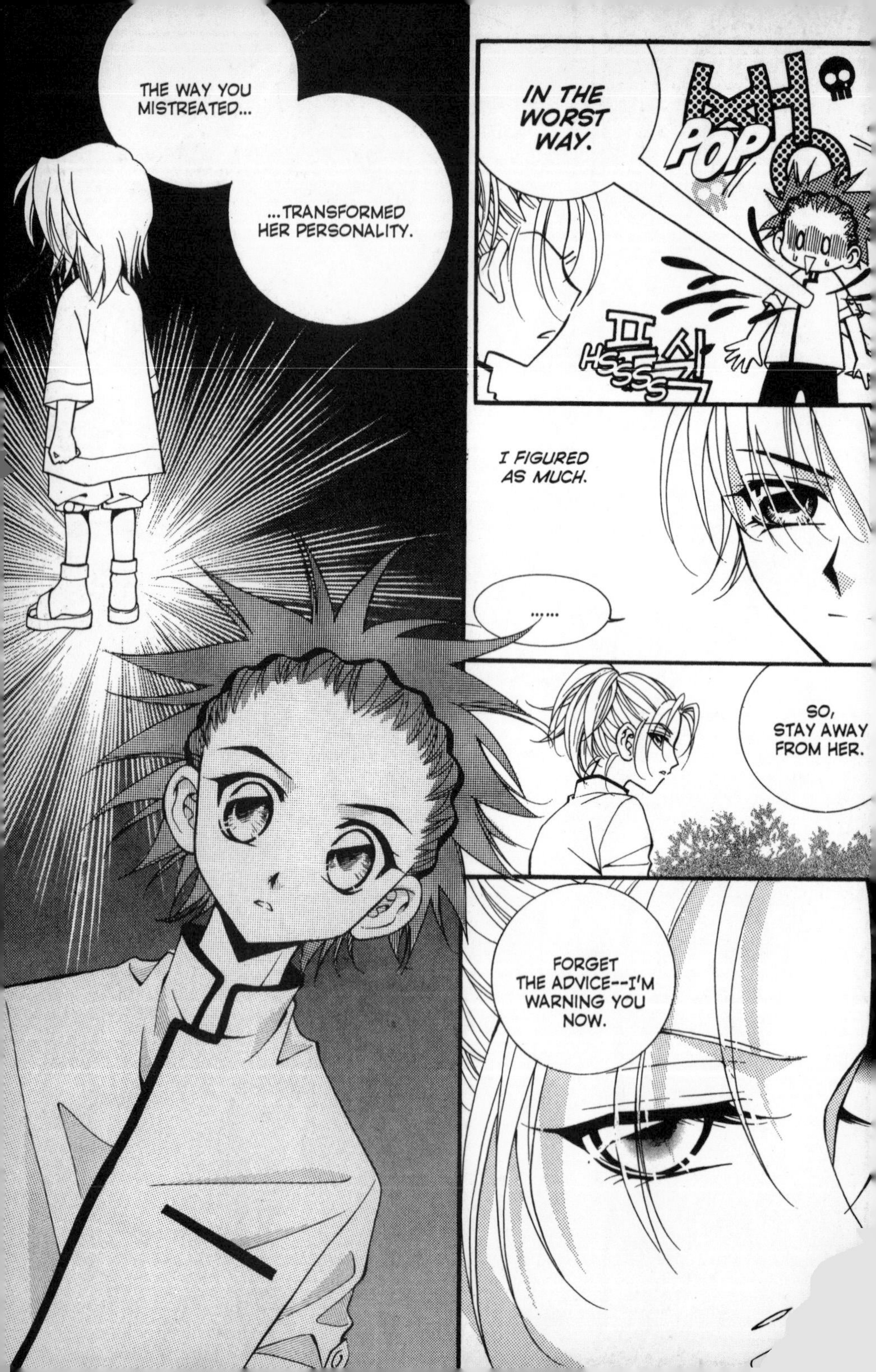
THE WAY YOU MISTREATED...
...TRANSFORMED HER PERSONALITY.
IN THE WORST WAY.
POP
HSSSSS
피식
I FIGURED AS MUCH.
......
SO, STAY AWAY FROM HER.
FORGET THE ADVICE--I'M WARNING YOU NOW.

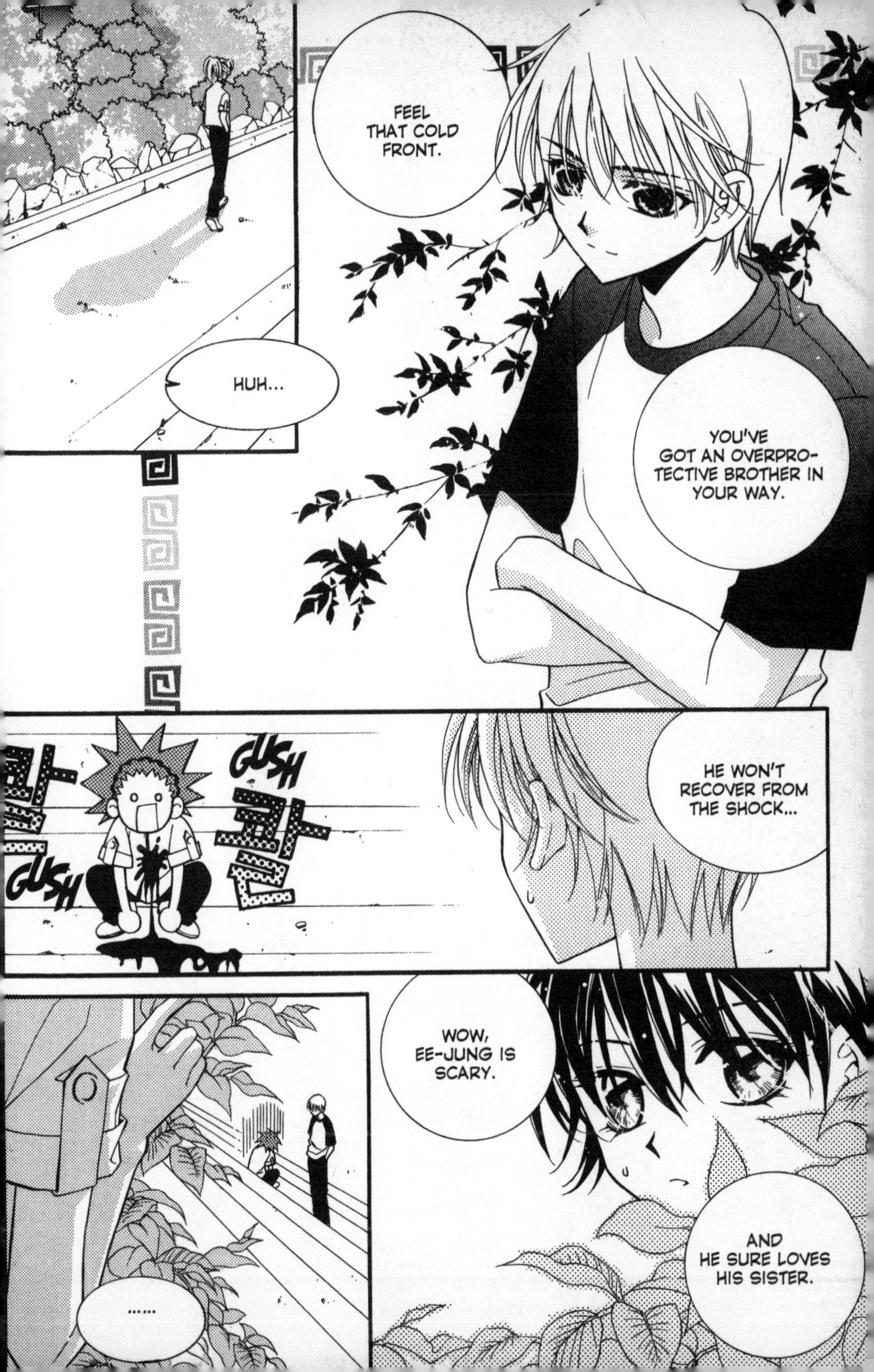
HUH...
FEEL THAT COLD FRONT.
YOU'VE GOT AN OVERPROTECTIVE BROTHER IN YOUR WAY.
GUSH
GUSH
HE WON'T RECOVER FROM THE SHOCK...
......
WOW, EE-JUNG IS SCARY.
AND HE SURE LOVES HIS SISTER.

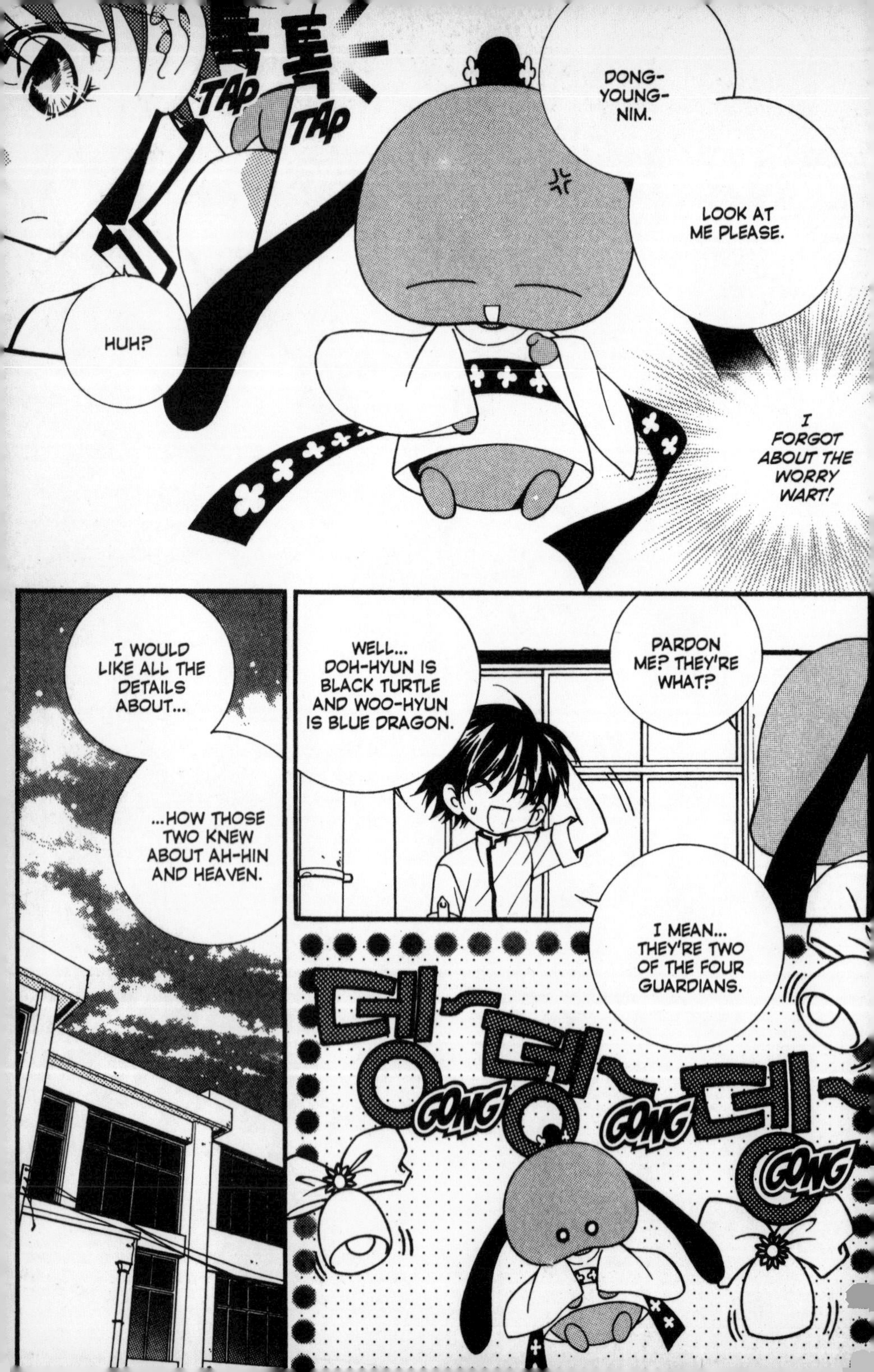
톡톡
TAP TAP
DONG-YOUNG-NIM.
LOOK AT ME PLEASE.
HUH?
I FORGOT ABOUT THE WORRY WART!
I WOULD LIKE ALL THE DETAILS ABOUT...
...HOW THOSE TWO KNEW ABOUT AH-HIN AND HEAVEN.
WELL... DOH-HYUN IS BLACK TURTLE AND WOO-HYUN IS BLUE DRAGON.
PARDON ME? THEY'RE WHAT?
I MEAN... THEY'RE TWO OF THE FOUR GUARDIANS.
뎅~ 뎅~ 뎅~
GONG GONG GONG

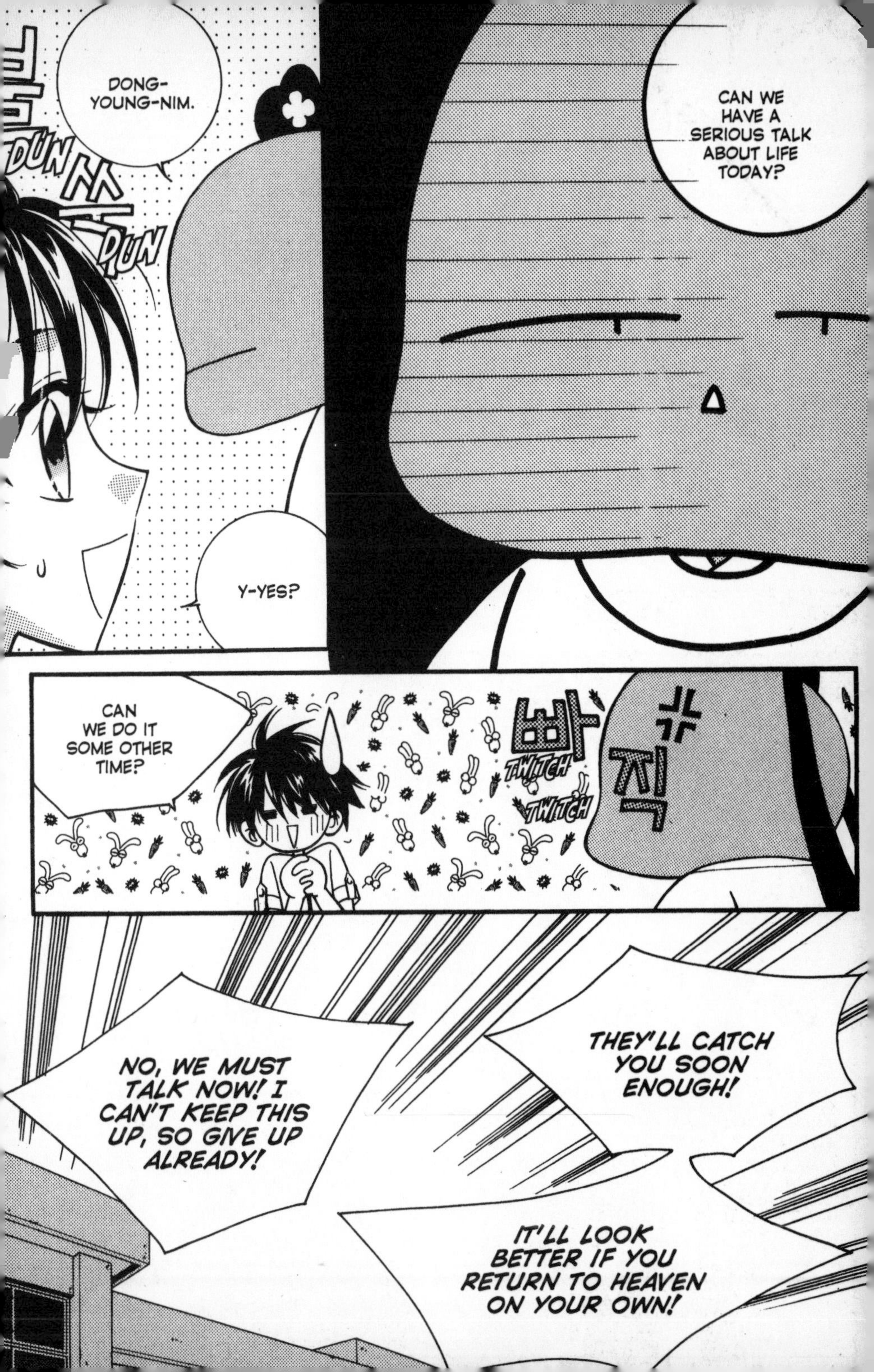
DUN
DUN
DONG-YOUNG-NIM.
Y-YES?
CAN WE HAVE A SERIOUS TALK ABOUT LIFE TODAY?
CAN WE DO IT SOME OTHER TIME?
빠직
TWITCH
TWITCH
NO, WE MUST TALK NOW! I CAN'T KEEP THIS UP, SO GIVE UP ALREADY!
THEY'LL CATCH YOU SOON ENOUGH!
IT'LL LOOK BETTER IF YOU RETURN TO HEAVEN ON YOUR OWN!

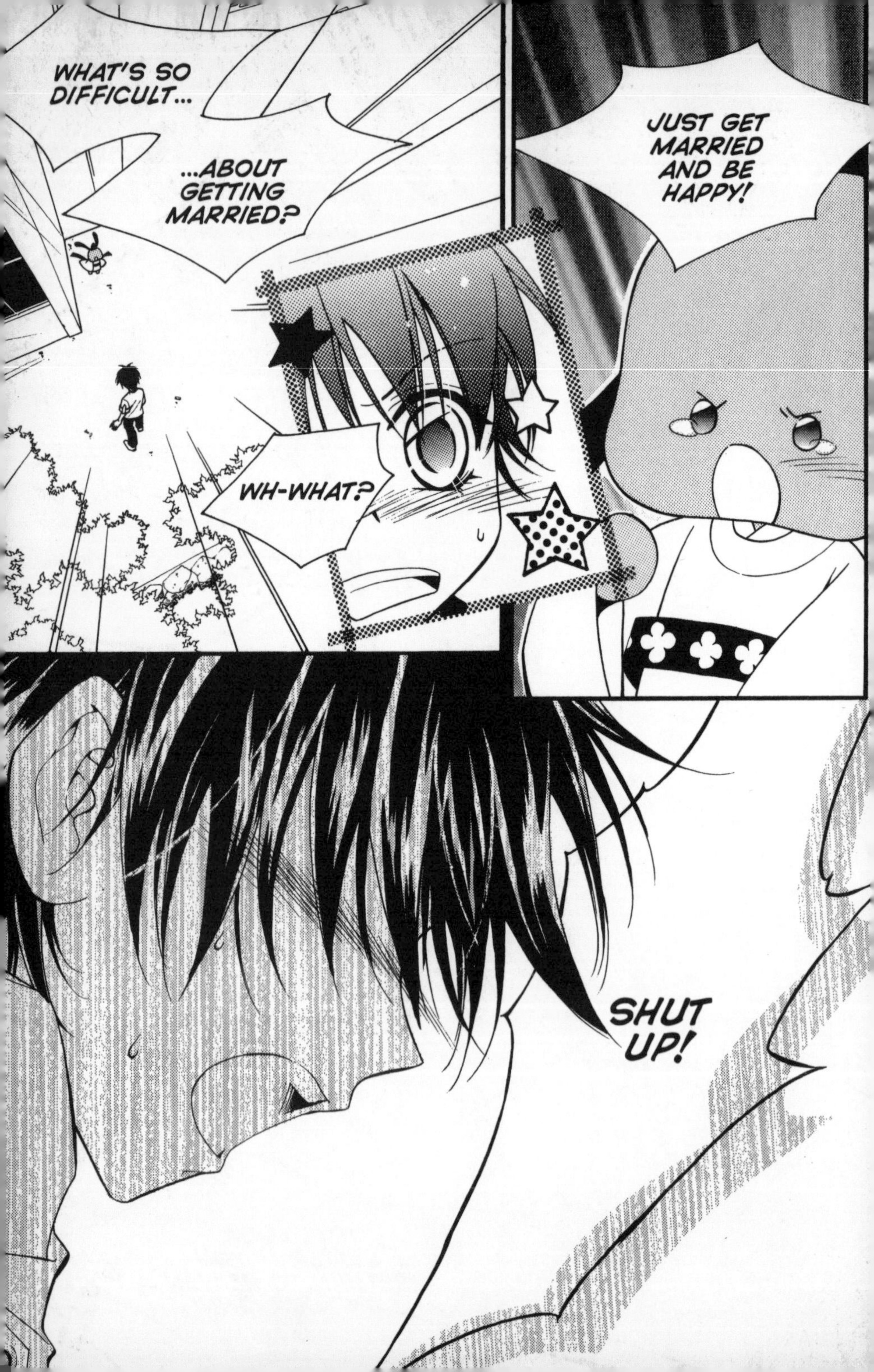
WHAT'S SO DIFFICULT...
...ABOUT GETTING MARRIED?
JUST GET MARRIED AND BE HAPPY!
WH-WHAT?
SHUT UP!

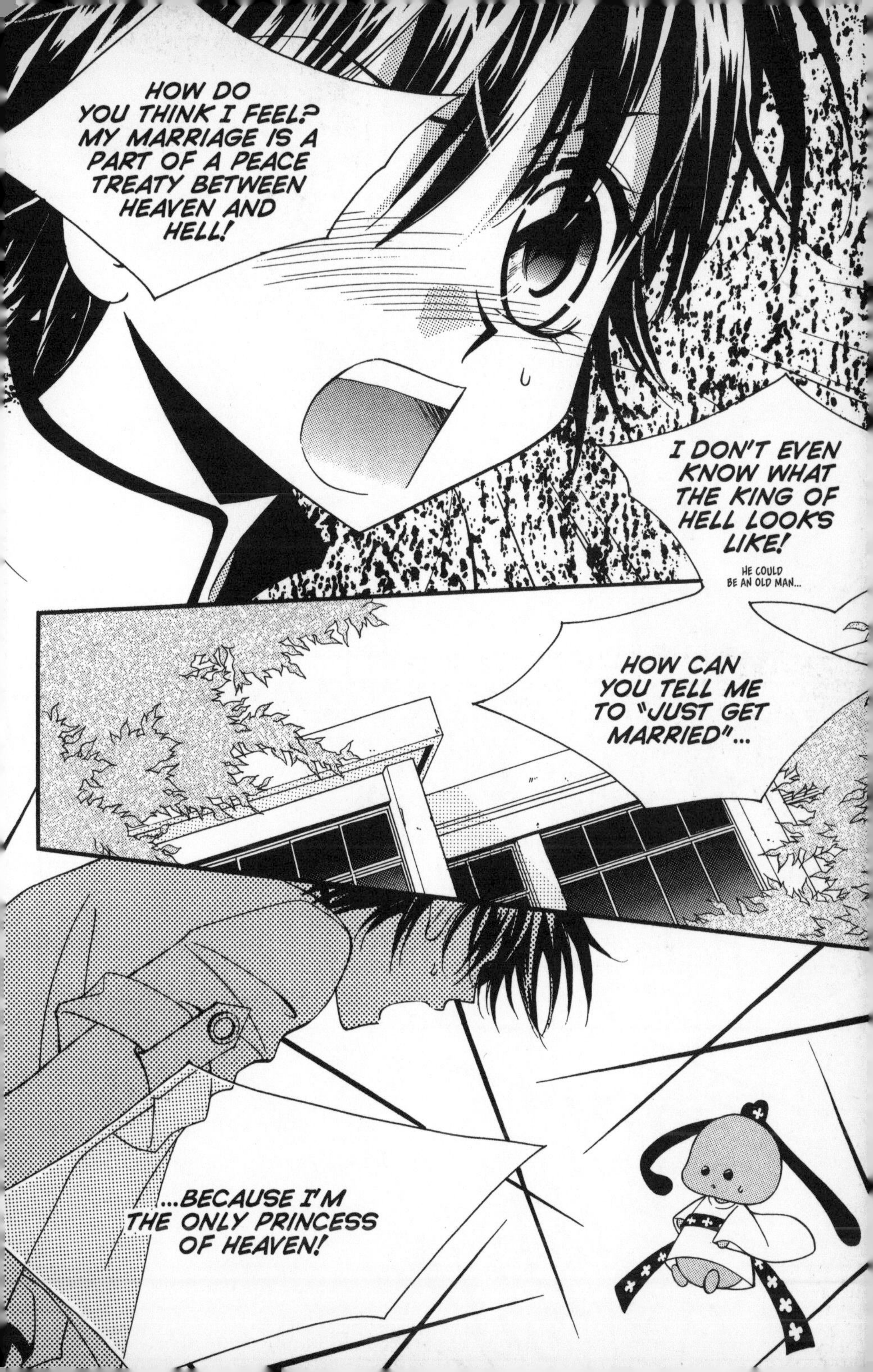
HOW DO YOU THINK I FEEL? MY MARRIAGE IS A PART OF A PEACE TREATY BETWEEN HEAVEN AND HELL!
I DON'T EVEN KNOW WHAT THE KING OF HELL LOOKS LIKE!
HE COULD BE AN OLD MAN...
HOW CAN YOU TELL ME TO "JUST GET MARRIED"...
...BECAUSE I'M THE ONLY PRINCESS OF HEAVEN!

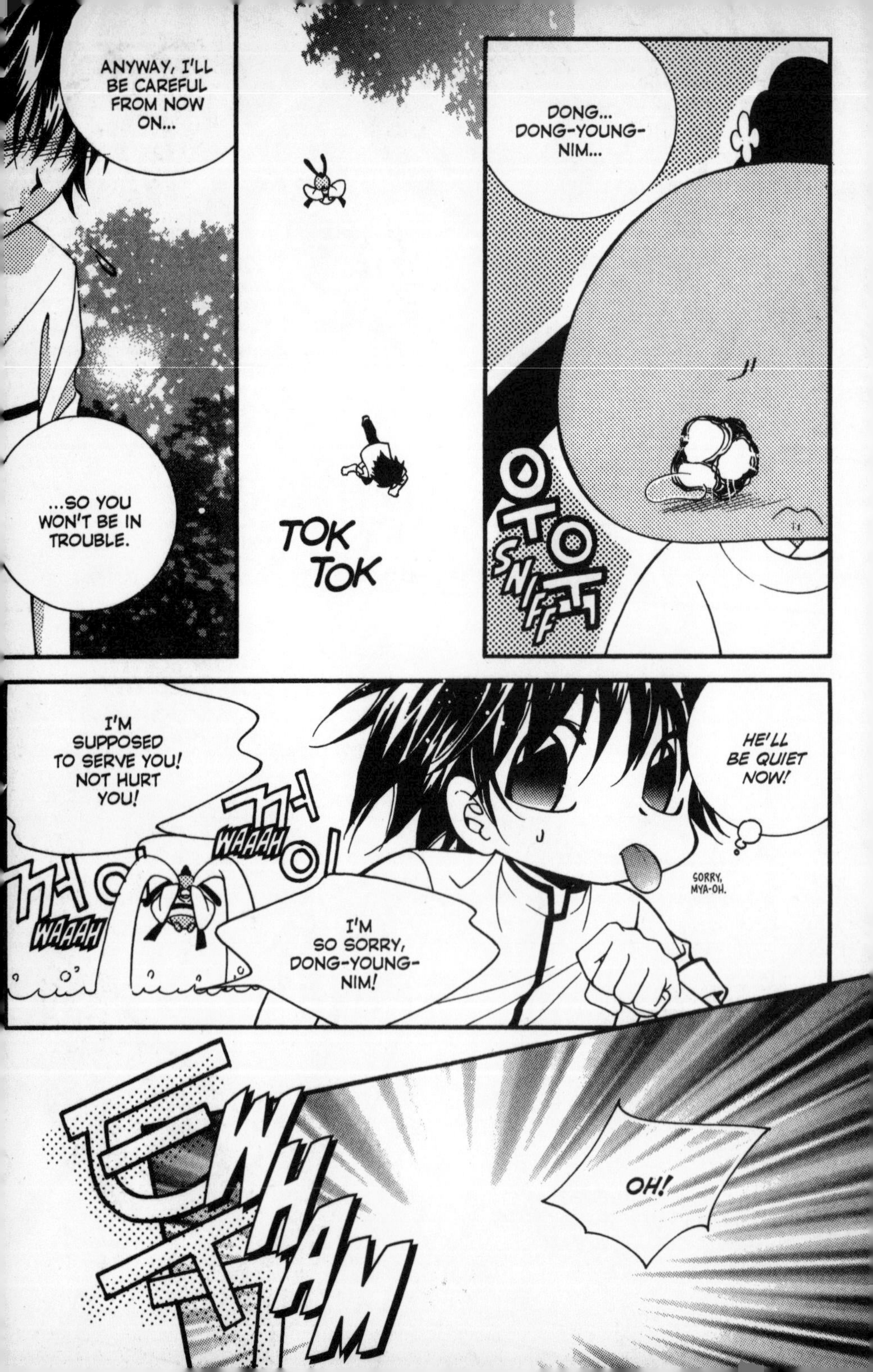
ANYWAY, I'LL BE CAREFUL FROM NOW ON...
...SO YOU WON'T BE IN TROUBLE.
TOK TOK
DONG... DONG-YOUNG-NIM...
SNIFF
I'M SUPPOSED TO SERVE YOU! NOT HURT YOU!
WAAAH
WAAAH
I'M SO SORRY, DONG-YOUNG-NIM!
HE'LL BE QUIET NOW!
SORRY, MYA-OH.
WHAM
OH!

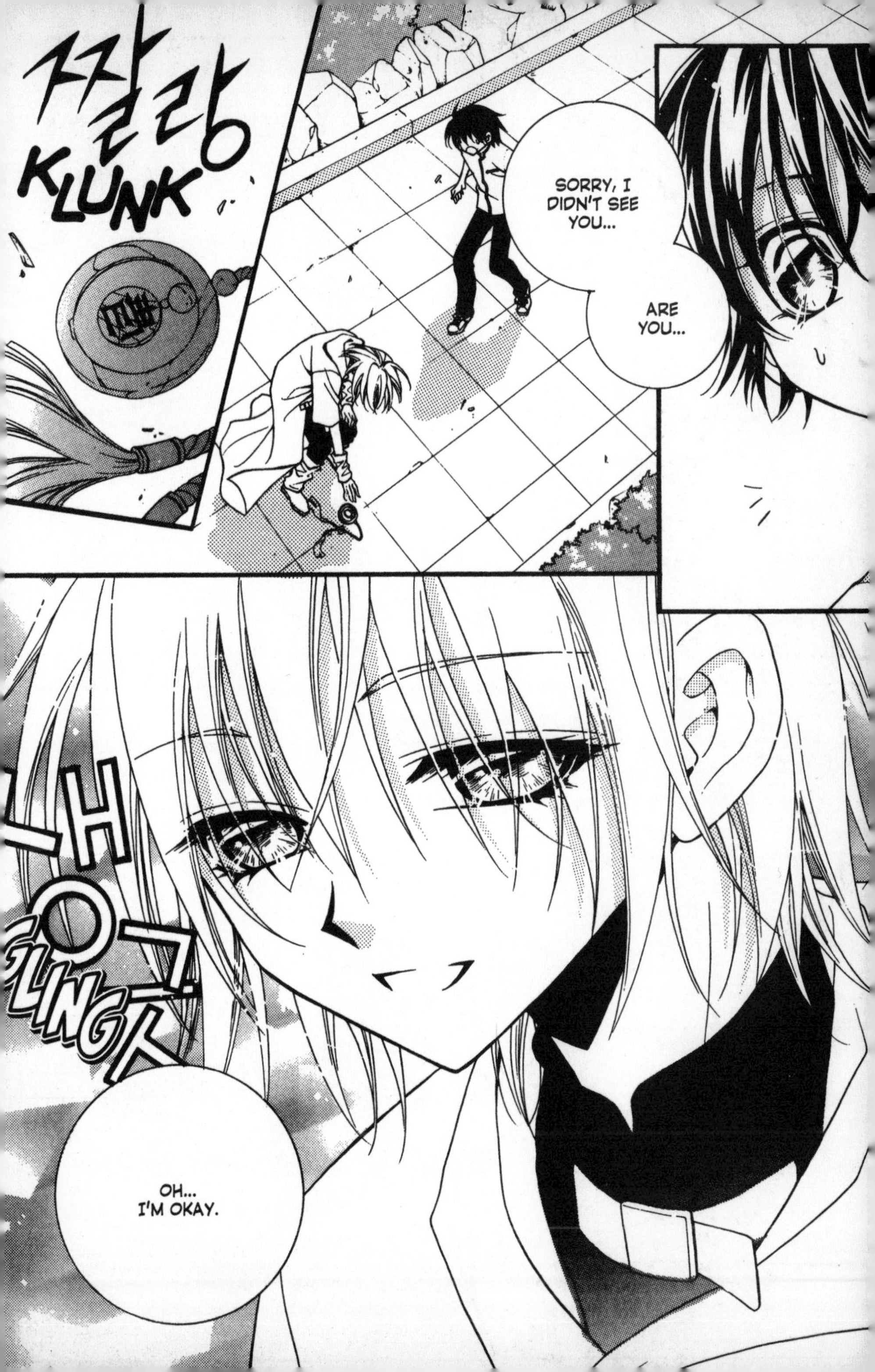
짤랑
KLUNK
SORRY, I DIDN'T SEE YOU...
ARE YOU...
OH... I'M OKAY.

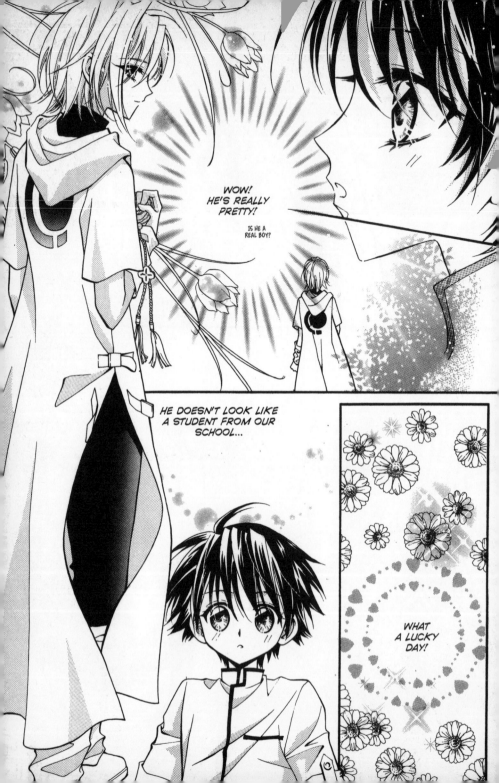

WOW!
HE'S REALLY
PRETTY!

IS HE A
REAL BOY?

HE DOESN'T LOOK LIKE
A STUDENT FROM OUR
SCHOOL...

WHAT
A LUCKY
DAY!

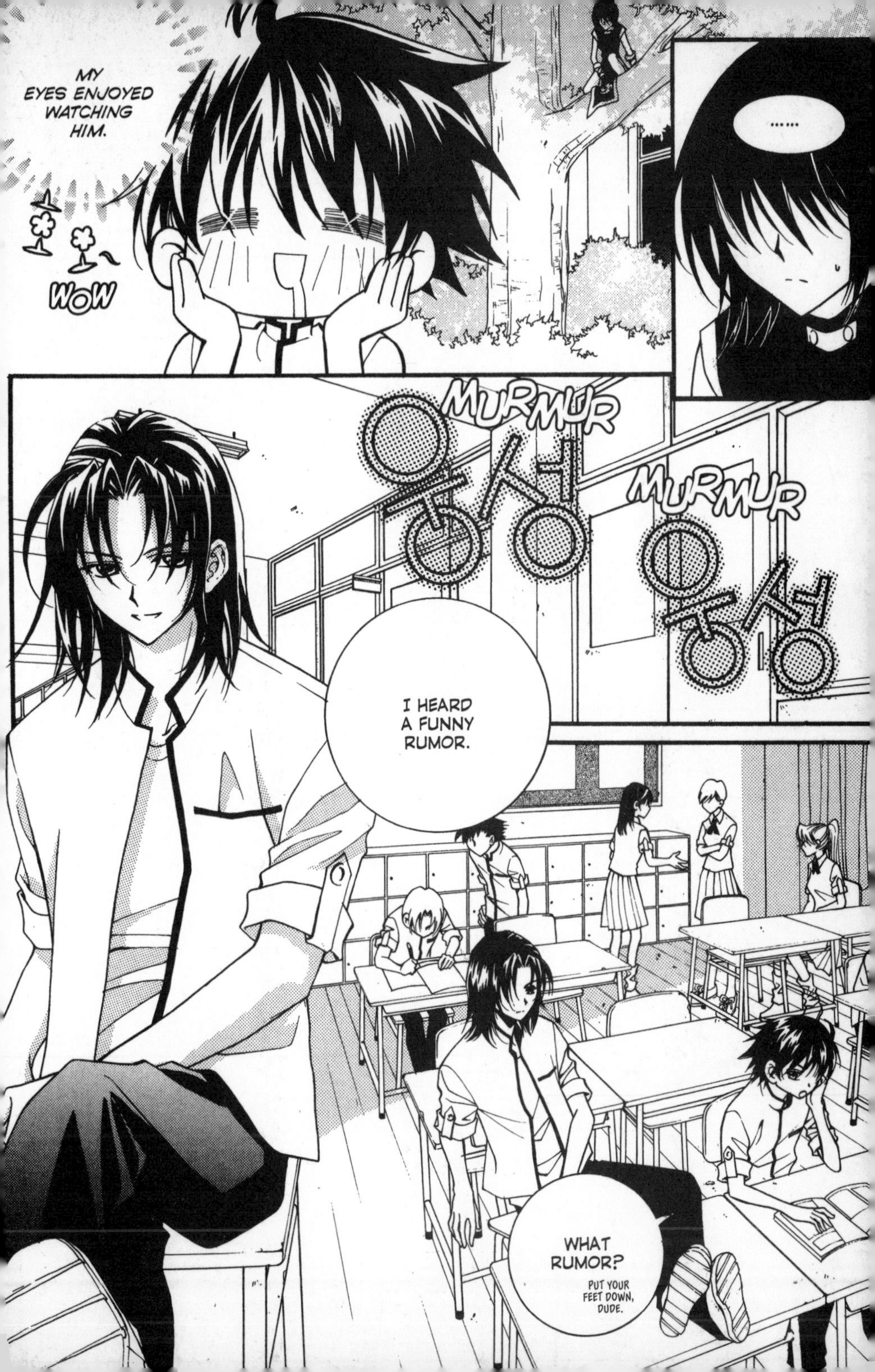
MY EYES ENJOYED WATCHING HIM.
WOW
......
MURMUR
MURMUR
I HEARD A FUNNY RUMOR.
WHAT RUMOR?
PUT YOUR FEET DOWN, DUDE.

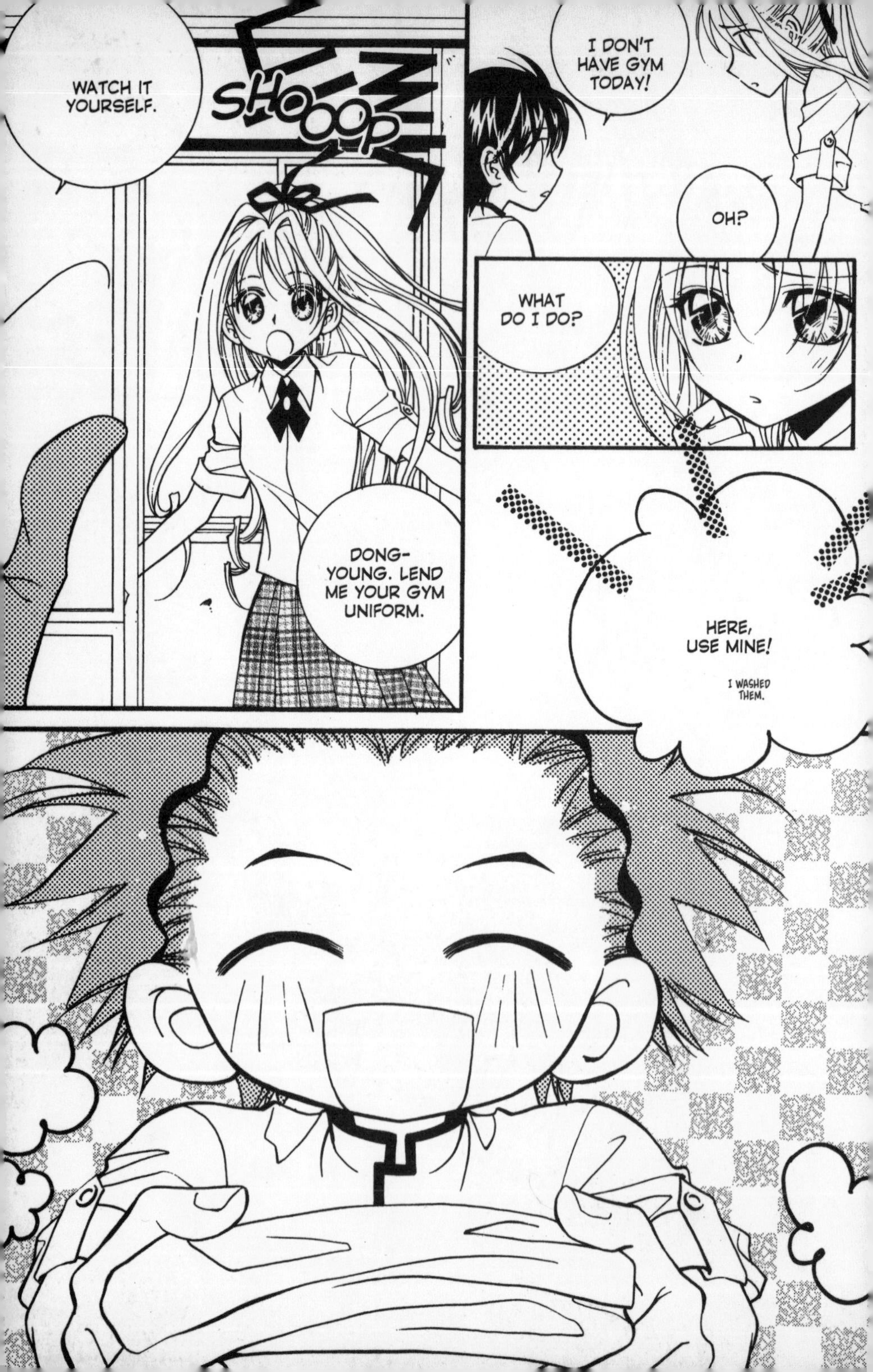

WATCH IT YOURSELF.
SHOOOP
DONG-YOUNG. LEND ME YOUR GYM UNIFORM.
I DON'T HAVE GYM TODAY!
OH?
WHAT DO I DO?
HERE, USE MINE!
I WASHED THEM.

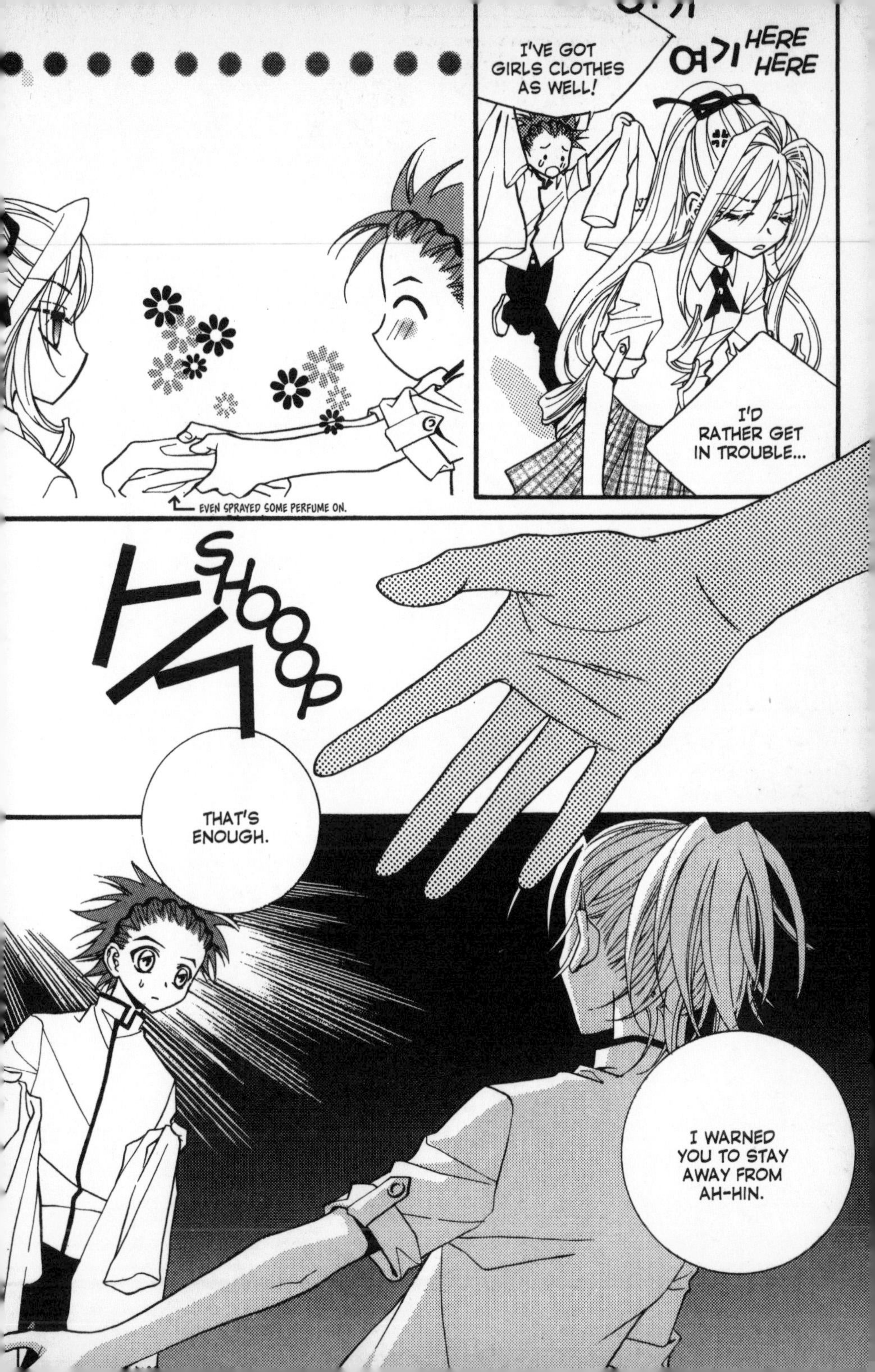
EVEN SPRAYED SOME PERFUME ON.
I'VE GOT GIRLS CLOTHES AS WELL!
여기 HERE
HERE
I'D RATHER GET IN TROUBLE...
SHOOOP
THAT'S ENOUGH.
I WARNED YOU TO STAY AWAY FROM AH-HIN.

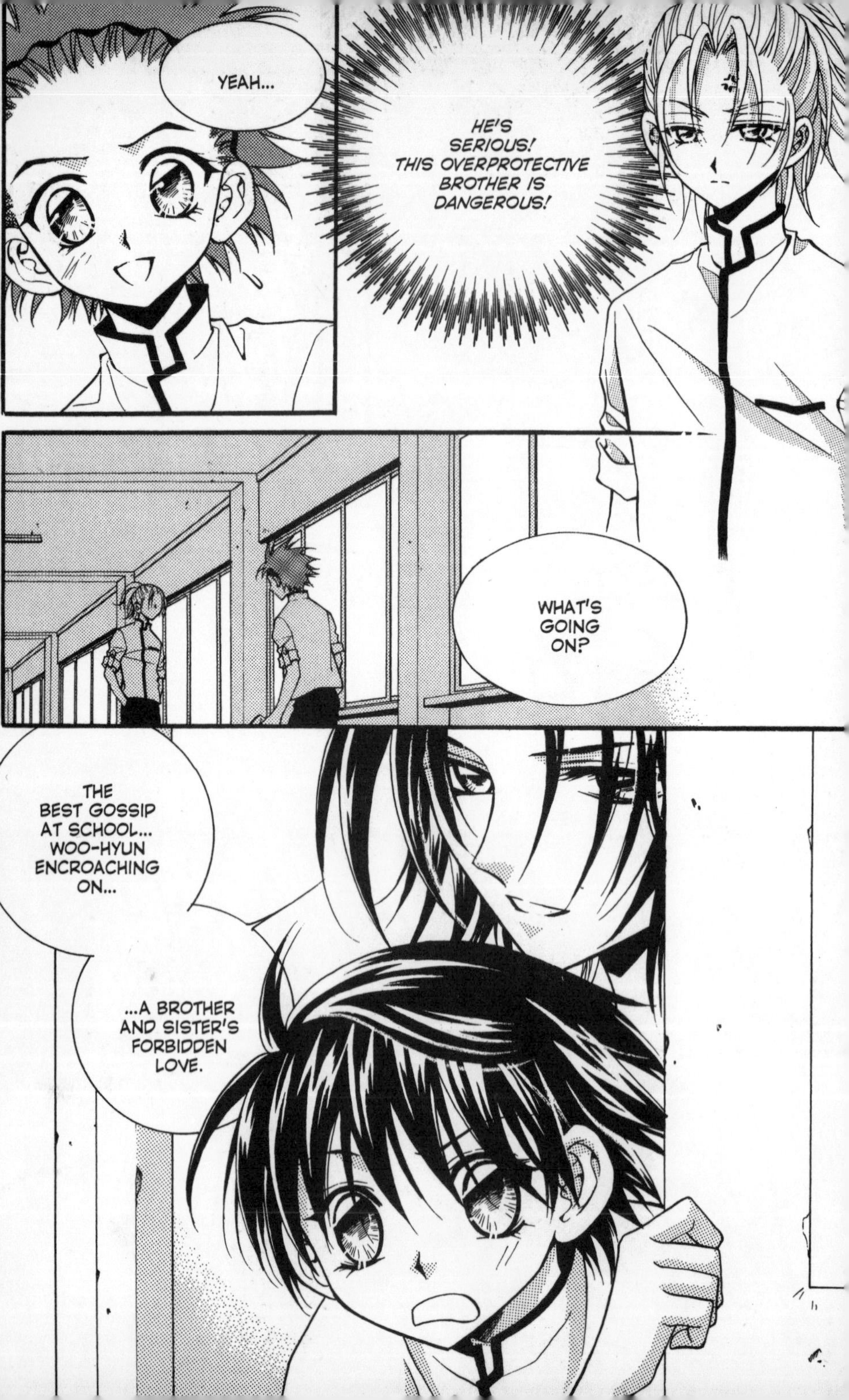
YEAH...
HE'S SERIOUS! THIS OVERPROTECTIVE BROTHER IS DANGEROUS!
WHAT'S GOING ON?
THE BEST GOSSIP AT SCHOOL... WOO-HYUN ENCROACHING ON...
...A BROTHER AND SISTER'S FORBIDDEN LOVE.

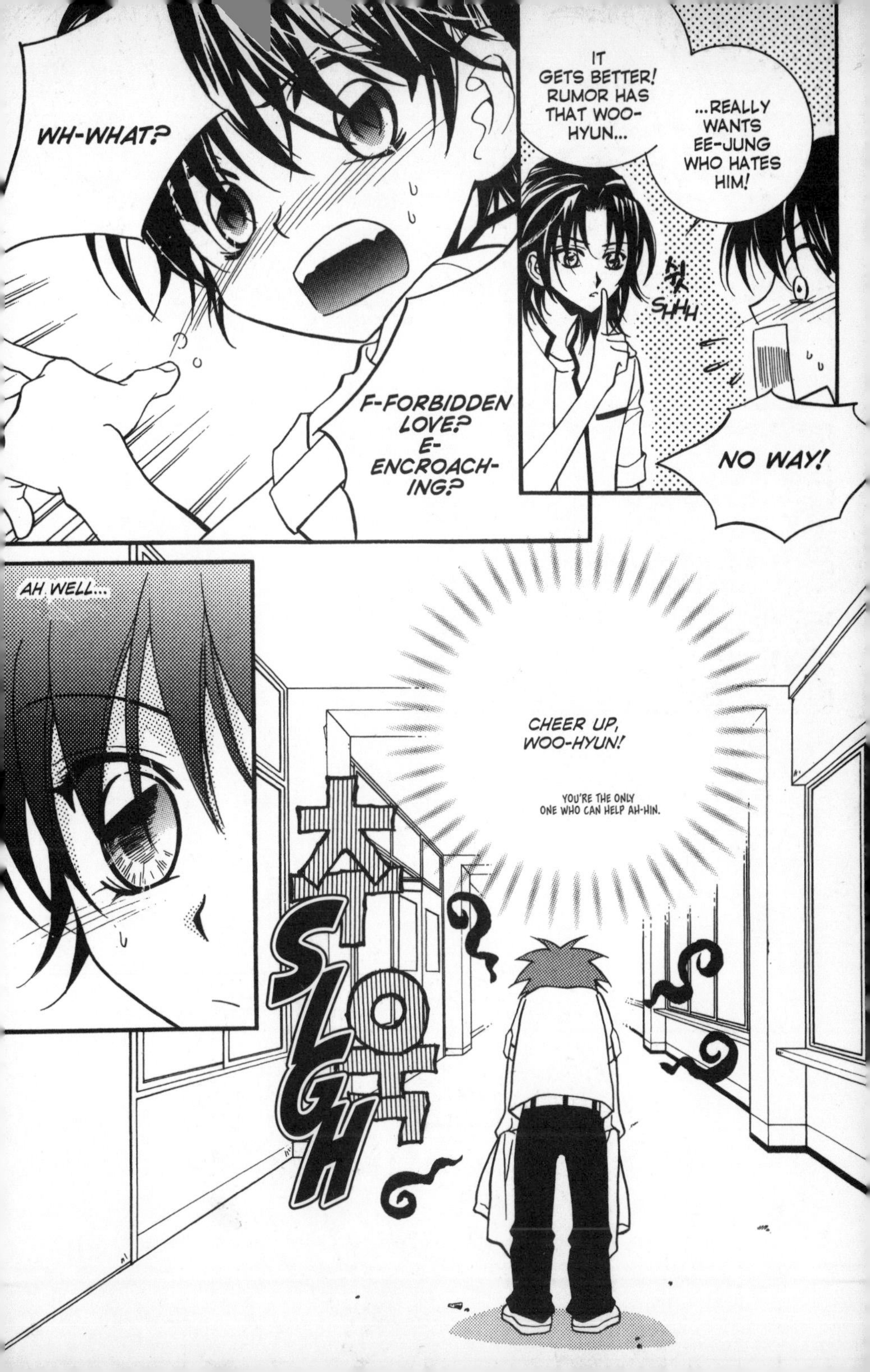
WH-WHAT?
F-FORBIDDEN LOVE? E-ENCROACHING?
IT GETS BETTER! RUMOR HAS THAT WOO-HYUN...
...REALLY WANTS EE-JUNG WHO HATES HIM!
SHHH
NO WAY!
AH WELL...
CHEER UP, WOO-HYUN!
YOU'RE THE ONLY ONE WHO CAN HELP AH-HIN.
SIGH

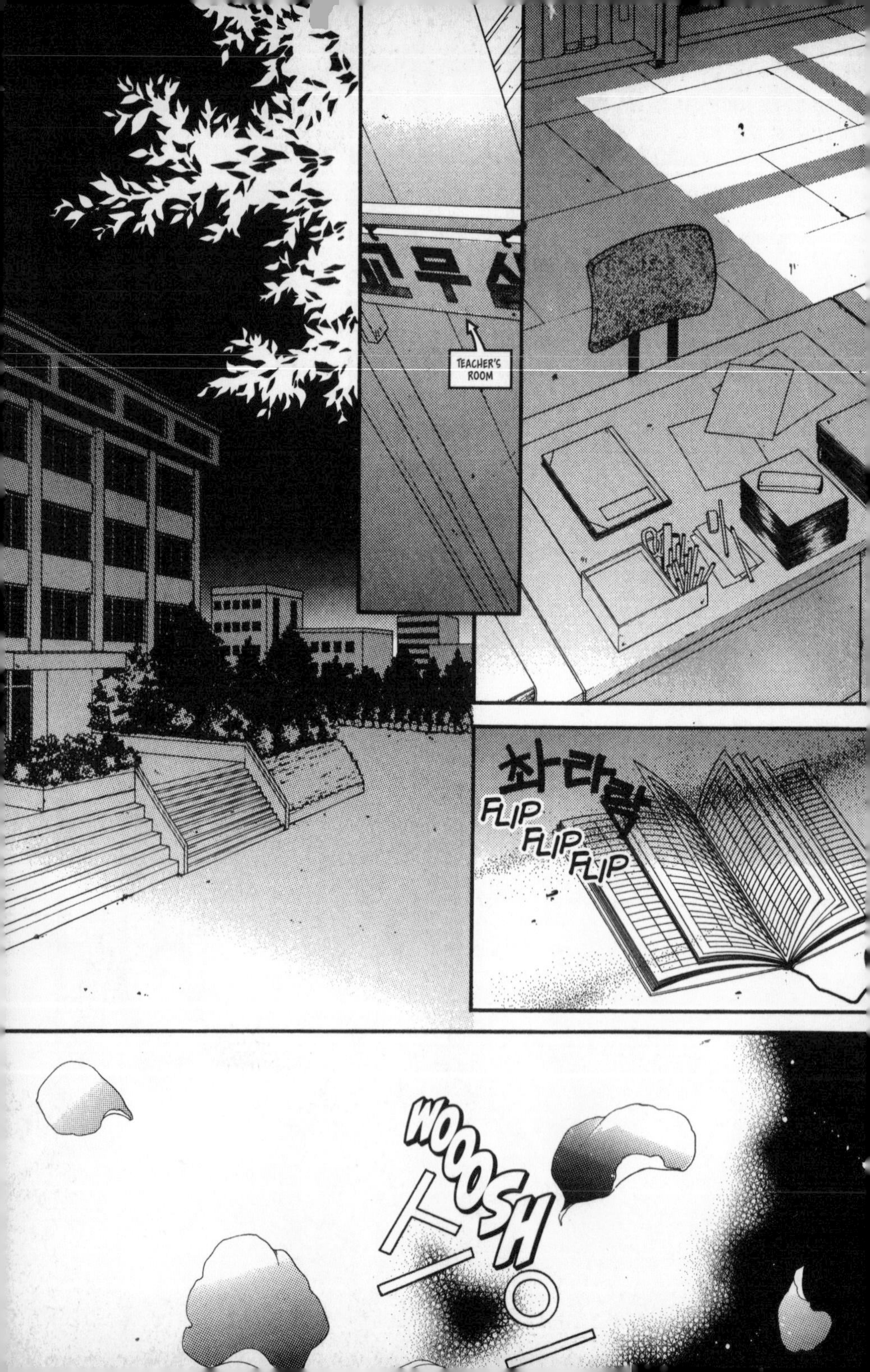
TEACHER'S ROOM
FLIP FLIP FLIP
WOOOSH

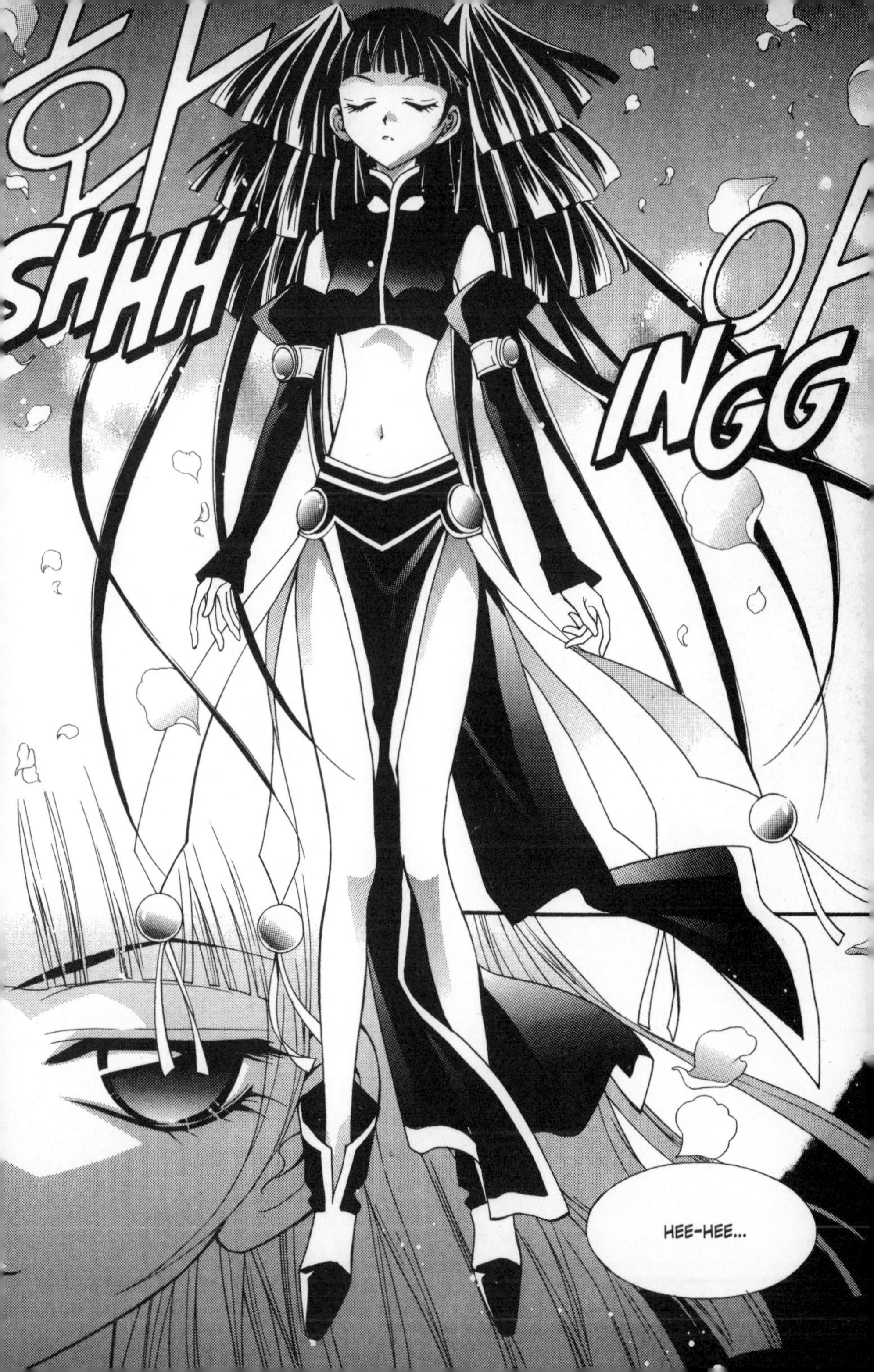
SHHH
INGG
HEE-HEE...

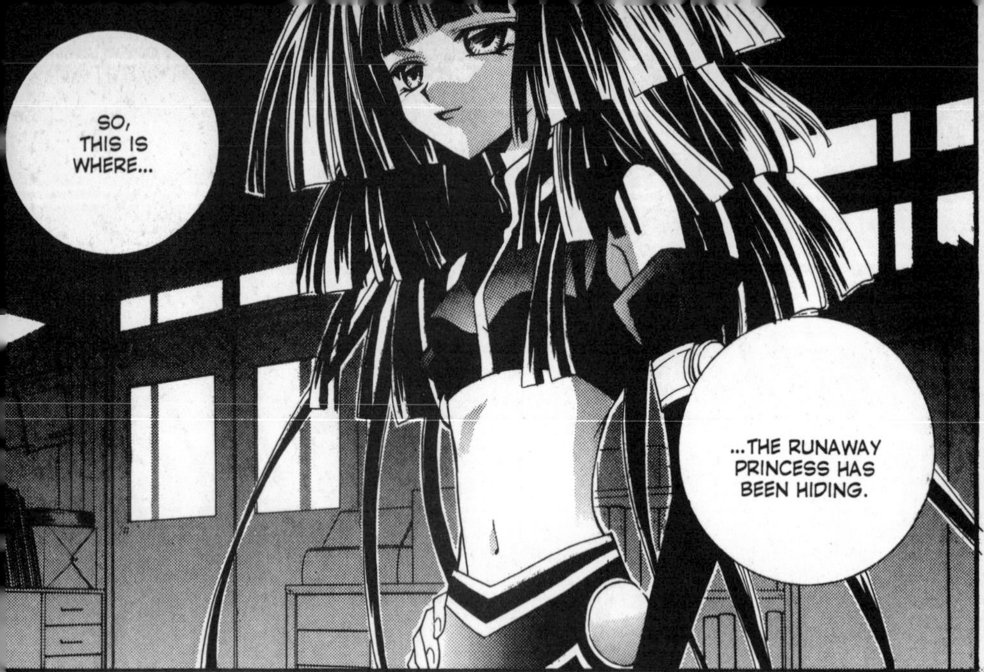
SO, THIS IS WHERE...
...THE RUNAWAY PRINCESS HAS BEEN HIDING.

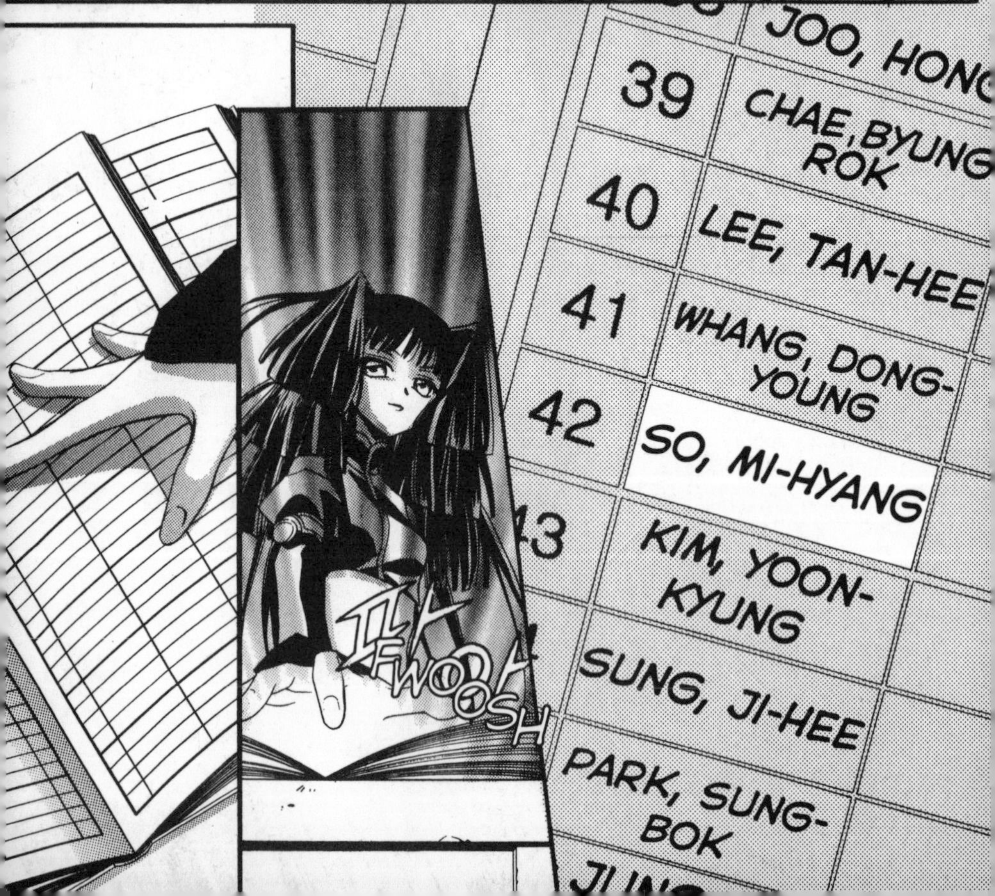
FWOOSH
39 CHAE, BYUNG ROK
40 LEE, TAN-HEE
41 WHANG, DONG-YOUNG
42 SO, MI-HYANG
43 KIM, YOON-KYUNG
SUNG, JI-HEE
PARK, SUNG-BOK

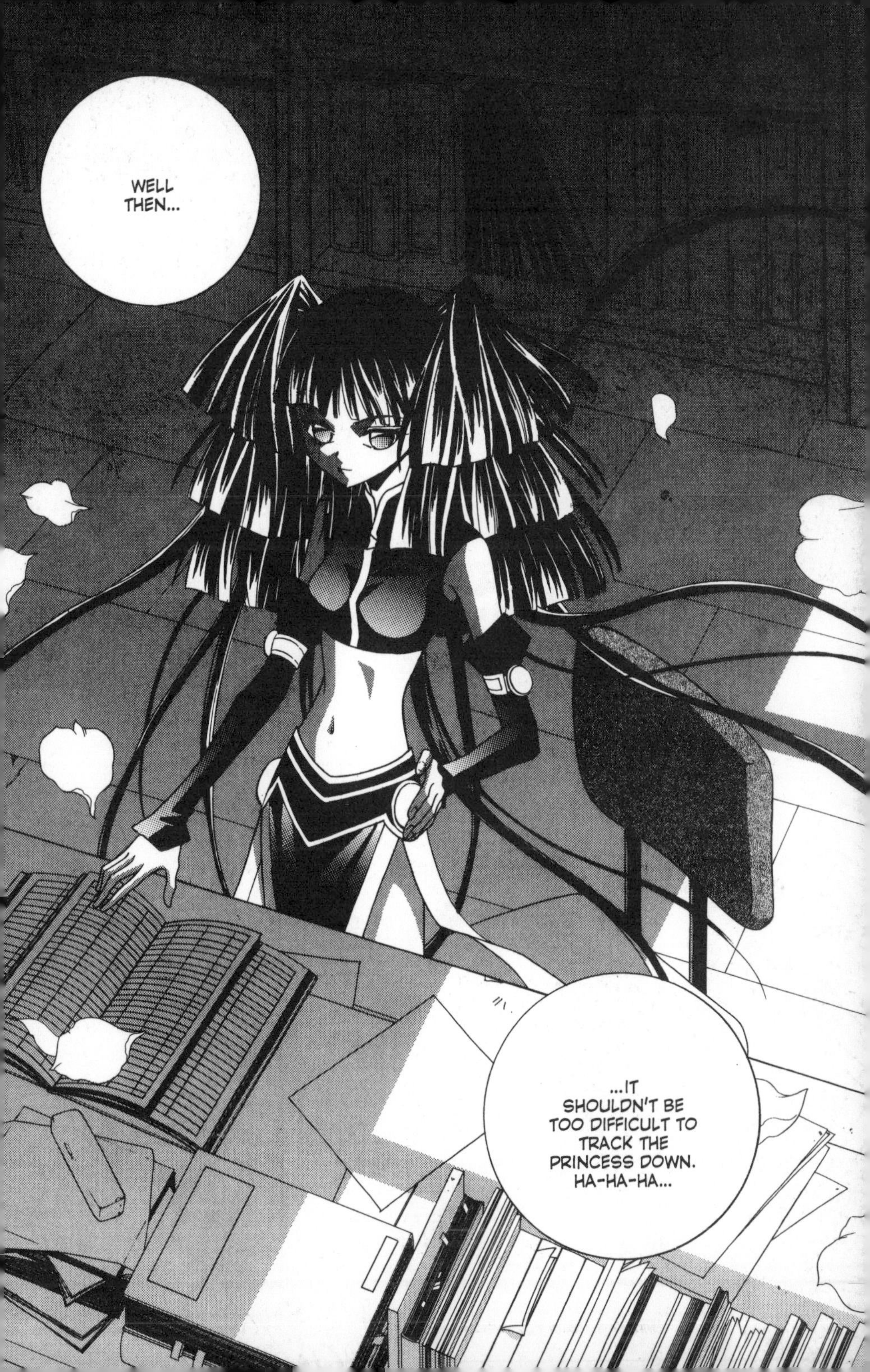
WELL THEN...
...IT SHOULDN'T BE TOO DIFFICULT TO TRACK THE PRINCESS DOWN. HA-HA-HA...

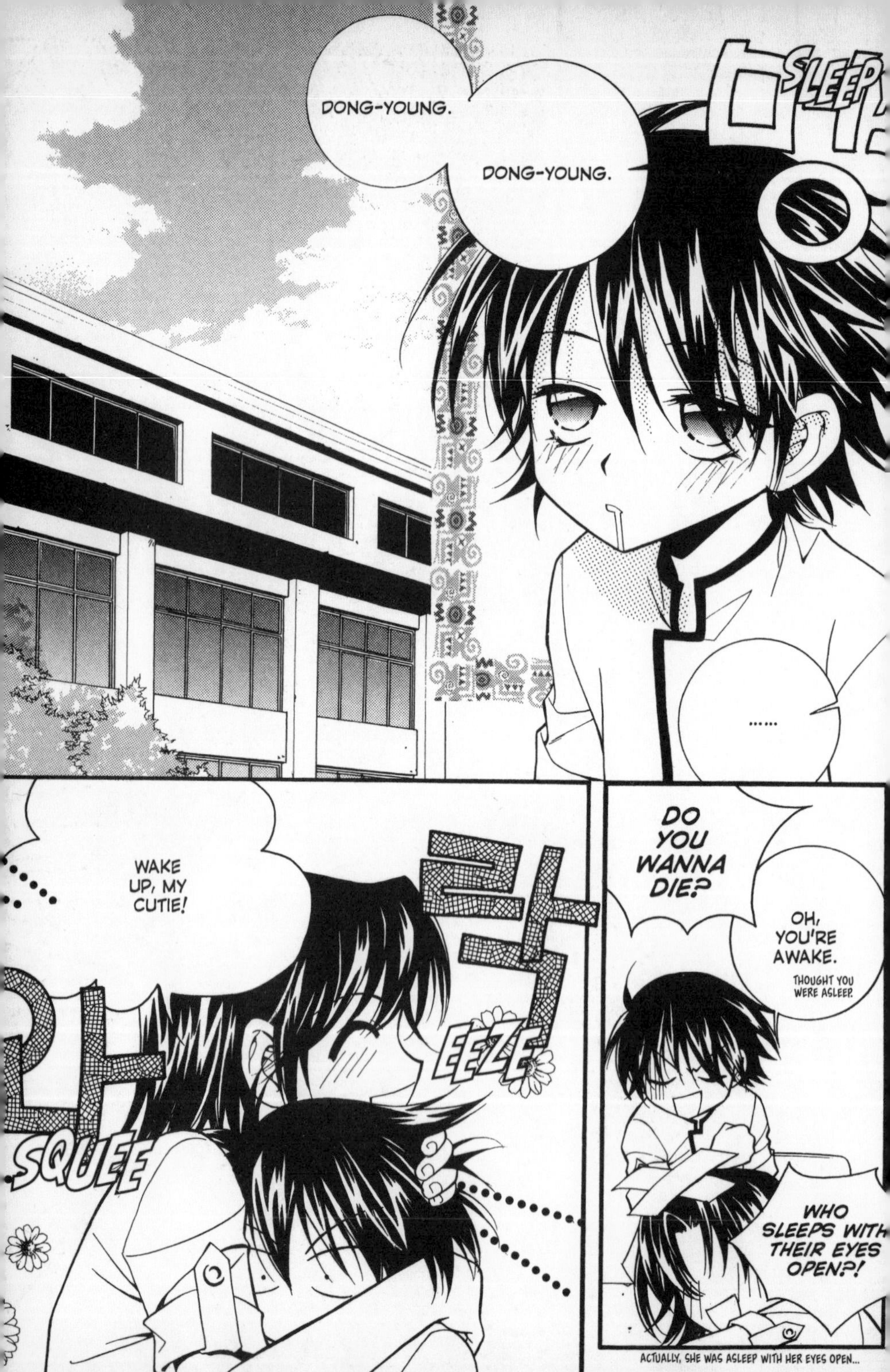
DONG-YOUNG.
DONG-YOUNG.
SLEEP
......
WAKE UP, MY CUTIE!
SQUEE
EEZE
DO YOU WANNA DIE?
OH, YOU'RE AWAKE.
THOUGHT YOU WERE ASLEEP.
WHO SLEEPS WITH THEIR EYES OPEN?!
ACTUALLY, SHE WAS ASLEEP WITH HER EYES OPEN...

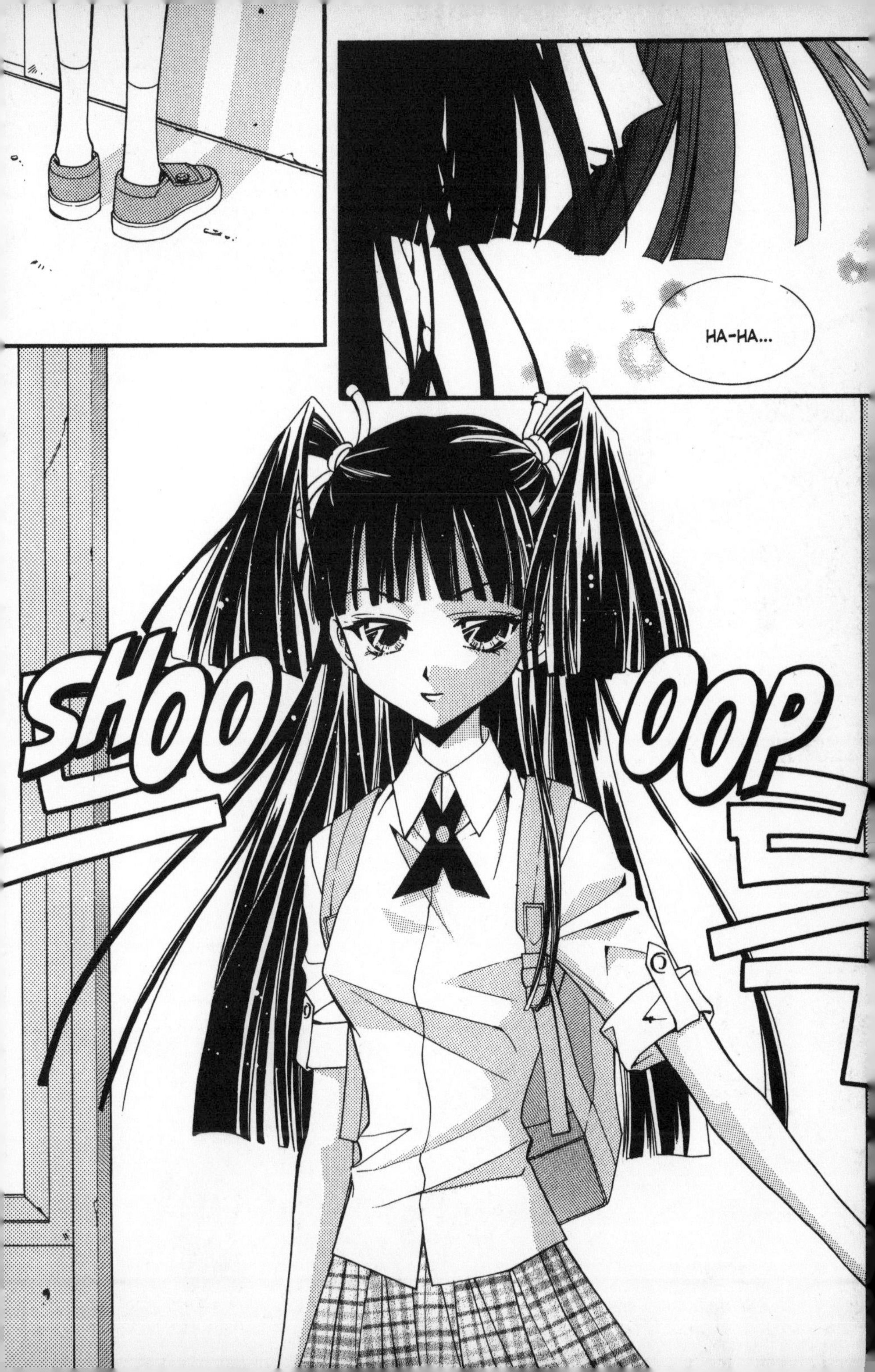
HA-HA...
SHOO
OOP

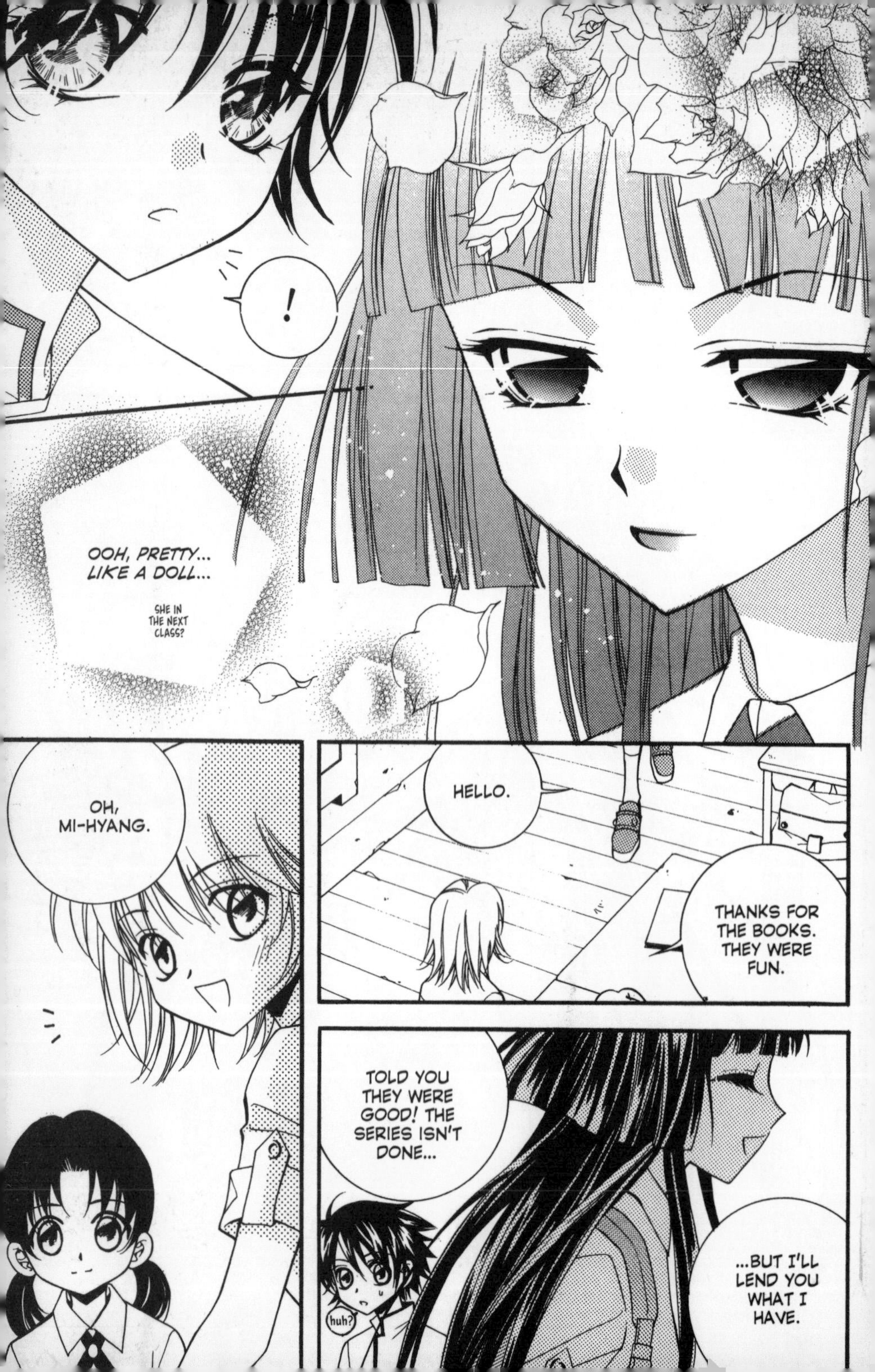
!
OOH, PRETTY... LIKE A DOLL...
SHE IN THE NEXT CLASS?
OH, MI-HYANG.
HELLO.
THANKS FOR THE BOOKS. THEY WERE FUN.
TOLD YOU THEY WERE GOOD! THE SERIES ISN'T DONE...
huh?
...BUT I'LL LEND YOU WHAT I HAVE.

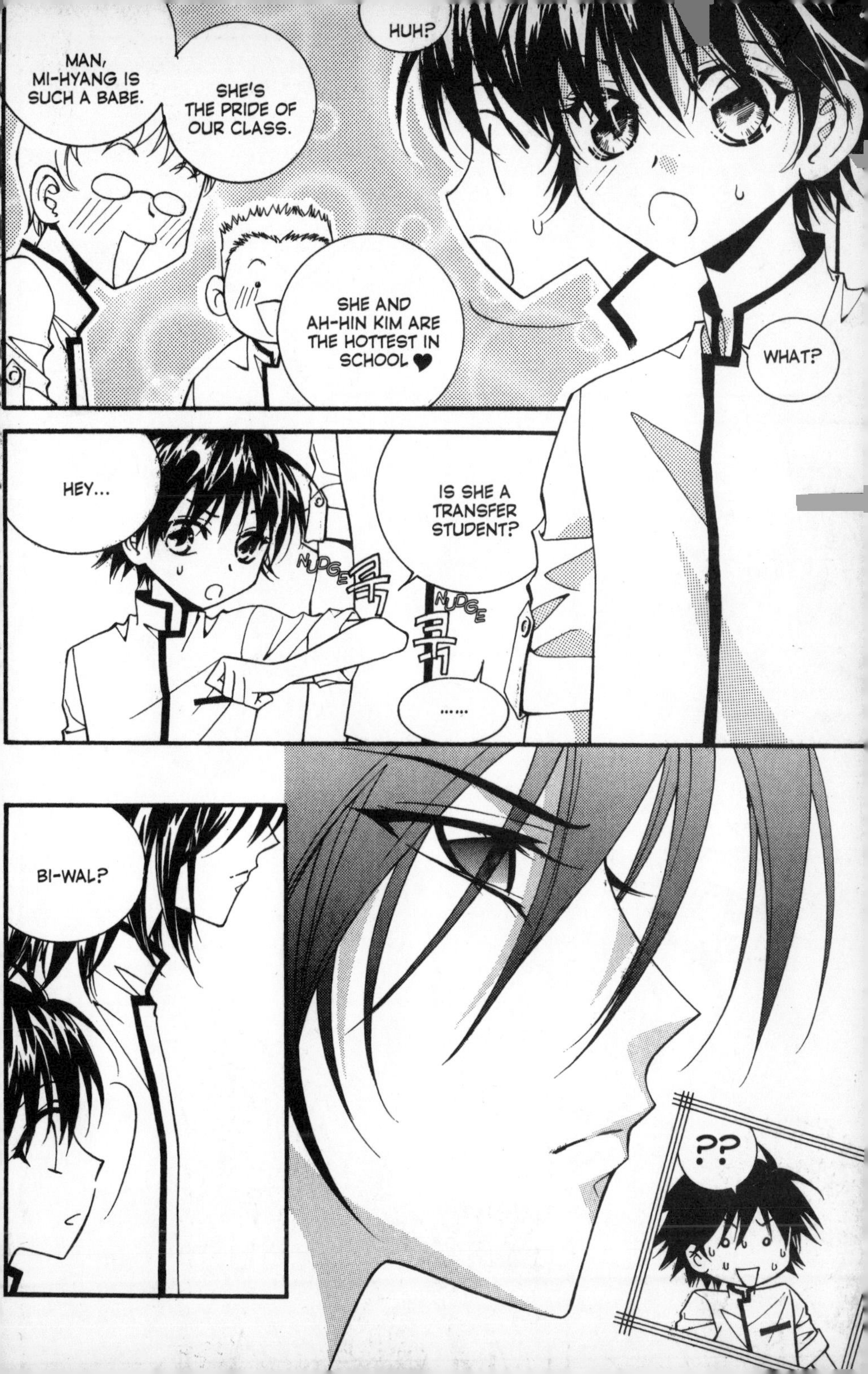
MAN, MI-HYANG IS SUCH A BABE.
SHE'S THE PRIDE OF OUR CLASS.
SHE AND AH-HIN KIM ARE THE HOTTEST IN SCHOOL ♥
HUH?
WHAT?
HEY...
NUDGE
IS SHE A TRANSFER STUDENT?
NUDGE
......
BI-WAL?
??

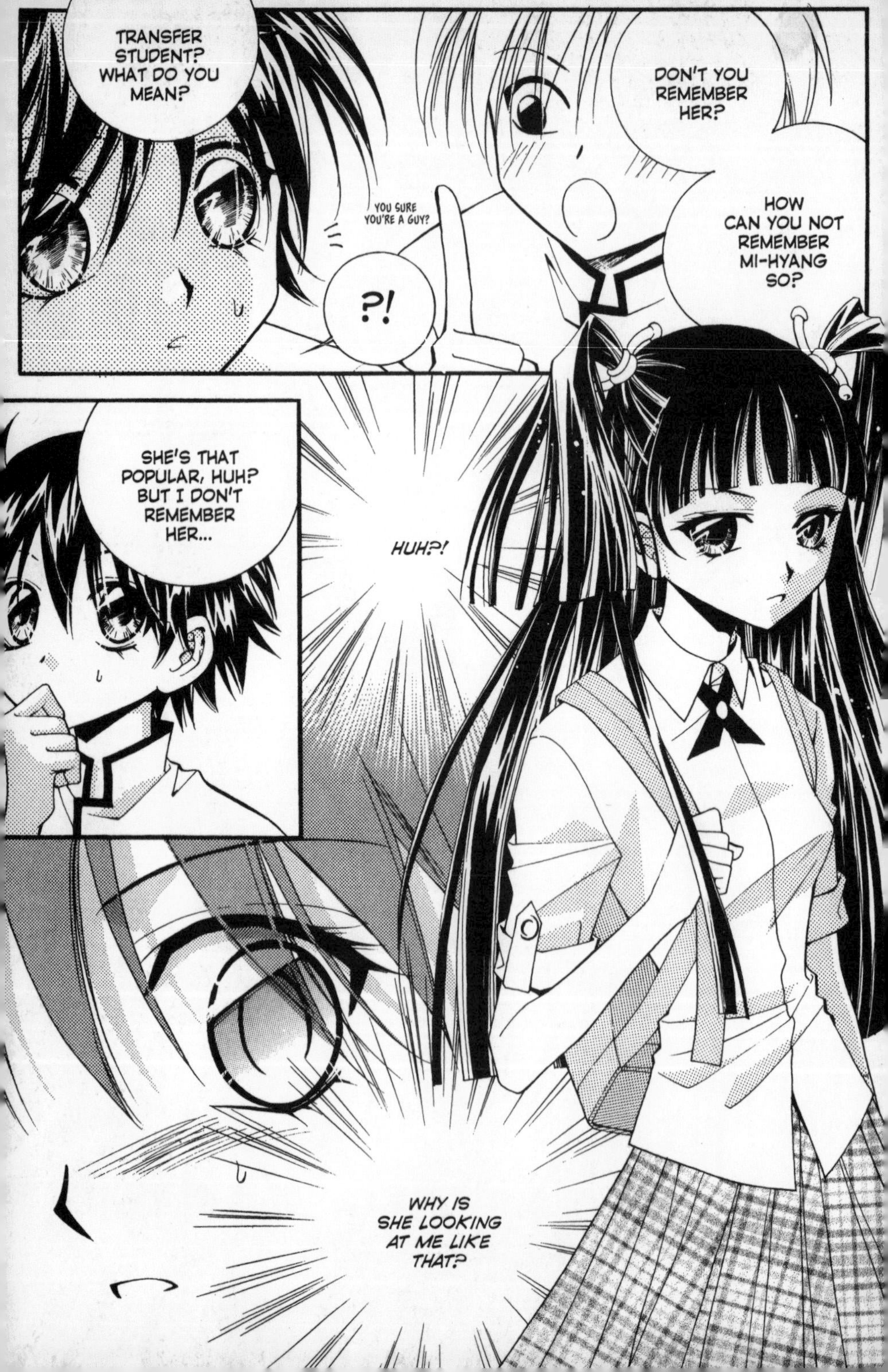
TRANSFER STUDENT? WHAT DO YOU MEAN?
YOU SURE YOU'RE A GUY?
?!
DON'T YOU REMEMBER HER?
HOW CAN YOU NOT REMEMBER MI-HYANG SO?
SHE'S THAT POPULAR, HUH? BUT I DON'T REMEMBER HER...
HUH?!
WHY IS SHE LOOKING AT ME LIKE THAT?

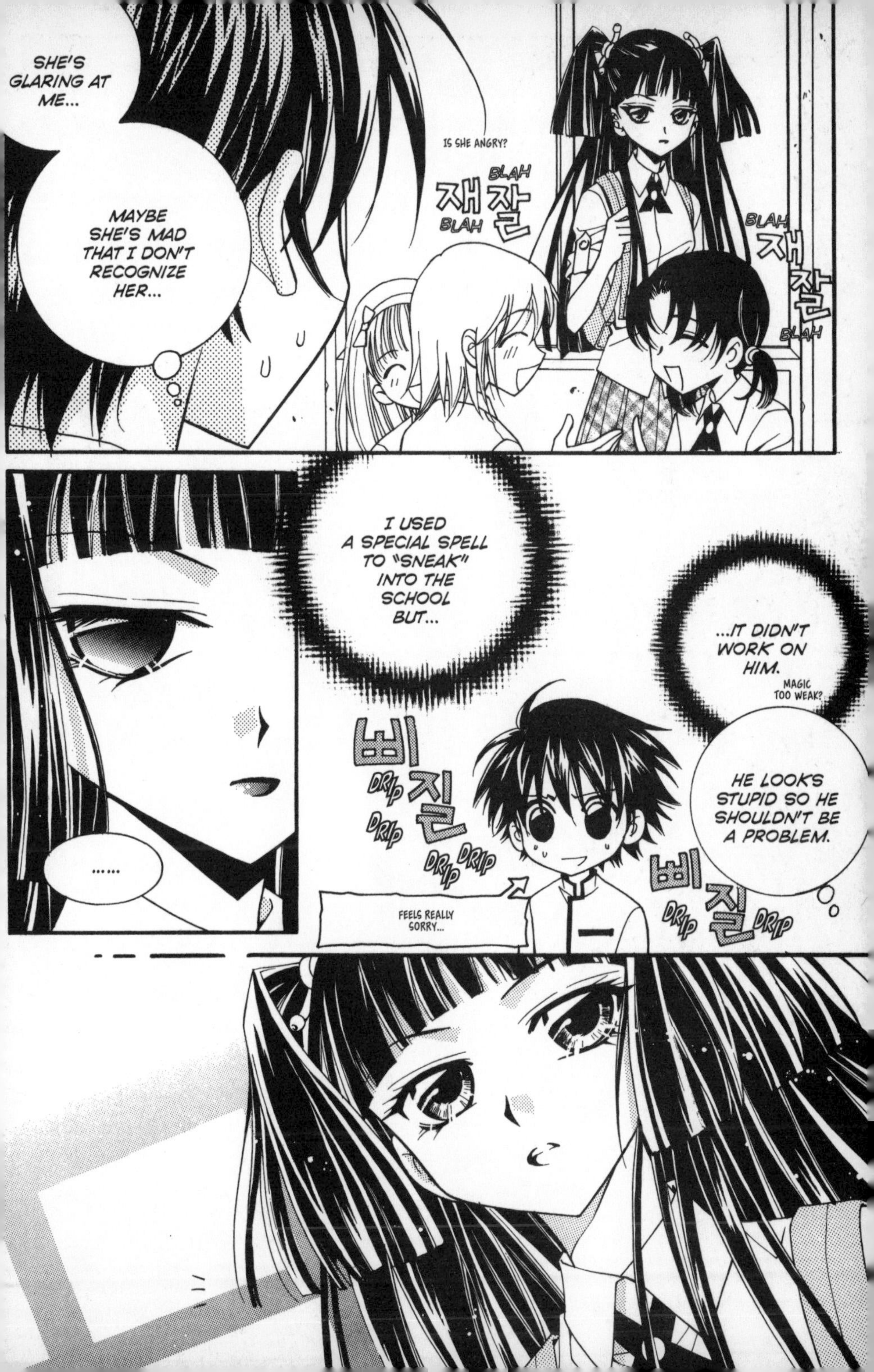
SHE'S GLARING AT ME...
MAYBE SHE'S MAD THAT I DON'T RECOGNIZE HER...
IS SHE ANGRY?
재잘 BLAH BLAH
재잘 BLAH BLAH
......
I USED A SPECIAL SPELL TO "SNEAK" INTO THE SCHOOL BUT...
...IT DIDN'T WORK ON HIM.
MAGIC TOO WEAK?
삐질 DRIP DRIP DRIP DRIP
HE LOOKS STUPID SO HE SHOULDN'T BE A PROBLEM.
FEELS REALLY SORRY...
삐질 DRIP DRIP

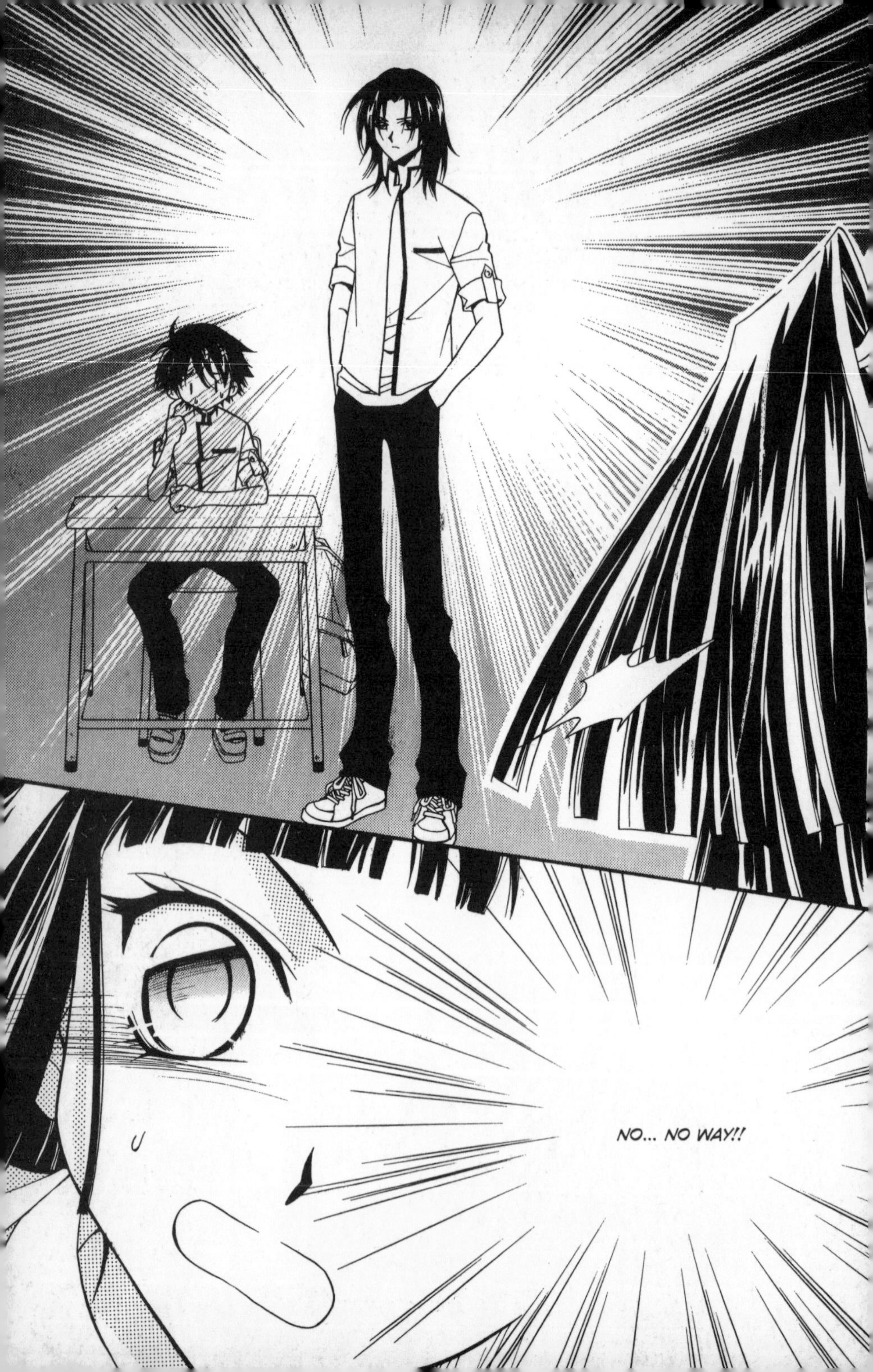
NO... NO WAY!!

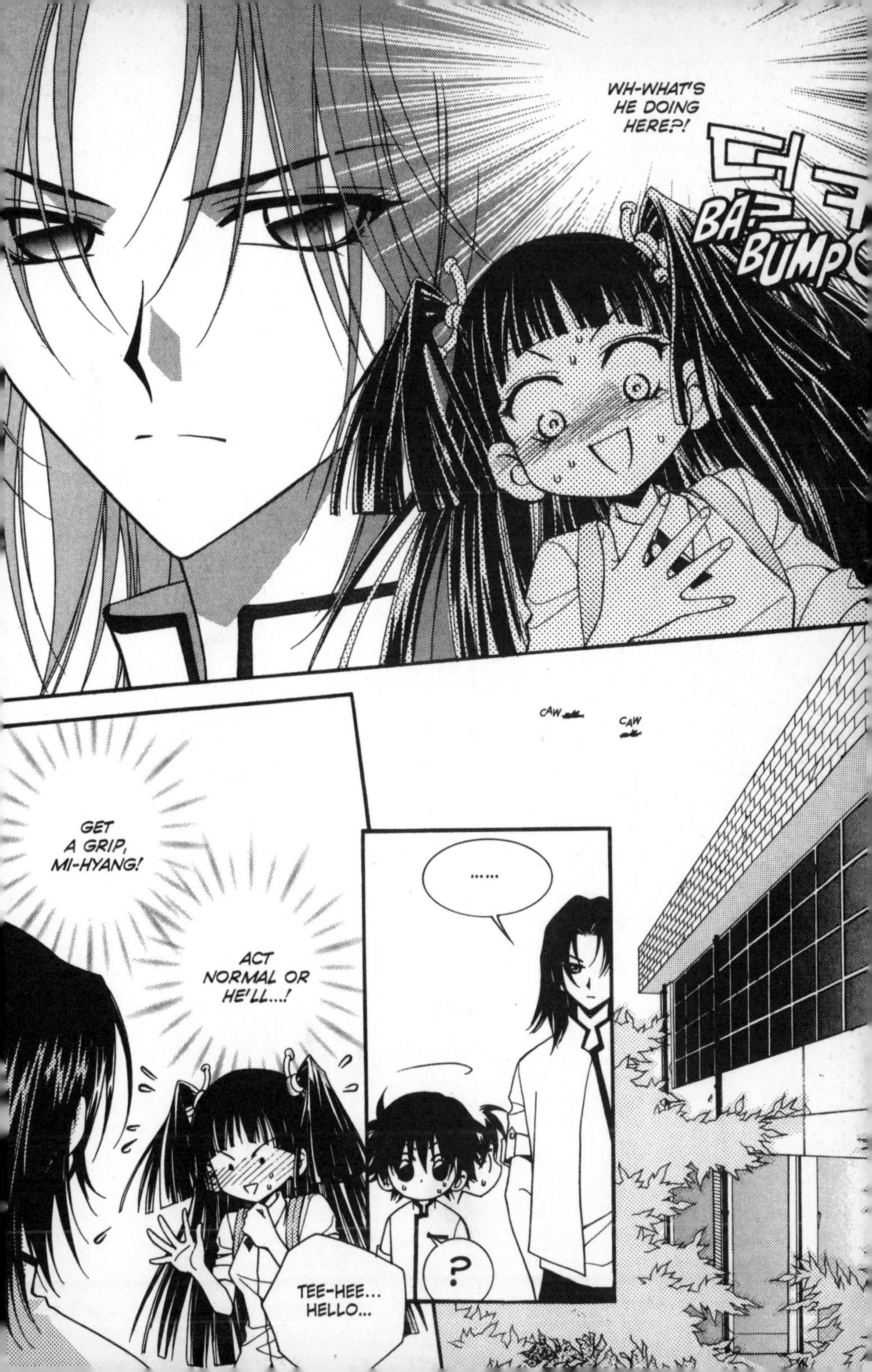
WH-WHAT'S HE DOING HERE?!
BA-BUMP
CAW
CAW
GET A GRIP, MI-HYANG!
ACT NORMAL OR HE'LL...!
TEE-HEE... HELLO...
?
......

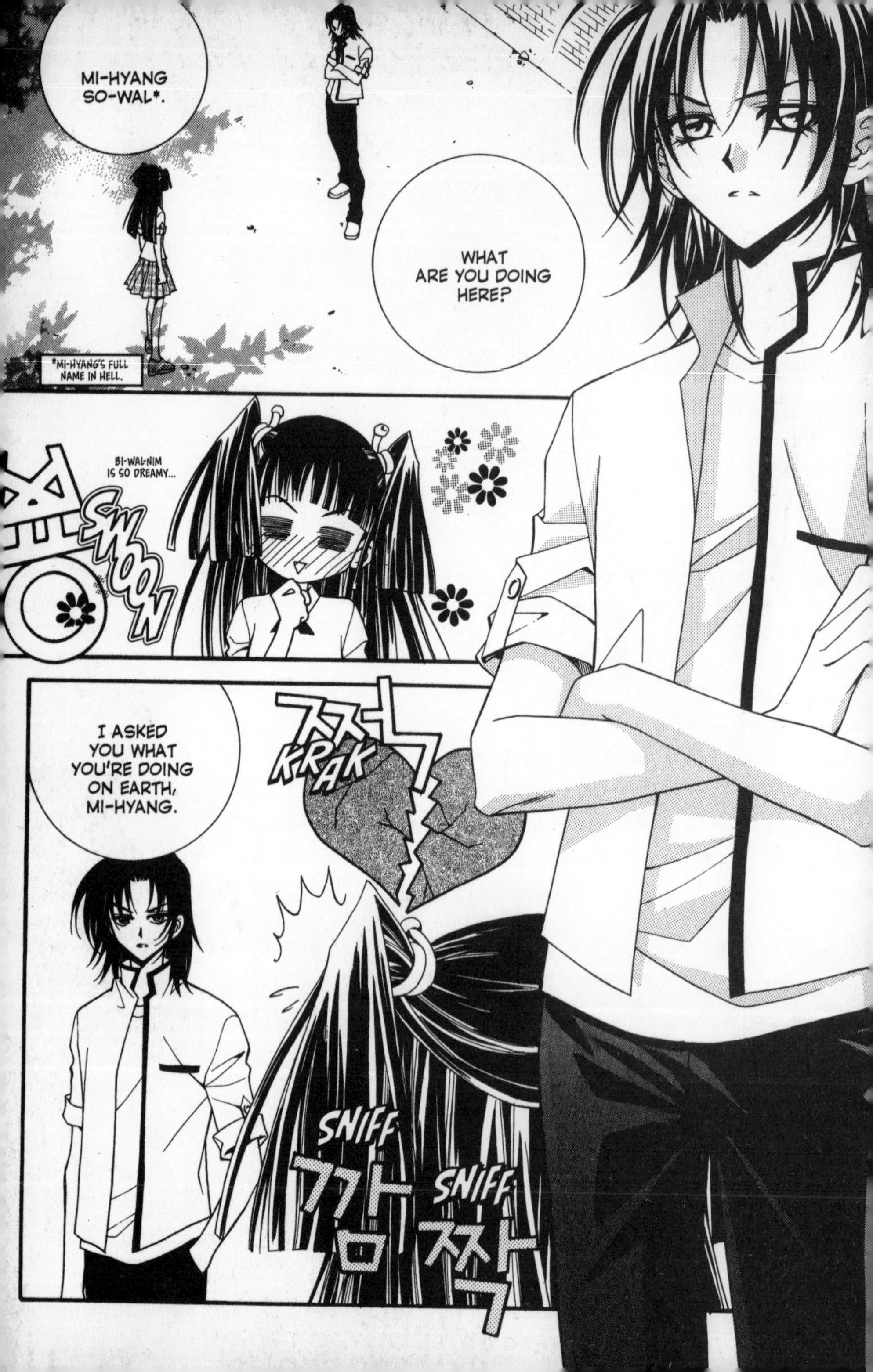
MI-HYANG SO-WAL*.
*MI-HYANG'S FULL NAME IN HELL.
WHAT ARE YOU DOING HERE?
BI-WAL-NIM IS SO DREAMY...
SWOON
I ASKED YOU WHAT YOU'RE DOING ON EARTH, MI-HYANG.
KRAK
SNIFF
SNIFF

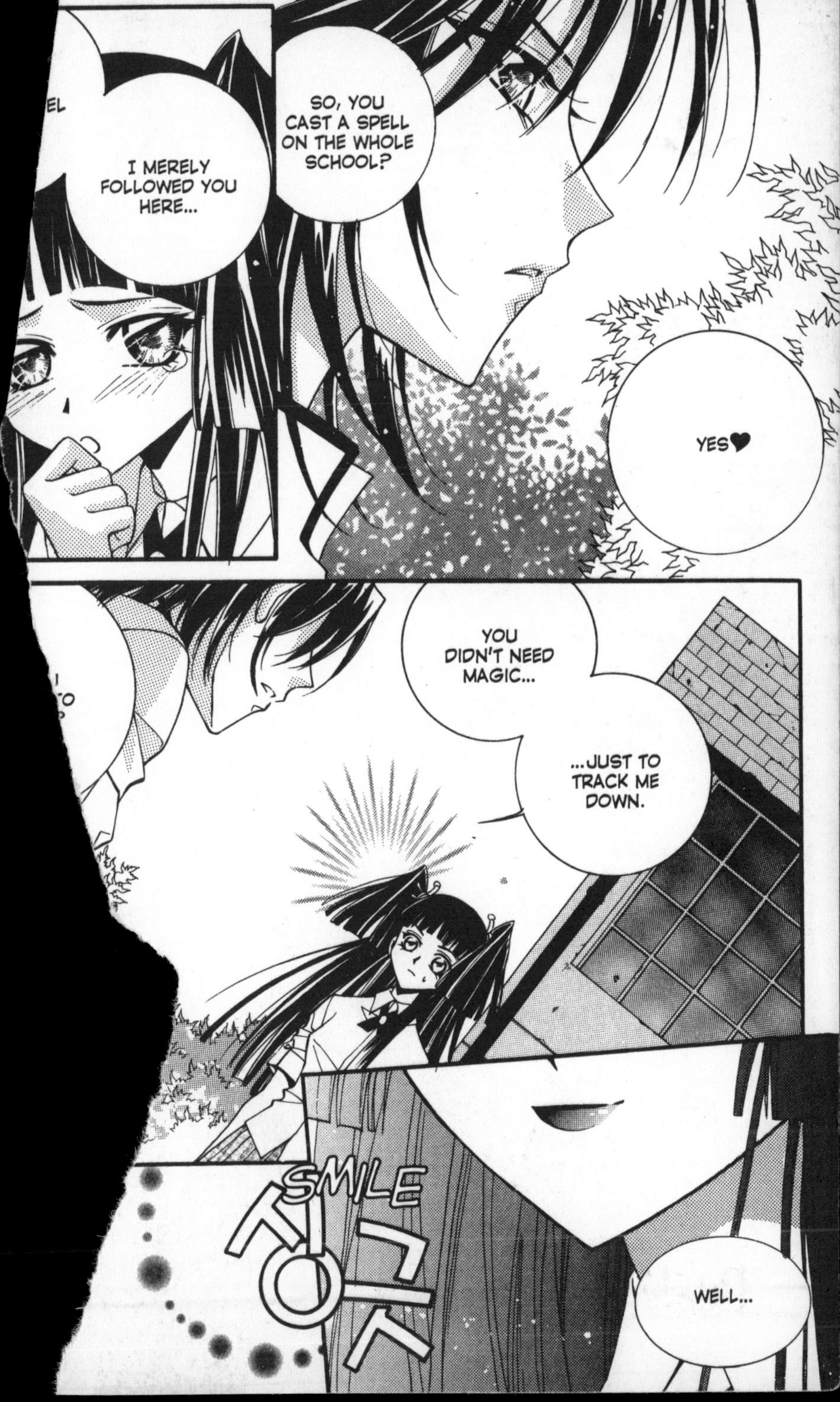
I MERELY FOLLOWED YOU HERE...
SO, YOU CAST A SPELL ON THE WHOLE SCHOOL?
YES♥
YOU DIDN'T NEED MAGIC...
...JUST TO TRACK ME DOWN.
SMILE
WELL...

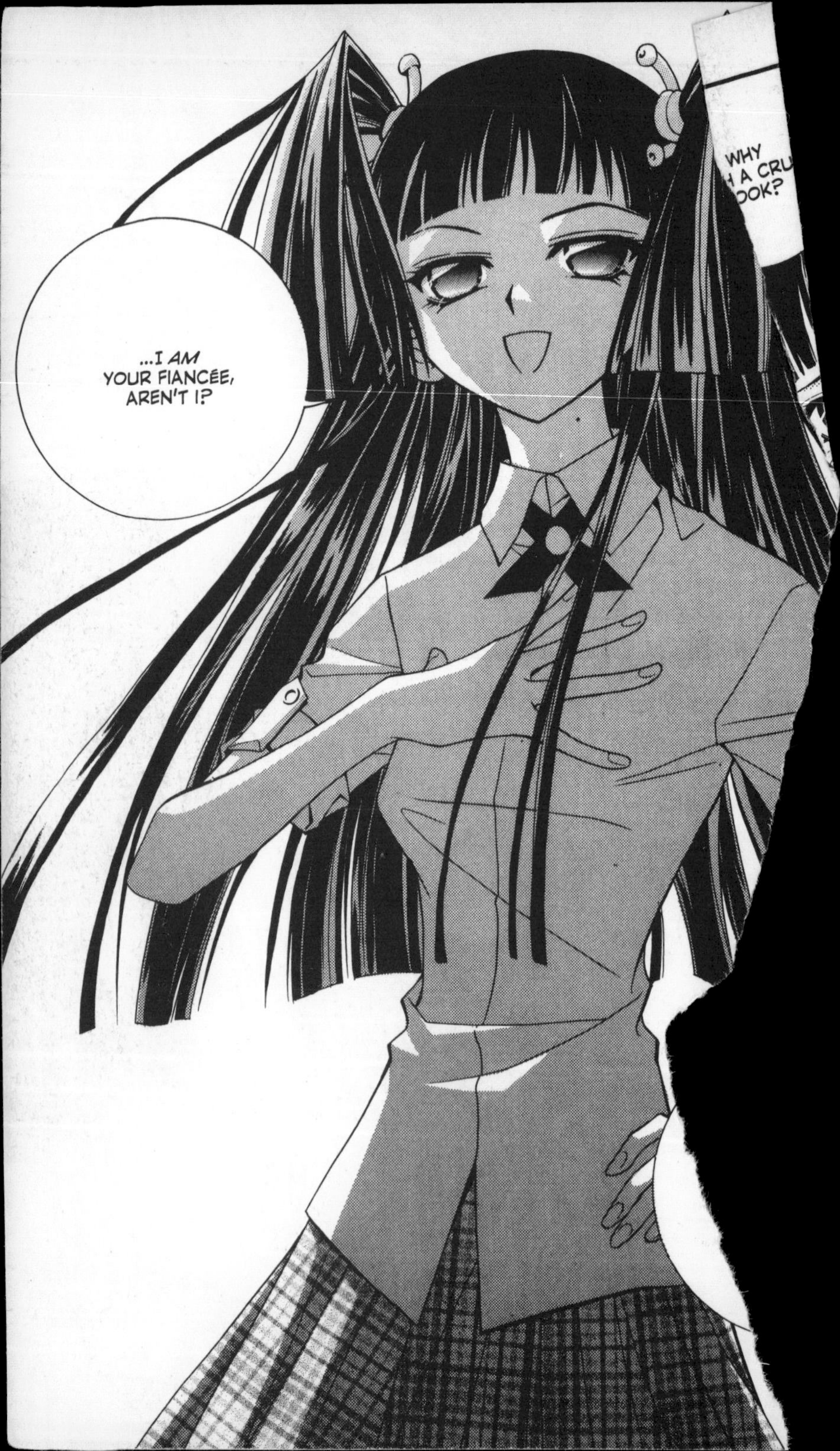
...I AM YOUR FIANCÉE, AREN'T I?
WHY H A CRU OOK?

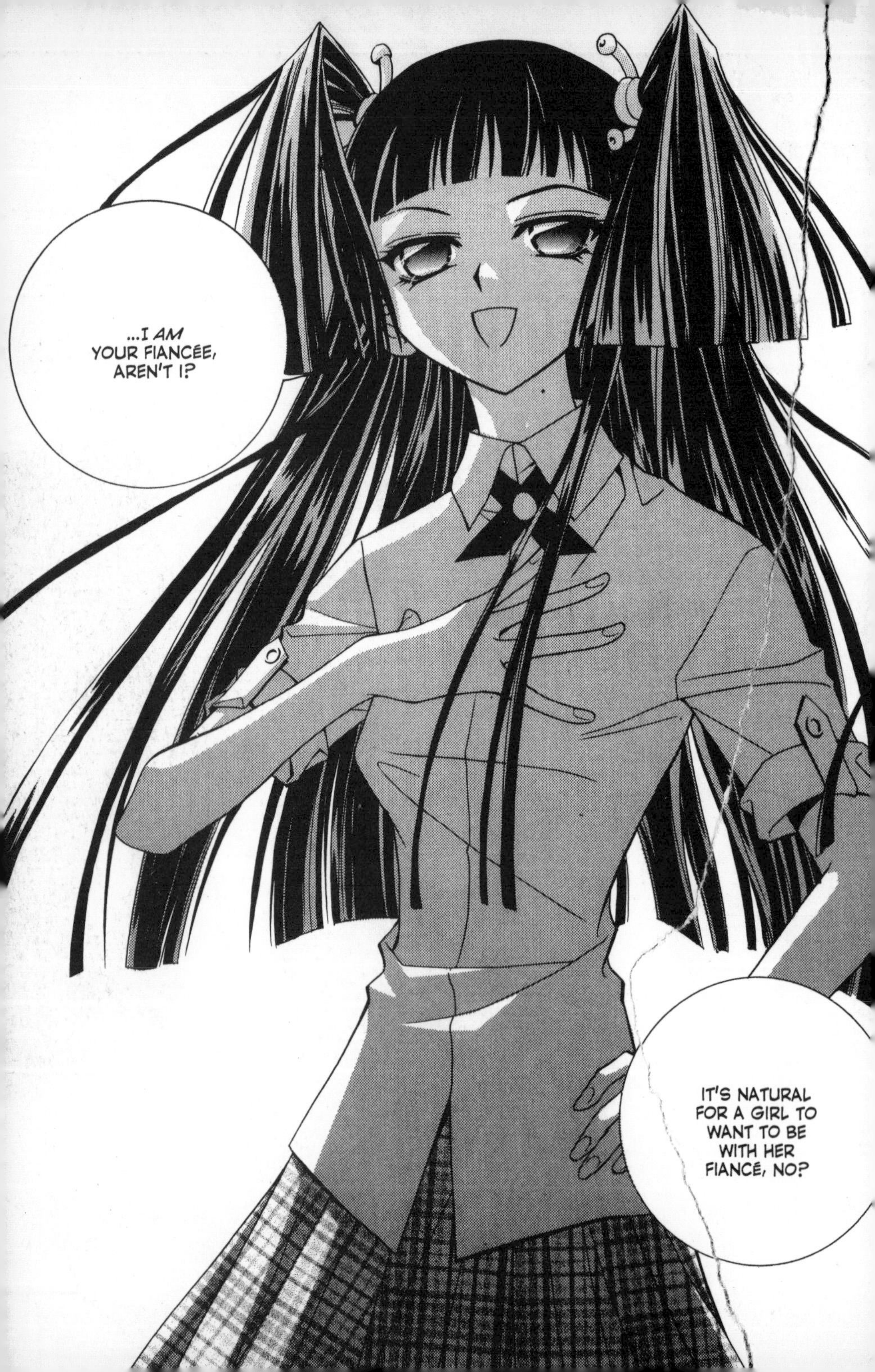
...I *AM* YOUR FIANCÉE, AREN'T I?
IT'S NATURAL FOR A GIRL TO WANT TO BE WITH HER FIANCÉ, NO?

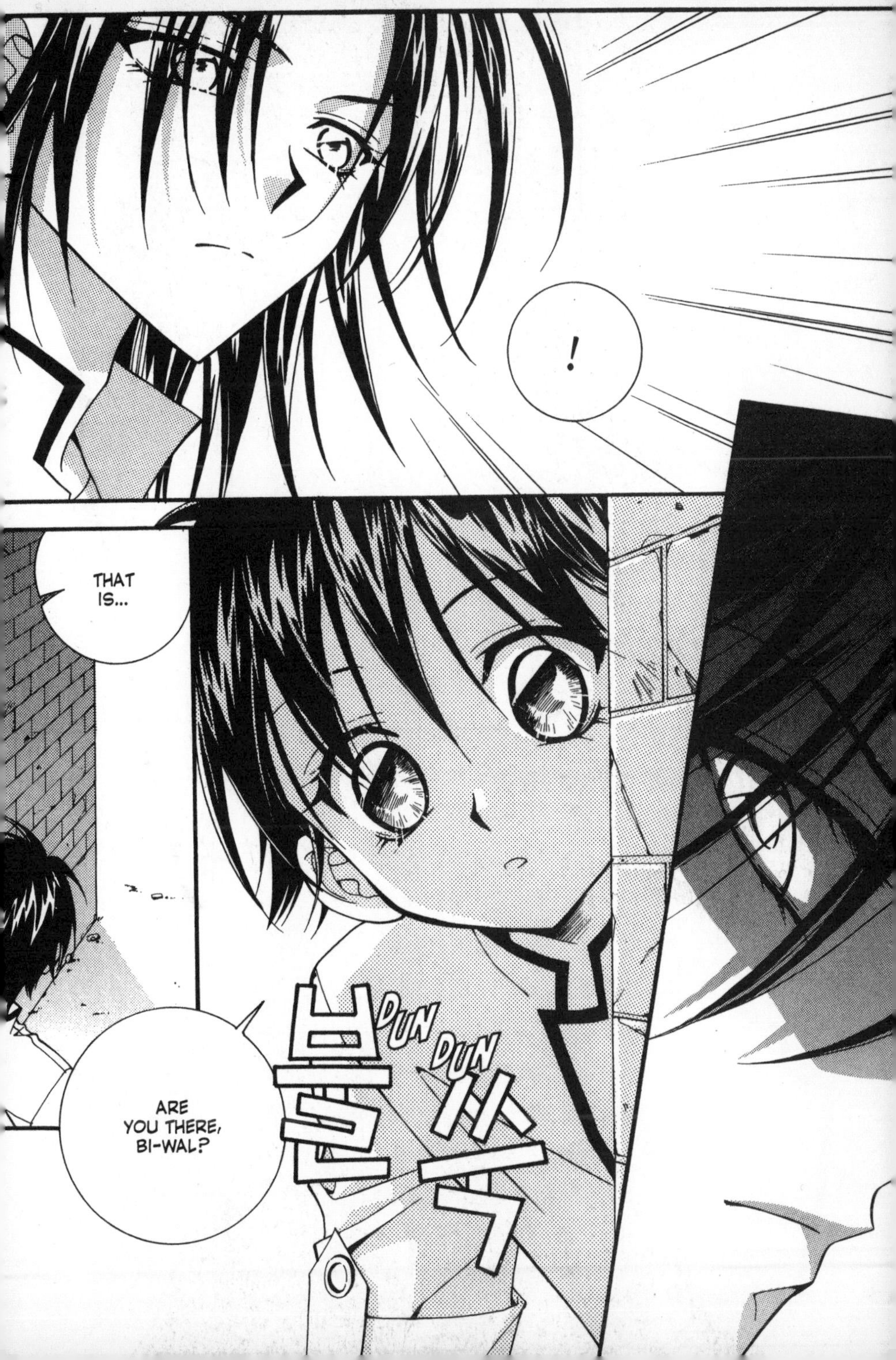
!
THAT IS...
DUN DUN
ARE YOU THERE, BI-WAL?

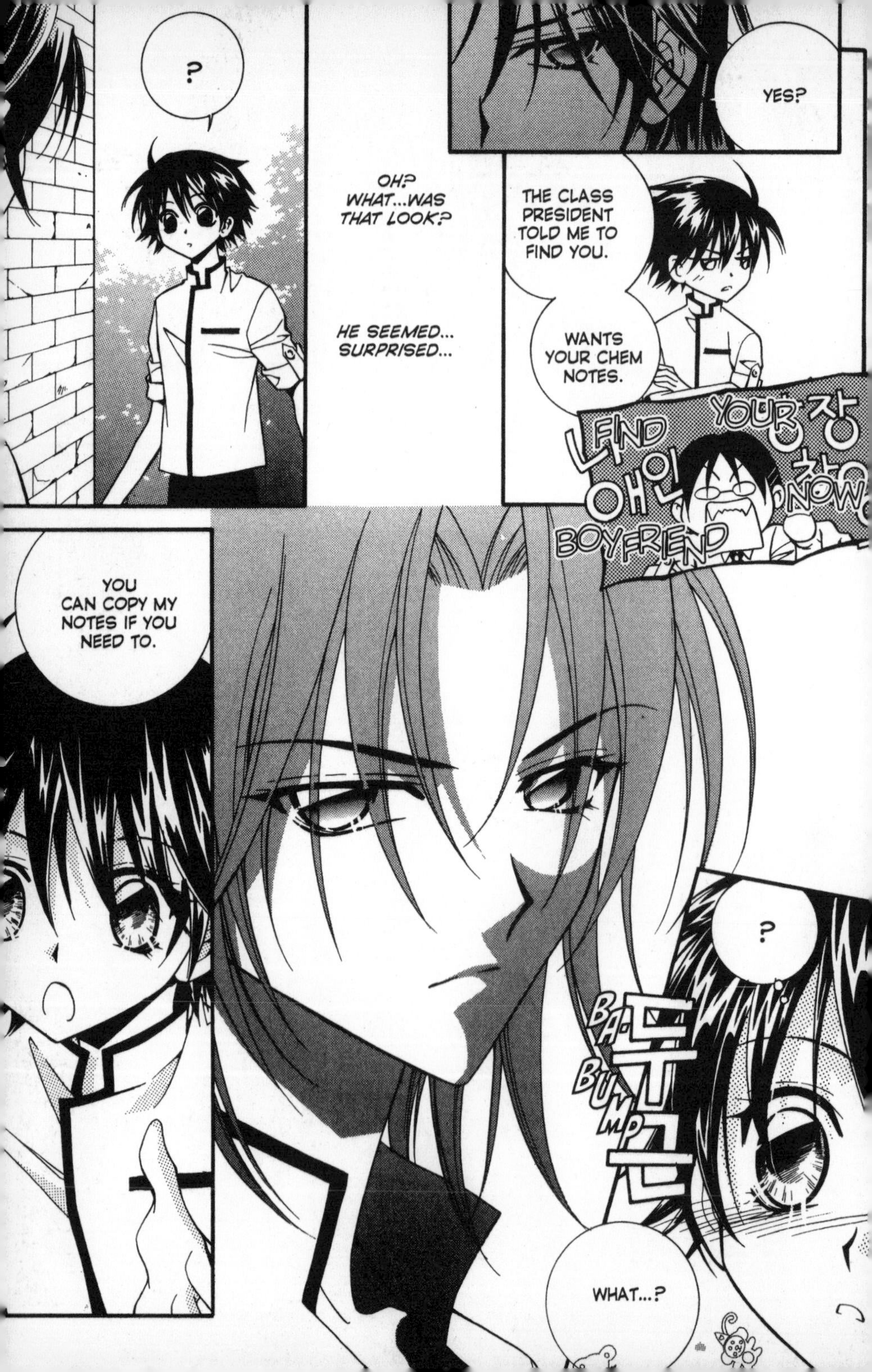
?
OH? WHAT...WAS THAT LOOK?
HE SEEMED... SURPRISED...
YES?
THE CLASS PRESIDENT TOLD ME TO FIND YOU.
WANTS YOUR CHEM NOTES.
FIND YOUR BOYFRIEND NOW
YOU CAN COPY MY NOTES IF YOU NEED TO.
?
BA-BUMP
WHAT...?

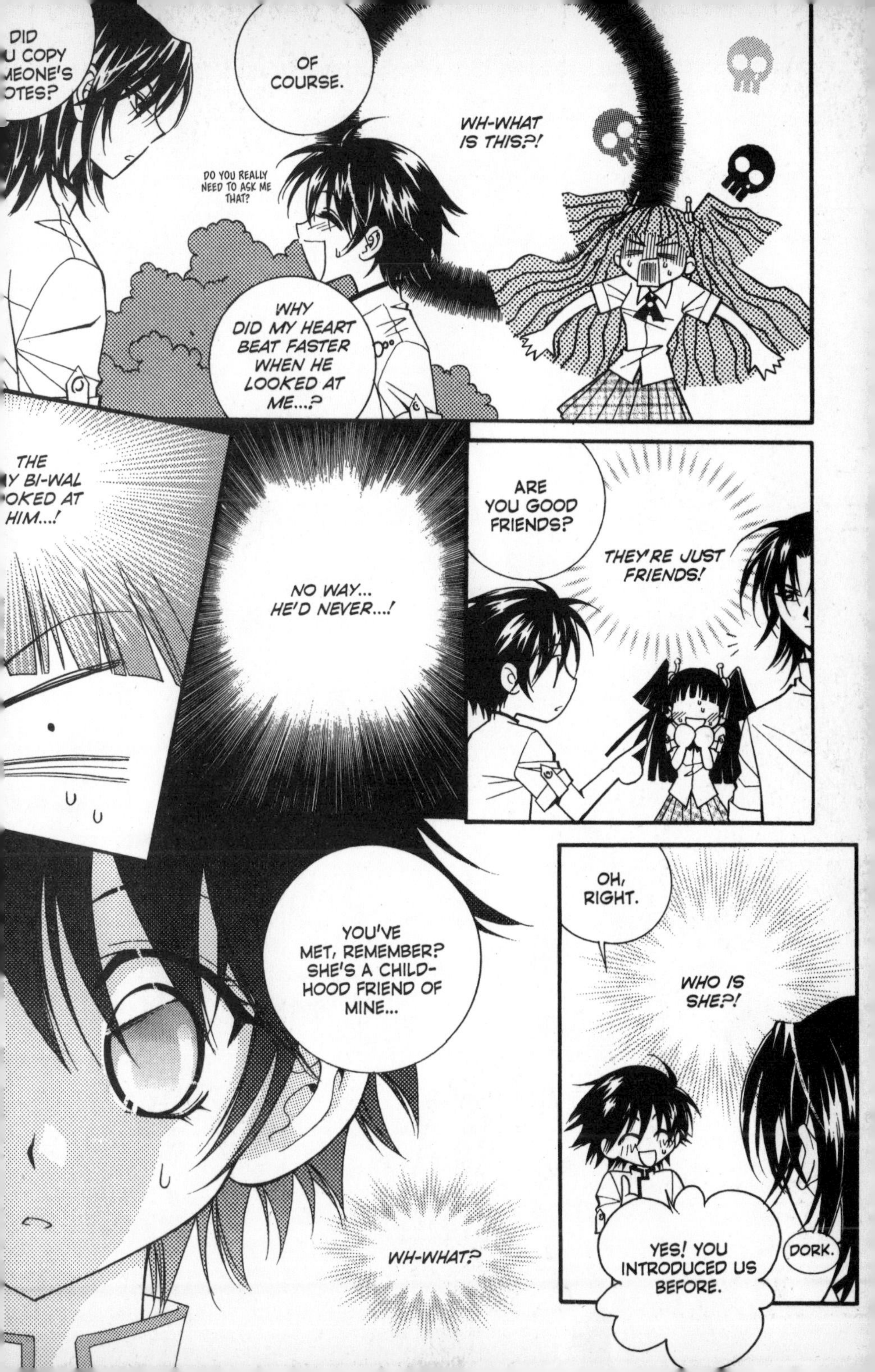
DID U COPY MEONE'S OTES?
OF COURSE.
DO YOU REALLY NEED TO ASK ME THAT?
WHY DID MY HEART BEAT FASTER WHEN HE LOOKED AT ME...?
WH-WHAT IS THIS?!
THE Y BI-WAL OKED AT HIM...!
NO WAY... HE'D NEVER...!
ARE YOU GOOD FRIENDS?
THEY'RE JUST FRIENDS!
YOU'VE MET, REMEMBER? SHE'S A CHILD-HOOD FRIEND OF MINE...
WH-WHAT?
OH, RIGHT.
WHO IS SHE?!
YES! YOU INTRODUCED US BEFORE.
DORK.

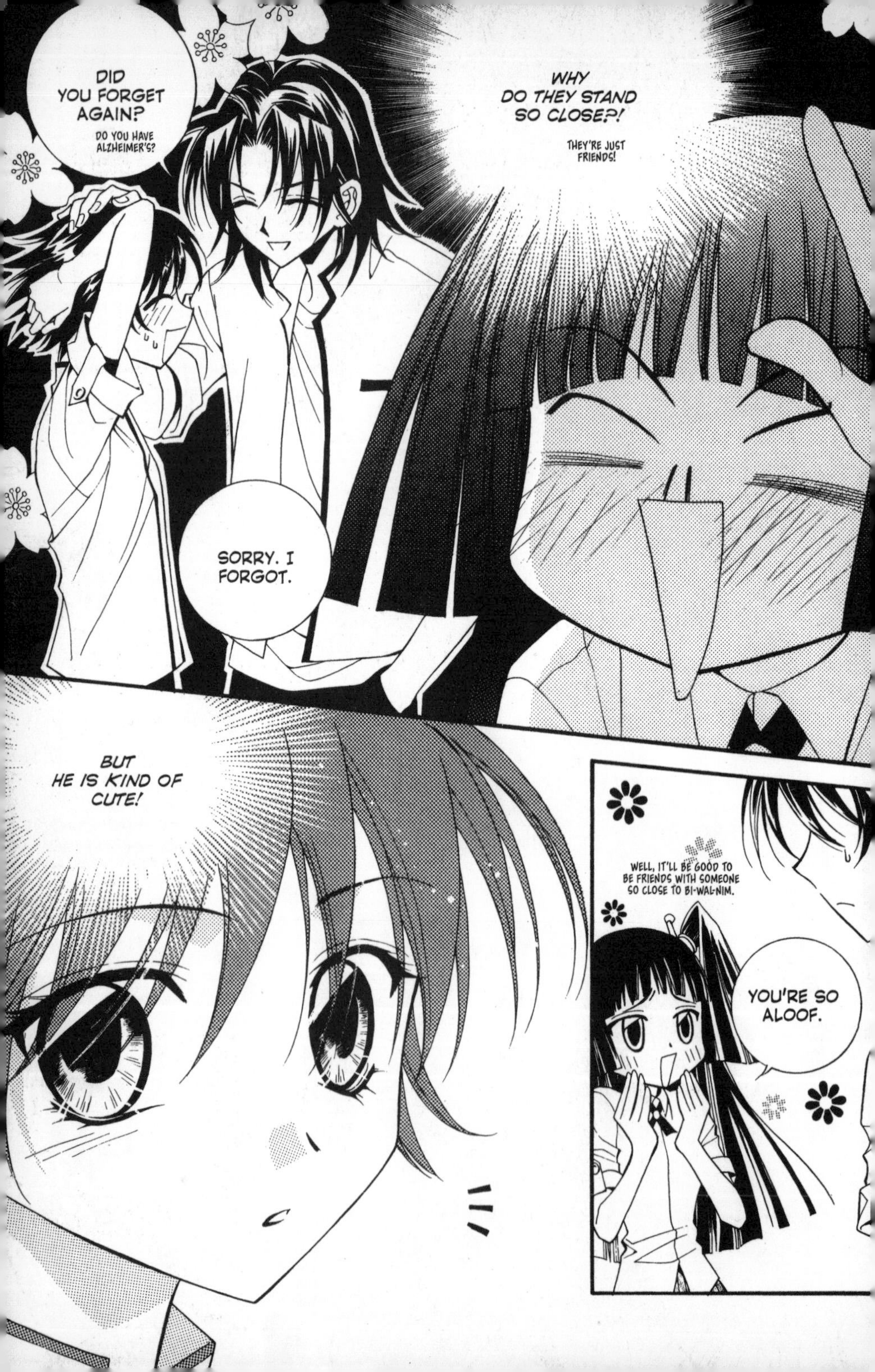
DID YOU FORGET AGAIN?
DO YOU HAVE ALZHEIMER'S?
SORRY. I FORGOT.
WHY DO THEY STAND SO CLOSE?!
THEY'RE JUST FRIENDS!
BUT HE IS KIND OF CUTE!
WELL, IT'LL BE GOOD TO BE FRIENDS WITH SOMEONE SO CLOSE TO BI-WAL-NIM.
YOU'RE SO ALOOF.

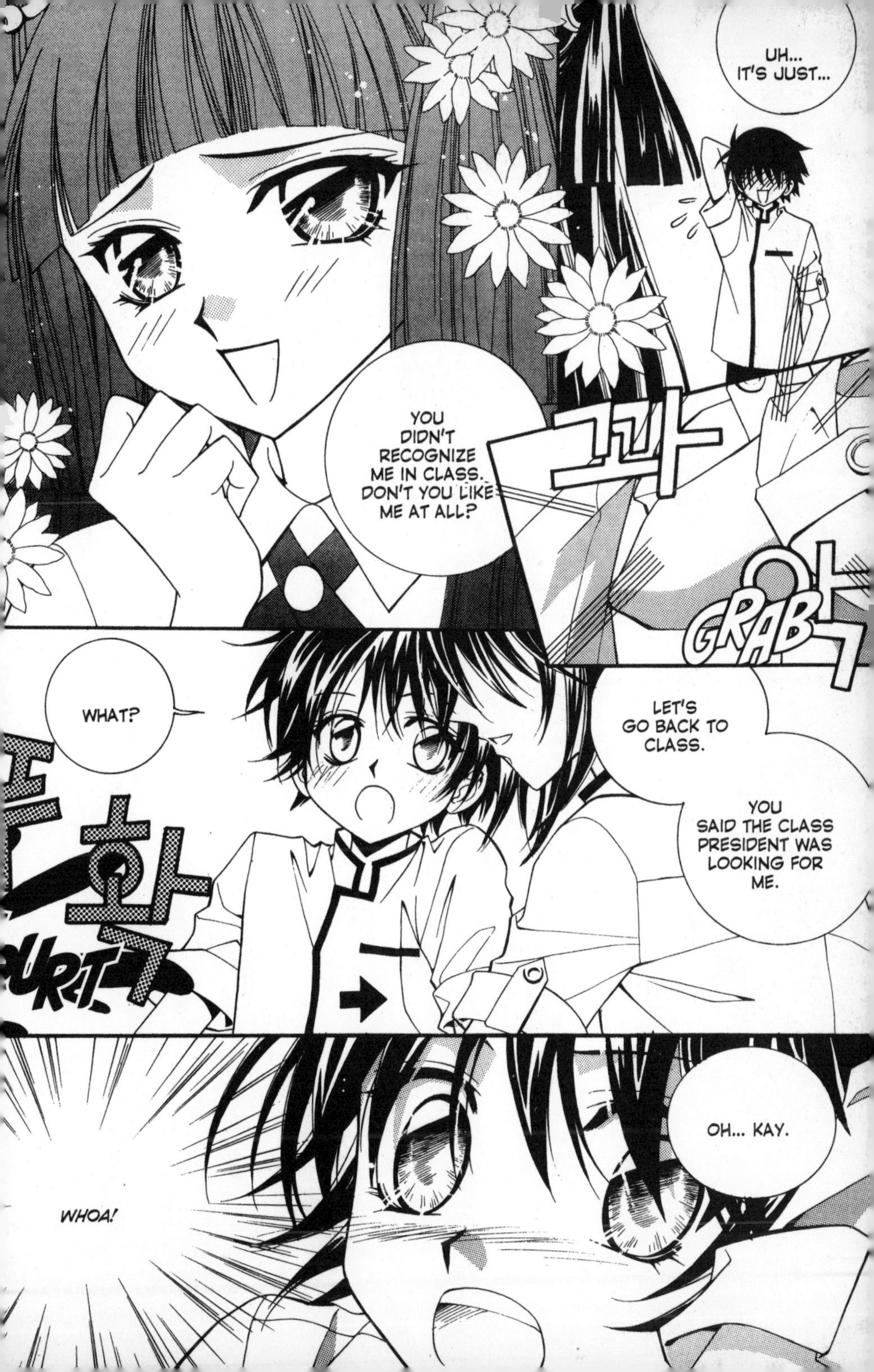
YOU DIDN'T RECOGNIZE ME IN CLASS. DON'T YOU LIKE ME AT ALL?
UH... IT'S JUST...
GRAB
WHAT?
LET'S GO BACK TO CLASS.
YOU SAID THE CLASS PRESIDENT WAS LOOKING FOR ME.
WHOA!
OH... KAY.

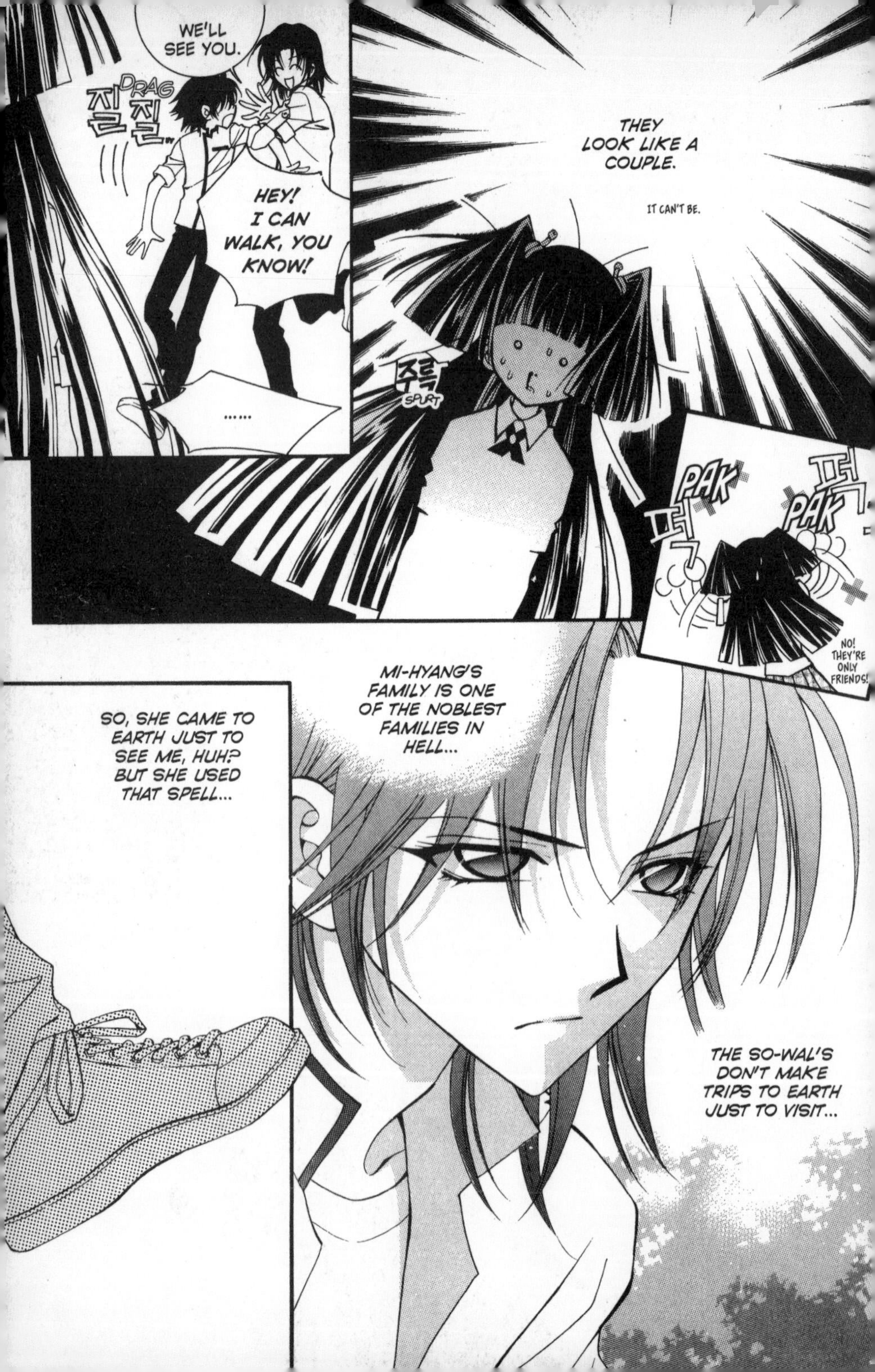
WE'LL SEE YOU.
DRAG
질질
HEY! I CAN WALK, YOU KNOW!
......
THEY LOOK LIKE A COUPLE.
IT CAN'T BE.
주륵
SPURT
PAK
퍽
PAK
퍽
NO! THEY'RE ONLY FRIENDS!
SO, SHE CAME TO EARTH JUST TO SEE ME, HUH? BUT SHE USED THAT SPELL...
MI-HYANG'S FAMILY IS ONE OF THE NOBLEST FAMILIES IN HELL...
THE SO-WAL'S DON'T MAKE TRIPS TO EARTH JUST TO VISIT...

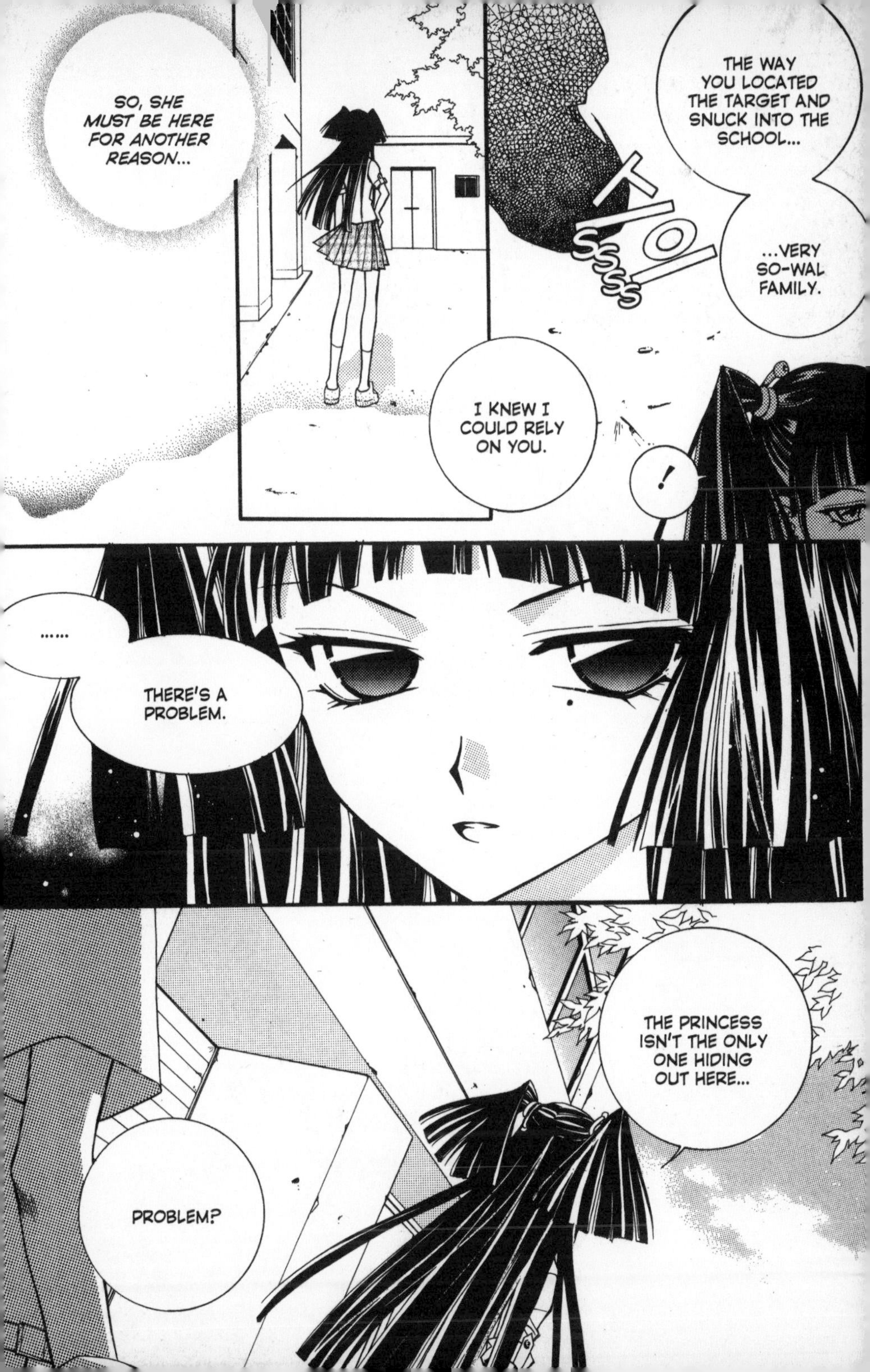

SO, SHE MUST BE HERE FOR ANOTHER REASON...
THE WAY YOU LOCATED THE TARGET AND SNUCK INTO THE SCHOOL...
...VERY SO-WAL FAMILY.
I KNEW I COULD RELY ON YOU.
!
......
THERE'S A PROBLEM.
PROBLEM?
THE PRINCESS ISN'T THE ONLY ONE HIDING OUT HERE...

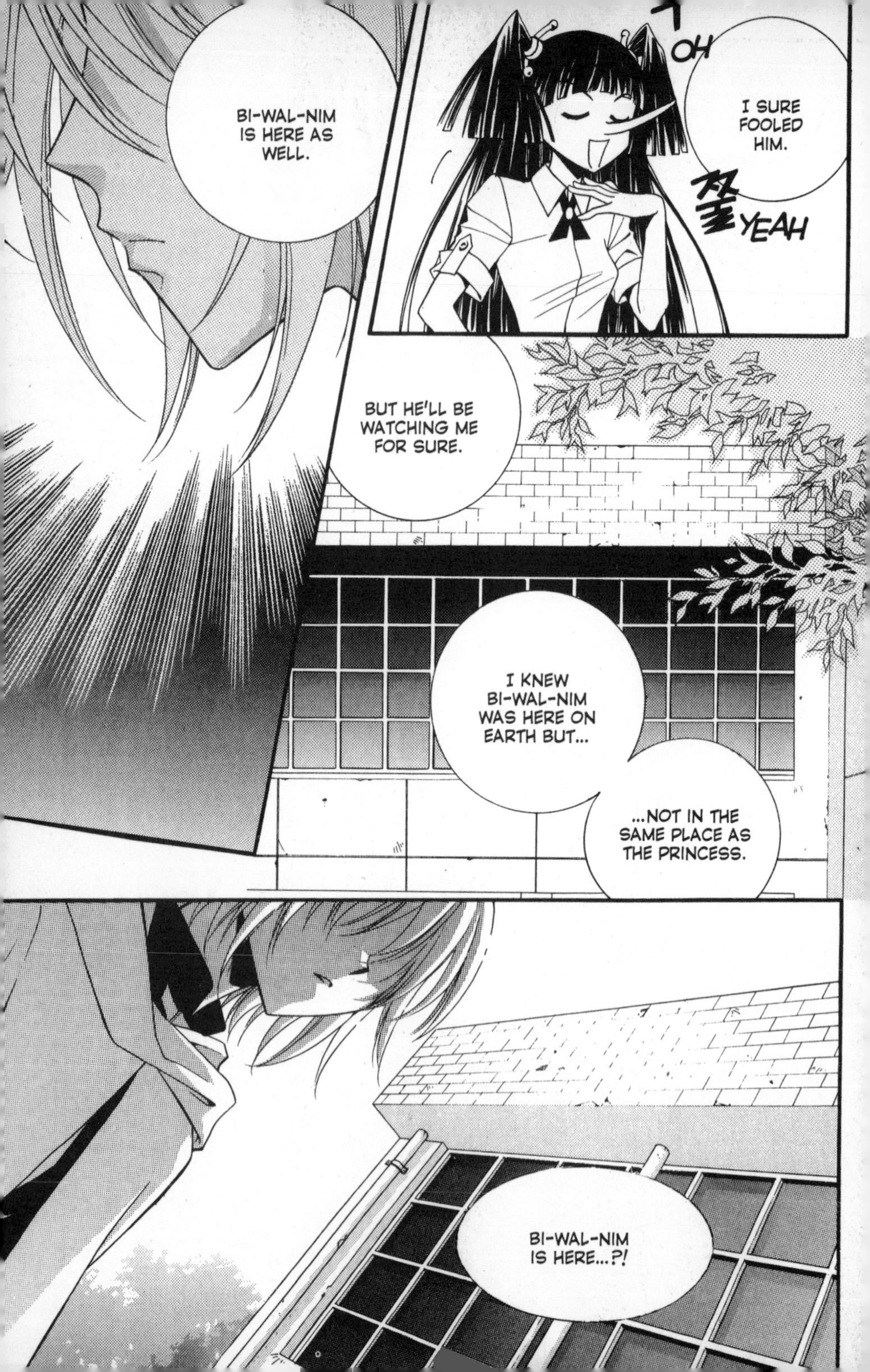
BI-WAL-NIM IS HERE AS WELL.
OH
I SURE FOOLED HIM.
YEAH
BUT HE'LL BE WATCHING ME FOR SURE.
I KNEW BI-WAL-NIM WAS HERE ON EARTH BUT...
...NOT IN THE SAME PLACE AS THE PRINCESS.
BI-WAL-NIM IS HERE...?!

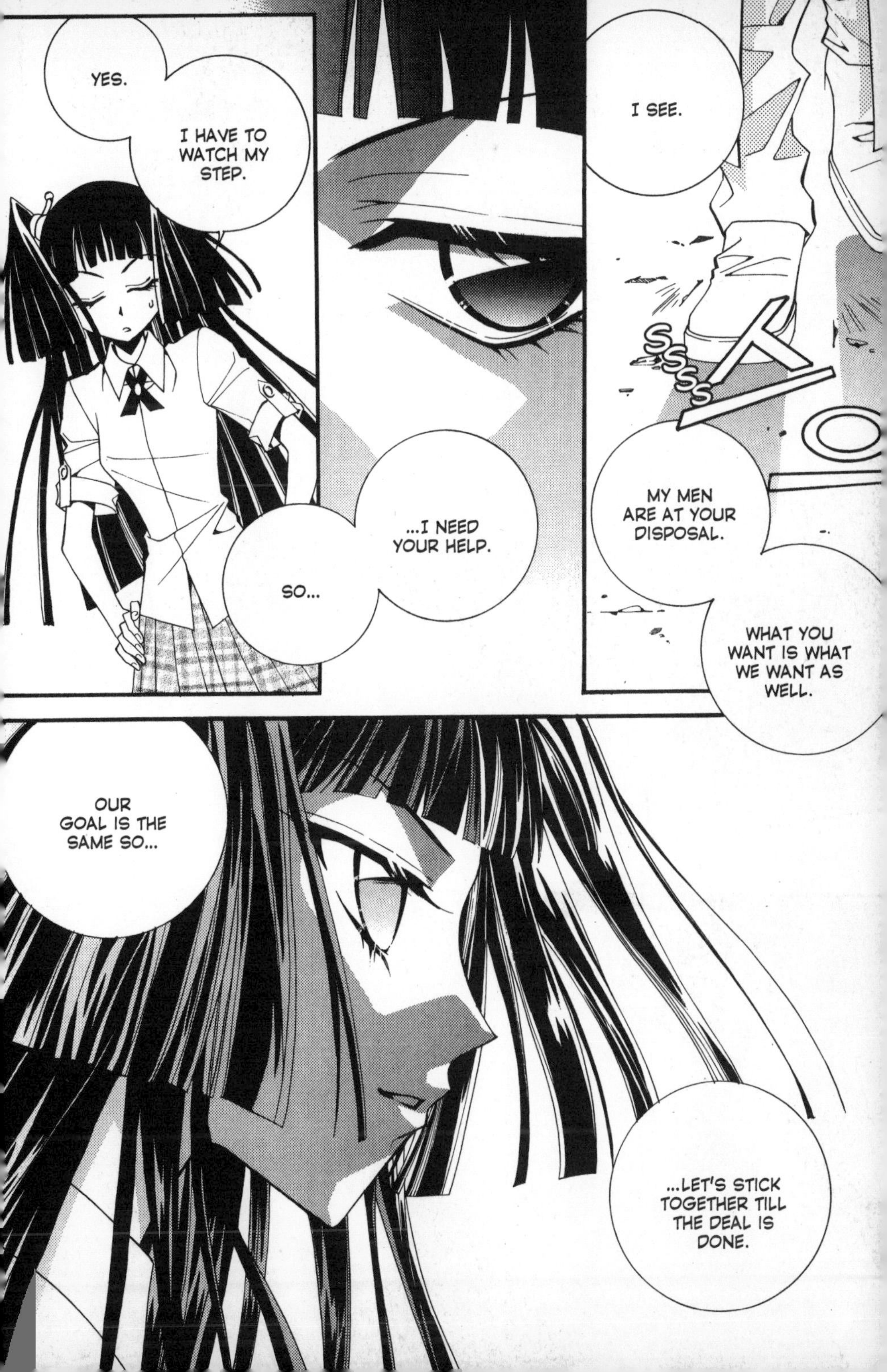
YES.
I HAVE TO WATCH MY STEP.
SO...
...I NEED YOUR HELP.
I SEE.
SSSS
MY MEN ARE AT YOUR DISPOSAL.
WHAT YOU WANT IS WHAT WE WANT AS WELL.
OUR GOAL IS THE SAME SO...
...LET'S STICK TOGETHER TILL THE DEAL IS DONE.

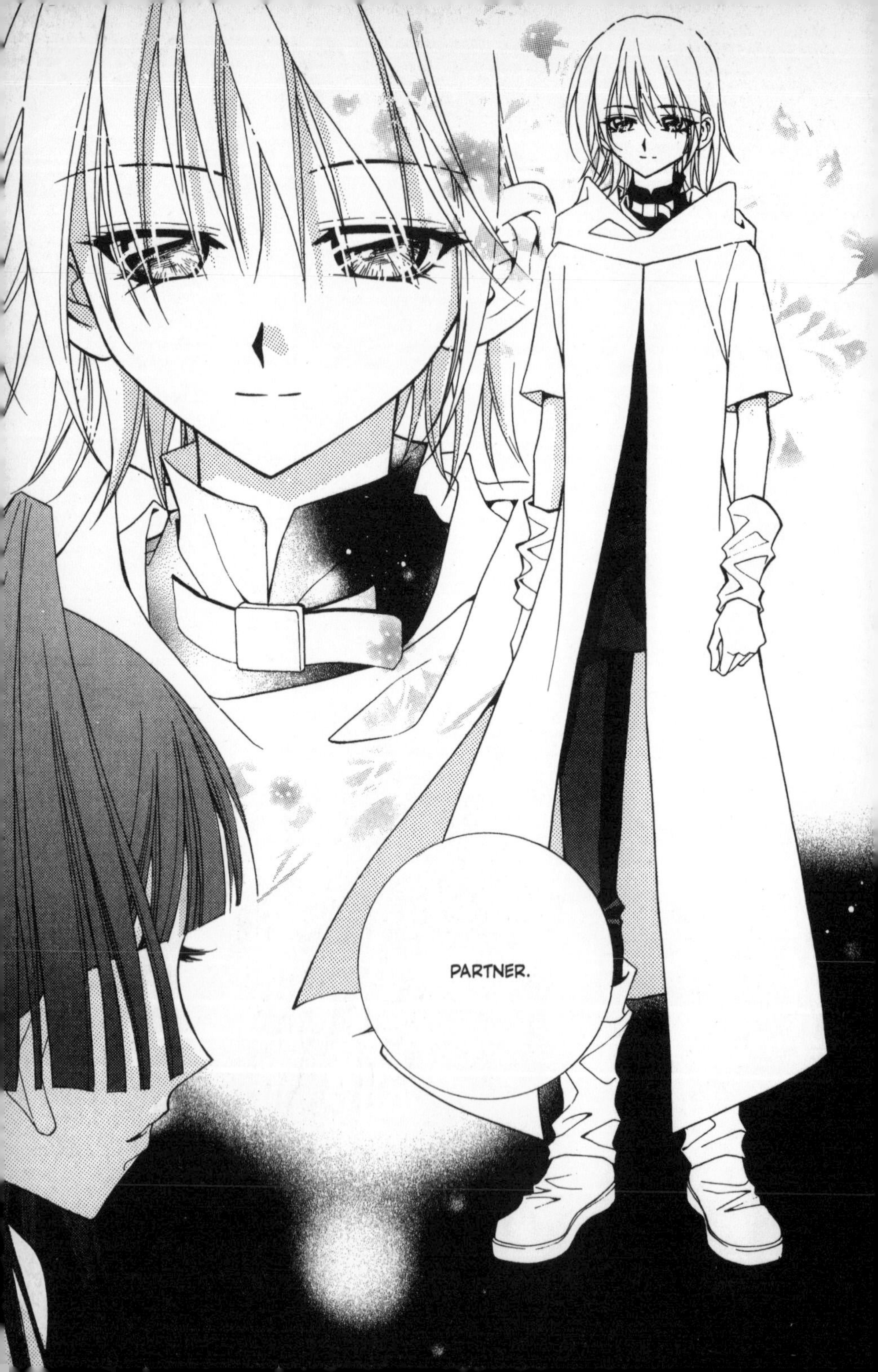
PARTNER.

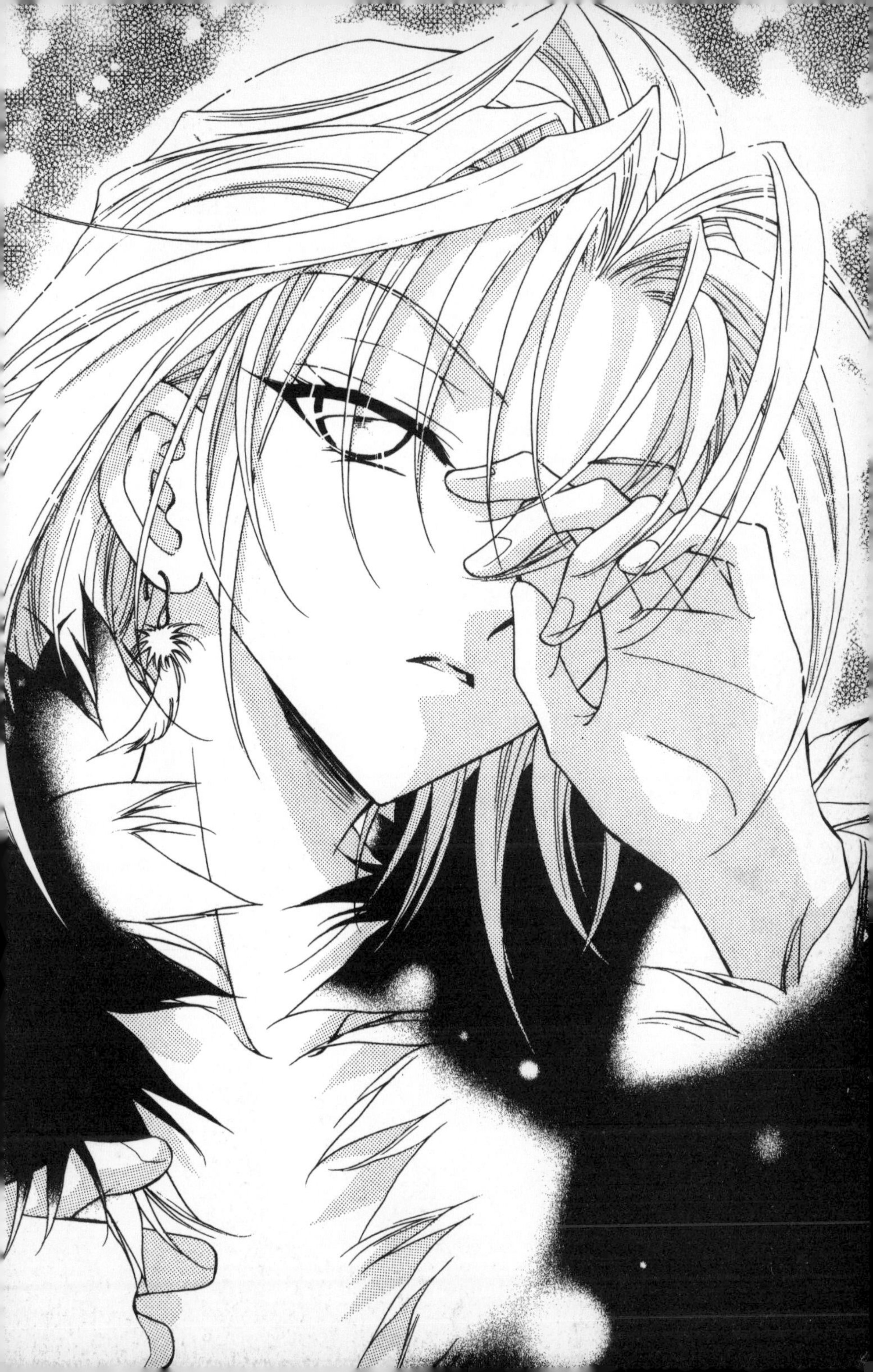

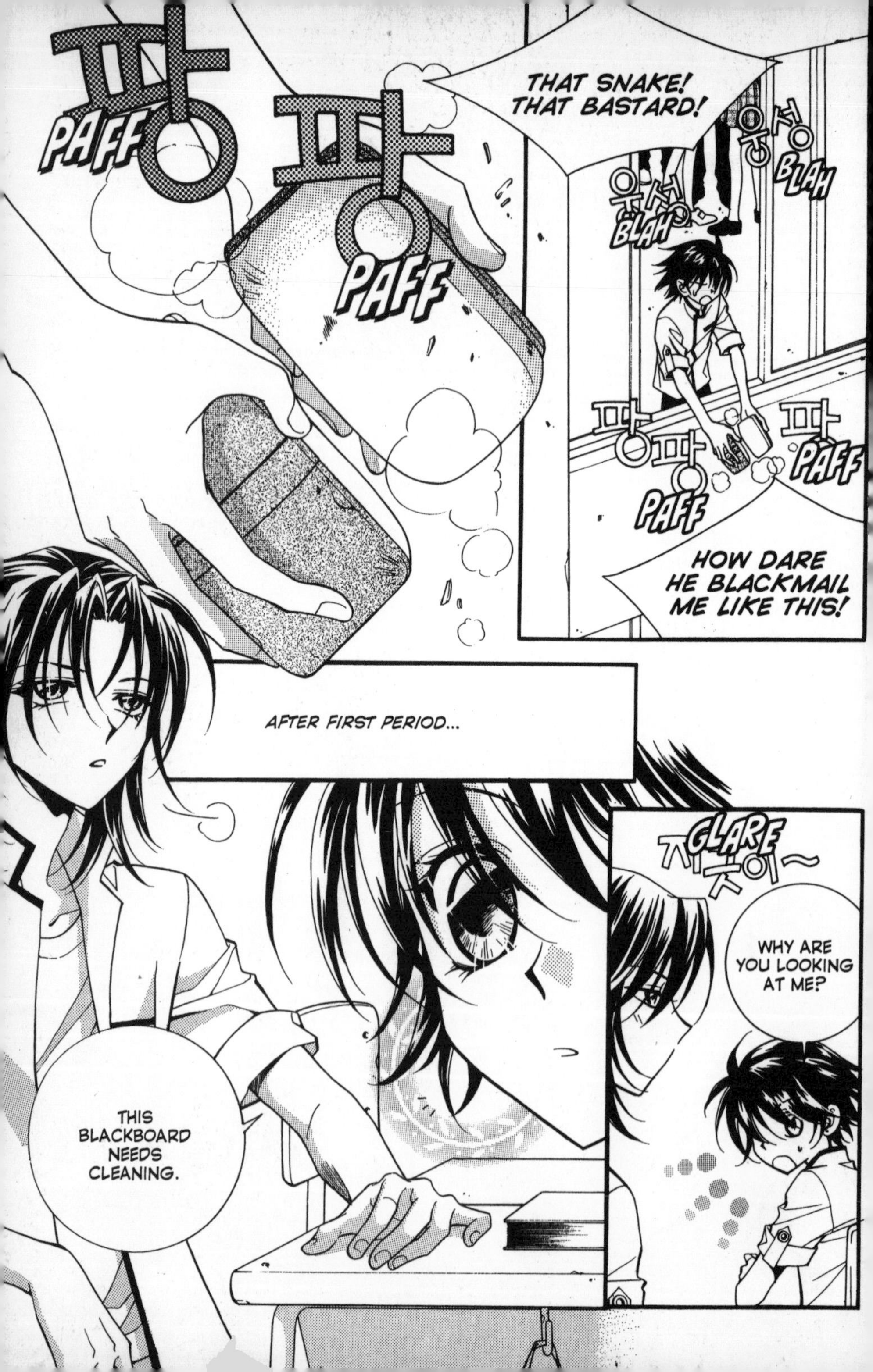
PAFF
PAFF
THAT SNAKE! THAT BASTARD!
BLAH
BLAH
PAFF
PAFF
HOW DARE HE BLACKMAIL ME LIKE THIS!
AFTER FIRST PERIOD...
THIS BLACKBOARD NEEDS CLEANING.
GLARE
WHY ARE YOU LOOKING AT ME?

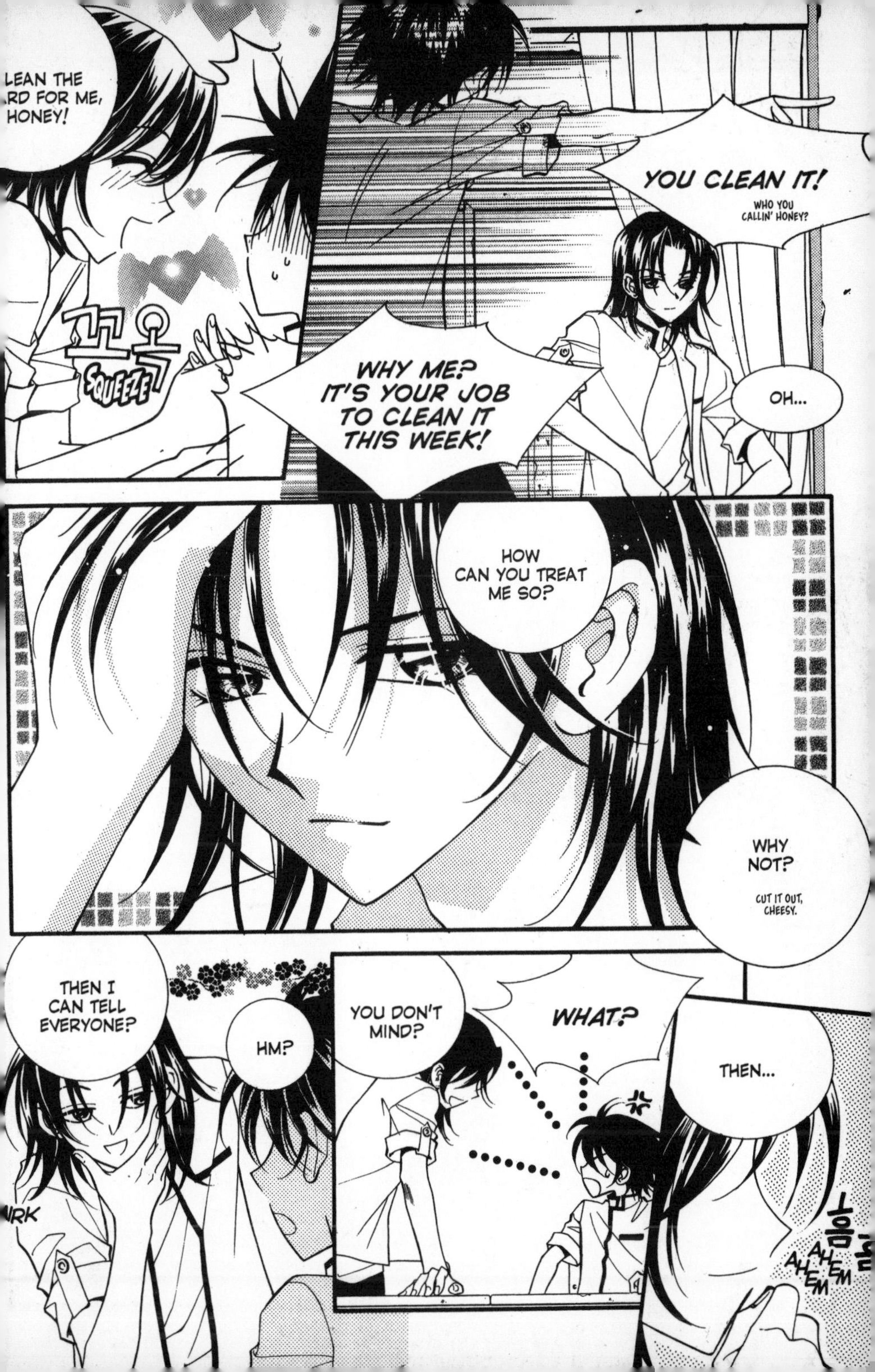
LEAN THE
RD FOR ME,
HONEY!
꼬옥
SQUEEZE
YOU CLEAN IT!
WHO YOU CALLIN' HONEY?
WHY ME? IT'S YOUR JOB TO CLEAN IT THIS WEEK!
OH...
HOW CAN YOU TREAT ME SO?
WHY NOT?
CUT IT OUT, CHEESY.
THEN I CAN TELL EVERYONE?
HM?
YOU DON'T MIND?
WHAT?
THEN...
AHEM
AHEM

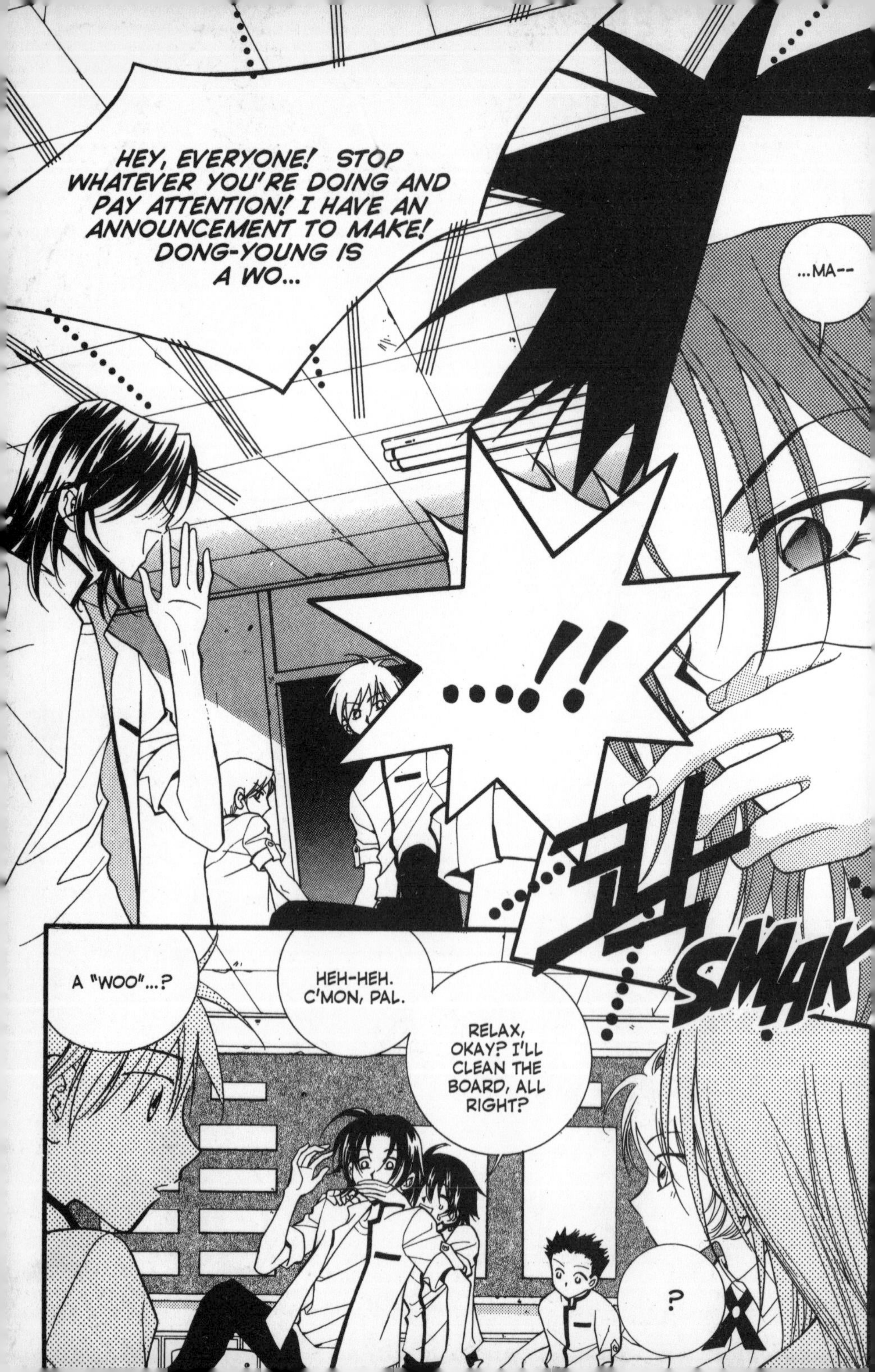
HEY, EVERYONE! STOP WHATEVER YOU'RE DOING AND PAY ATTENTION! I HAVE AN ANNOUNCEMENT TO MAKE! DONG-YOUNG IS A WO...
...MA--
...!!
SMAK
A "WOO"...?
HEH-HEH. C'MON, PAL.
RELAX, OKAY? I'LL CLEAN THE BOARD, ALL RIGHT?
?

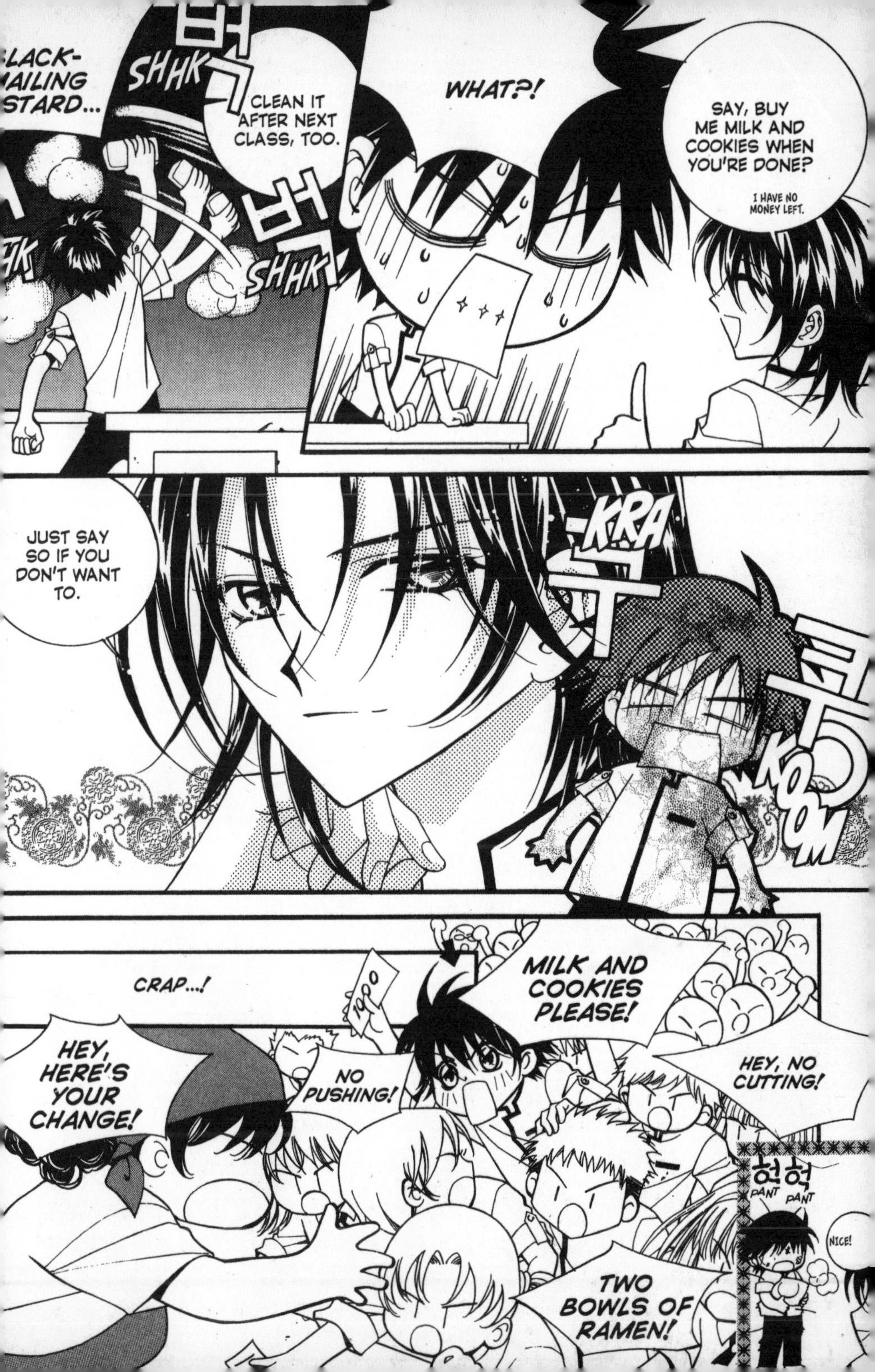
LACK-MAILING STARD...
SHHK
CLEAN IT AFTER NEXT CLASS, TOO.
SHHK
WHAT?!
SAY, BUY ME MILK AND COOKIES WHEN YOU'RE DONE?
I HAVE NO MONEY LEFT.
JUST SAY SO IF YOU DON'T WANT TO.
KRA
KOOM
CRAP...!
HEY, HERE'S YOUR CHANGE!
NO PUSHING!
1000
MILK AND COOKIES PLEASE!
HEY, NO CUTTING!
TWO BOWLS OF RAMEN!
헉헉
PANT PANT
NICE!

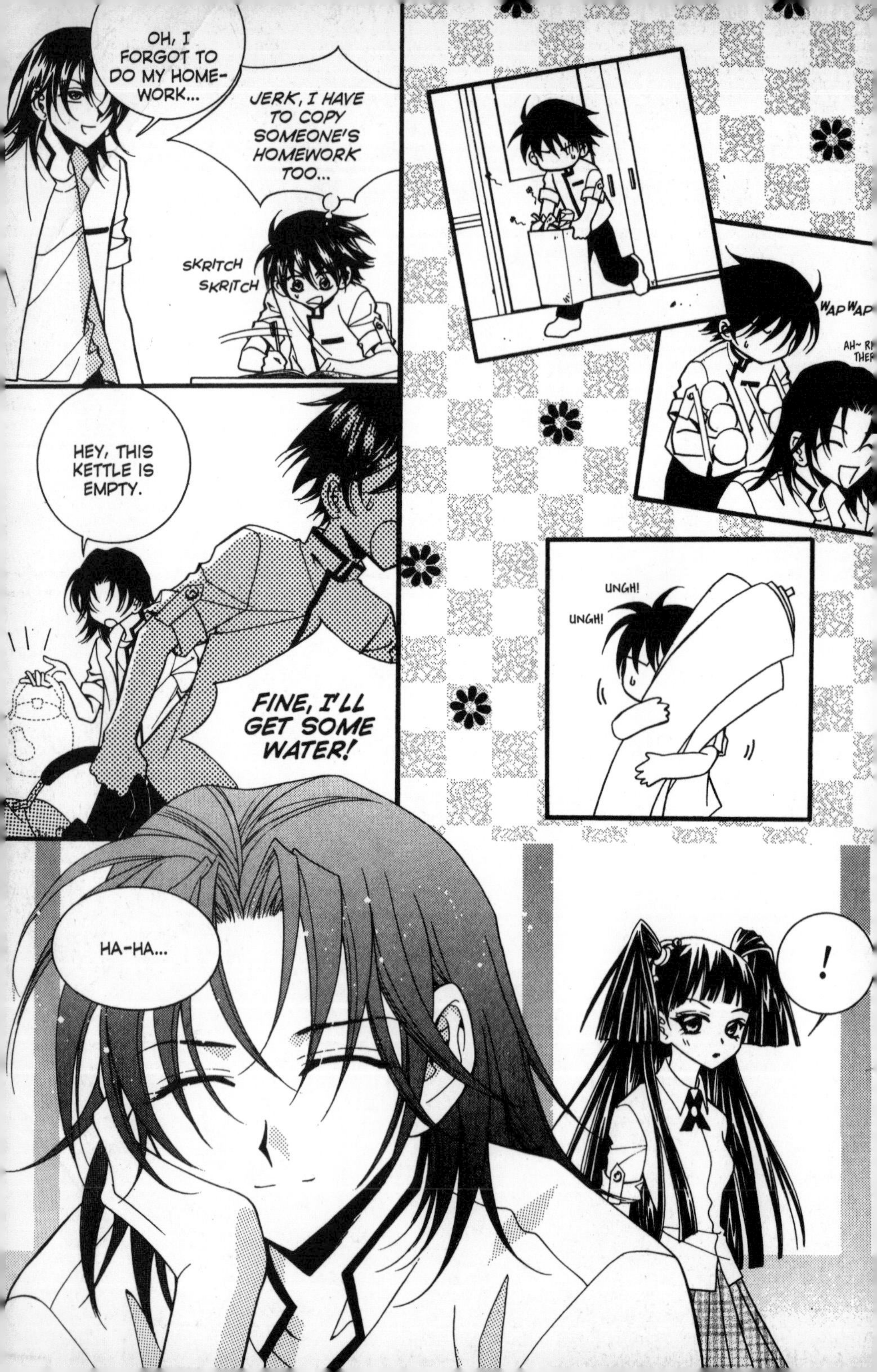
OH, I FORGOT TO DO MY HOME-WORK...
JERK, I HAVE TO COPY SOMEONE'S HOMEWORK TOO...
SKRITCH SKRITCH
HEY, THIS KETTLE IS EMPTY.
FINE, I'LL GET SOME WATER!
WAP WAP
UNGH!
UNGH!
HA-HA...
!

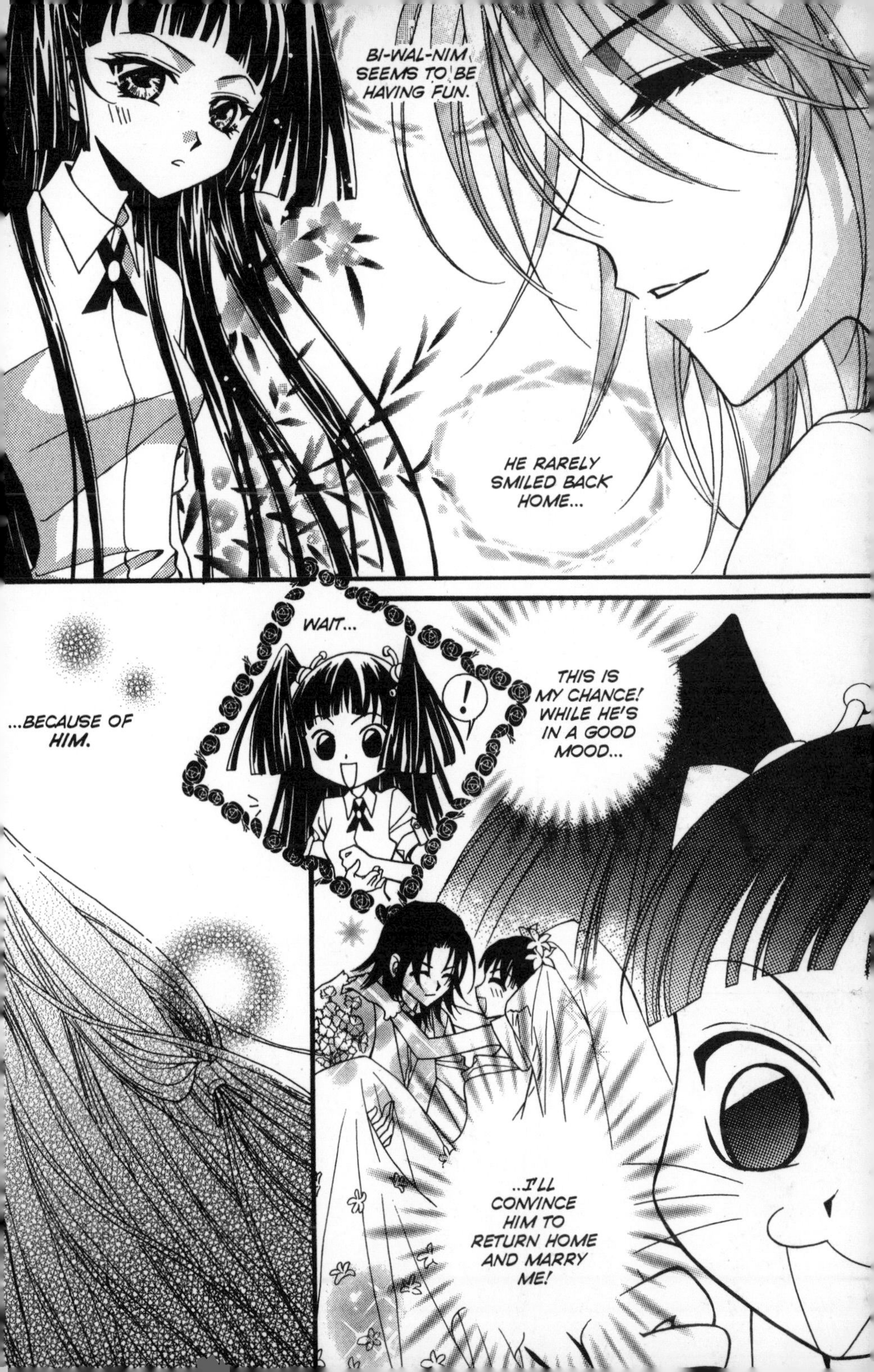
BI-WAL-NIM SEEMS TO BE HAVING FUN.
HE RARELY SMILED BACK HOME...
...BECAUSE OF HIM.
WAIT...
!
THIS IS MY CHANCE! WHILE HE'S IN A GOOD MOOD...
...I'LL CONVINCE HIM TO RETURN HOME AND MARRY ME!

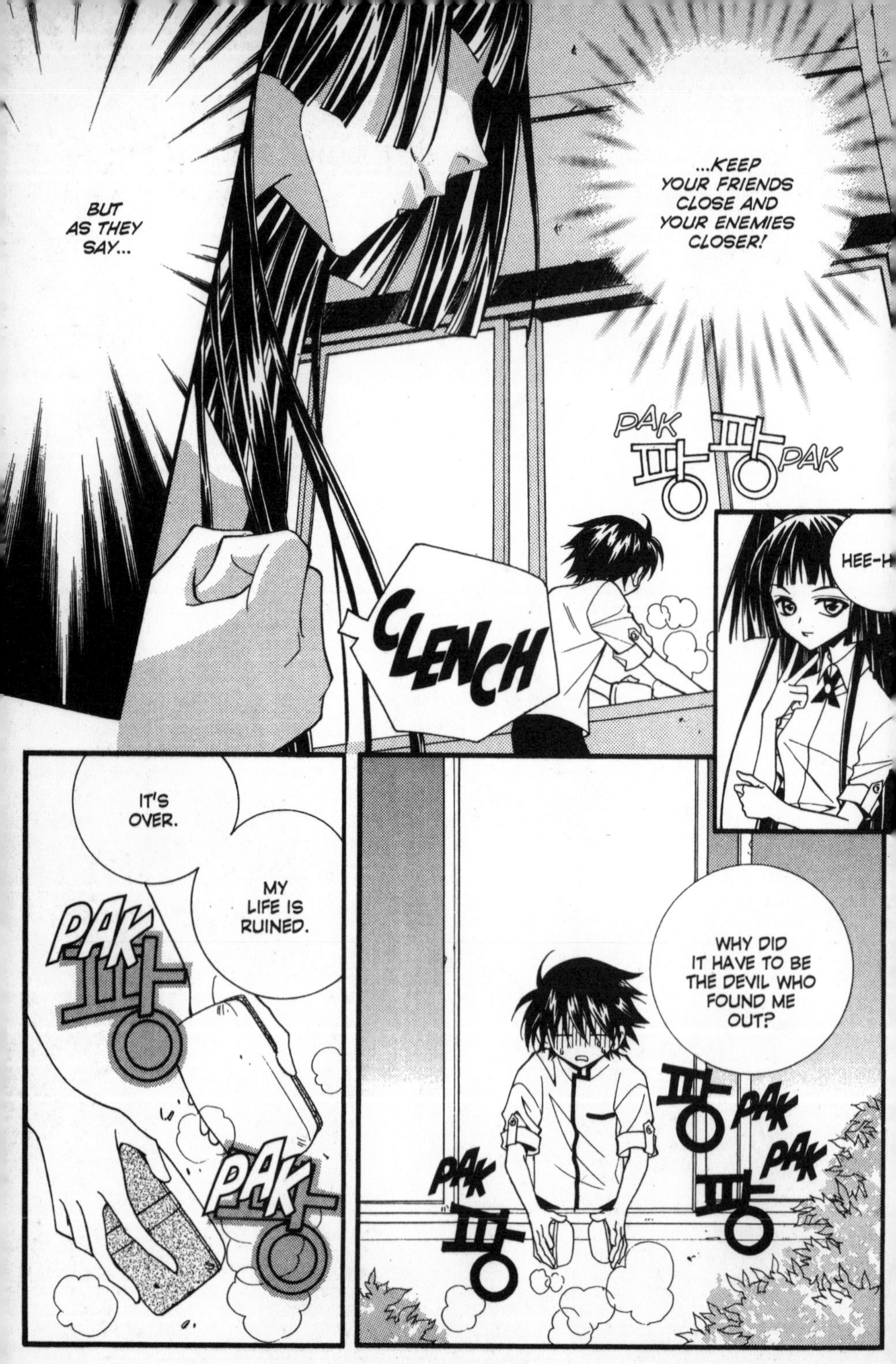
BUT AS THEY SAY...
...KEEP YOUR FRIENDS CLOSE AND YOUR ENEMIES CLOSER!
PAK 팡 팡 PAK
CLENCH
HEE-H
IT'S OVER.
MY LIFE IS RUINED.
PAK 팡
PAK 팡
WHY DID IT HAVE TO BE THE DEVIL WHO FOUND ME OUT?
팡 PAK
PAK 팡
PAK 팡

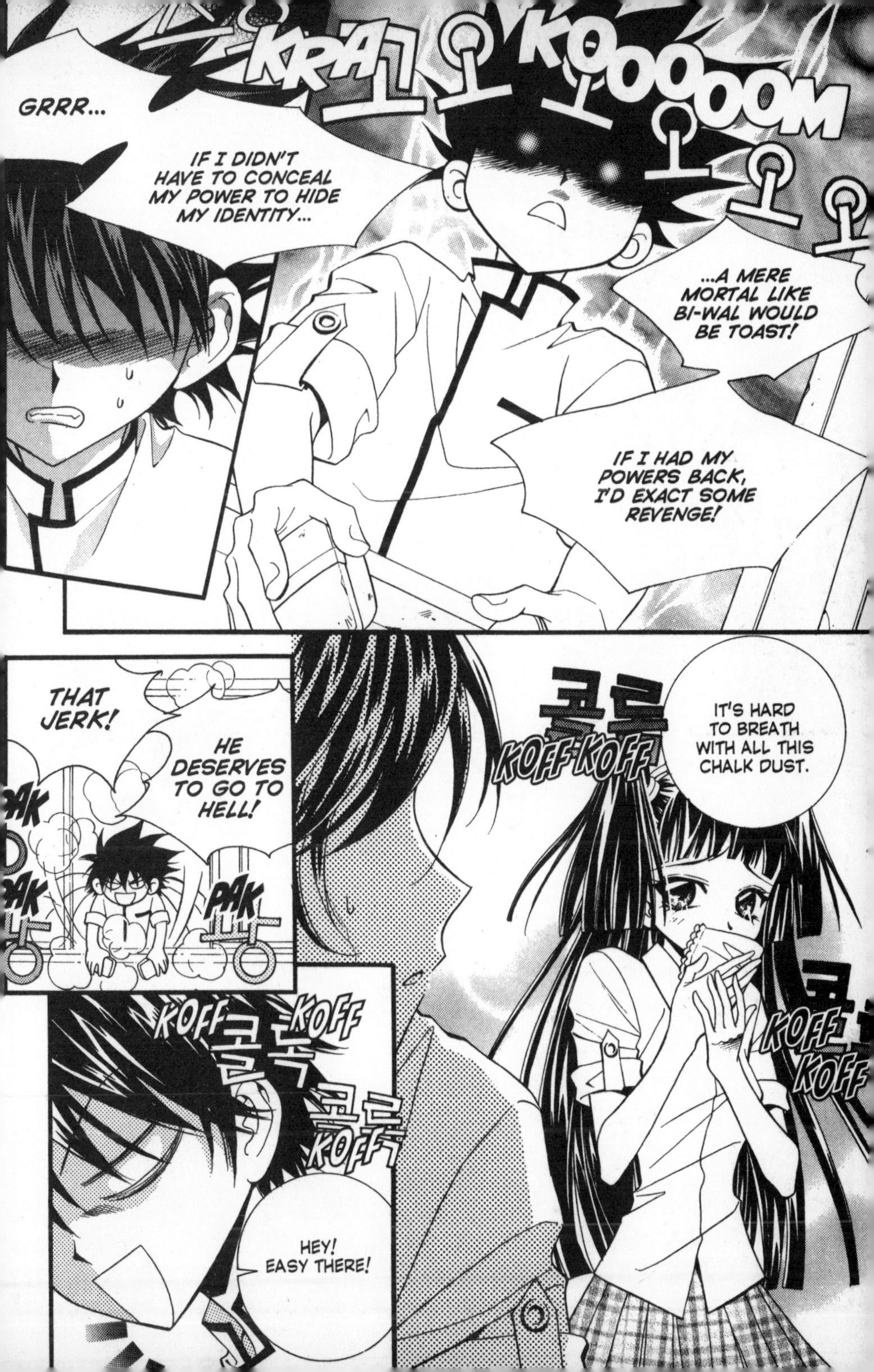
KRA
KOOOOOOM
GRRR...
IF I DIDN'T HAVE TO CONCEAL MY POWER TO HIDE MY IDENTITY...
...A MERE MORTAL LIKE BI-WAL WOULD BE TOAST!
IF I HAD MY POWERS BACK, I'D EXACT SOME REVENGE!
THAT JERK!
HE DESERVES TO GO TO HELL!
PAK
KOFF KOFF
IT'S HARD TO BREATH WITH ALL THIS CHALK DUST.
KOFF KOFF
KOFF KOFF
KOFF
HEY! EASY THERE!

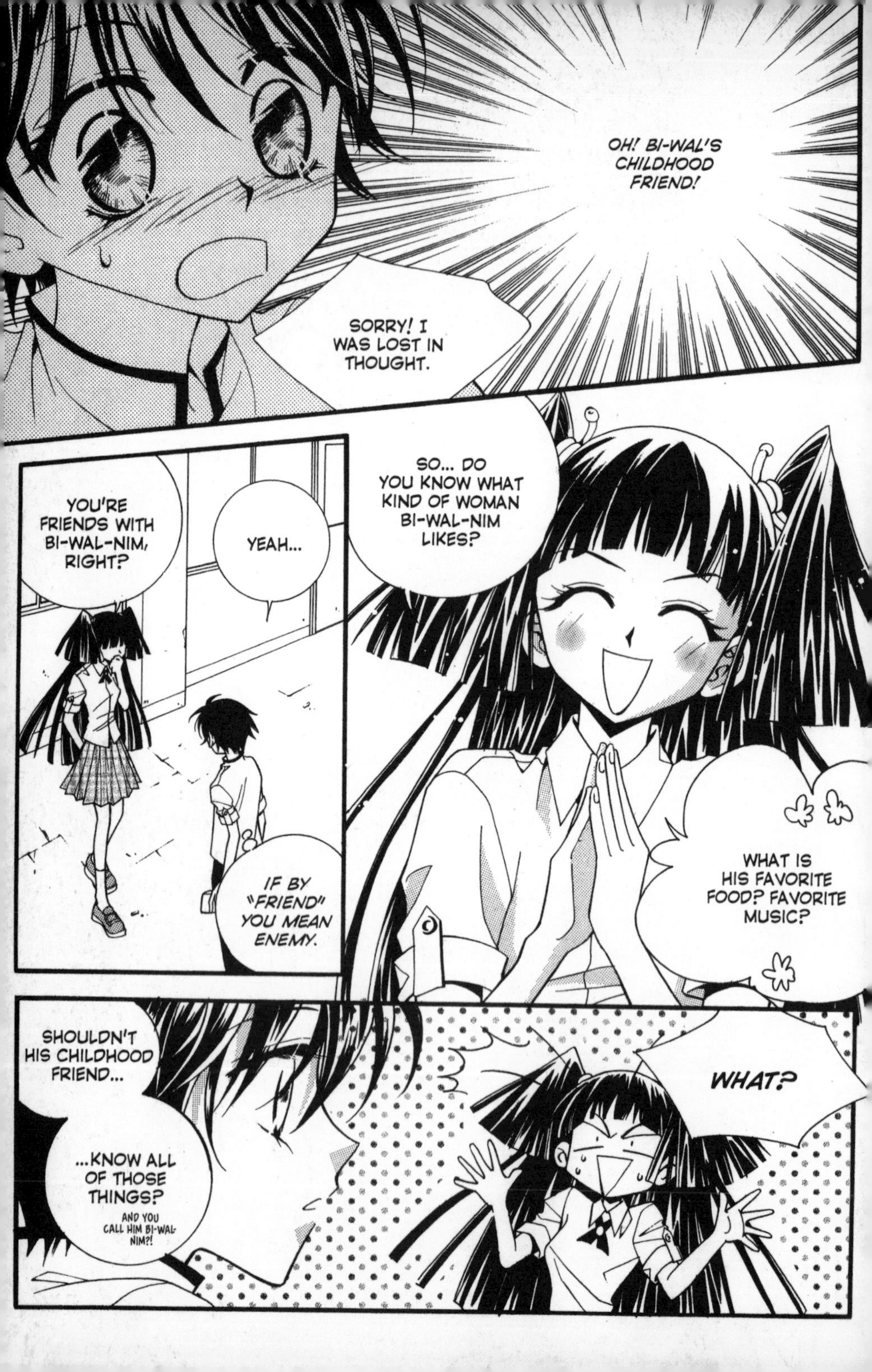
OH! BI-WAL'S CHILDHOOD FRIEND!
SORRY! I WAS LOST IN THOUGHT.
YOU'RE FRIENDS WITH BI-WAL-NIM, RIGHT?
YEAH...
IF BY "FRIEND" YOU MEAN ENEMY.
SO... DO YOU KNOW WHAT KIND OF WOMAN BI-WAL-NIM LIKES?
WHAT IS HIS FAVORITE FOOD? FAVORITE MUSIC?
SHOULDN'T HIS CHILDHOOD FRIEND...
...KNOW ALL OF THOSE THINGS?
AND YOU CALL HIM BI-WAL-NIM?!
WHAT?

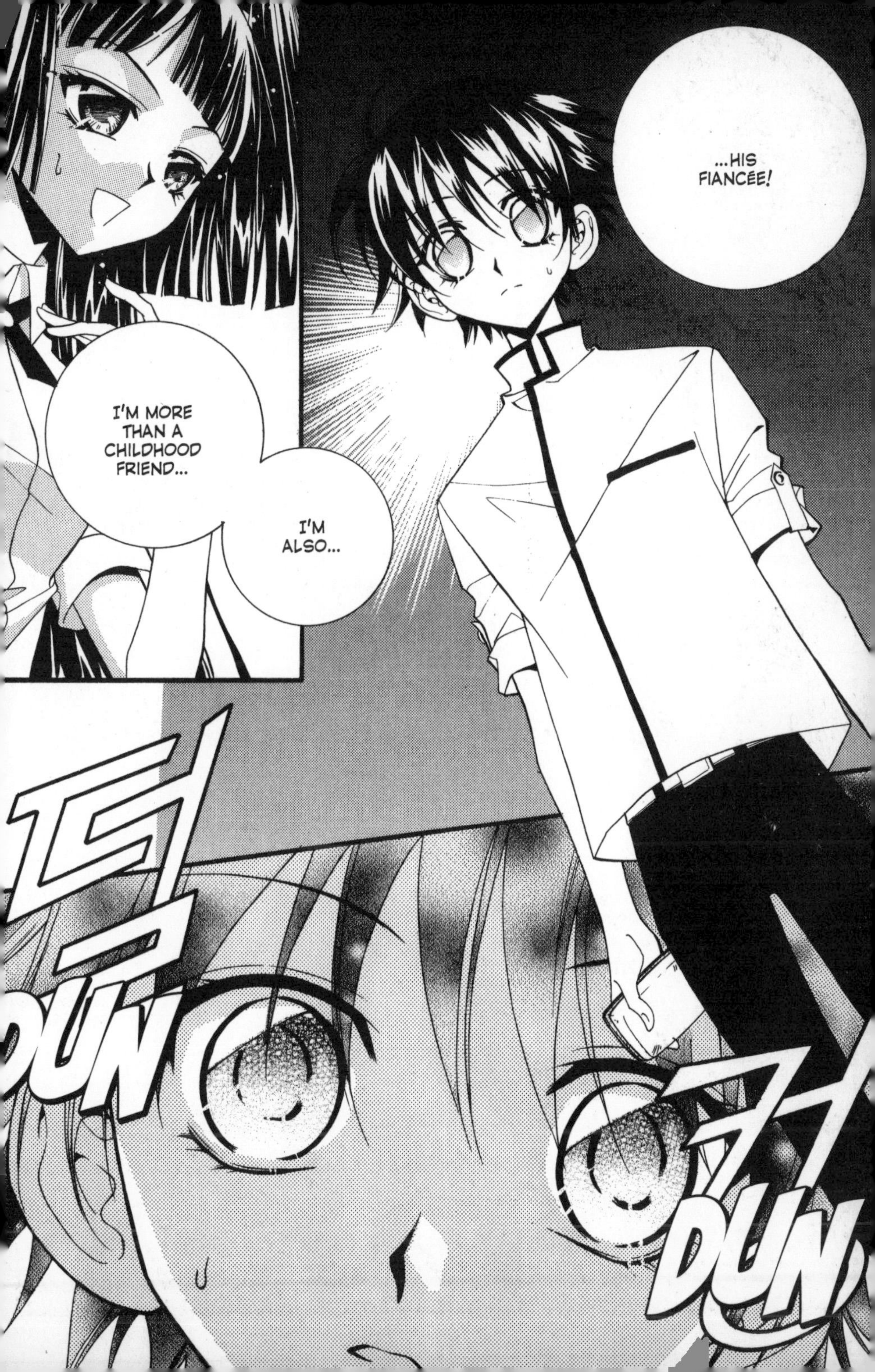
I'M MORE THAN A CHILDHOOD FRIEND...
I'M ALSO...
...HIS FIANCÉE!
DUN
DUN

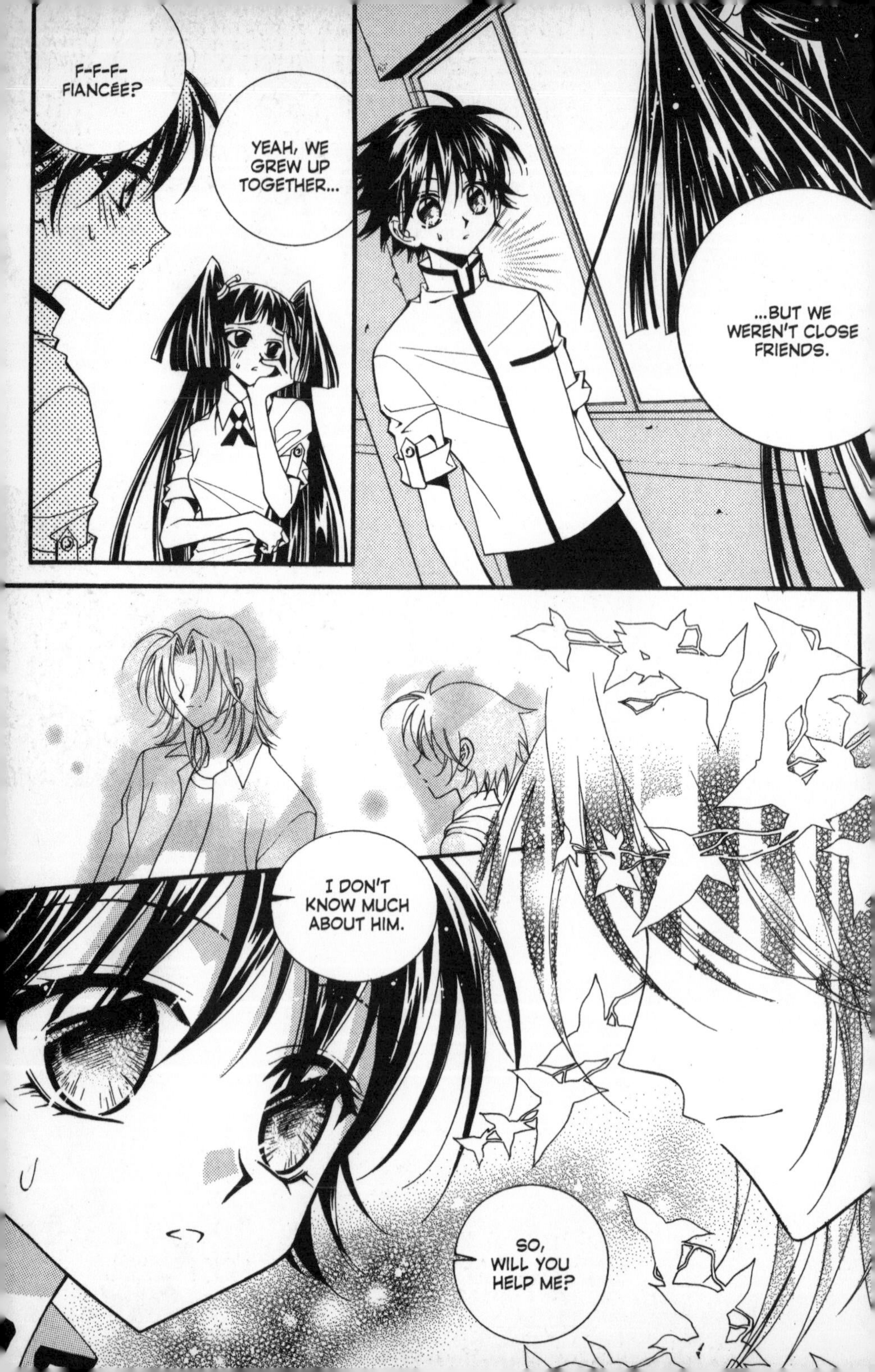
F-F-F-FIANCÉE?
YEAH, WE GREW UP TOGETHER...
...BUT WE WEREN'T CLOSE FRIENDS.
I DON'T KNOW MUCH ABOUT HIM.
SO, WILL YOU HELP ME?

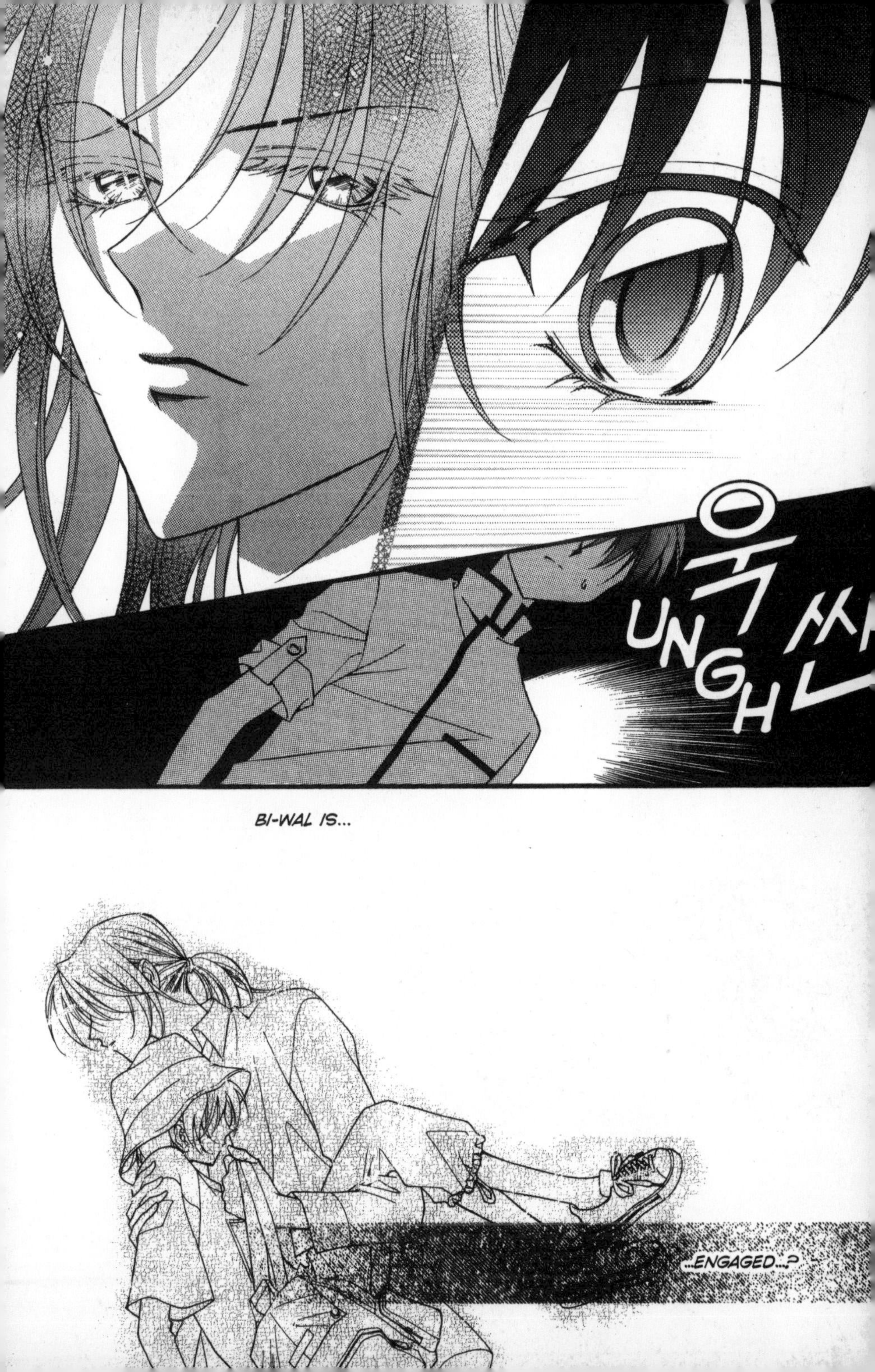

욱씬
UNGH
BI-WAL IS...
...ENGAGED...?

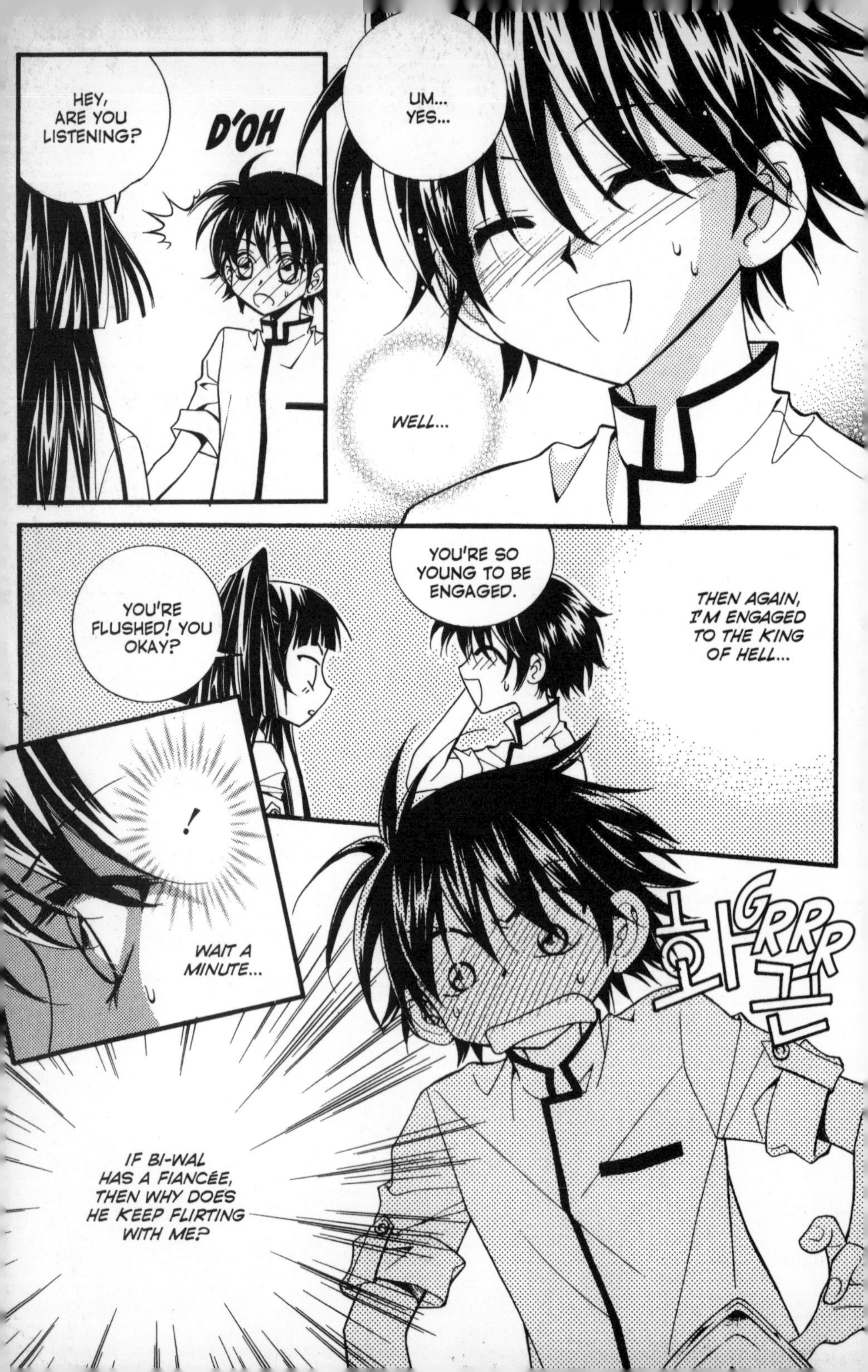
HEY, ARE YOU LISTENING?
D'OH
UM... YES...
WELL...
YOU'RE FLUSHED! YOU OKAY?
YOU'RE SO YOUNG TO BE ENGAGED.
THEN AGAIN, I'M ENGAGED TO THE KING OF HELL...
!
WAIT A MINUTE...
GRRR
IF BI-WAL HAS A FIANCÉE, THEN WHY DOES HE KEEP FLIRTING WITH ME?

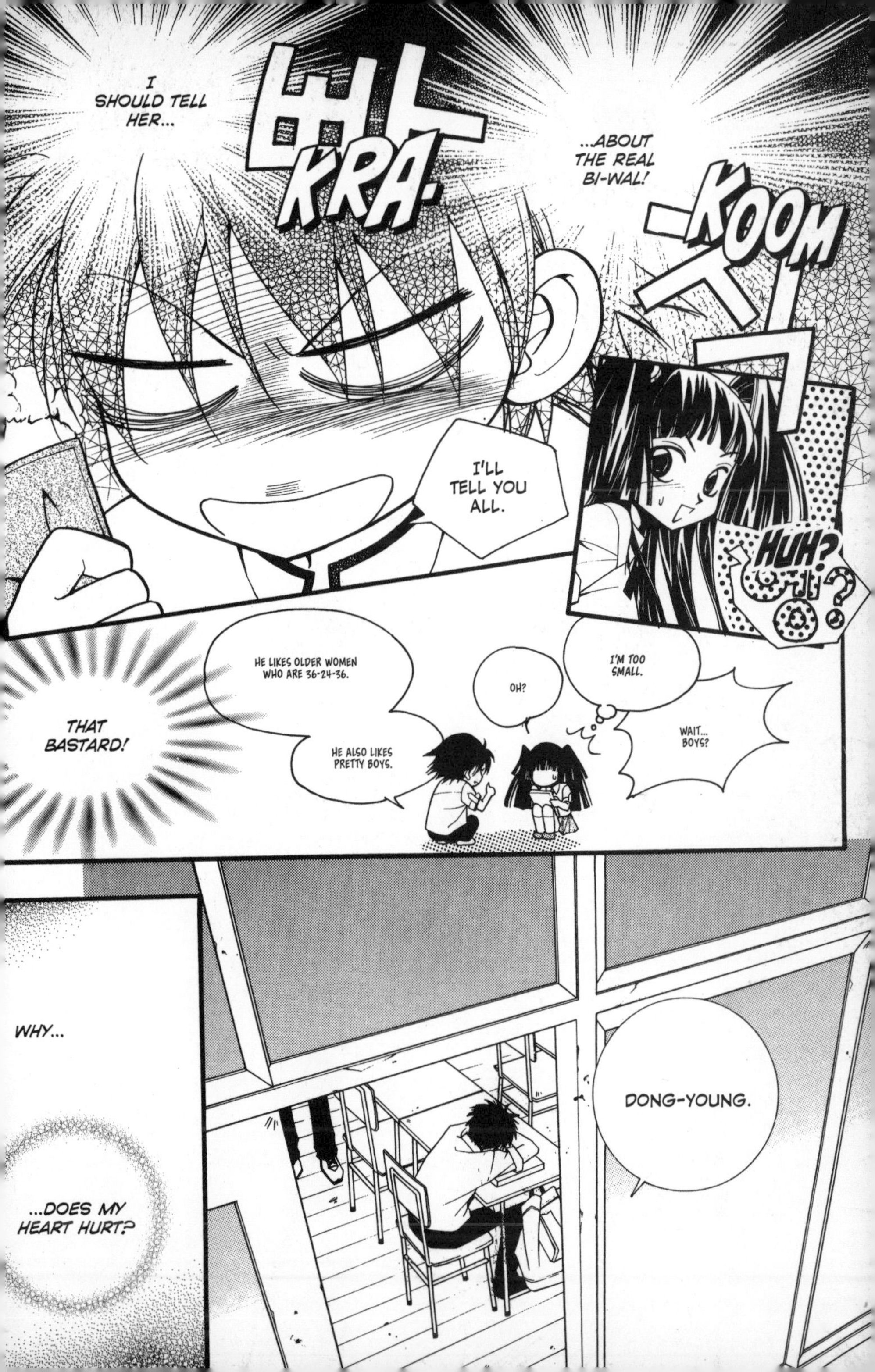
I SHOULD TELL HER...
KRA-
...ABOUT THE REAL BI-WAL!
-KOOM
I'LL TELL YOU ALL.
HUH?
THAT BASTARD!
HE LIKES OLDER WOMEN WHO ARE 36-24-36.
HE ALSO LIKES PRETTY BOYS.
OH?
I'M TOO SMALL.
WAIT... BOYS?
WHY...
...DOES MY HEART HURT?
DONG-YOUNG.

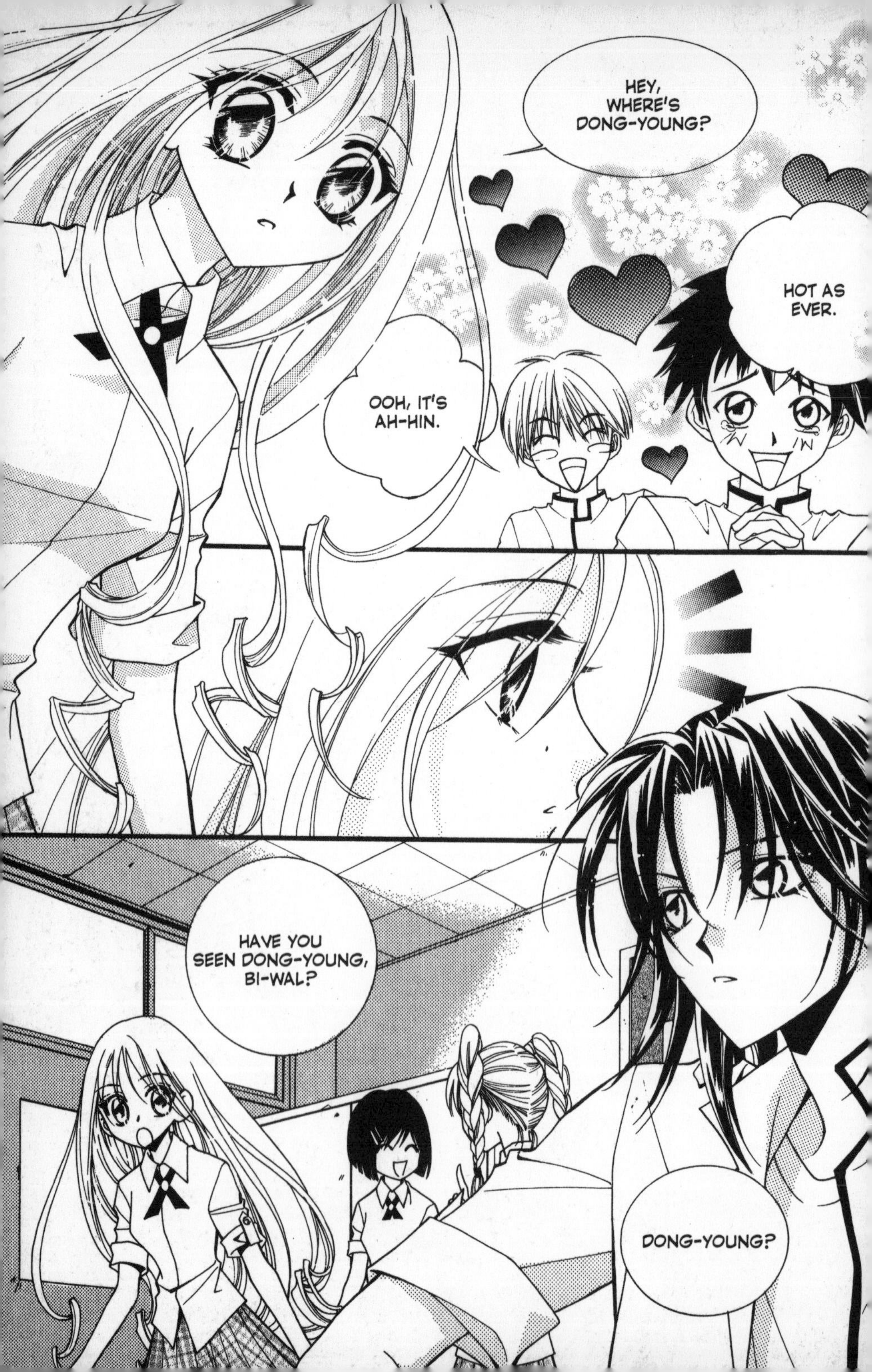
HEY, WHERE'S DONG-YOUNG?
OOH, IT'S AH-HIN.
HOT AS EVER.
HAVE YOU SEEN DONG-YOUNG, BI-WAL?
DONG-YOUNG?

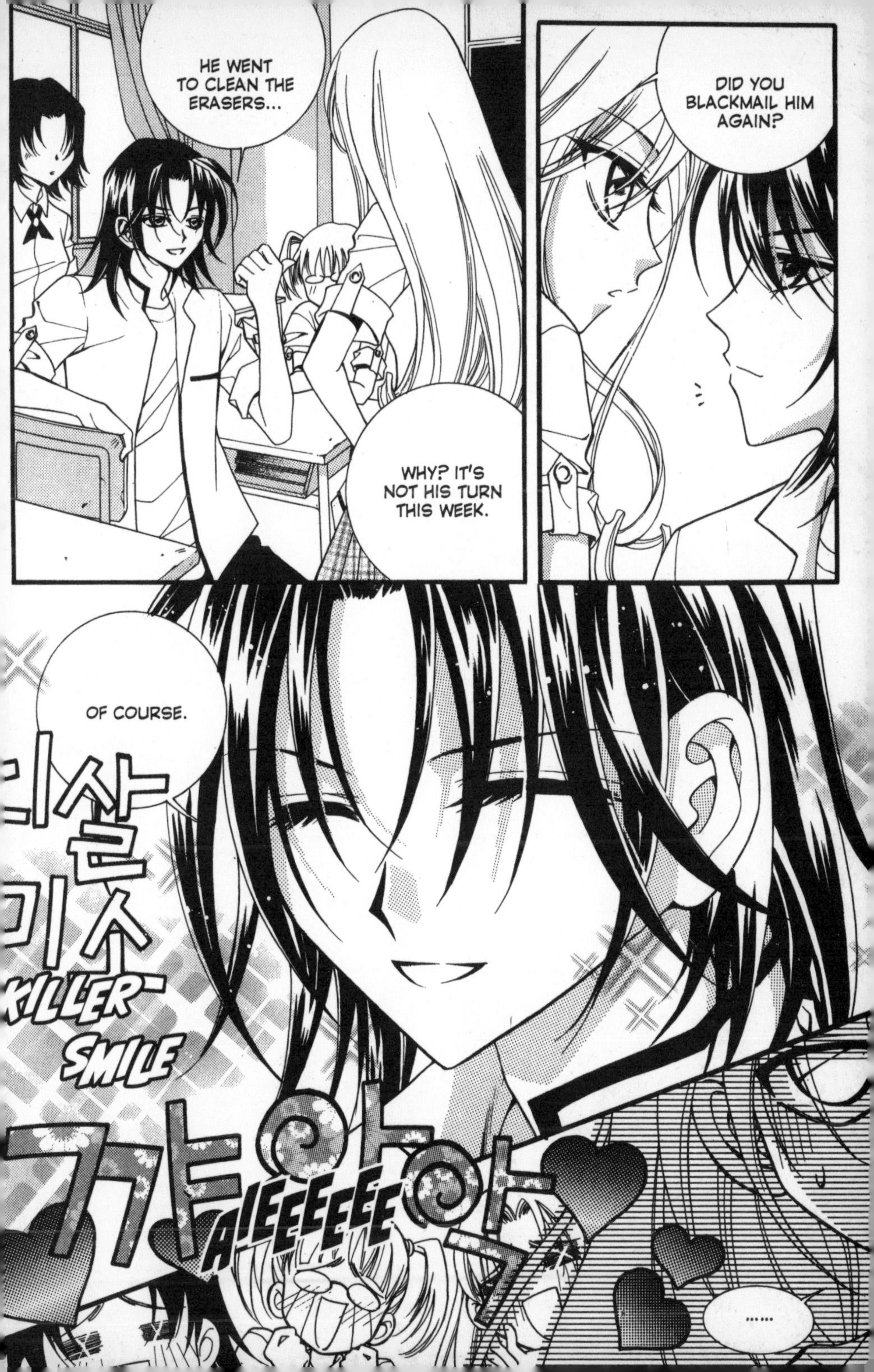
HE WENT TO CLEAN THE ERASERS...
WHY? IT'S NOT HIS TURN THIS WEEK.
DID YOU BLACKMAIL HIM AGAIN?
OF COURSE.
KILLER-SMILE
AIEEEEEE
......

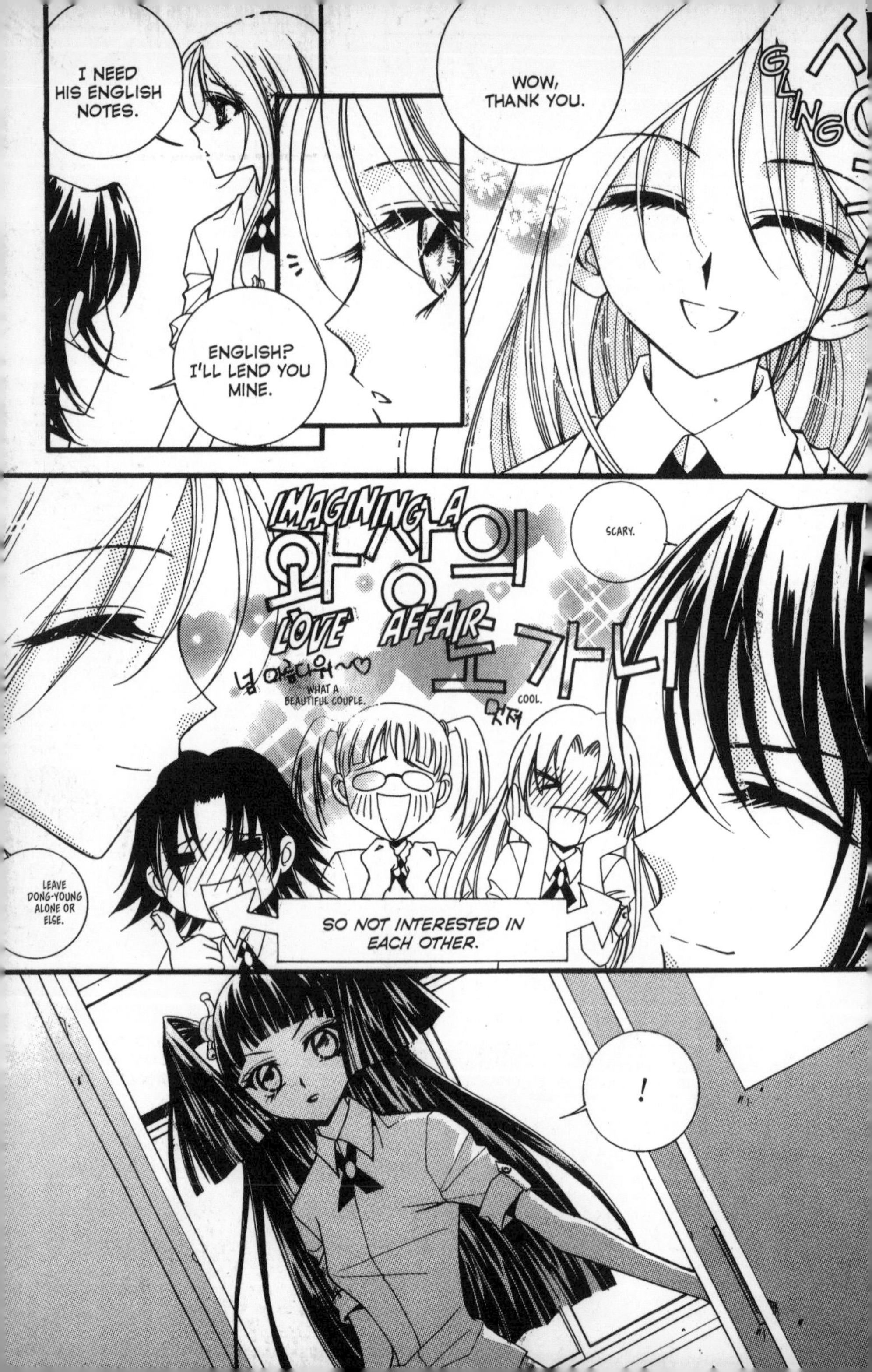
I NEED HIS ENGLISH NOTES.
ENGLISH? I'LL LEND YOU MINE.
WOW, THANK YOU.
GLING
IMAGINING A LOVE AFFAIR
WHAT A BEAUTIFUL COUPLE.
COOL.
SCARY.
LEAVE DONG-YOUNG ALONE OR ELSE.
SO NOT INTERESTED IN EACH OTHER.
!

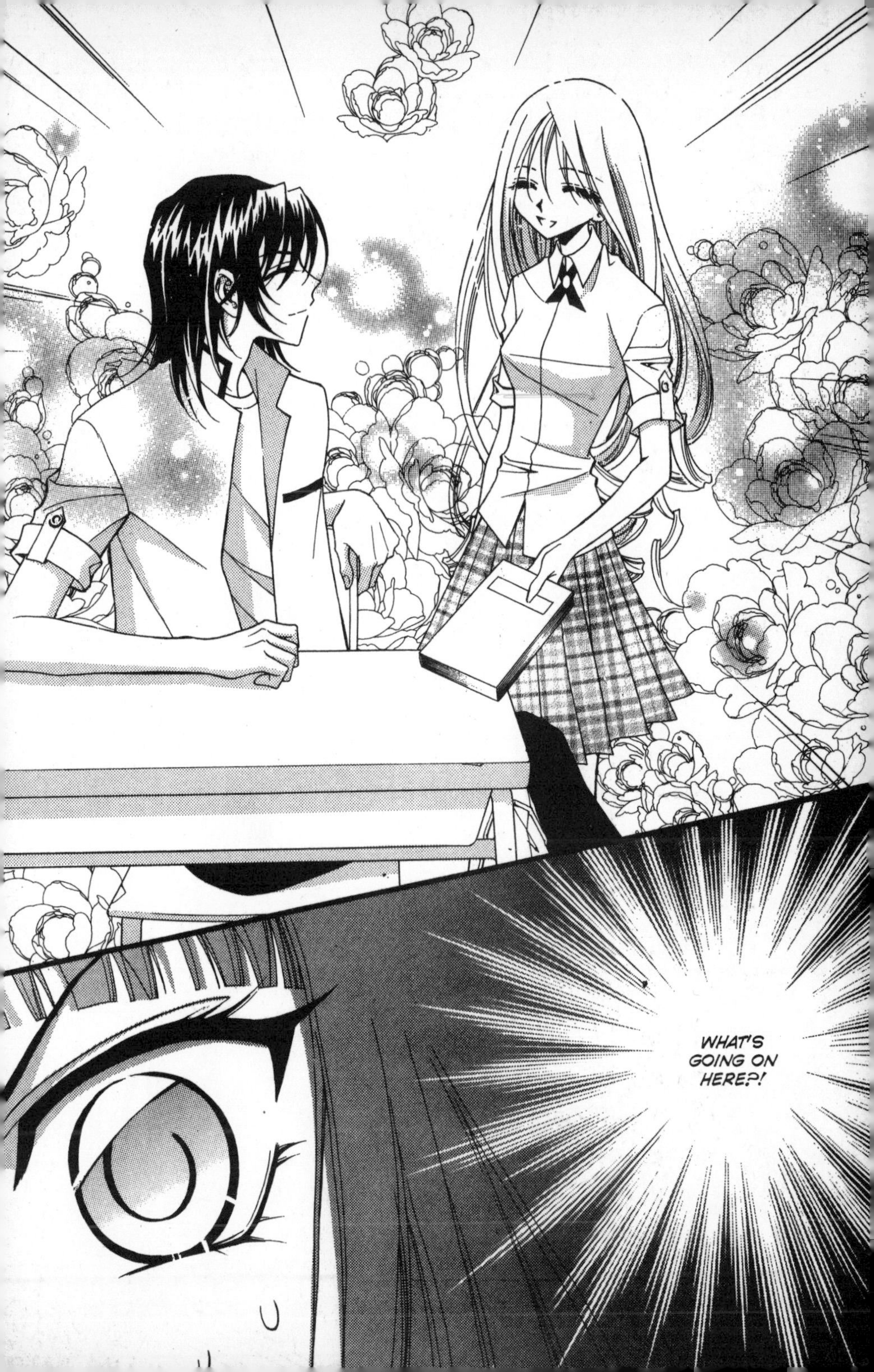
WHAT'S GOING ON HERE?!

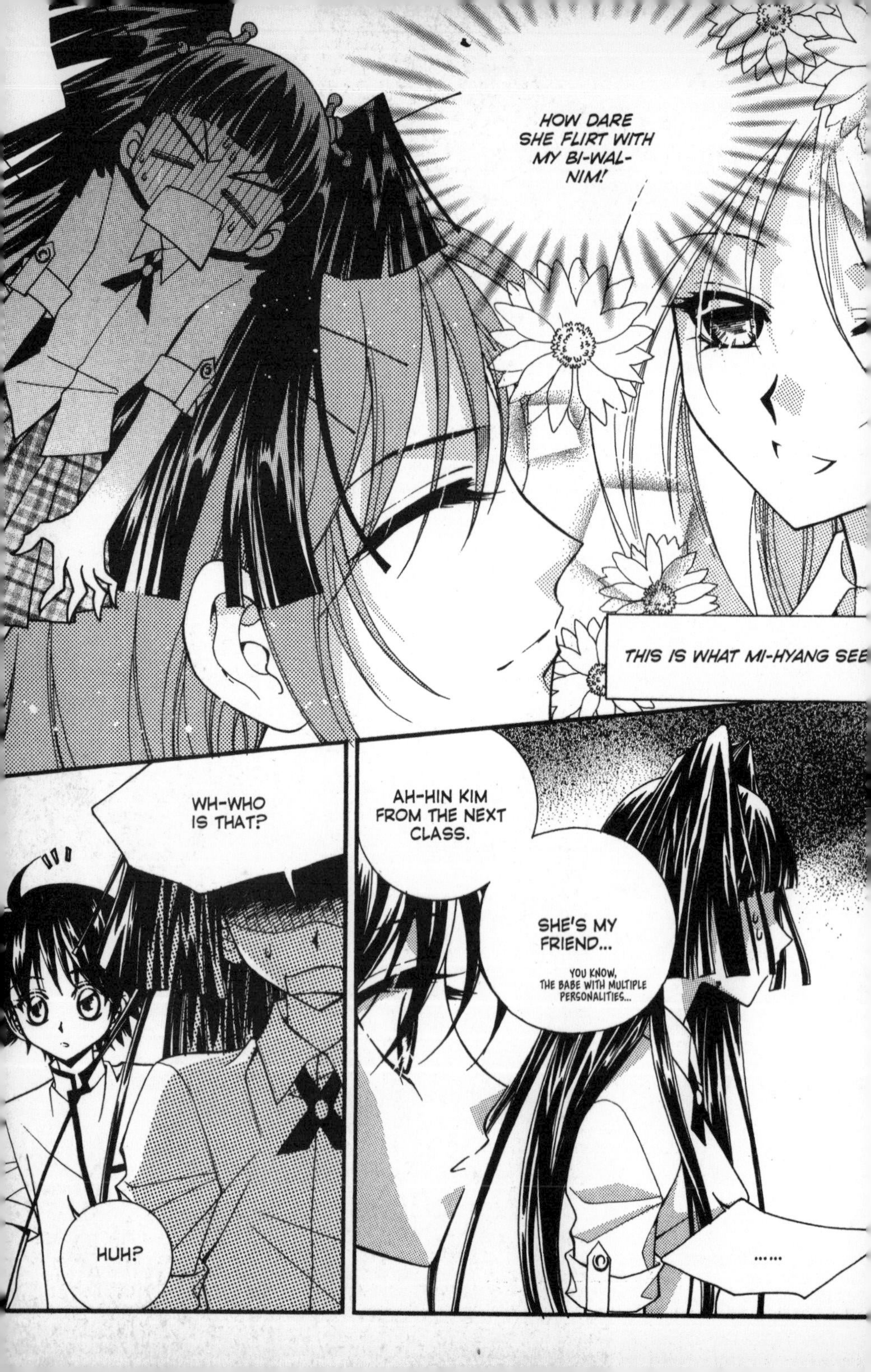
HOW DARE SHE FLIRT WITH MY BI-WAL-NIM!
THIS IS WHAT MI-HYANG SEE
WH-WHO IS THAT?
HUH?
AH-HIN KIM FROM THE NEXT CLASS.
SHE'S MY FRIEND...
YOU KNOW, THE BABE WITH MULTIPLE PERSONALITIES...
......

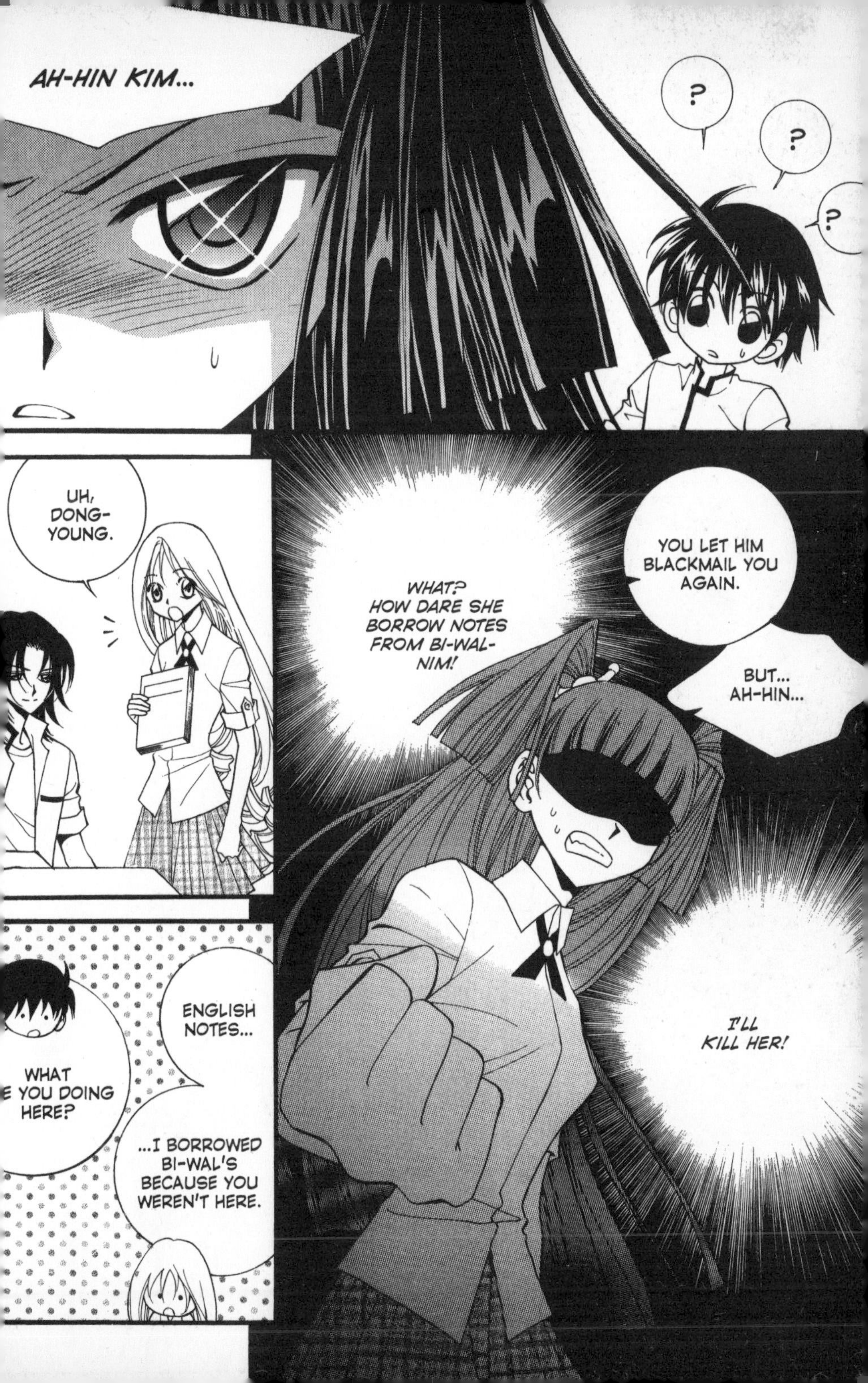

AH-HIN KIM...
?
?
?
UH, DONG-YOUNG.
WHAT E YOU DOING HERE?
ENGLISH NOTES...
...I BORROWED BI-WAL'S BECAUSE YOU WEREN'T HERE.
YOU LET HIM BLACKMAIL YOU AGAIN.
WHAT? HOW DARE SHE BORROW NOTES FROM BI-WAL-NIM!
BUT... AH-HIN...
I'LL KILL HER!

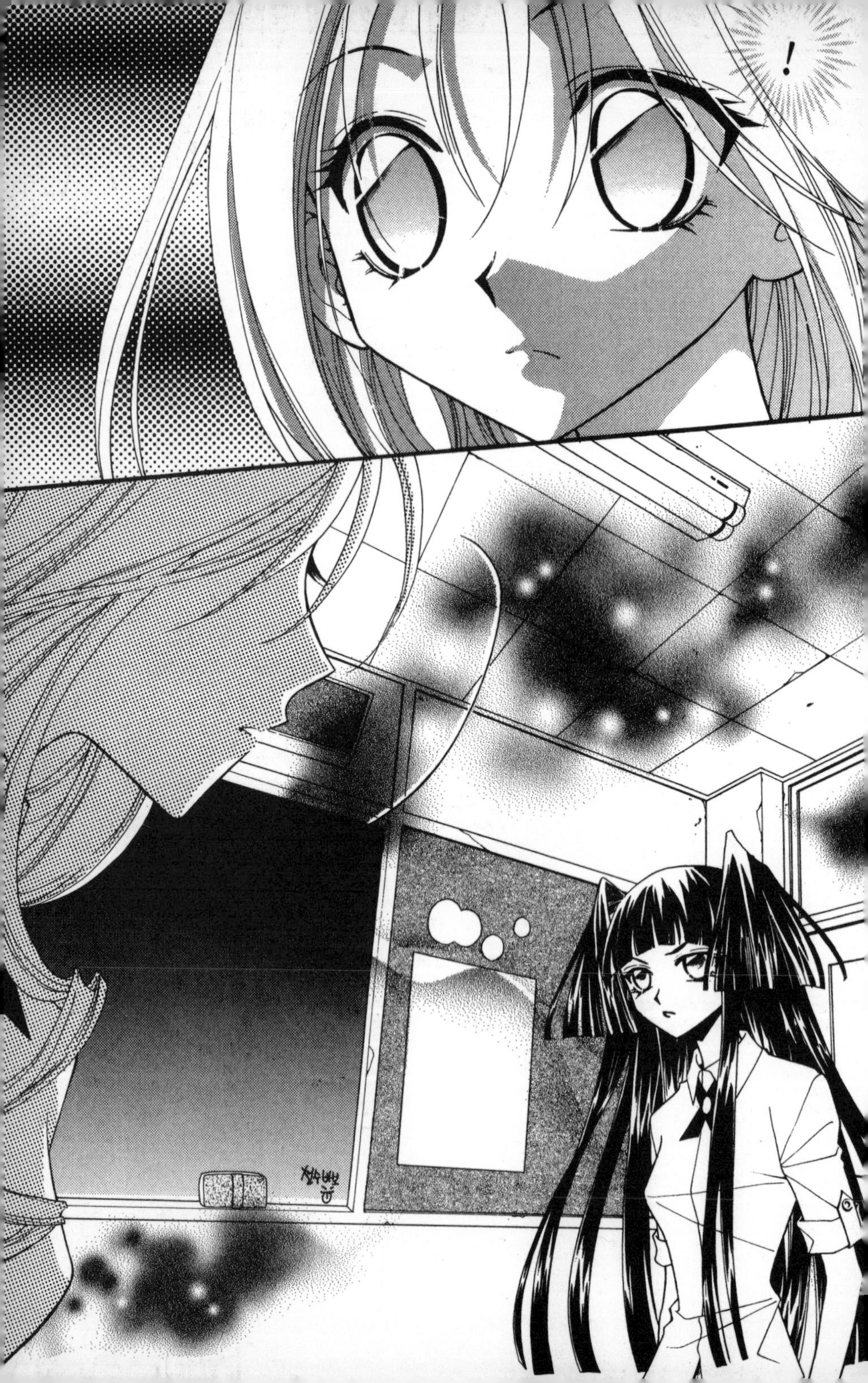
!

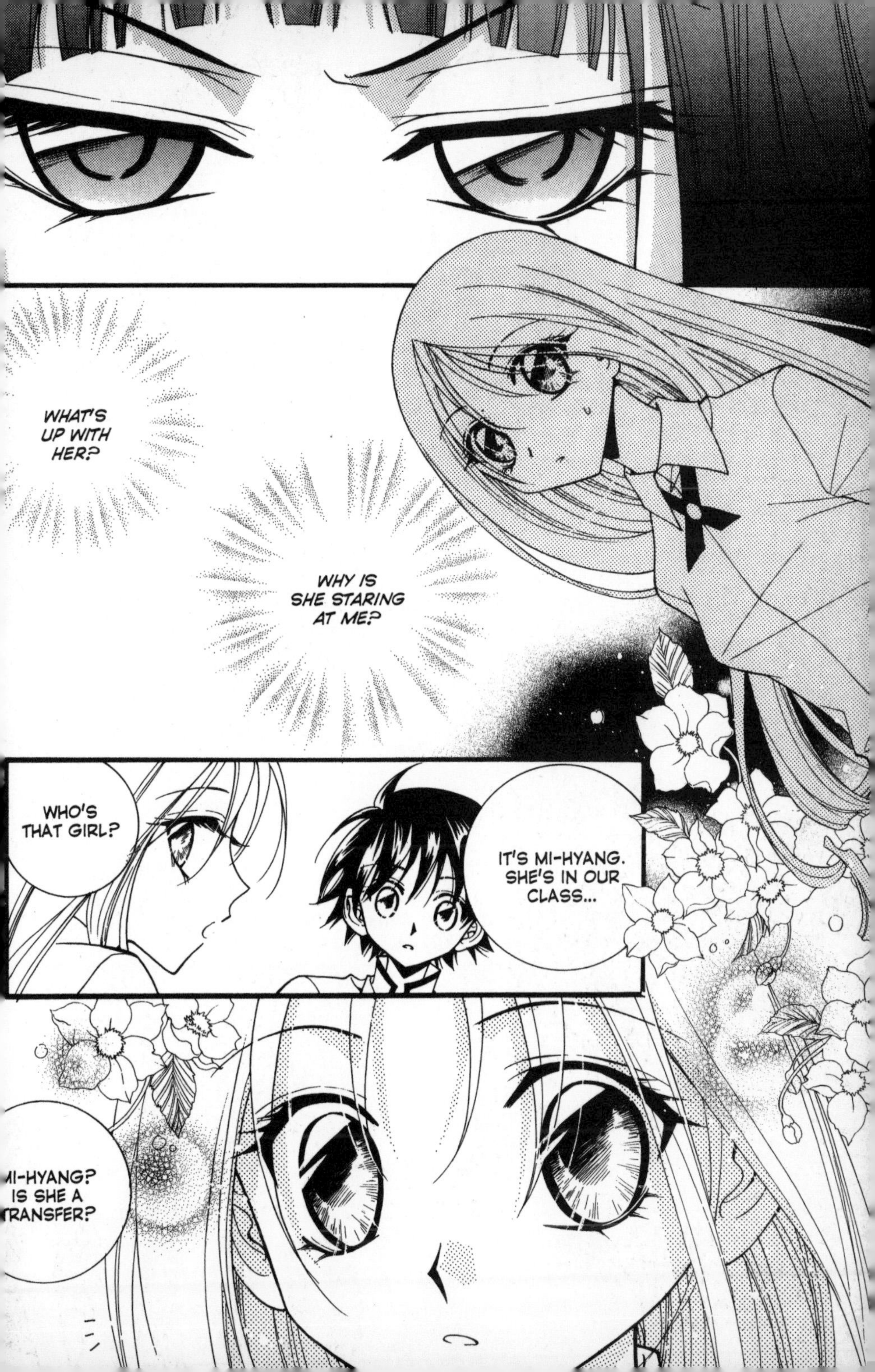
WHAT'S UP WITH HER?
WHY IS SHE STARING AT ME?
WHO'S THAT GIRL?
IT'S MI-HYANG. SHE'S IN OUR CLASS...
MI-HYANG? IS SHE A TRANSFER?

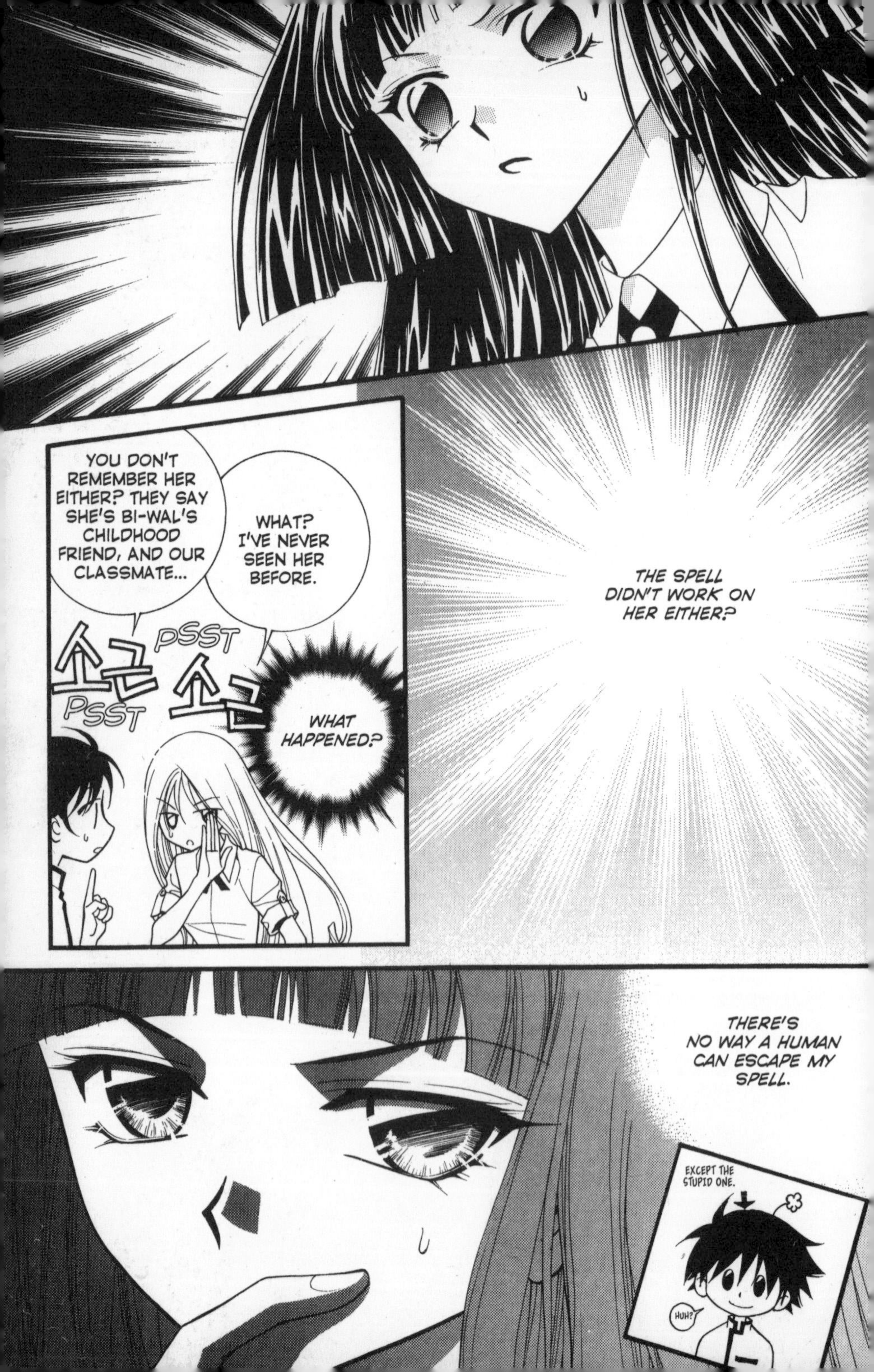
YOU DON'T REMEMBER HER EITHER? THEY SAY SHE'S BI-WAL'S CHILDHOOD FRIEND, AND OUR CLASSMATE...
WHAT? I'VE NEVER SEEN HER BEFORE.
소곤 PSST
소곤 PSST
WHAT HAPPENED?
THE SPELL DIDN'T WORK ON HER EITHER?
THERE'S NO WAY A HUMAN CAN ESCAPE MY SPELL.
EXCEPT THE STUPID ONE.
HUH?

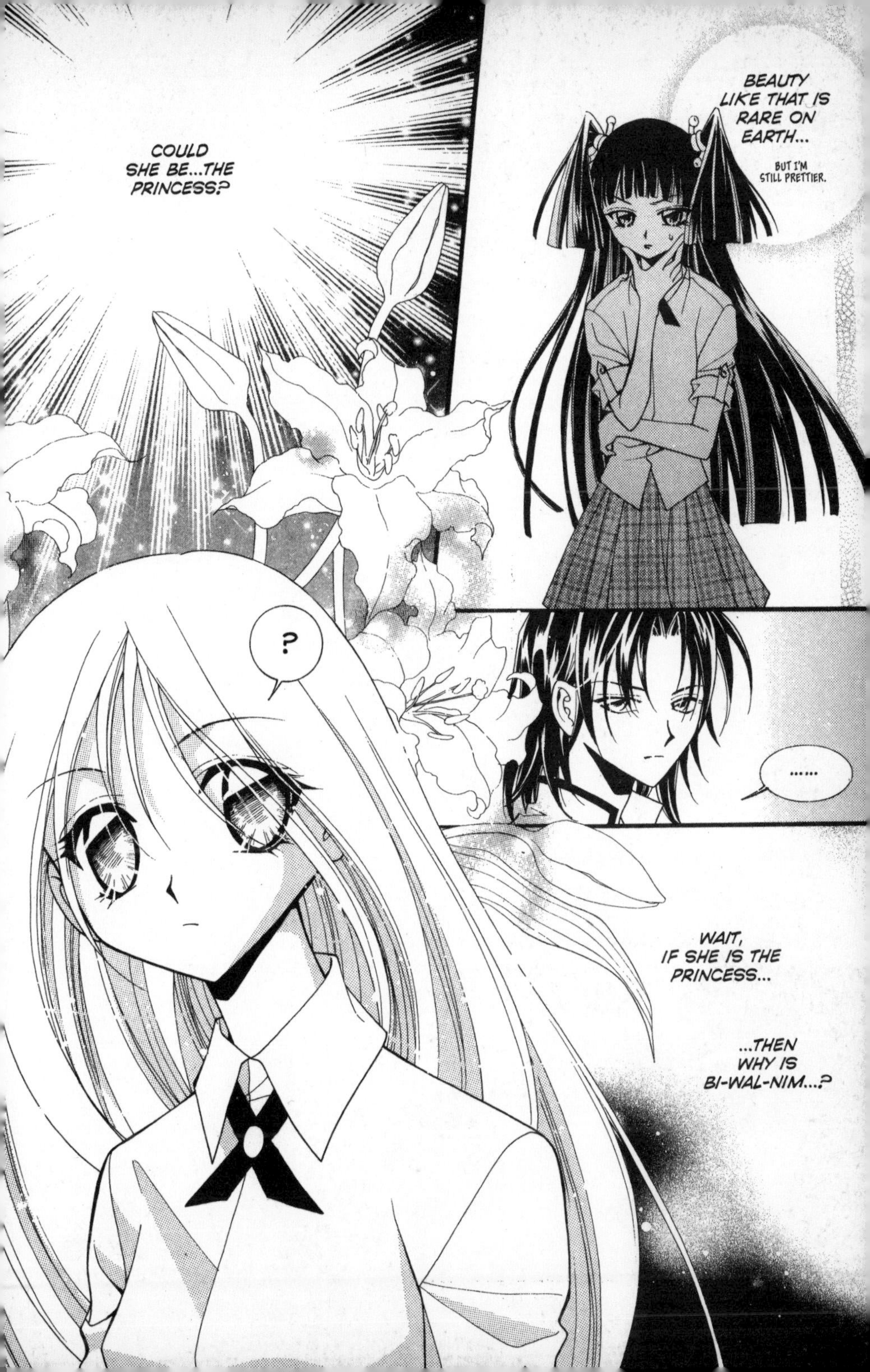
COULD SHE BE...THE PRINCESS?
BEAUTY LIKE THAT IS RARE ON EARTH...
BUT I'M STILL PRETTIER.
?
......
WAIT, IF SHE IS THE PRINCESS...
...THEN WHY IS BI-WAL-NIM...?

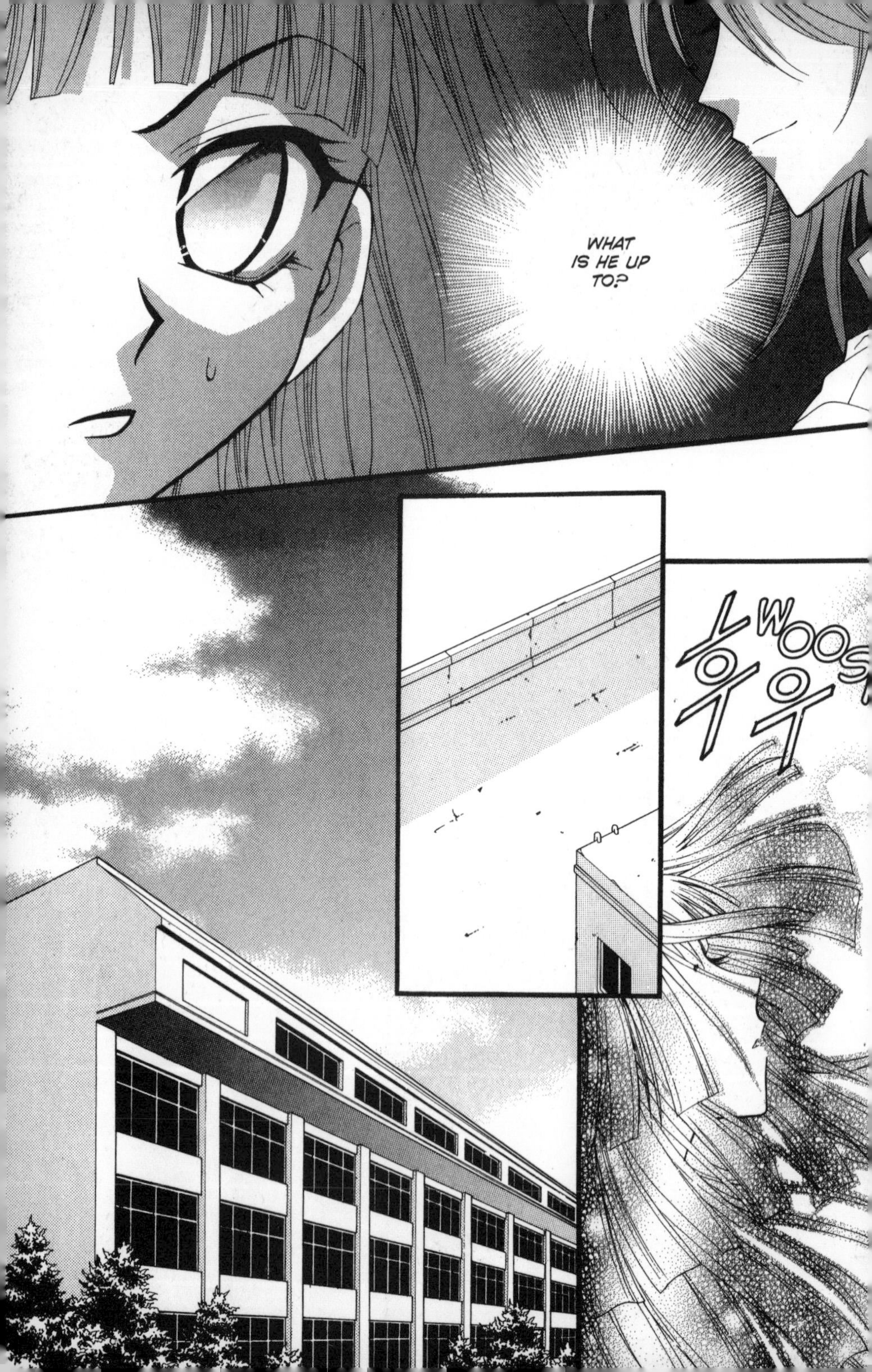
WHAT IS HE UP TO?
후우
WOOS

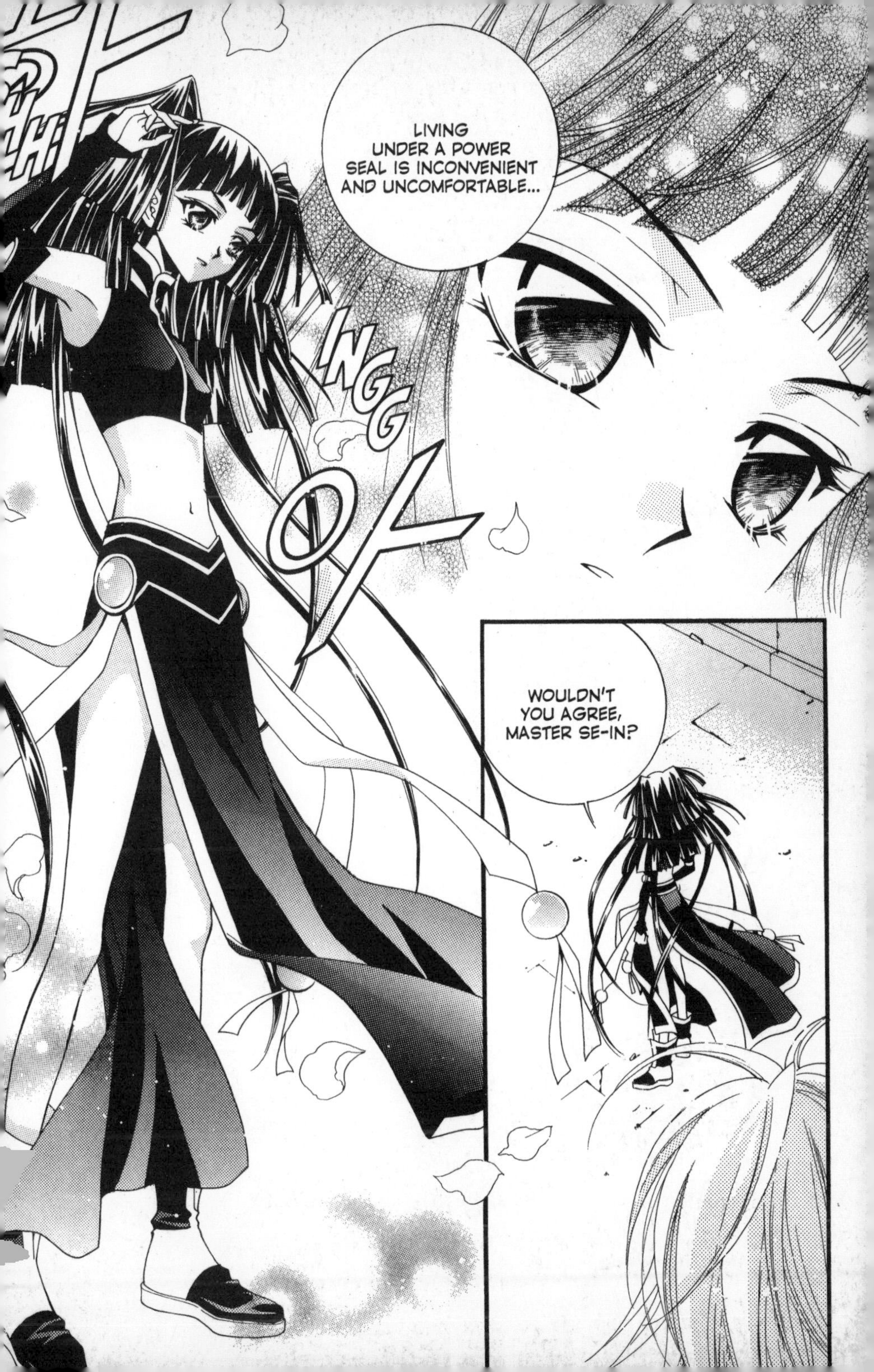
LIVING UNDER A POWER SEAL IS INCONVENIENT AND UNCOMFORTABLE...
INGG
WOULDN'T YOU AGREE, MASTER SE-IN?

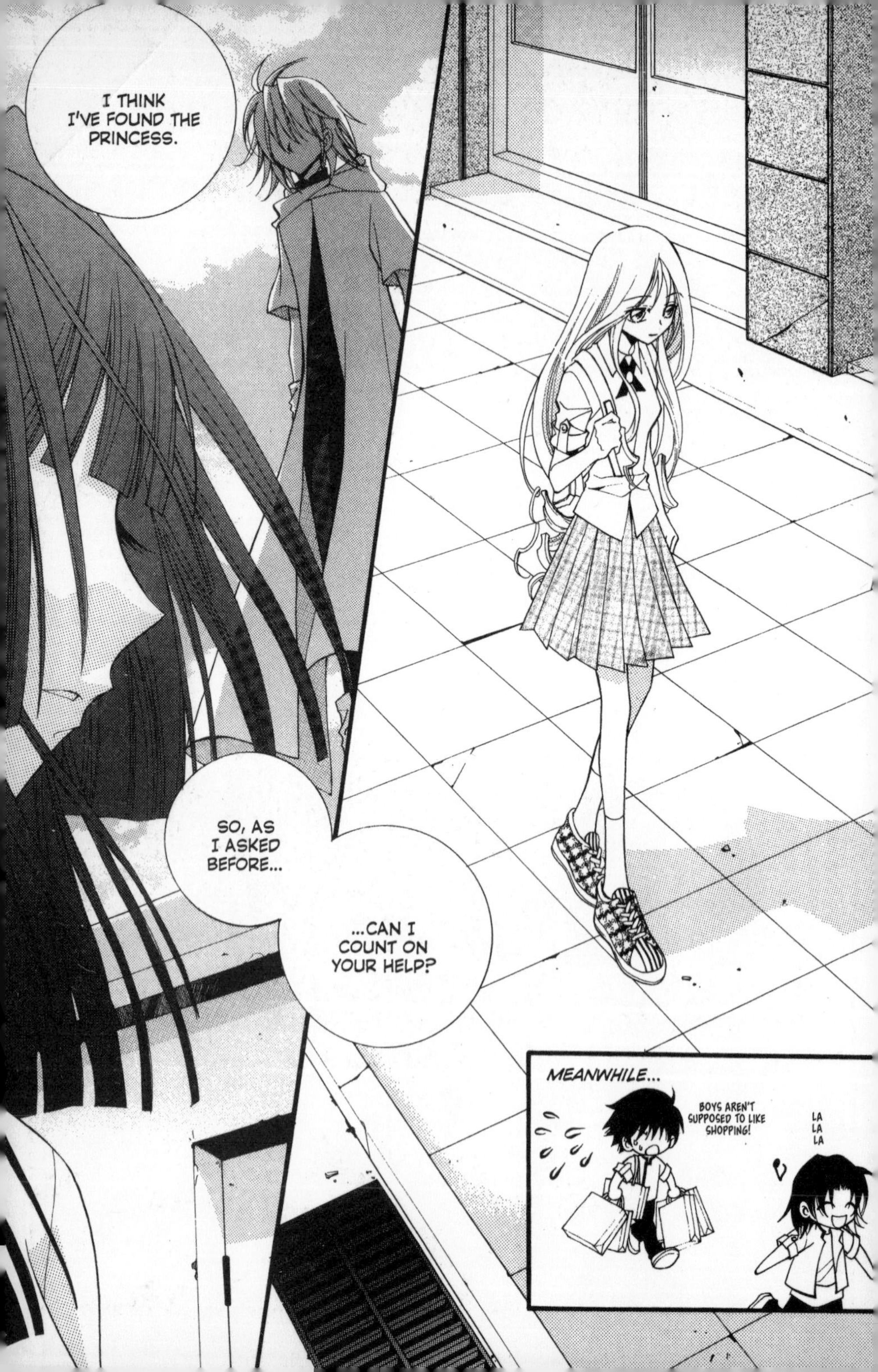
I THINK I'VE FOUND THE PRINCESS.
SO, AS I ASKED BEFORE...
...CAN I COUNT ON YOUR HELP?
MEANWHILE...
BOYS AREN'T SUPPOSED TO LIKE SHOPPING!
LA LA LA

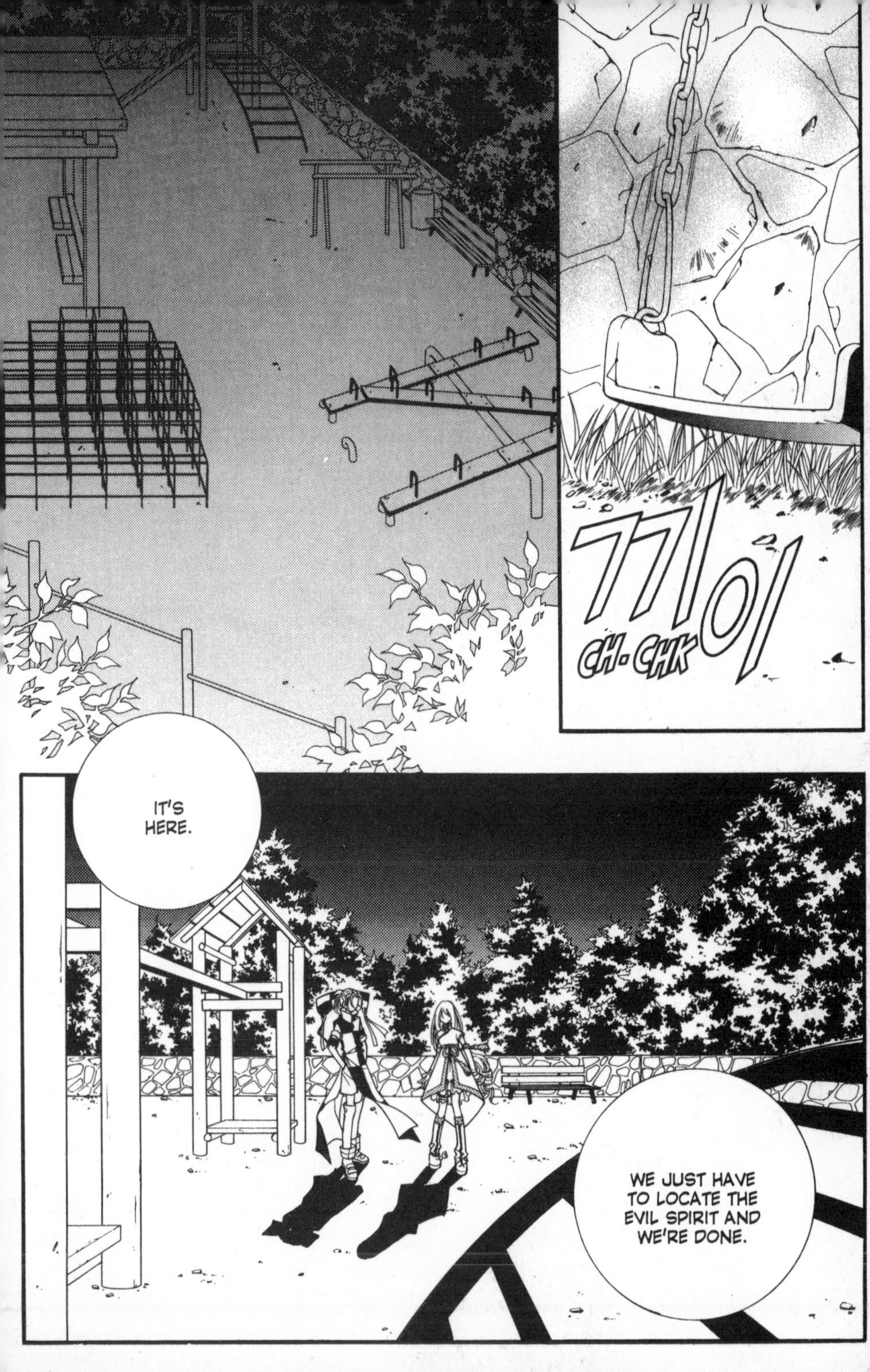
CH-CHK
IT'S HERE.
WE JUST HAVE TO LOCATE THE EVIL SPIRIT AND WE'RE DONE.

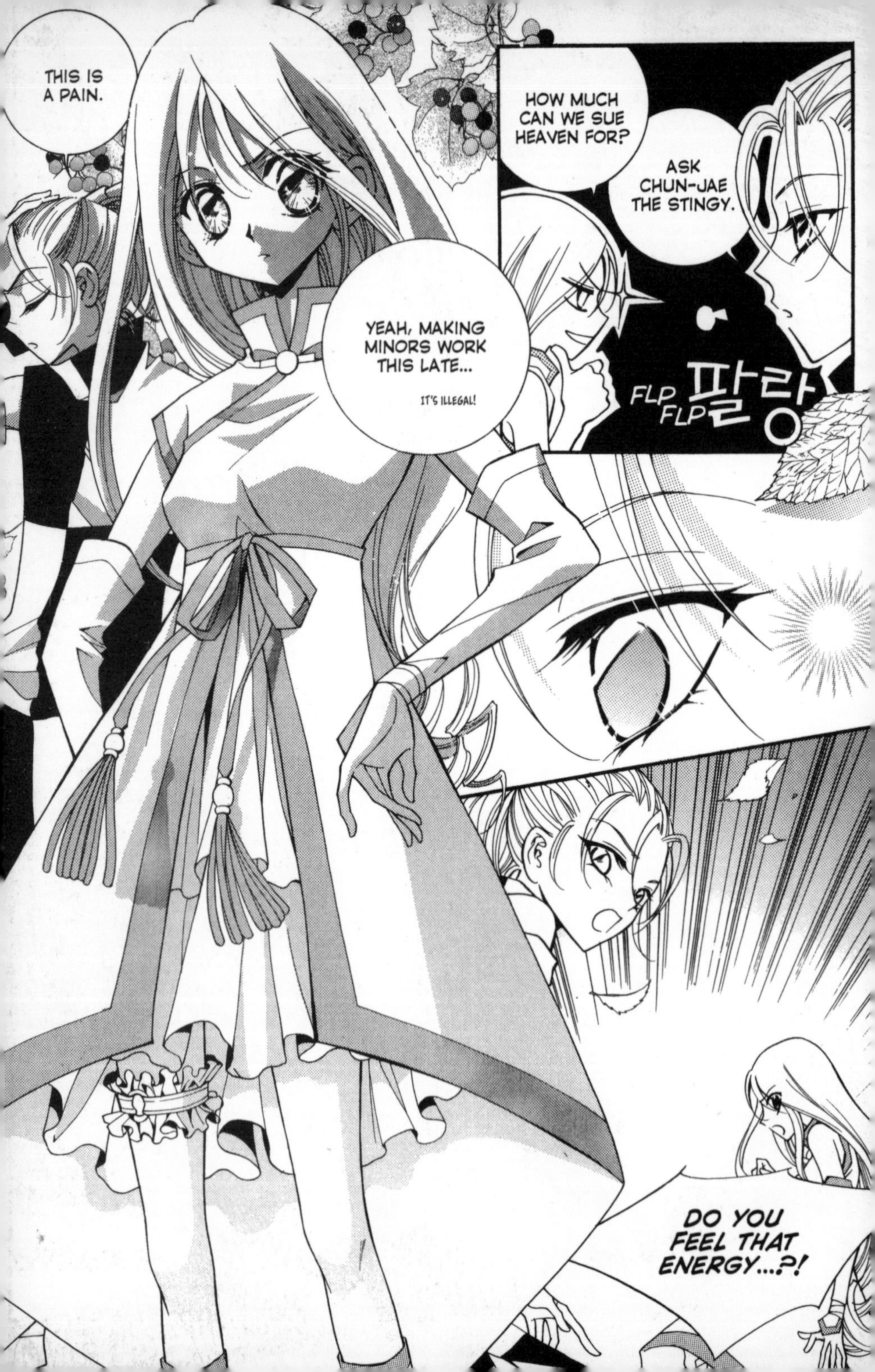
HOW MUCH CAN WE SUE HEAVEN FOR?
ASK CHUN-JAE THE STINGY.
FLP FLP 팔랑
THIS IS A PAIN.
YEAH, MAKING MINORS WORK THIS LATE...
IT'S ILLEGAL!
DO YOU FEEL THAT ENERGY...?!

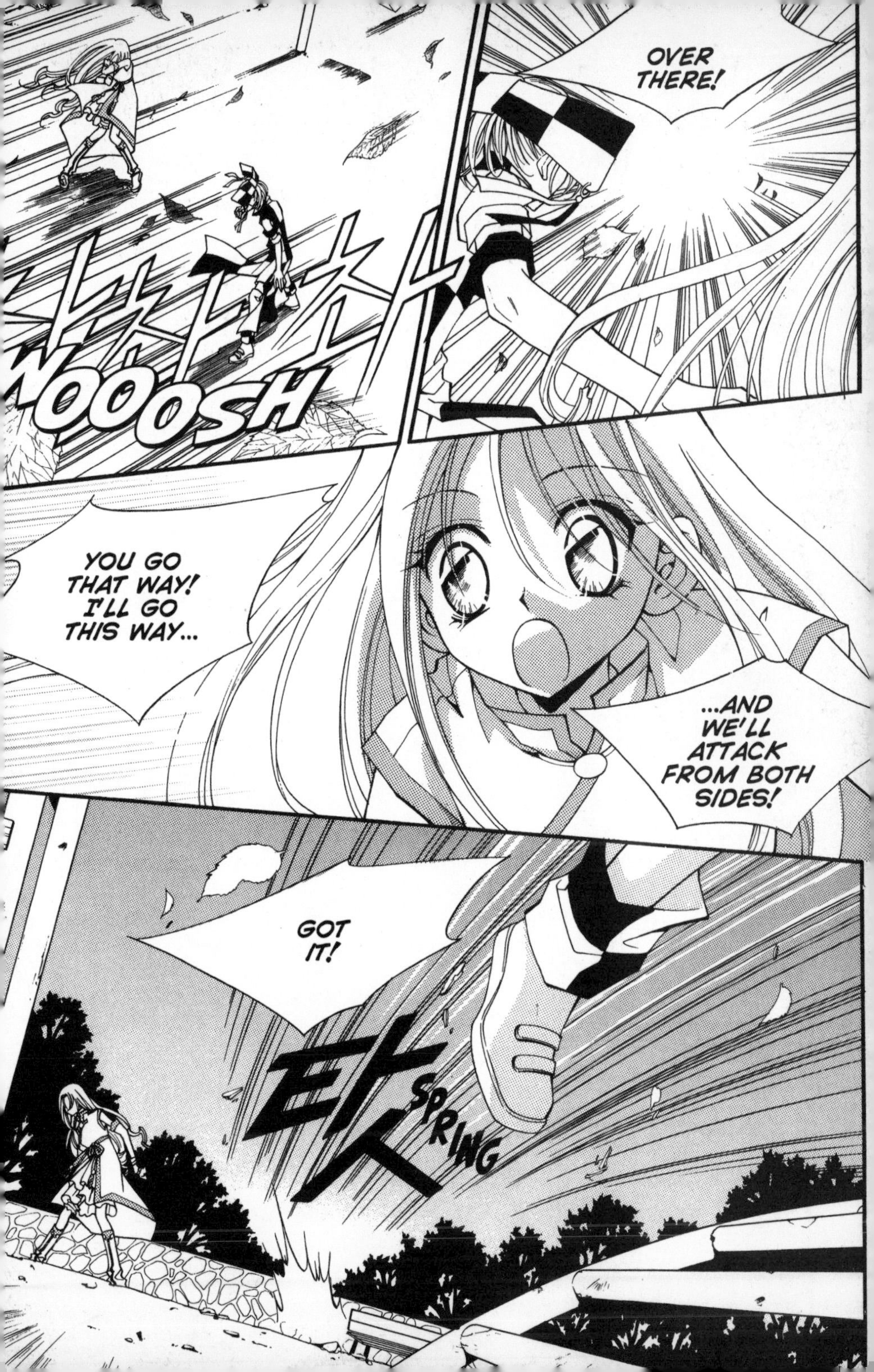
WHOOOSH
OVER THERE!
YOU GO THAT WAY! I'LL GO THIS WAY...
...AND WE'LL ATTACK FROM BOTH SIDES!
GOT IT!
SPRING

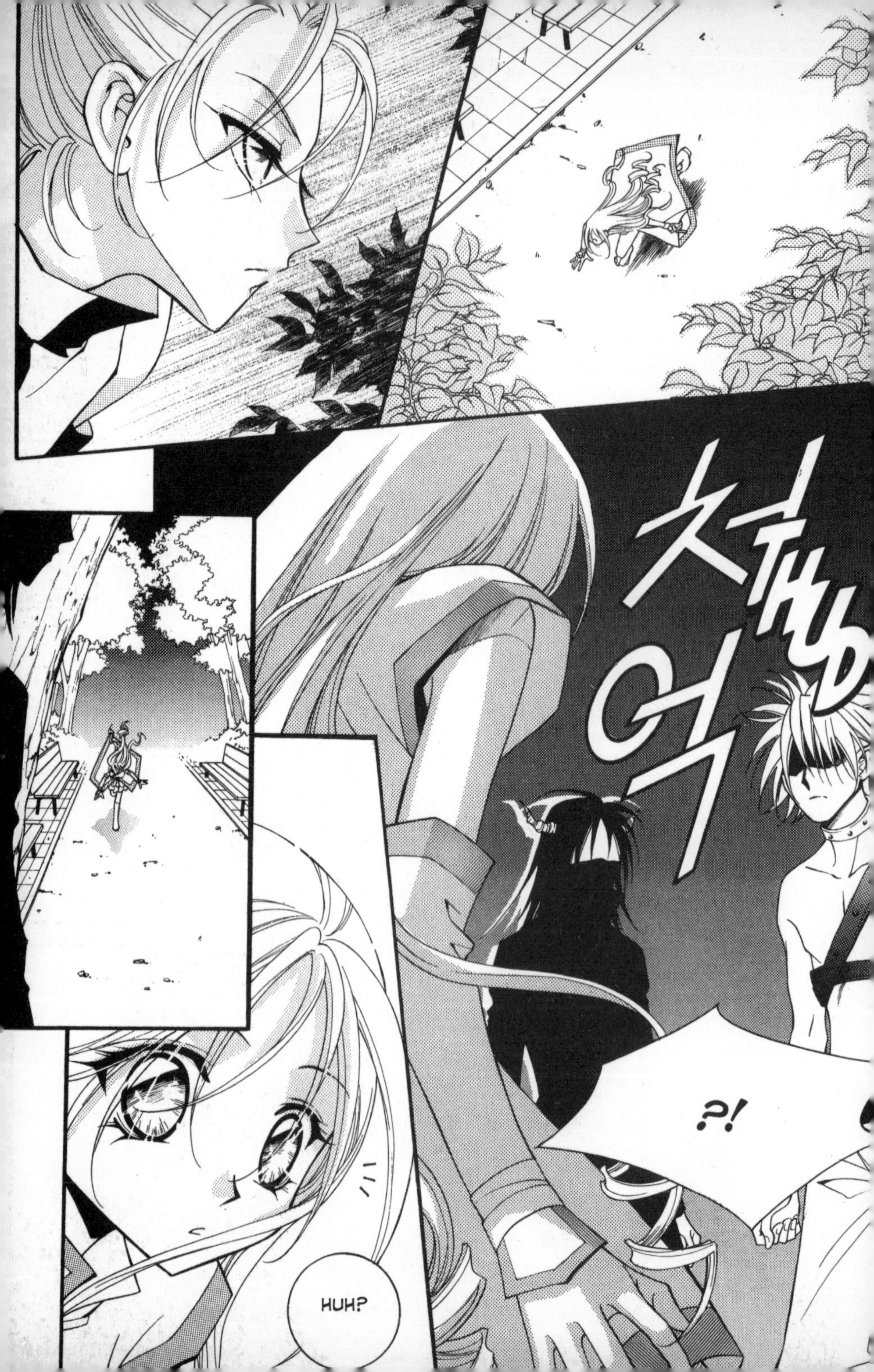
처억
THUD
?!
HUH?

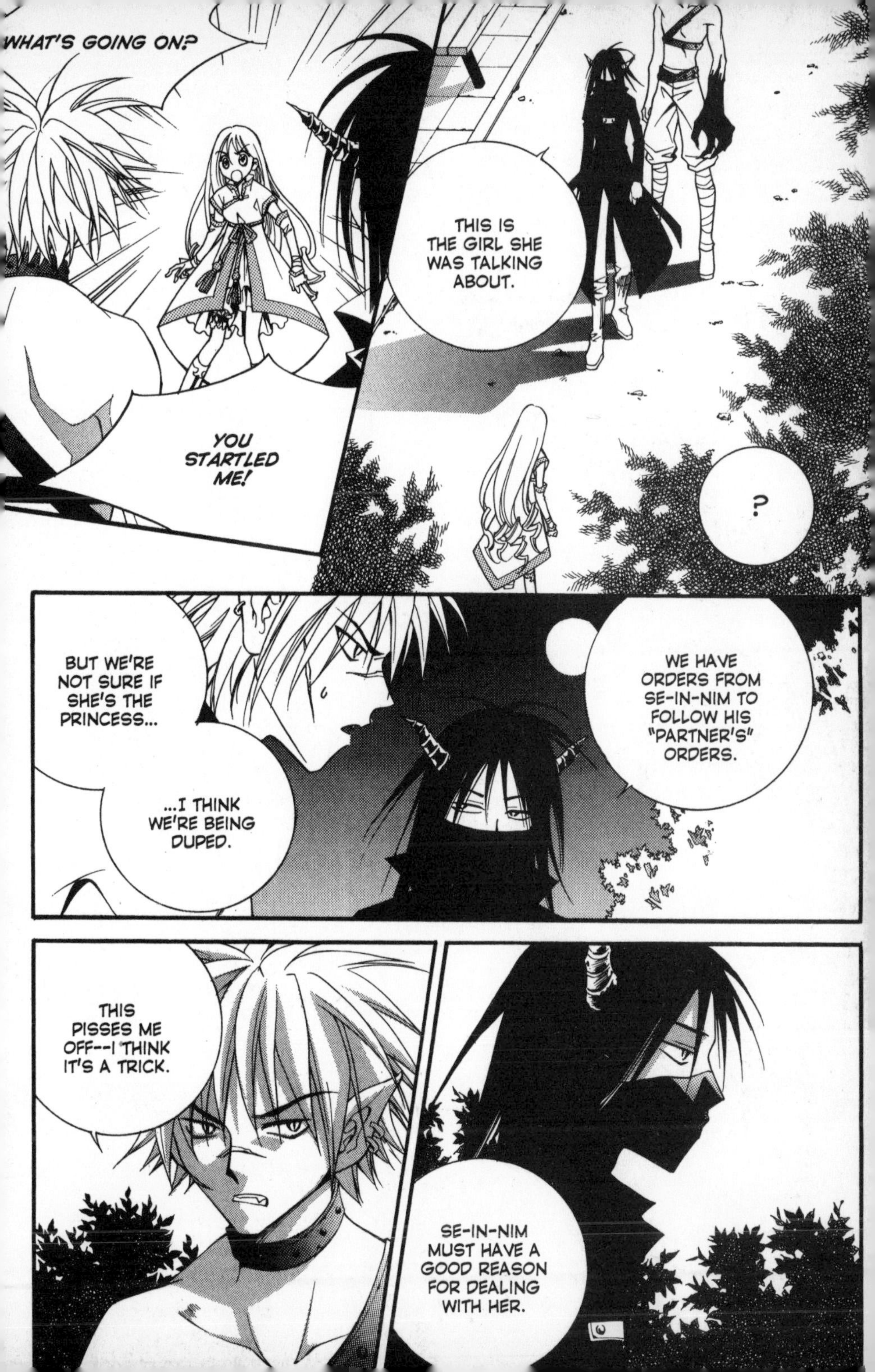
WHAT'S GOING ON?
YOU STARTLED ME!
THIS IS THE GIRL SHE WAS TALKING ABOUT.
?
BUT WE'RE NOT SURE IF SHE'S THE PRINCESS...
...I THINK WE'RE BEING DUPED.
WE HAVE ORDERS FROM SE-IN-NIM TO FOLLOW HIS "PARTNER'S" ORDERS.
THIS PISSES ME OFF--I THINK IT'S A TRICK.
SE-IN-NIM MUST HAVE A GOOD REASON FOR DEALING WITH HER.

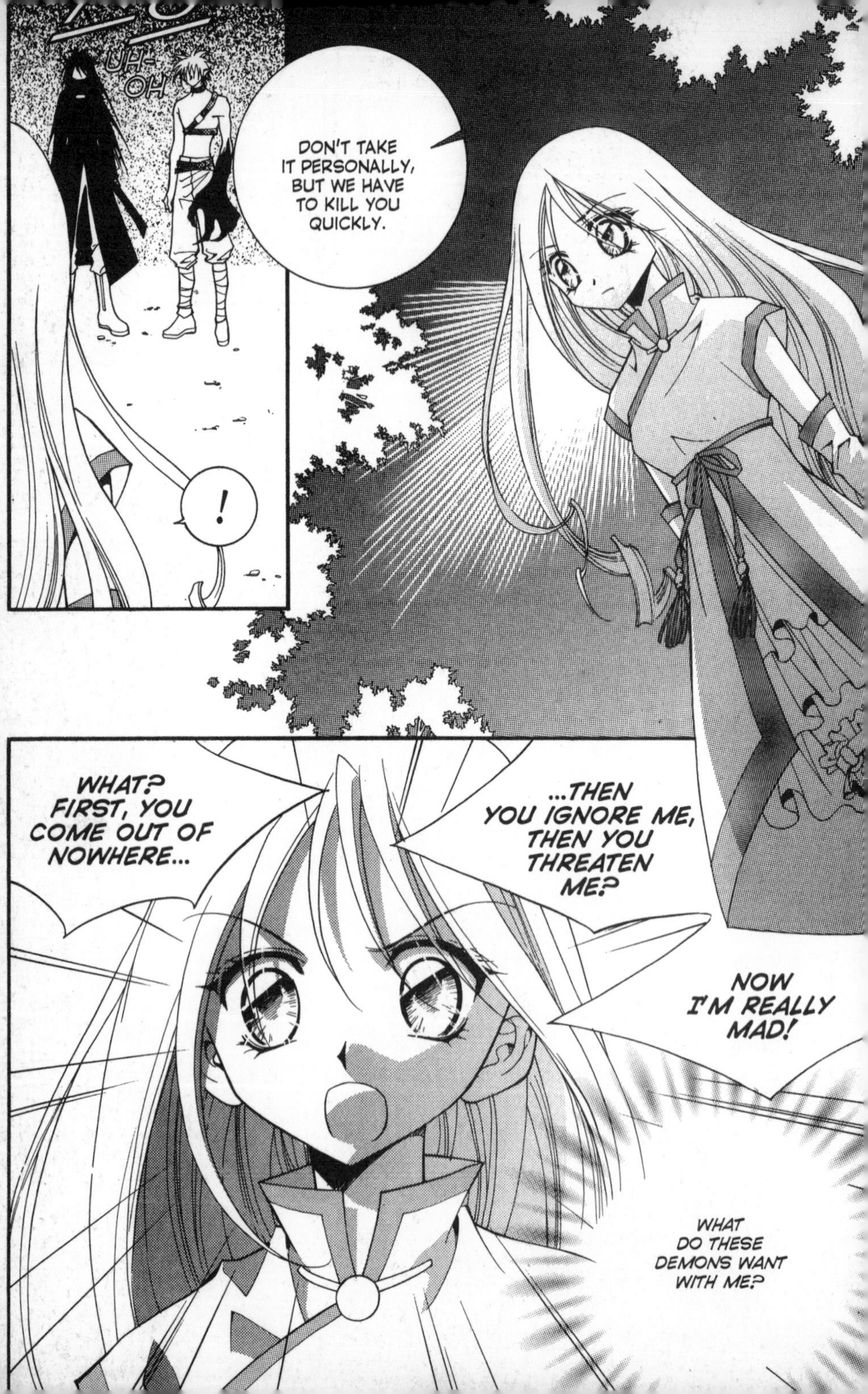
UH-OH
DON'T TAKE IT PERSONALLY, BUT WE HAVE TO KILL YOU QUICKLY.
!
WHAT? FIRST, YOU COME OUT OF NOWHERE...
...THEN YOU IGNORE ME, THEN YOU THREATEN ME?
NOW I'M REALLY MAD!
WHAT DO THESE DEMONS WANT WITH ME?

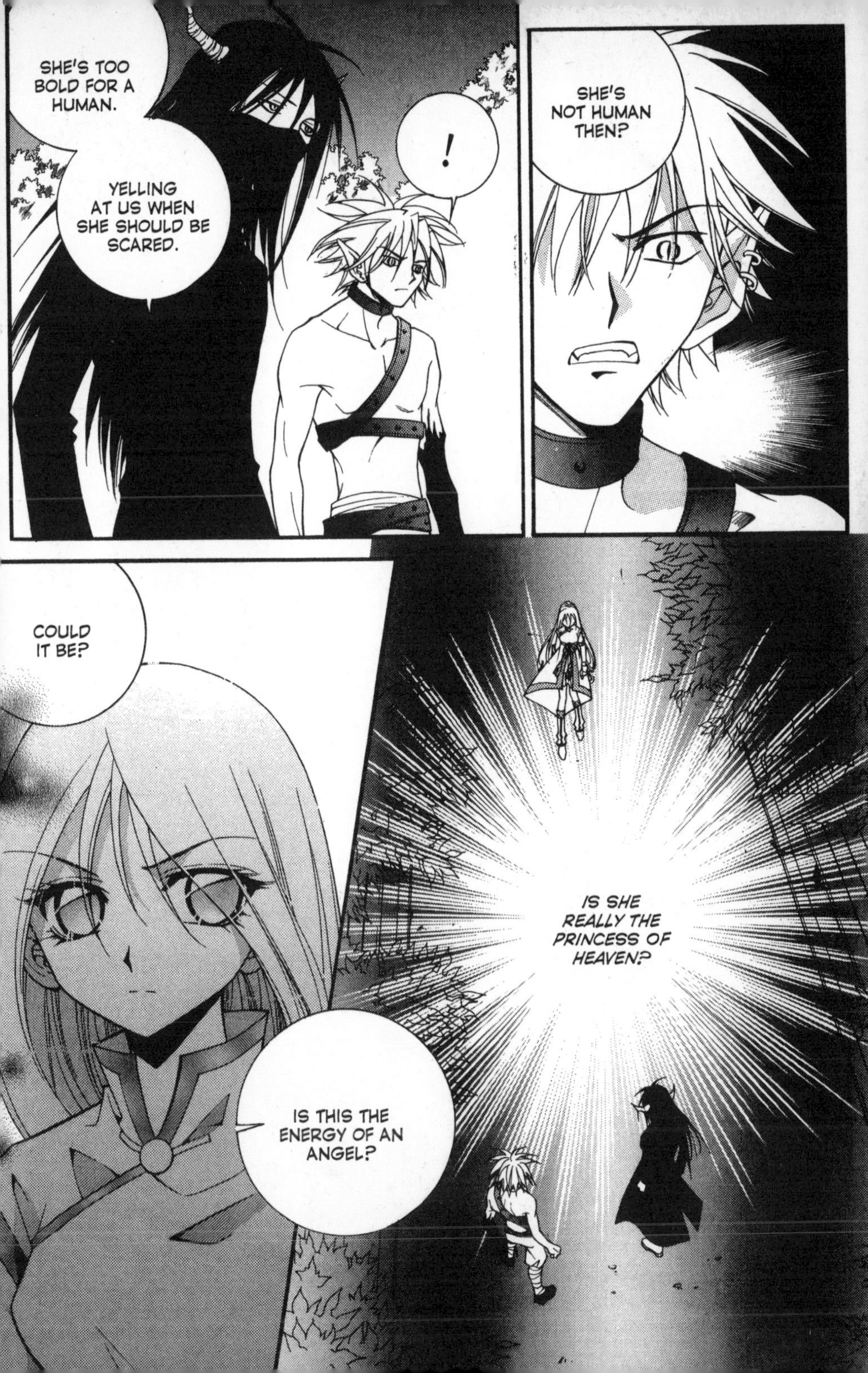
SHE'S TOO BOLD FOR A HUMAN.
YELLING AT US WHEN SHE SHOULD BE SCARED.
!
SHE'S NOT HUMAN THEN?
COULD IT BE?
IS SHE REALLY THE PRINCESS OF HEAVEN?
IS THIS THE ENERGY OF AN ANGEL?

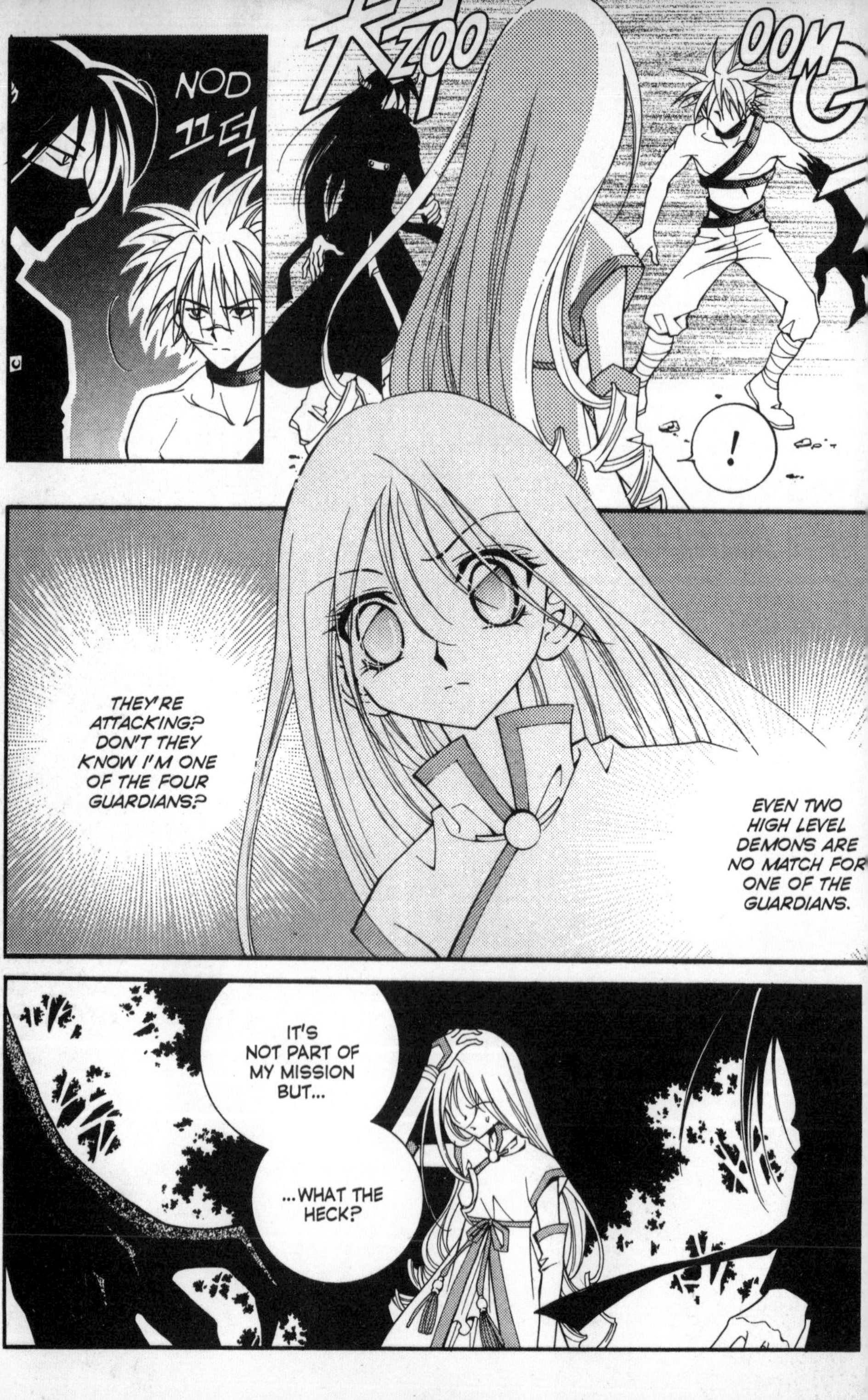
NOD
끄덕
ZOO
OOM
!
THEY'RE ATTACKING? DON'T THEY KNOW I'M ONE OF THE FOUR GUARDIANS?
EVEN TWO HIGH LEVEL DEMONS ARE NO MATCH FOR ONE OF THE GUARDIANS.
IT'S NOT PART OF MY MISSION BUT...
...WHAT THE HECK?

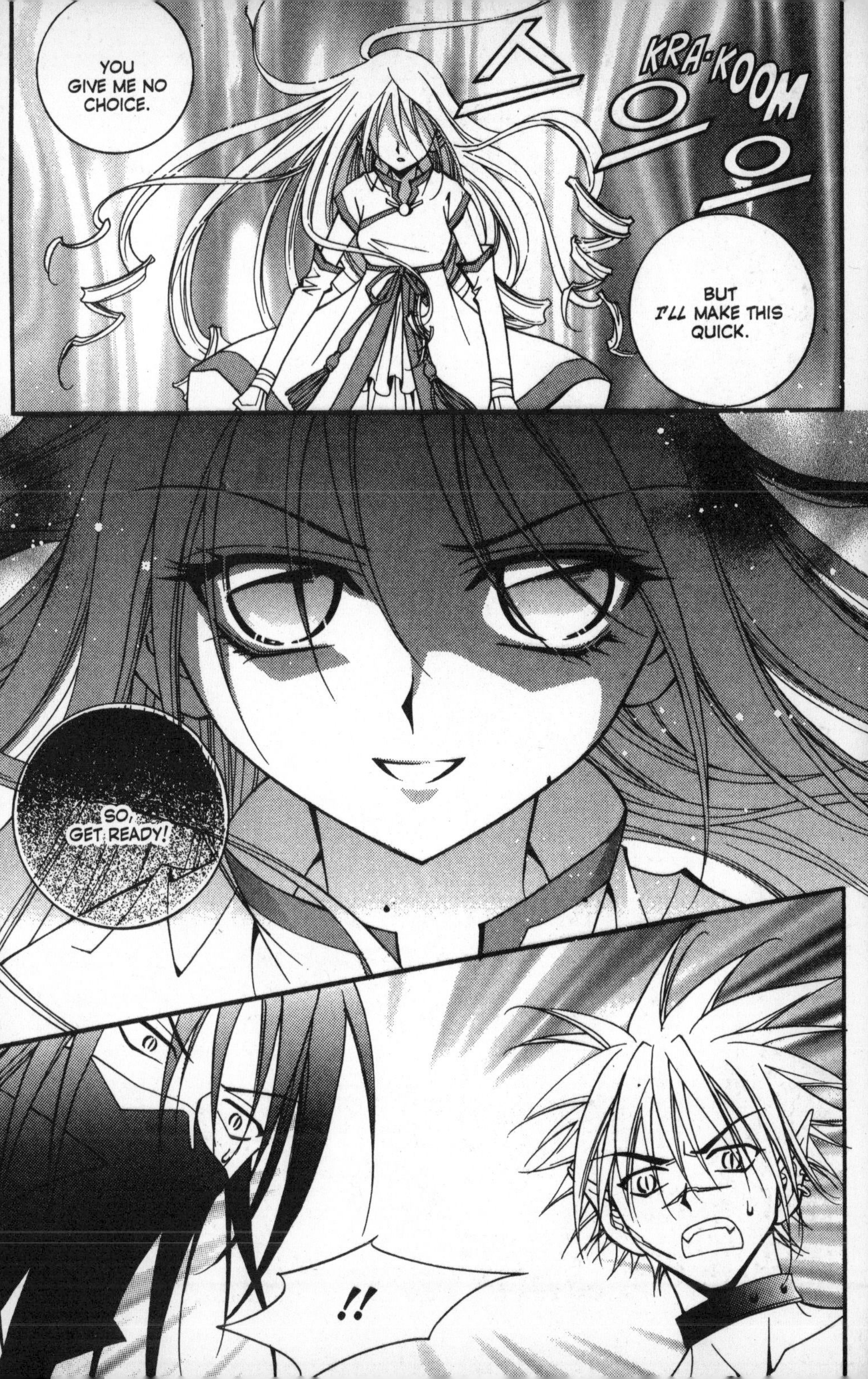
YOU GIVE ME NO CHOICE.
KRA-KOOM
BUT I'LL MAKE THIS QUICK.
SO, GET READY!
!!

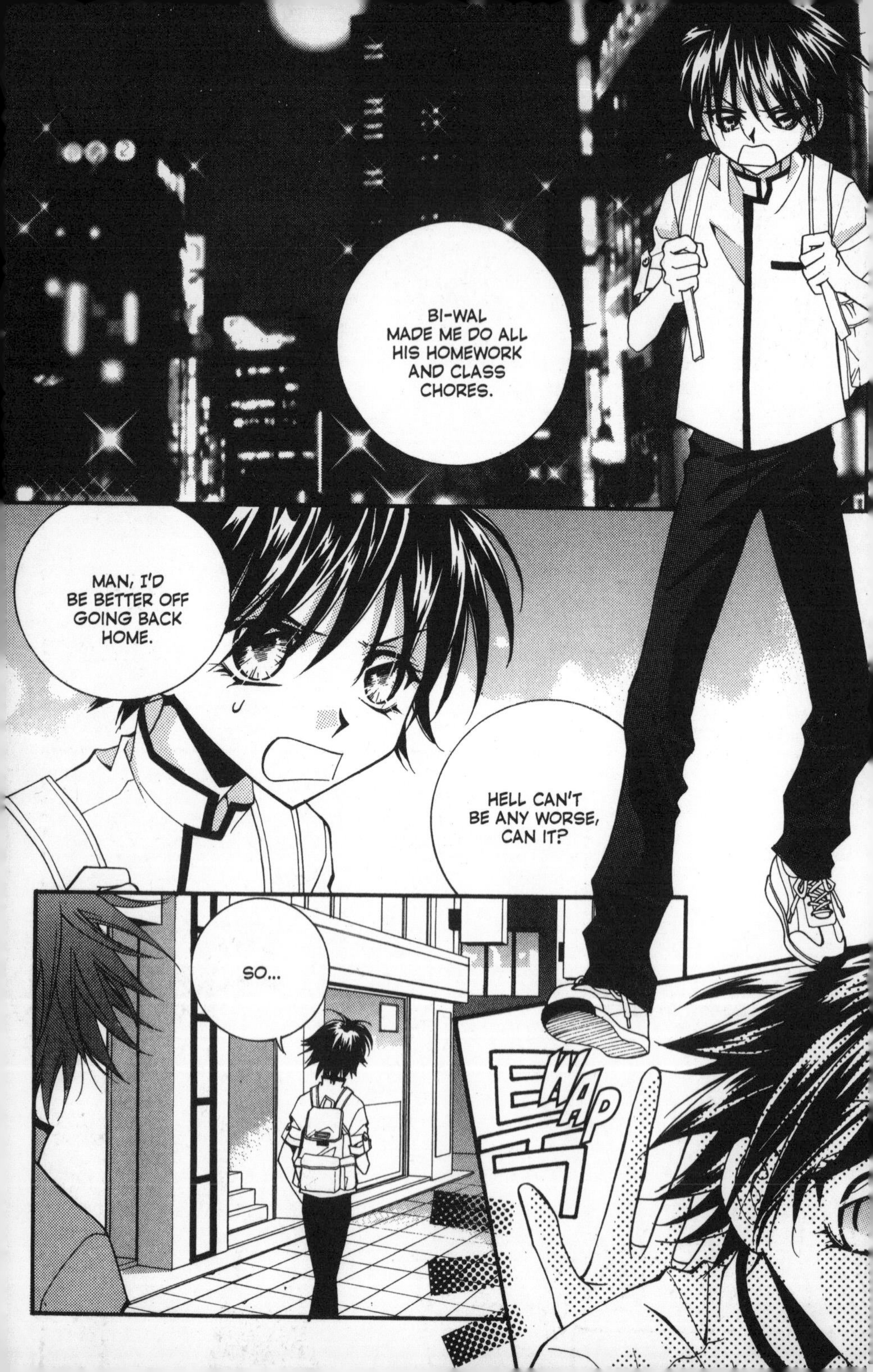
BI-WAL MADE ME DO ALL HIS HOMEWORK AND CLASS CHORES.
MAN, I'D BE BETTER OFF GOING BACK HOME.
HELL CAN'T BE ANY WORSE, CAN IT?
SO...
EWAAP

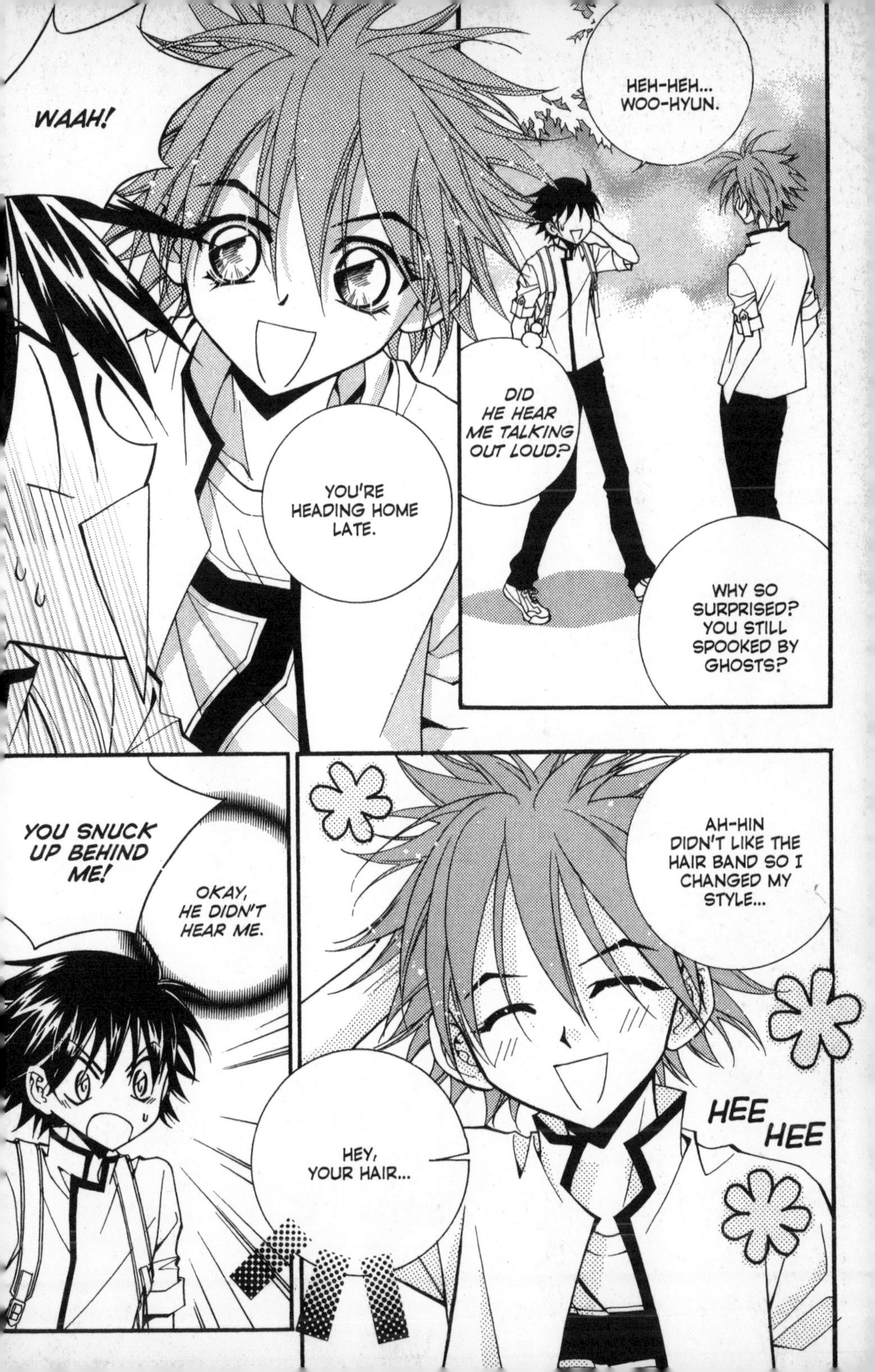
WAAH!
YOU'RE HEADING HOME LATE.
HEH-HEH... WOO-HYUN.
DID HE HEAR ME TALKING OUT LOUD?
WHY SO SURPRISED? YOU STILL SPOOKED BY GHOSTS?
YOU SNUCK UP BEHIND ME!
OKAY, HE DIDN'T HEAR ME.
AH-HIN DIDN'T LIKE THE HAIR BAND SO I CHANGED MY STYLE...
HEY, YOUR HAIR...
HEE HEE

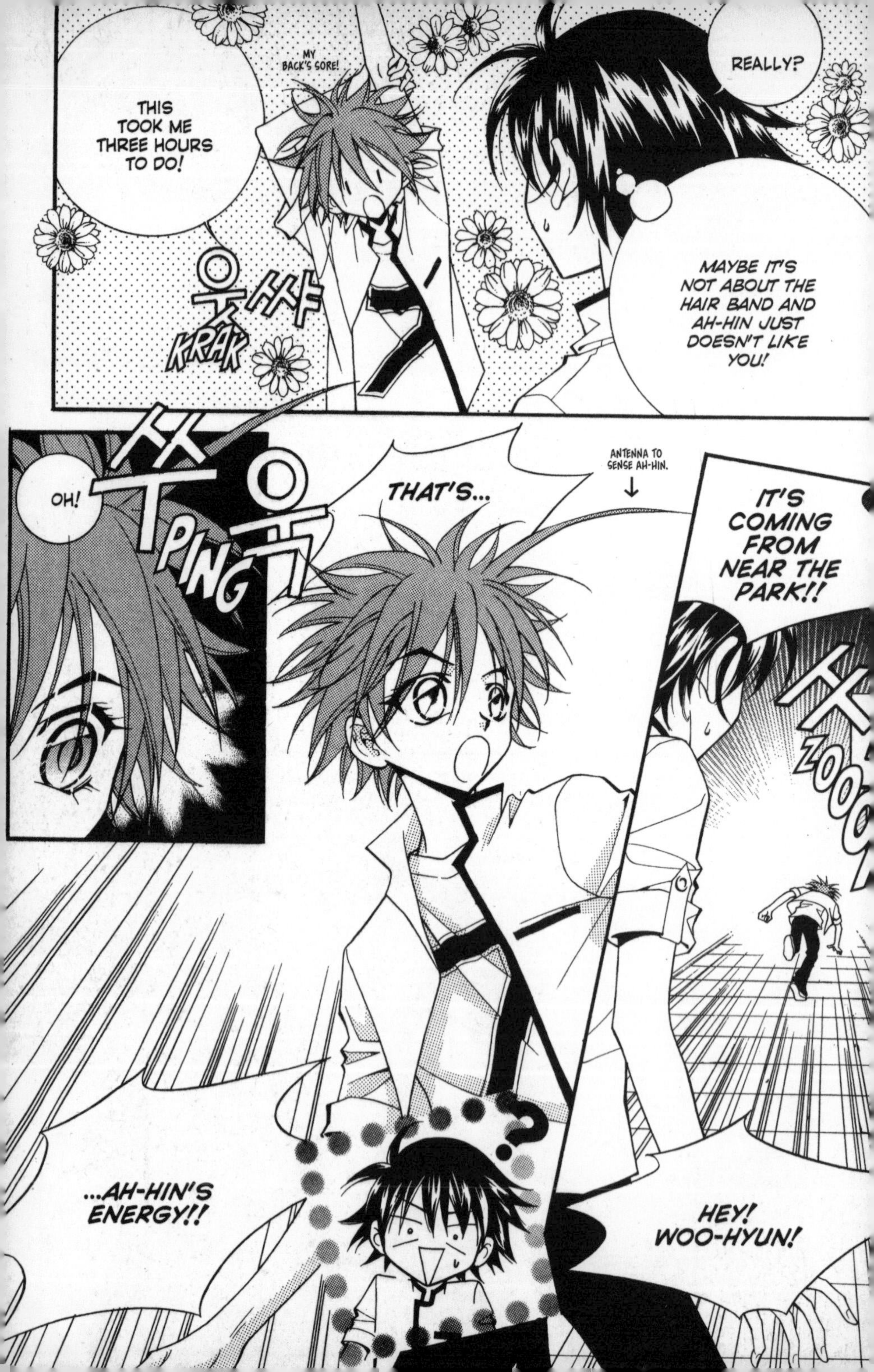
THIS TOOK ME THREE HOURS TO DO!
MY BACK'S SORE!
KRAK
REALLY?
MAYBE IT'S NOT ABOUT THE HAIR BAND AND AH-HIN JUST DOESN'T LIKE YOU!
OH!
PING
THAT'S...
ANTENNA TO SENSE AH-HIN.
...AH-HIN'S ENERGY!!
IT'S COMING FROM NEAR THE PARK!!
HEY! WOO-HYUN!

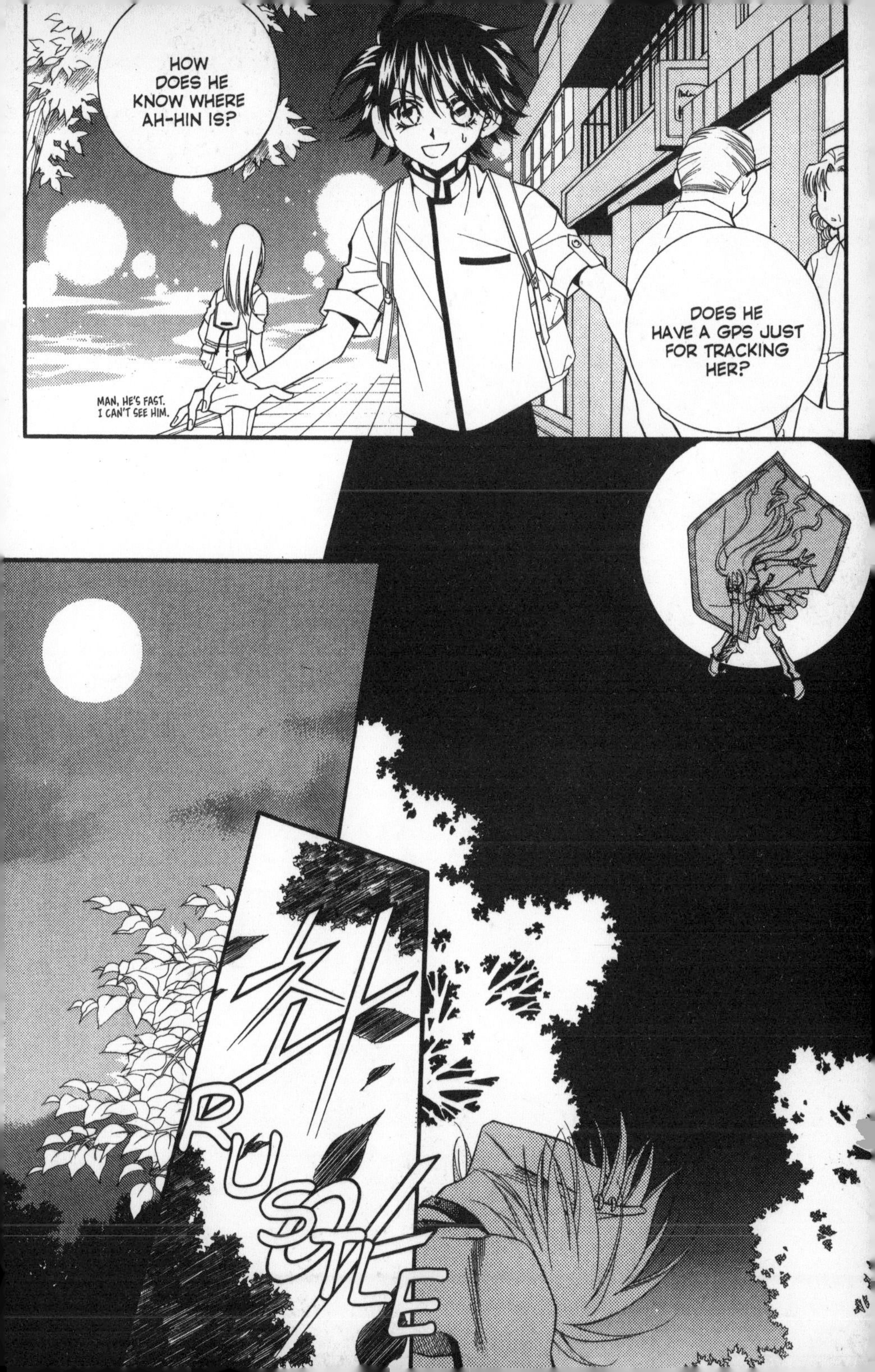
HOW DOES HE KNOW WHERE AH-HIN IS?
DOES HE HAVE A GPS JUST FOR TRACKING HER?
MAN, HE'S FAST. I CAN'T SEE HIM.
RUSTLE

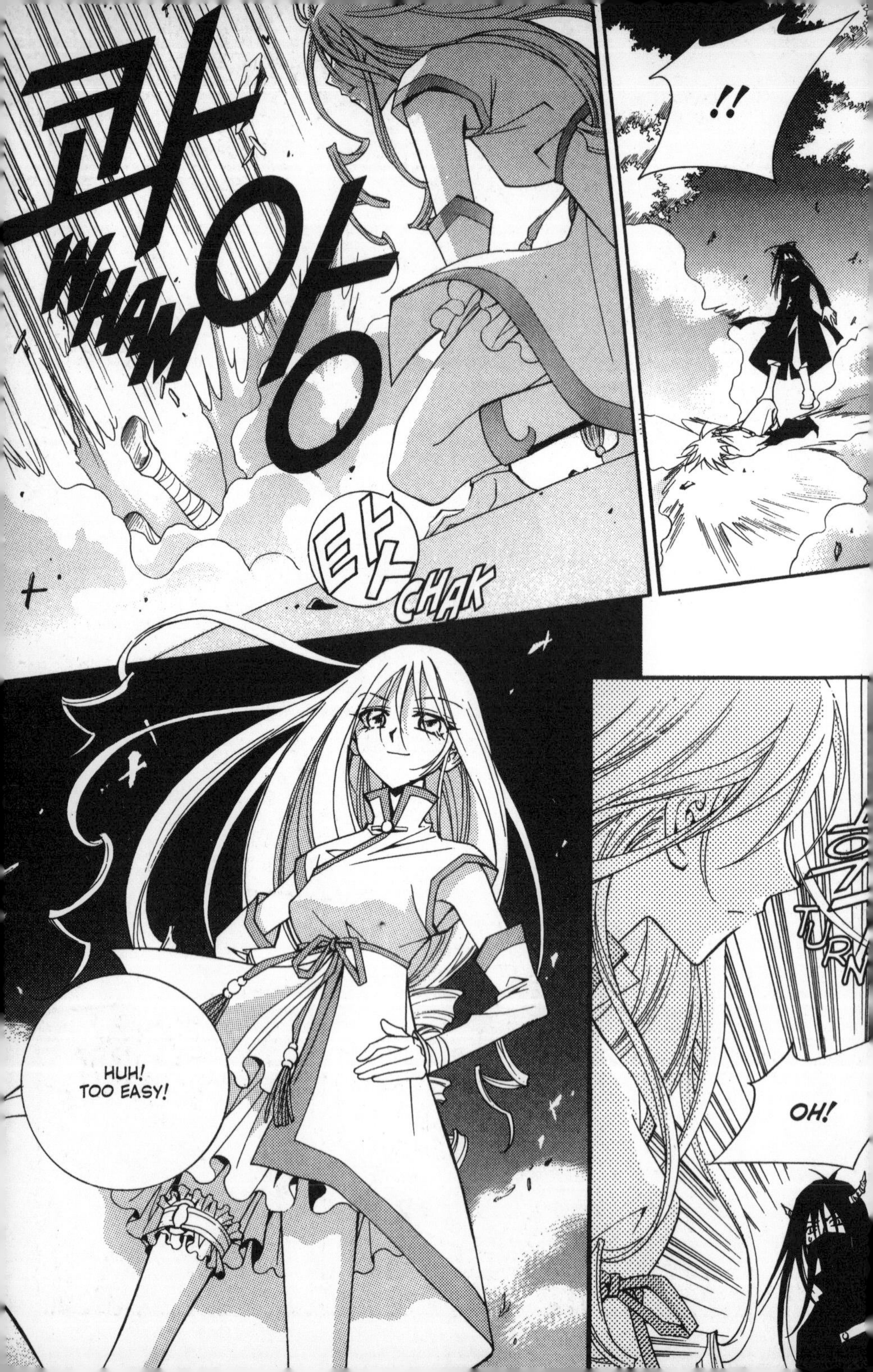
콰앙
WHAM
탁
CHAK
!!
HUH! TOO EASY!
TURN
OH!

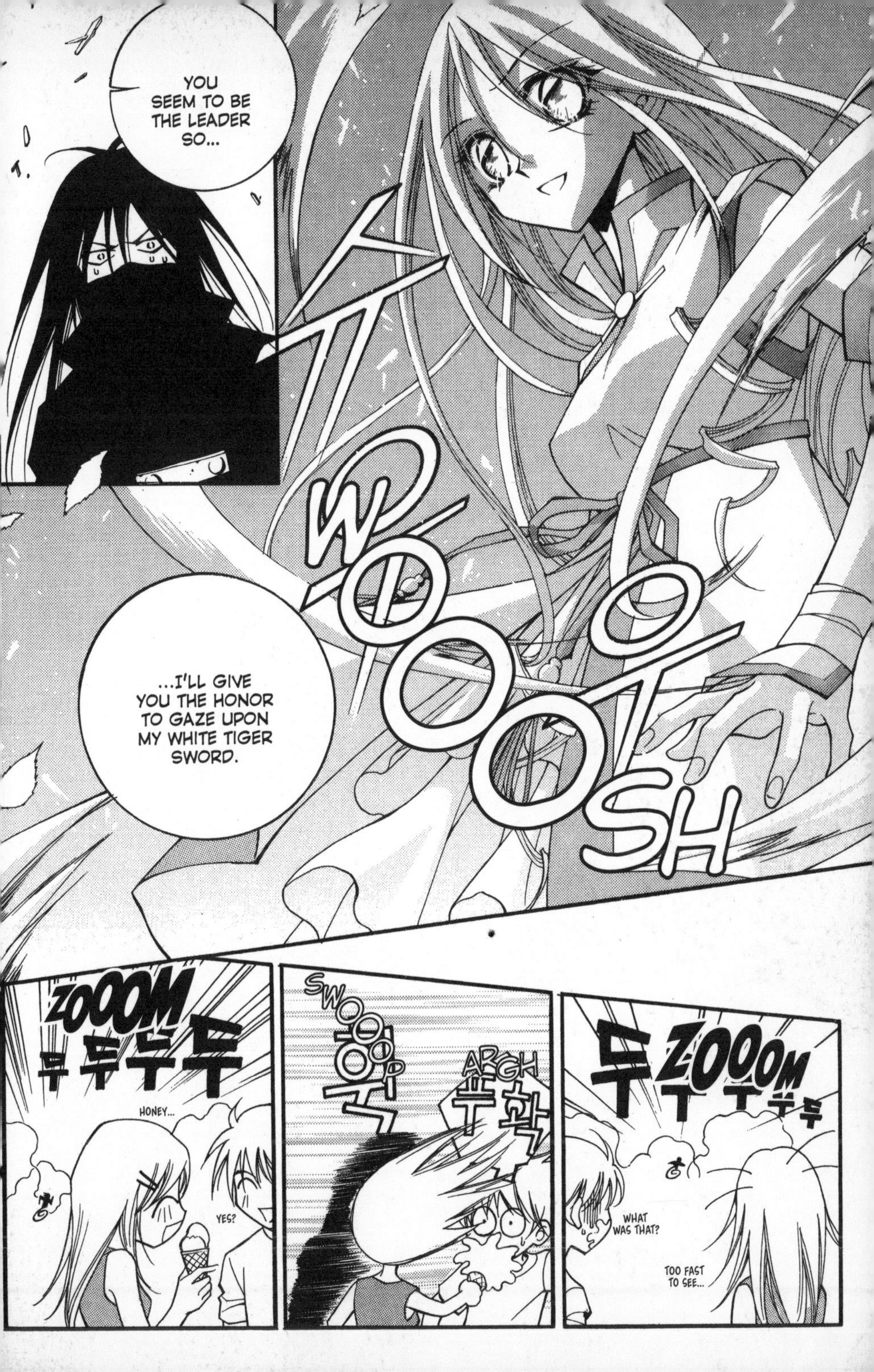
YOU SEEM TO BE THE LEADER SO...
...I'LL GIVE YOU THE HONOR TO GAZE UPON MY WHITE TIGER SWORD.
WOOOOOSH
ZOOOM
두두두두
HONEY...
YES?
SWOOOOP
ARGH
ZOOOM
WHAT WAS THAT?
TOO FAST TO SEE...

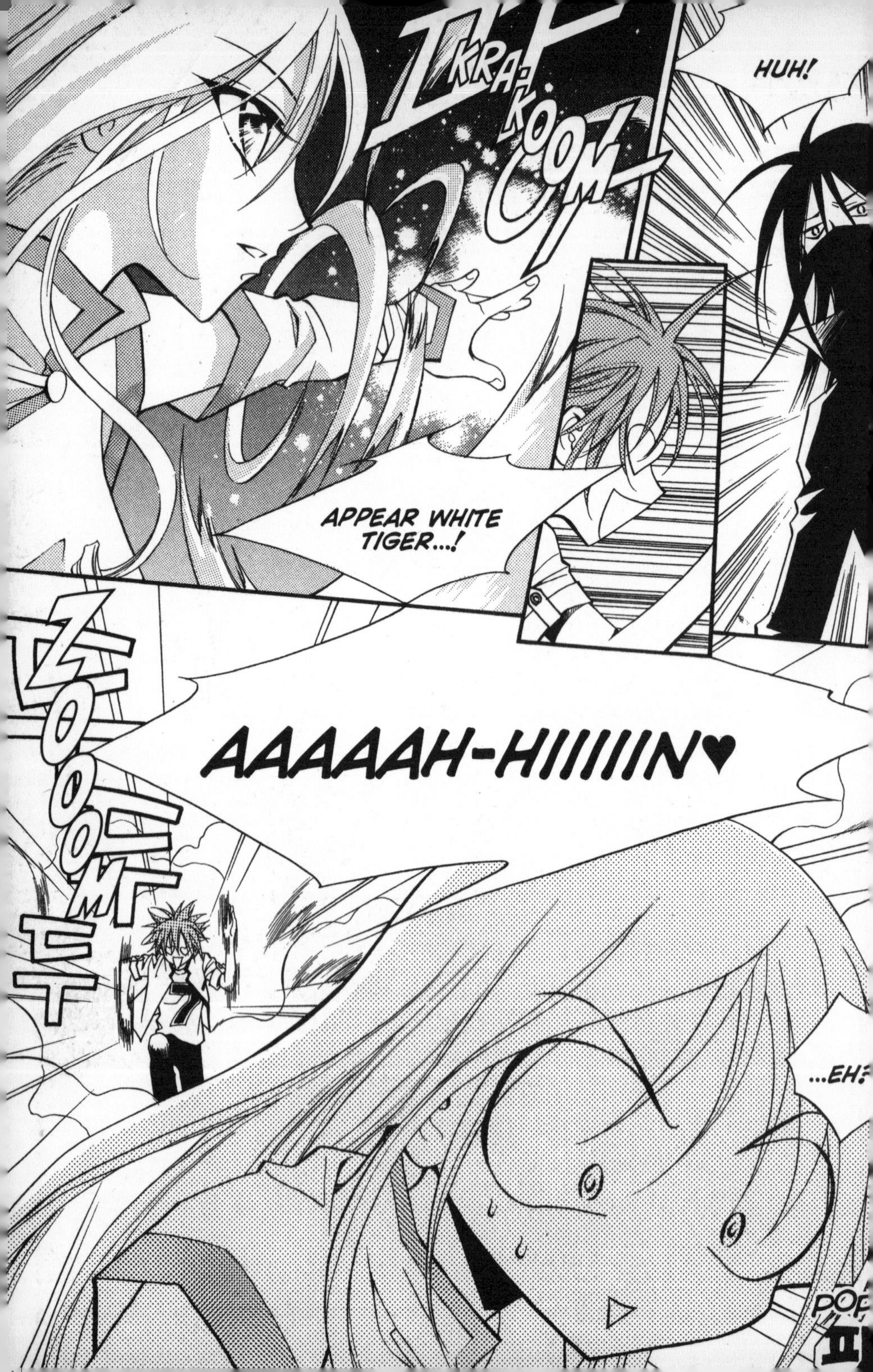
KRA-KOOM
HUH!
APPEAR WHITE TIGER...!
ZOOOOM
AAAAAH-HIIIIIN♥
...EH?
POP

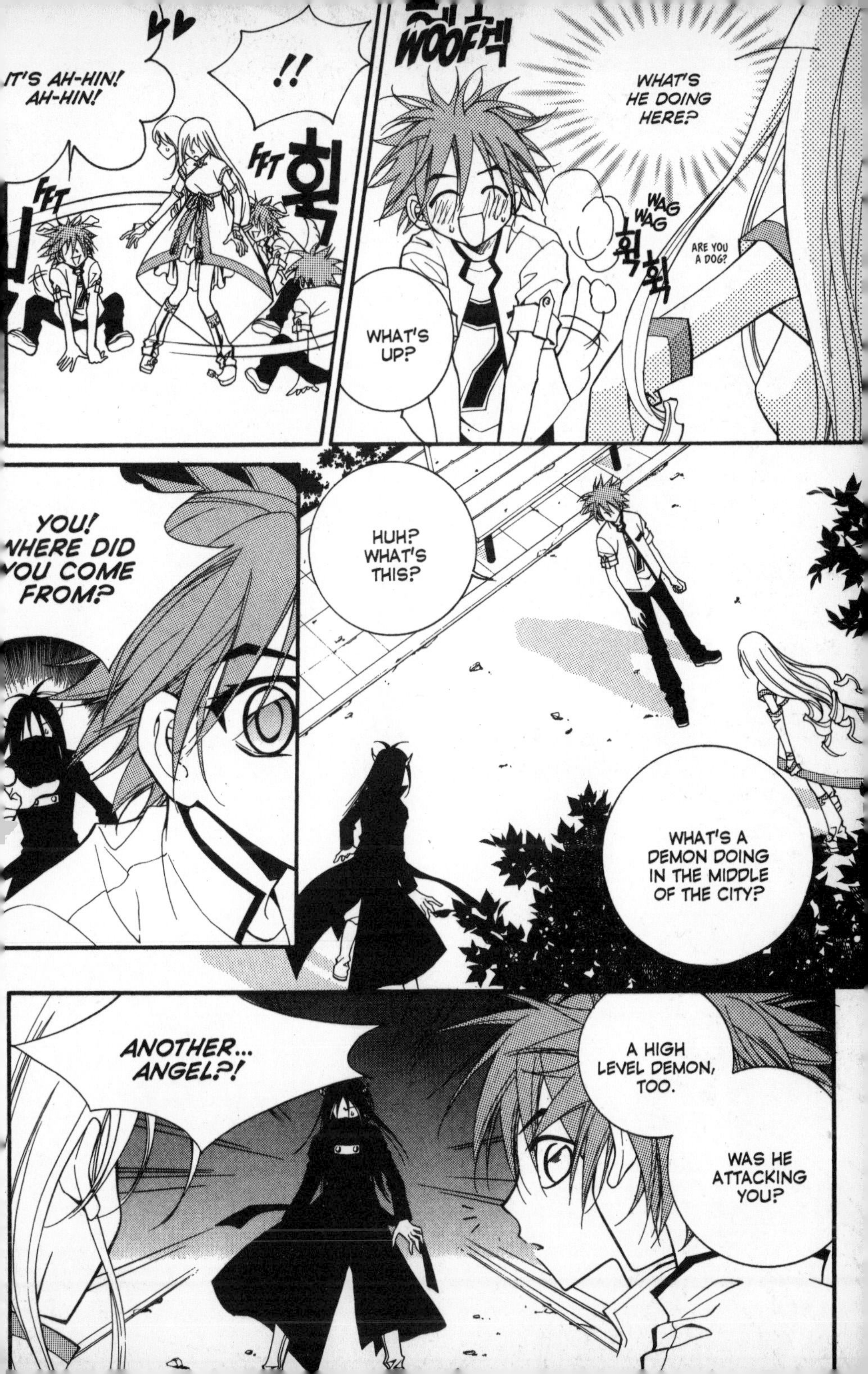
IT'S AH-HIN! AH-HIN!
!!
FFT
FFT 휙
WOOF
WHAT'S HE DOING HERE?
WHAT'S UP?
WAG WAG
휙휙
ARE YOU A DOG?
YOU! WHERE DID YOU COME FROM?
HUH? WHAT'S THIS?
WHAT'S A DEMON DOING IN THE MIDDLE OF THE CITY?
ANOTHER... ANGEL?!
A HIGH LEVEL DEMON, TOO.
WAS HE ATTACKING YOU?

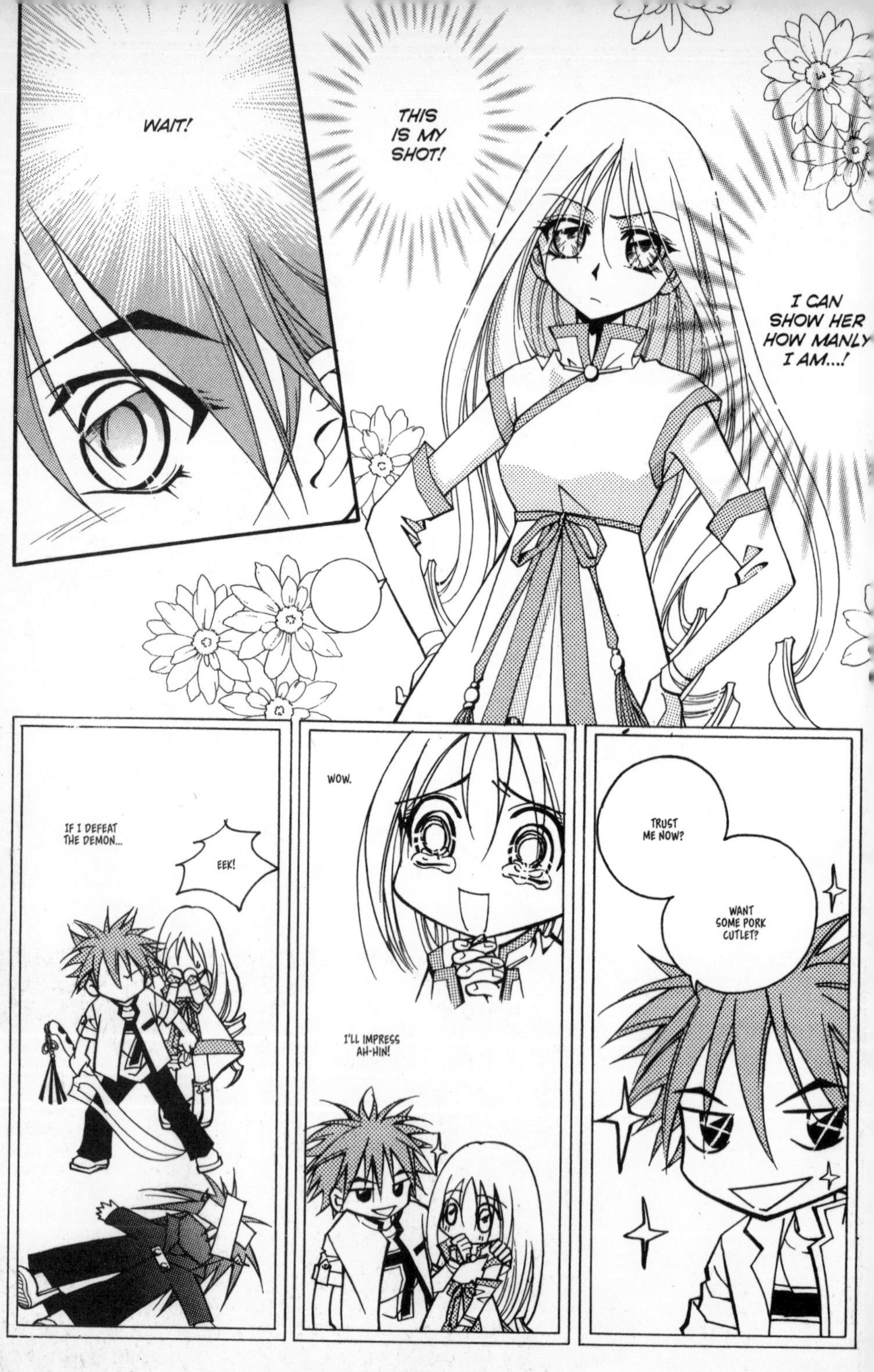
WAIT!
THIS IS MY SHOT!
I CAN SHOW HER HOW MANLY I AM...!
IF I DEFEAT THE DEMON...
EEK!
WOW.
I'LL IMPRESS AH-HIN!
TRUST ME NOW?
WANT SOME PORK CUTLET?

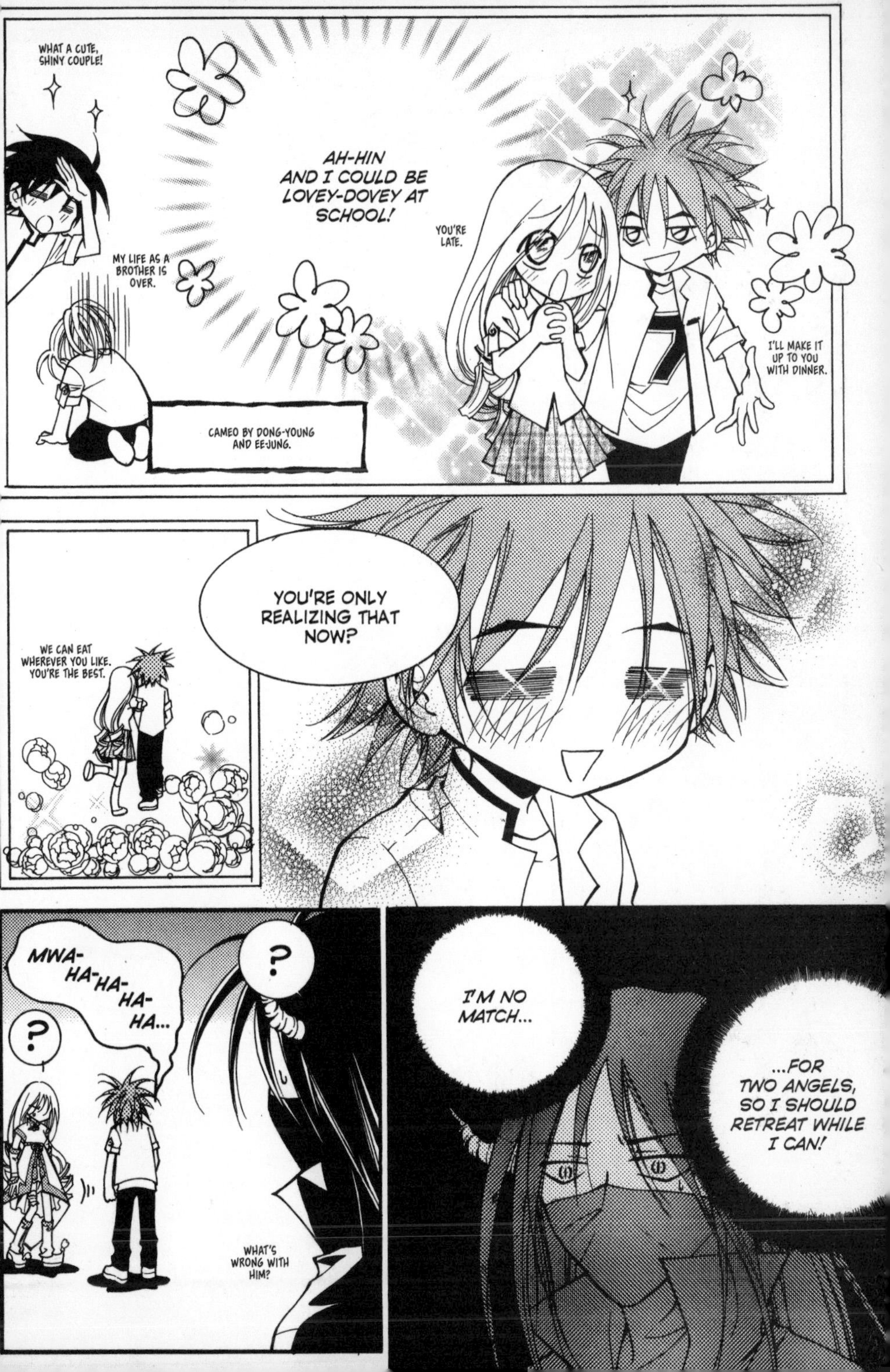
WHAT A CUTE, SHINY COUPLE!
AH-HIN AND I COULD BE LOVEY-DOVEY AT SCHOOL!
YOU'RE LATE.
MY LIFE AS A BROTHER IS OVER.
I'LL MAKE IT UP TO YOU WITH DINNER.
CAMEO BY DONG-YOUNG AND EE-JUNG.
WE CAN EAT WHEREVER YOU LIKE. YOU'RE THE BEST.
YOU'RE ONLY REALIZING THAT NOW?
MWA-HA-HA-HA-HA...
?
?
WHAT'S WRONG WITH HIM?
I'M NO MATCH...
...FOR TWO ANGELS, SO I SHOULD RETREAT WHILE I CAN!

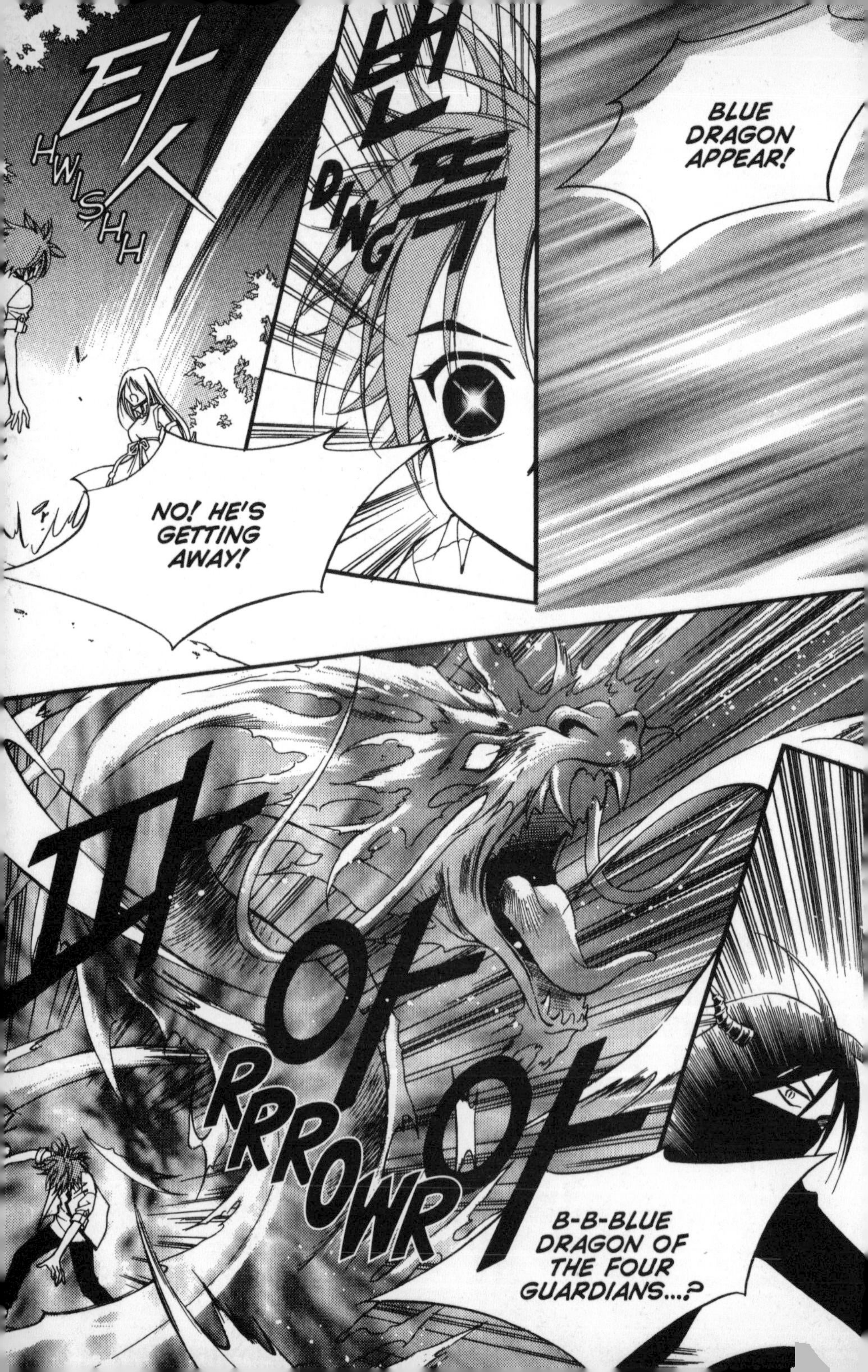
HWISHH
NO! HE'S GETTING AWAY!
DING
BLUE DRAGON APPEAR!
RRROWR
B-B-BLUE DRAGON OF THE FOUR GUARDIANS...?

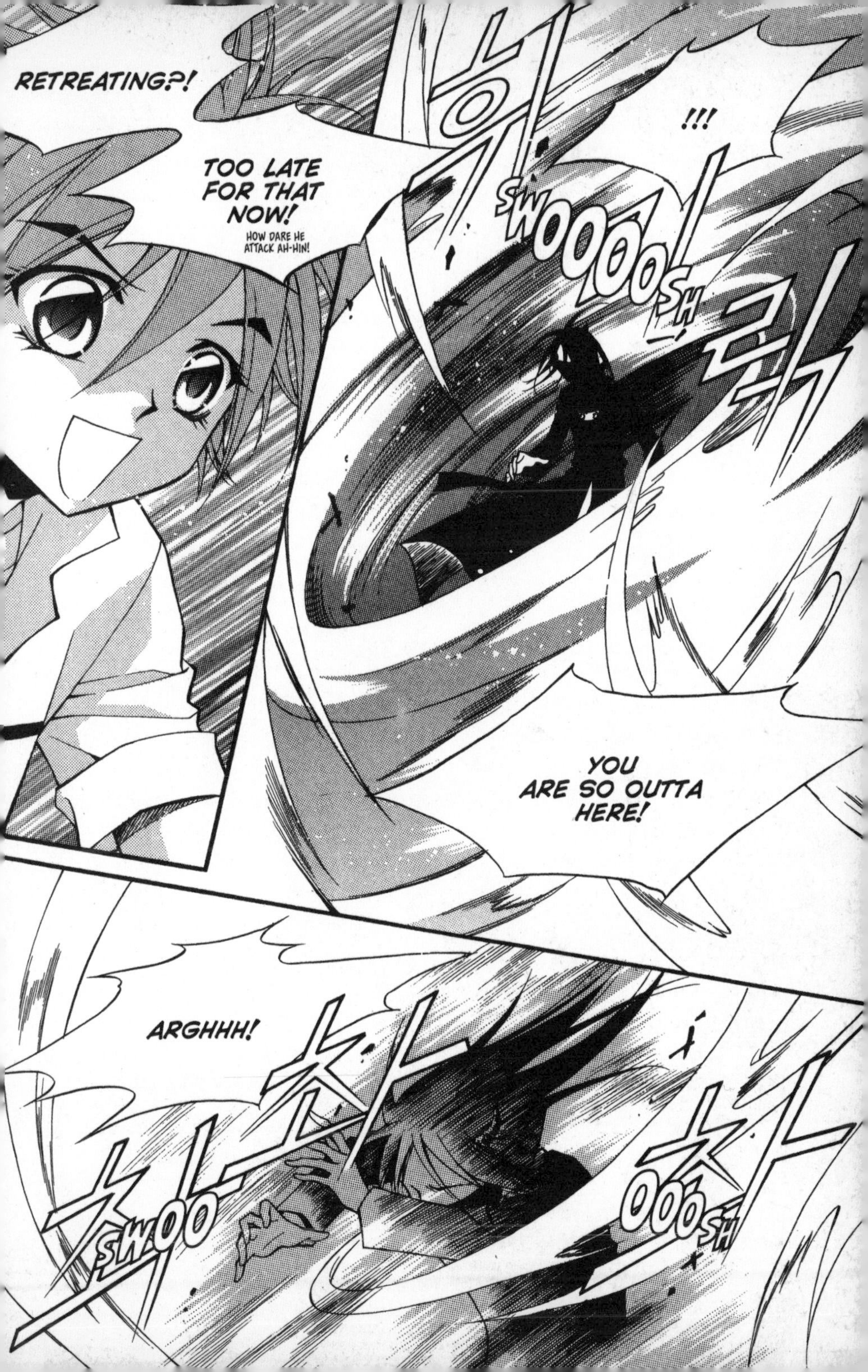

RETREATING?!
TOO LATE FOR THAT NOW!
HOW DARE HE ATTACK AH-HIN!
!!!
SWOOOOOSH
YOU ARE SO OUTTA HERE!
ARGHHH!
SWOOOOOSH

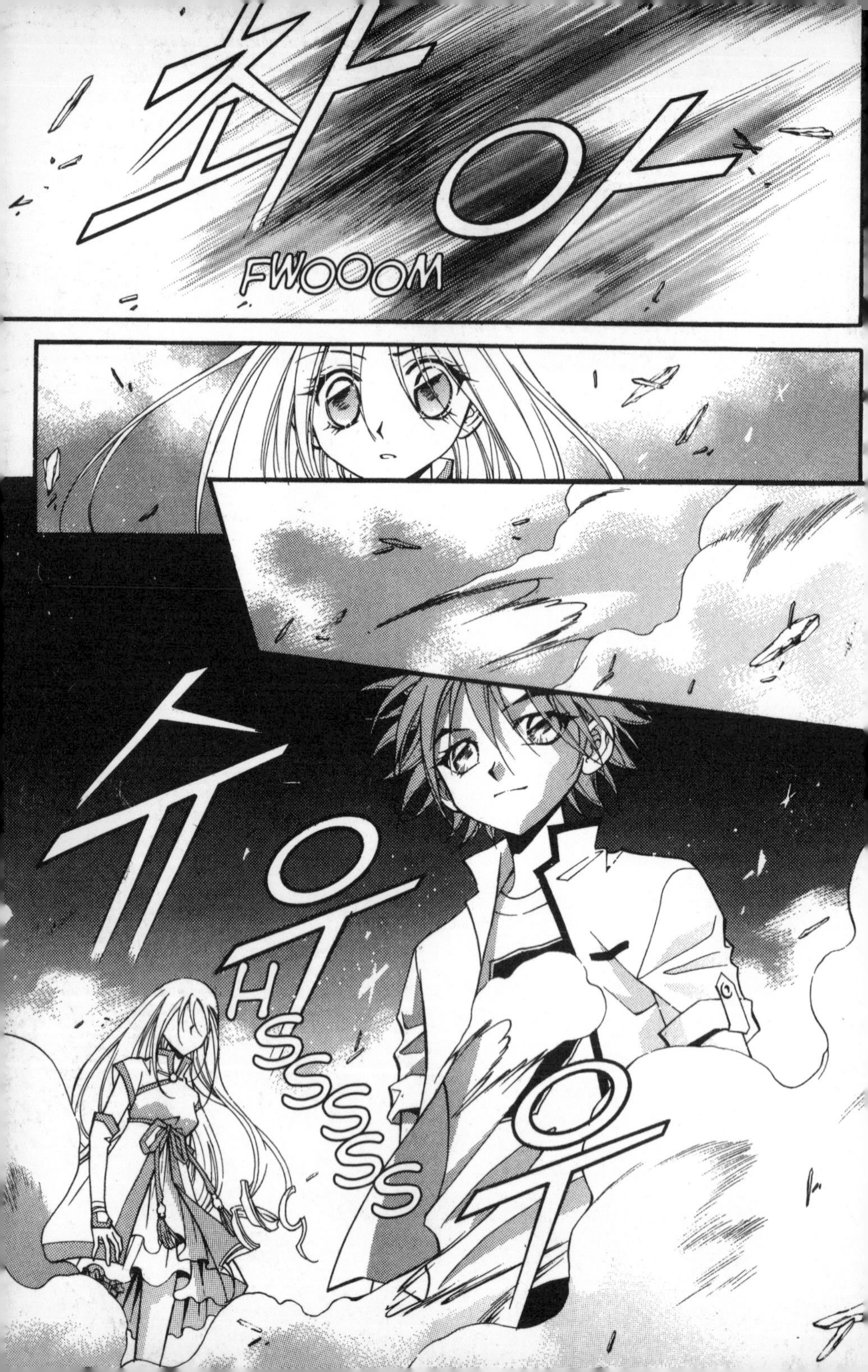
촤아
FWOOOM
슈우우
HSSSSSS

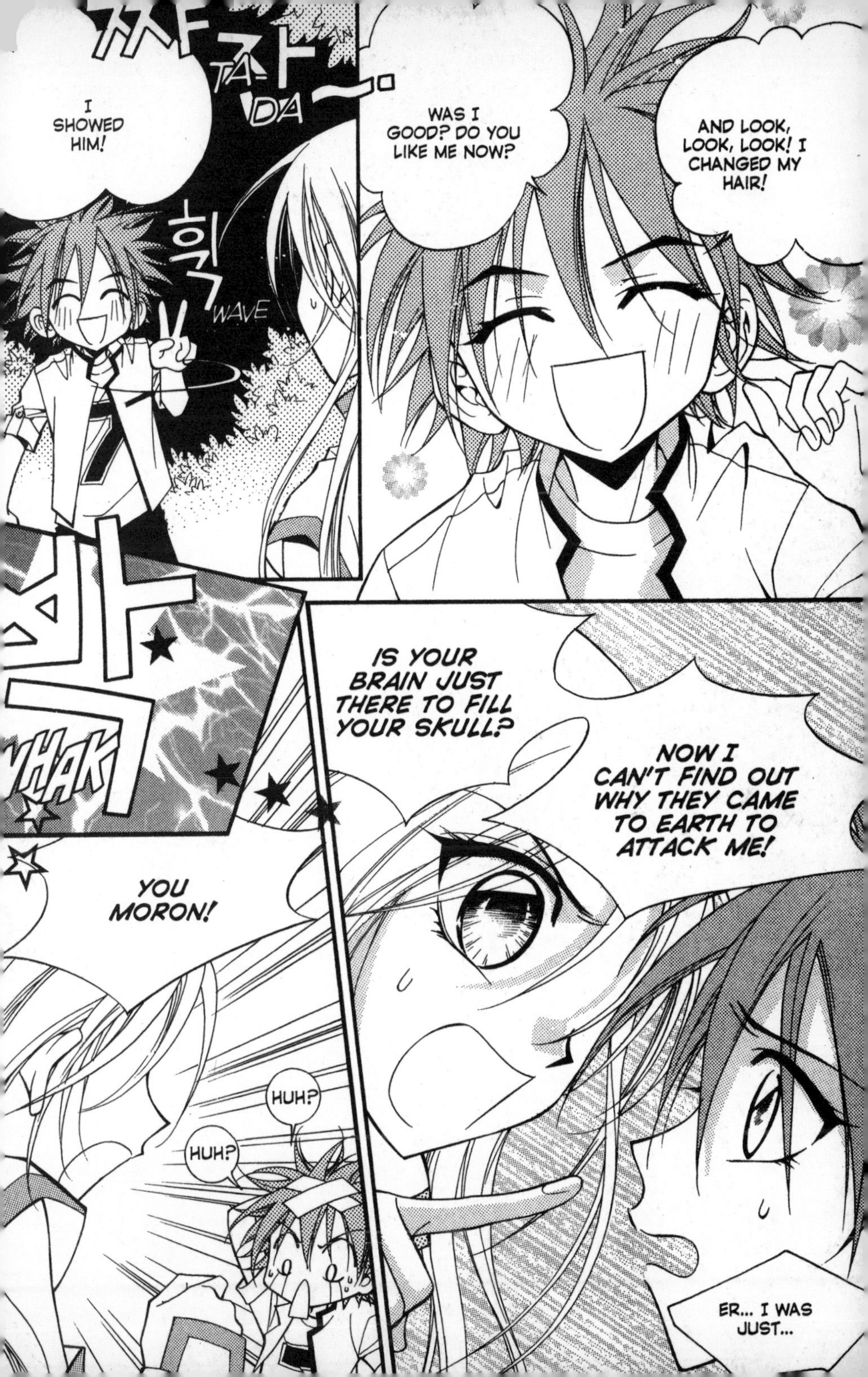
I SHOWED HIM!
TA-DA
WAVE
WAS I GOOD? DO YOU LIKE ME NOW?
AND LOOK, LOOK, LOOK! I CHANGED MY HAIR!
WHAK
YOU MORON!
HUH?
HUH?
IS YOUR BRAIN JUST THERE TO FILL YOUR SKULL?
NOW I CAN'T FIND OUT WHY THEY CAME TO EARTH TO ATTACK ME!
ER... I WAS JUST...

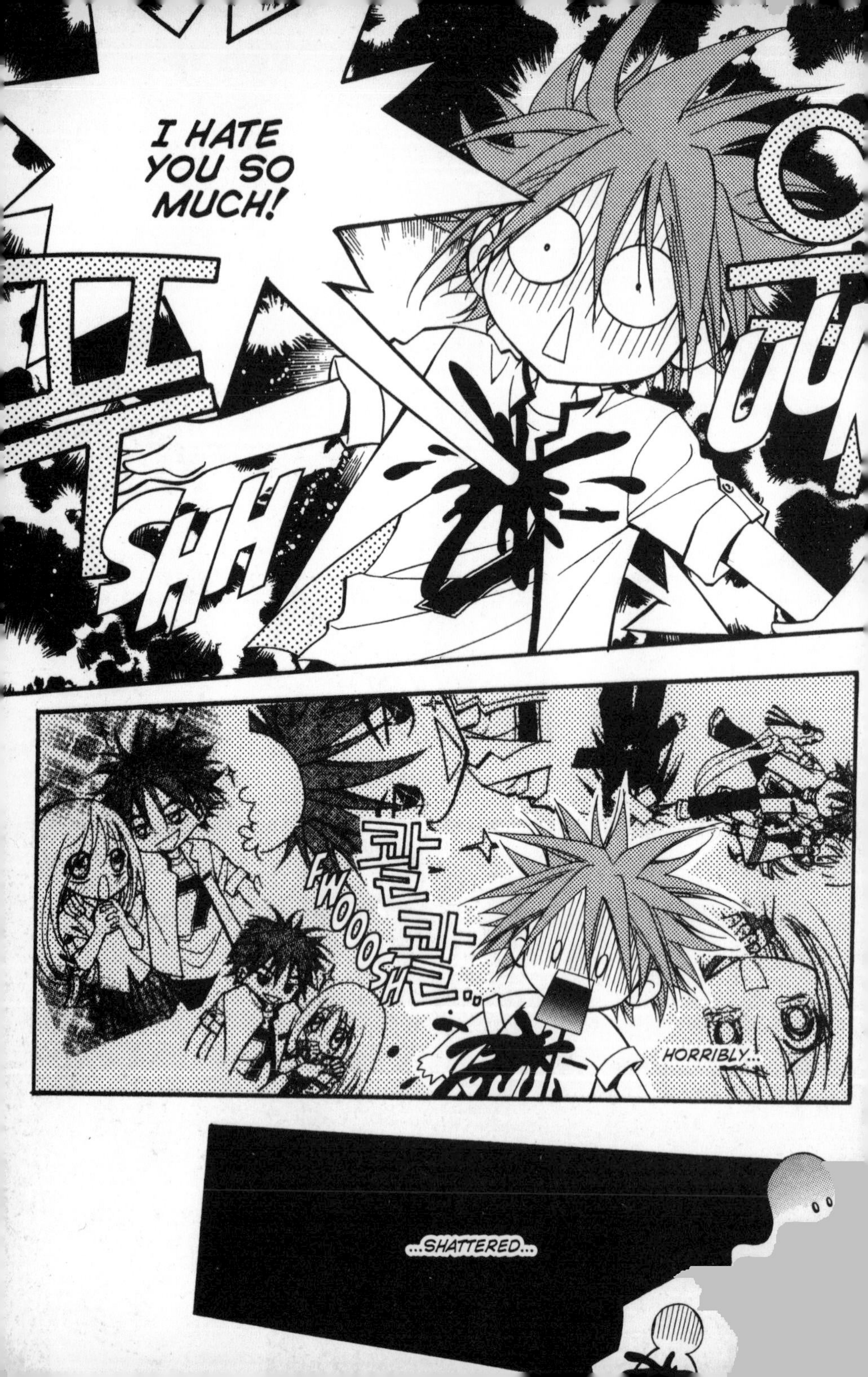
I HATE YOU SO MUCH!
SHH
FWOOOSH
HORRIBLY...
...SHATTERED...

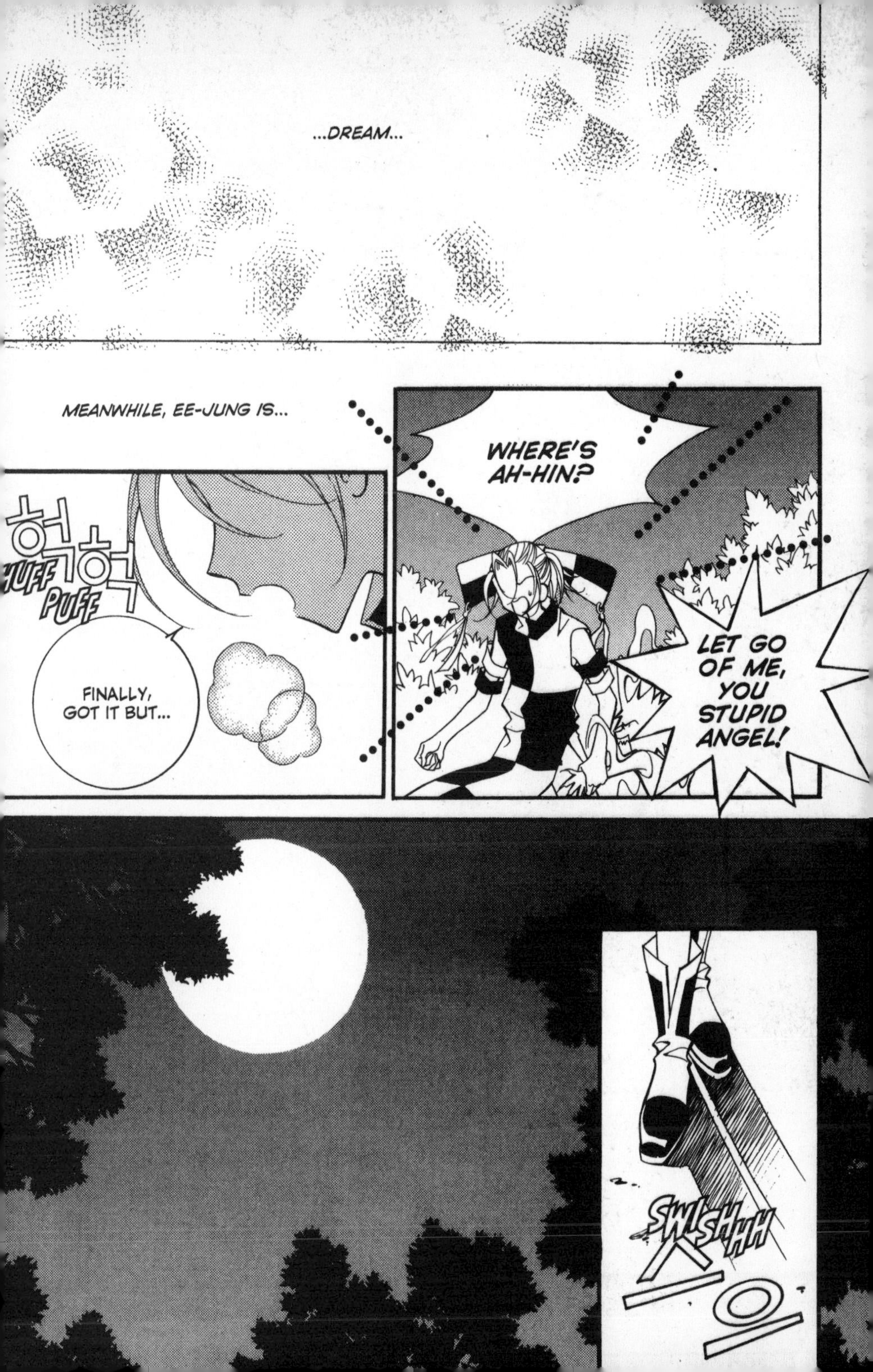
...DREAM...
MEANWHILE, EE-JUNG IS...
헉헉
HUFF PUFF
FINALLY, GOT IT BUT...
WHERE'S AH-HIN?
LET GO OF ME, YOU STUPID ANGEL!
SWISHHH

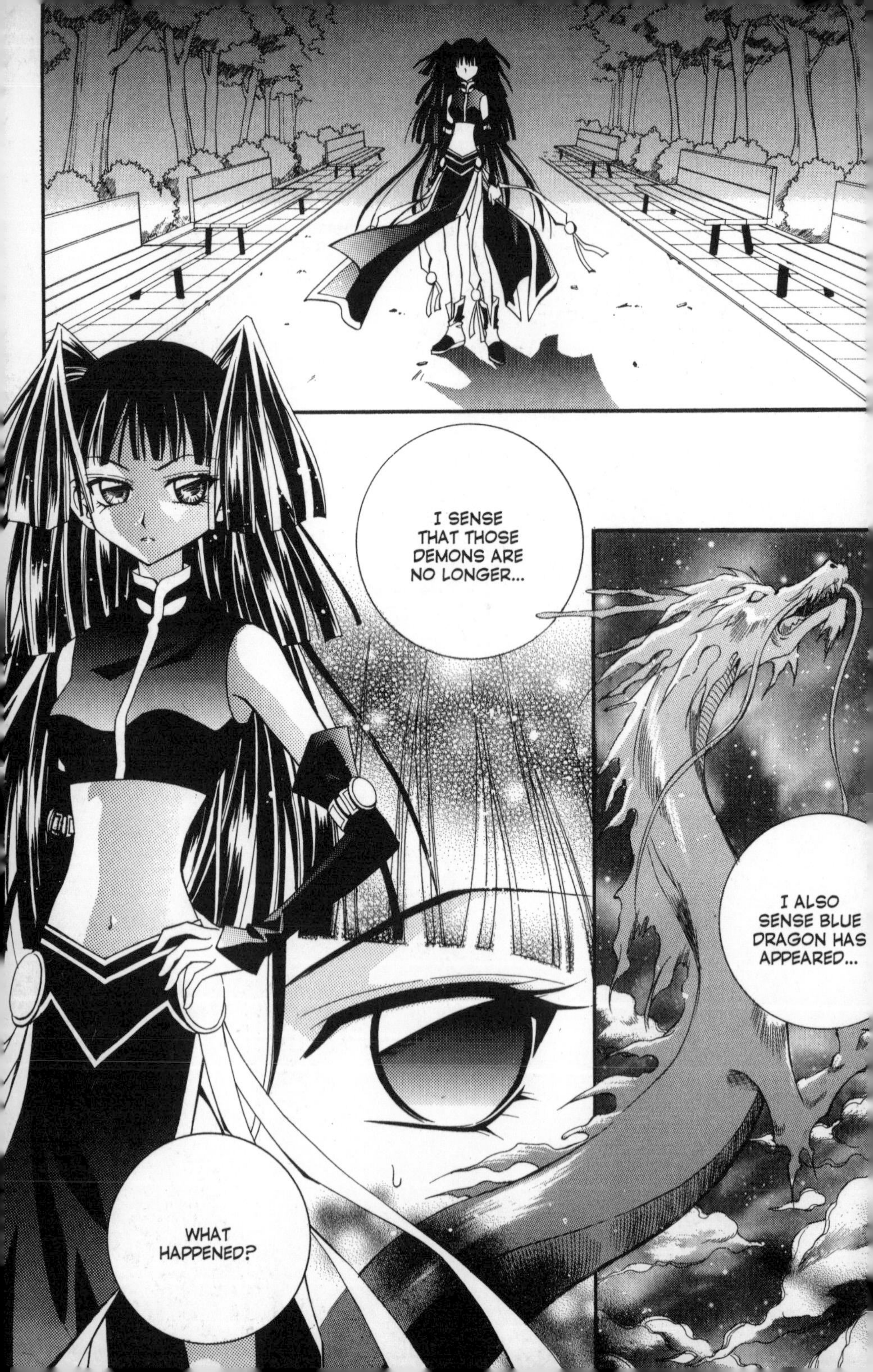
I SENSE THAT THOSE DEMONS ARE NO LONGER...
I ALSO SENSE BLUE DRAGON HAS APPEARED...
WHAT HAPPENED?

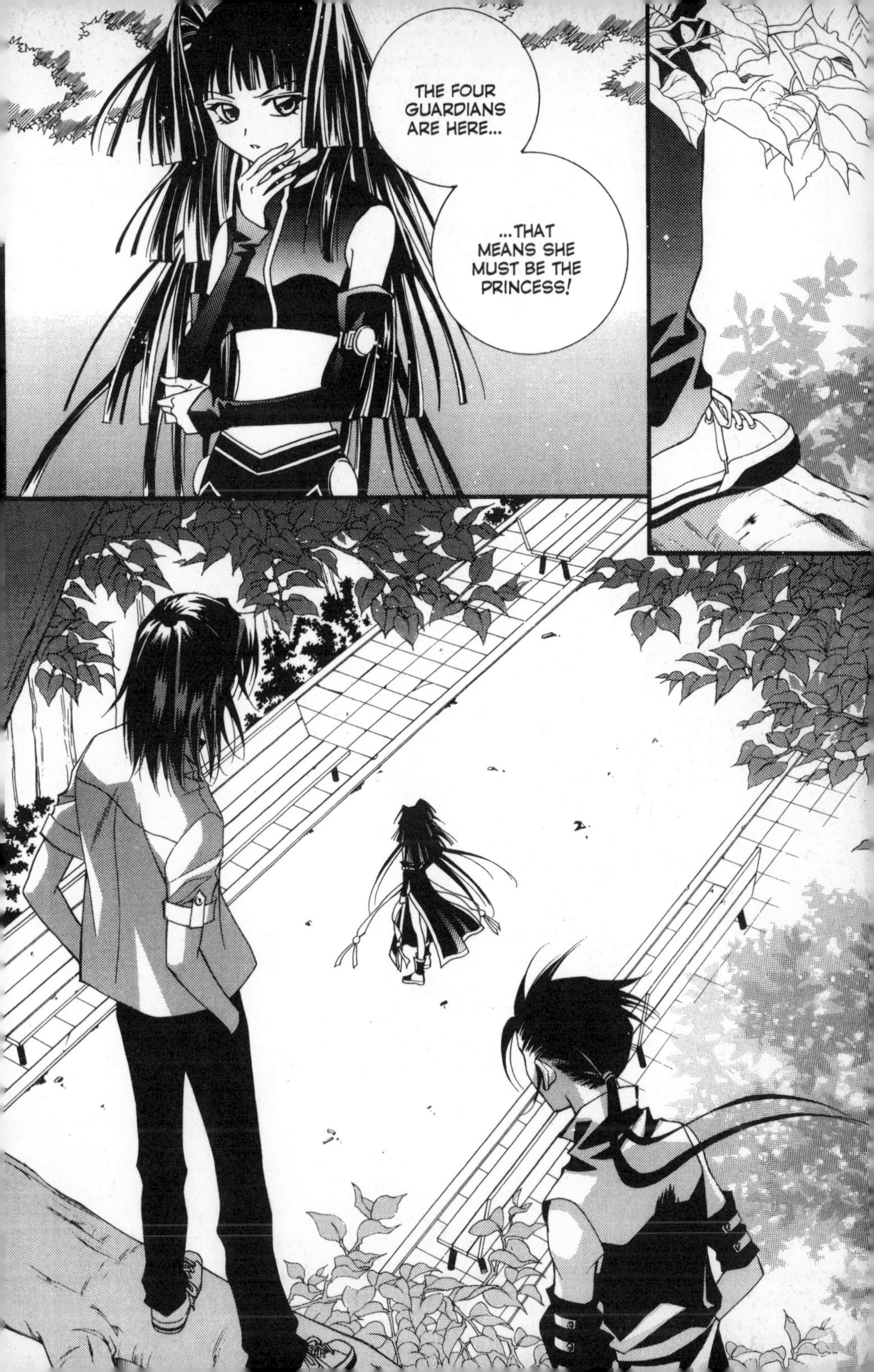
THE FOUR GUARDIANS ARE HERE...
...THAT MEANS SHE MUST BE THE PRINCESS!

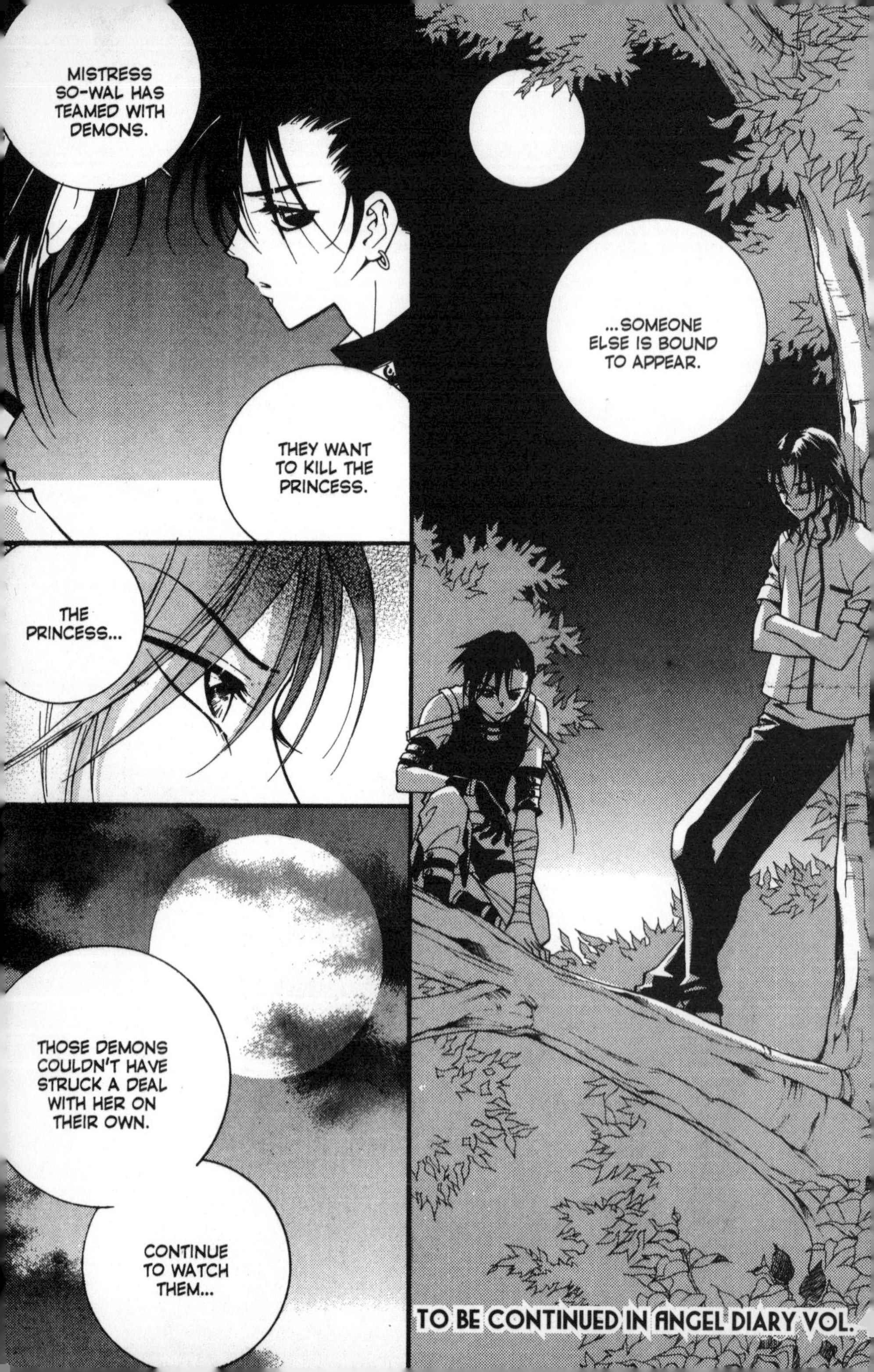
MISTRESS SO-WAL HAS TEAMED WITH DEMONS.
THEY WANT TO KILL THE PRINCESS.
THE PRINCESS...
THOSE DEMONS COULDN'T HAVE STRUCK A DEAL WITH HER ON THEIR OWN.
CONTINUE TO WATCH THEM...
...SOMEONE ELSE IS BOUND TO APPEAR.
TO BE CONTINUED IN ANGEL DIARY VOL.

THE COSMOLOGY OF "ANGEL DIARY"

WHICH MAKES "ANGEL DIARY" MORE INTERESTING

THE SYSTEM OF HEAVEN, EARTH AND HELL

ALL LIVING THINGS ON EARTH EVENTUALLY DIE. THEIR SPIRITS WILL THEN GO TO HELL WHERE THEIR KARMA WILL BE CLEANSED. IF A SPIRIT IS PARTICULARLY BAD, IT WILL TAKE A LONG TIME TO CLEANSE. ONCE A SPIRIT IS CLEANSED, IT ASCENDS TO HEAVEN. THERE THE SPIRIT RESTS FOR A TIME UNTIL IT IS BORN AGAIN AS A HUMAN ON EARTH. THIS IS THE BALANCE MAINTAINED BY HEAVEN, EARTH AND HELL.

BOTH HEAVEN AND HELL AFFECT EARTH. POWER STRUGGLES BETWEEN HEAVEN AND HELL HAVE DAMAGED BOTH SIDES AS WELL. BUT THE TWO REALMS EVENTUALLY SIGNED A "PEACE TREATY" AND THIS PACT WAS TO BE FURTHER SEALED BY AN ARRANGED MARRIAGE BETWEEN HEAVEN AND HELL.

"ANGEL DIARY" IS THE STORY OF THE RUNAWAY PRINCESS OF HEAVEN WHO REFUSED THIS ARRANGED MARRIAGE.

THE STORY OF HEAVEN

CHUN-JAE IS THE KING OF HEAVEN AND HE RULES WITH ABSOLUTE POWER. CHUN-JAE HAS THE RIGHT TO HAVE SEVERAL WIVES BUT CURRENTLY ONLY HAS ONE, QUEEN HONG. HE HAD THREE PREVIOUS WIVES BUT THEY ALL PASSED AWAY BEFORE HE MARRIED THE CURRENT QUEEN.

CHUN-JAE IS A FATHER TO SIX PRINCES AND THREE PRINCESSES. THE PRINCES AND THE PRINCESSES ARE NOT THE CHILDREN OF QUEEN HONG BUT THEY ARE VERY CLOSE TO HER. TWO OF THE PRINCESSES ARE MARRIED SO CHUN-YOO (DONG-YOUNG'S PROPER NAME) WAS BETROTHED TO THE KING OF HELL AS A PART OF THE PEACE TREATY.

THE FOUR GUARDIANS ARE ANGELS WHO PROTECT THE FOUR CARDINAL POINTS OF HEAVEN AND THERE ARE FOUR ANGEL GENERALS WHO CONTROL SPRING, SUMMER, FALL AND WINTER. THESE ANGELS WIELD SWORDS (WHICH EVEN CIVIL OFFICIALS CAN USE) AND ONE YEAR TO THEM IS EQUIVALENT TO TEN HUMAN YEARS.

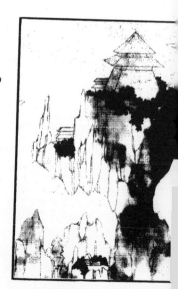

THE STORY OF HELL

THE PEOPLE OF HELL DO NOT ACKNOWLEDGE THE ENGAGEMENT BETWEEN THEIR KING AND THE PRINCESS OF HEAVEN BECAUSE OF BAD HISTORY BETWEEN THEM.

THE KING OF HELL DOES NOT REVEAL HIMSELF VERY OFTEN SO NOT MUCH IS KNOWN ABOUT HIM, BUT THERE ARE MANY RUMORS SURROUNDING HIM.

JUCK-WAL, CHUNG-WAL, BAECK-WAL, AND HUK-WAL ARE THE NAME OF THE FAMILIES THAT PROTECT THE FOUR CARDINAL CORNERS OF HELL. NOBLE FAMILIES LIKE SO-WAL, DAE-WAL, JIN-WAL, AND MOO-WAL PROTECT THE CENTER. ALL OF THESE FAMILIES HAVE "WAL" (MEANING "MOON") IN THEIR NAMES BECAUSE THEY HONOR THE MOON.

THESE FAMILIES AFFECT THE POLITICS AND POWER STRUGGLES IN HELL BUT THE KING IS THE ULTIMATE RULER.

UNLIKE IN HEAVEN, THE PEOPLE OF HELL EMPLOY SORCERY, ASTROLOGY AND PROPHECY.

DEMONS

DEMONS ARE BEINGS WHICH EXIST OUTSIDE OF THE SYSTEM OF HEAVEN, EARTH AND HELL. THEY ARE BORN FROM EVIL SPIRITS THAT EXERT THEIR OWN DARK WILL. THEY LIVE IN DARK PLACES ON EARTH AND ARE OFFICIALLY REJECTED BY BOTH HEAVEN AND HELL. HOWEVER, CERTAIN PARTIES FROM HELL EMPLOY THEM WHILE ANGELS TEND TO CONSIDER THEM THE MOST CORRUPT BEINGS IN THE WORLD.

THE FOUR GUARDIANS OF HEAVEN OFTEN STAY ON EARTH TO GET RID OF BAD SPIRITS BEFORE THEY BECOME DEMONS. FROM THIS ONE REALIZES THAT HEAVEN CONSIDERS DEMONS AS THEIR ENEMIES.

THERE ARE THREE DIFFERENT LEVELS OF DEMONS: HIGH, MIDDLE AND LOW LEVEL. AS THEIR LEVEL GOES UP, THEIR APPEARANCE BECOMES MORE AND MORE HUMAN. THEIR RELATIONSHIPS ARE GOVERNED BY POWER SO IF A DEMON IS WEAKER THAN ANOTHER, THEY MUST OBEY THE MORE POWERFUL DEMON.

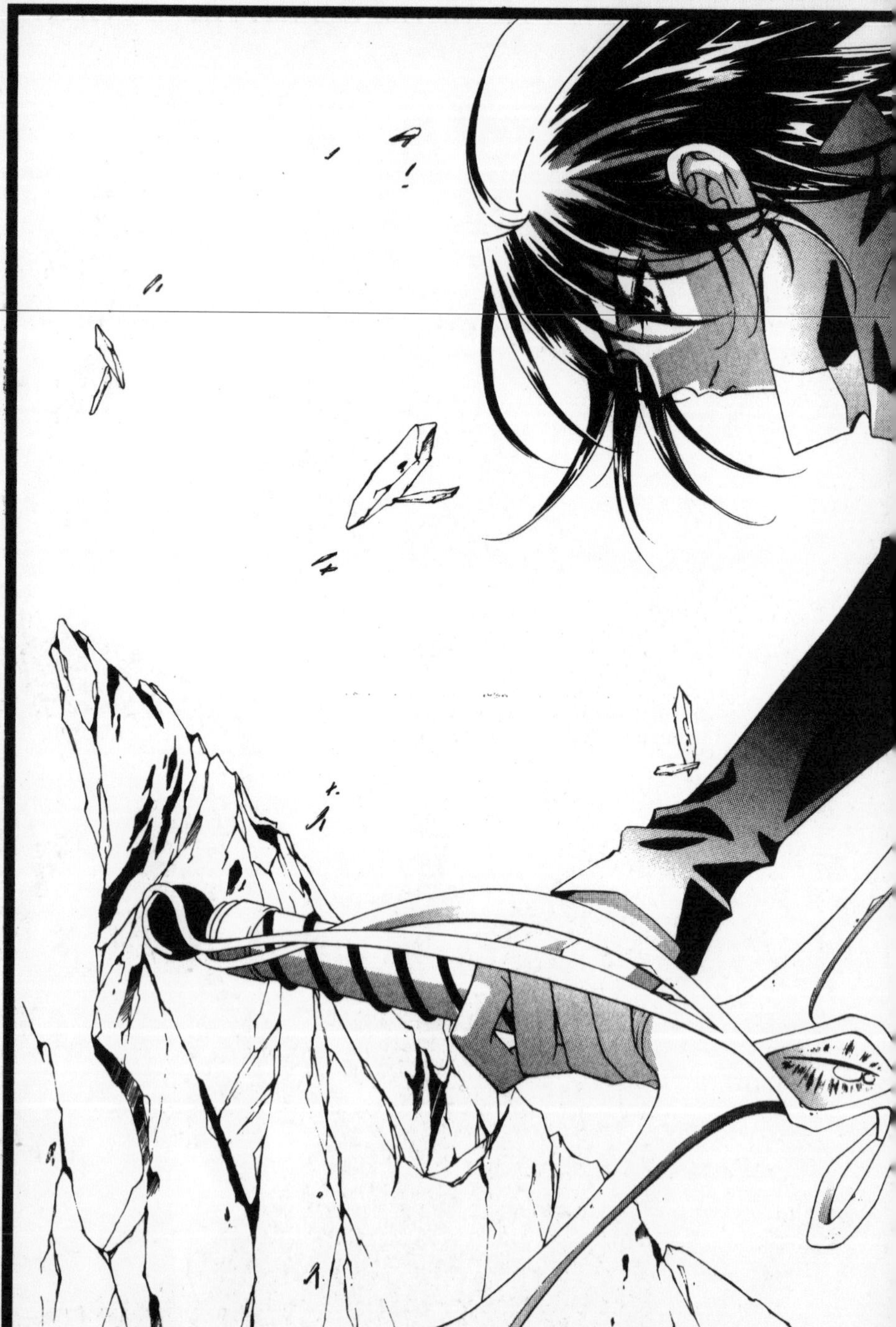

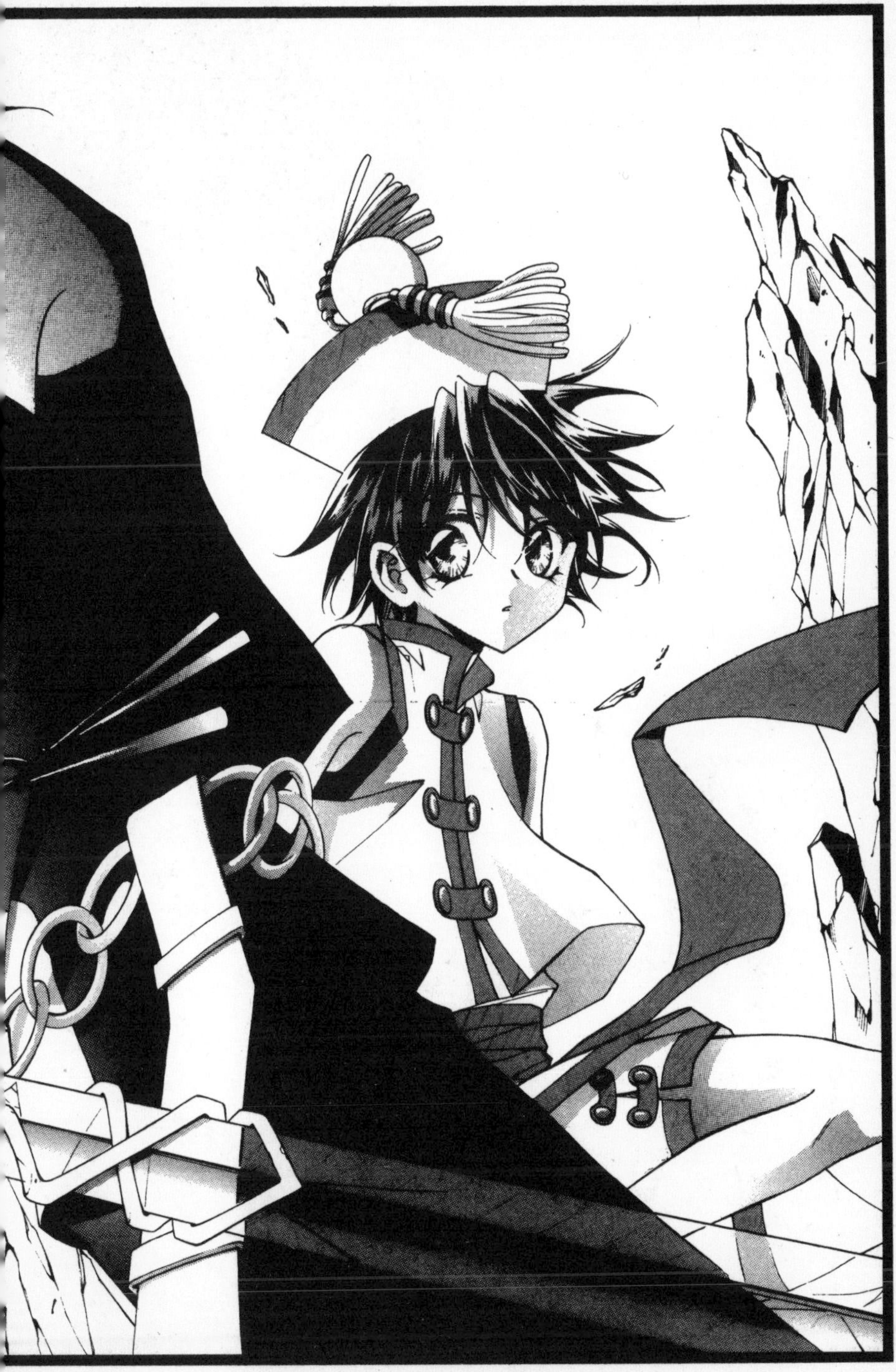

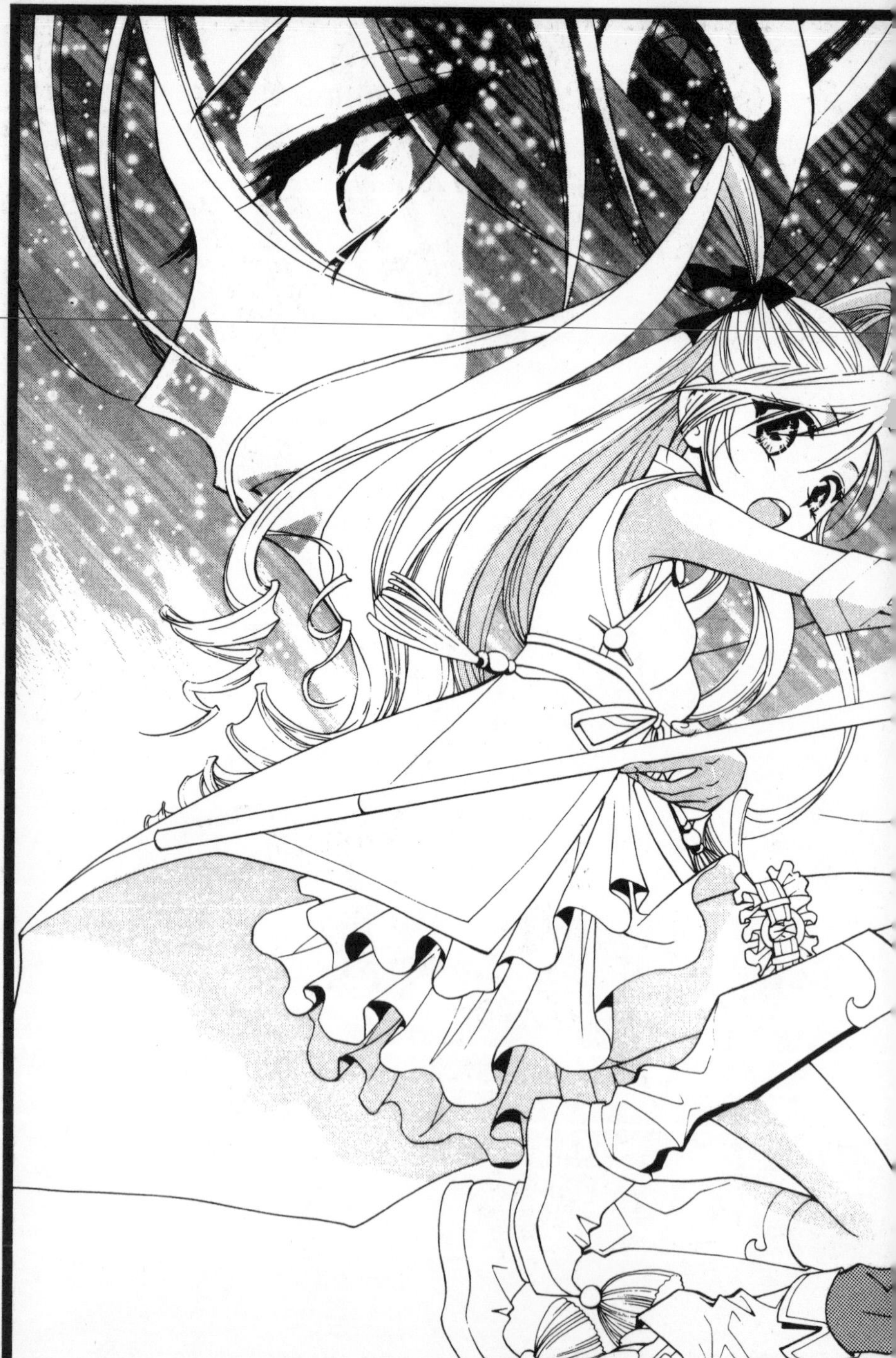

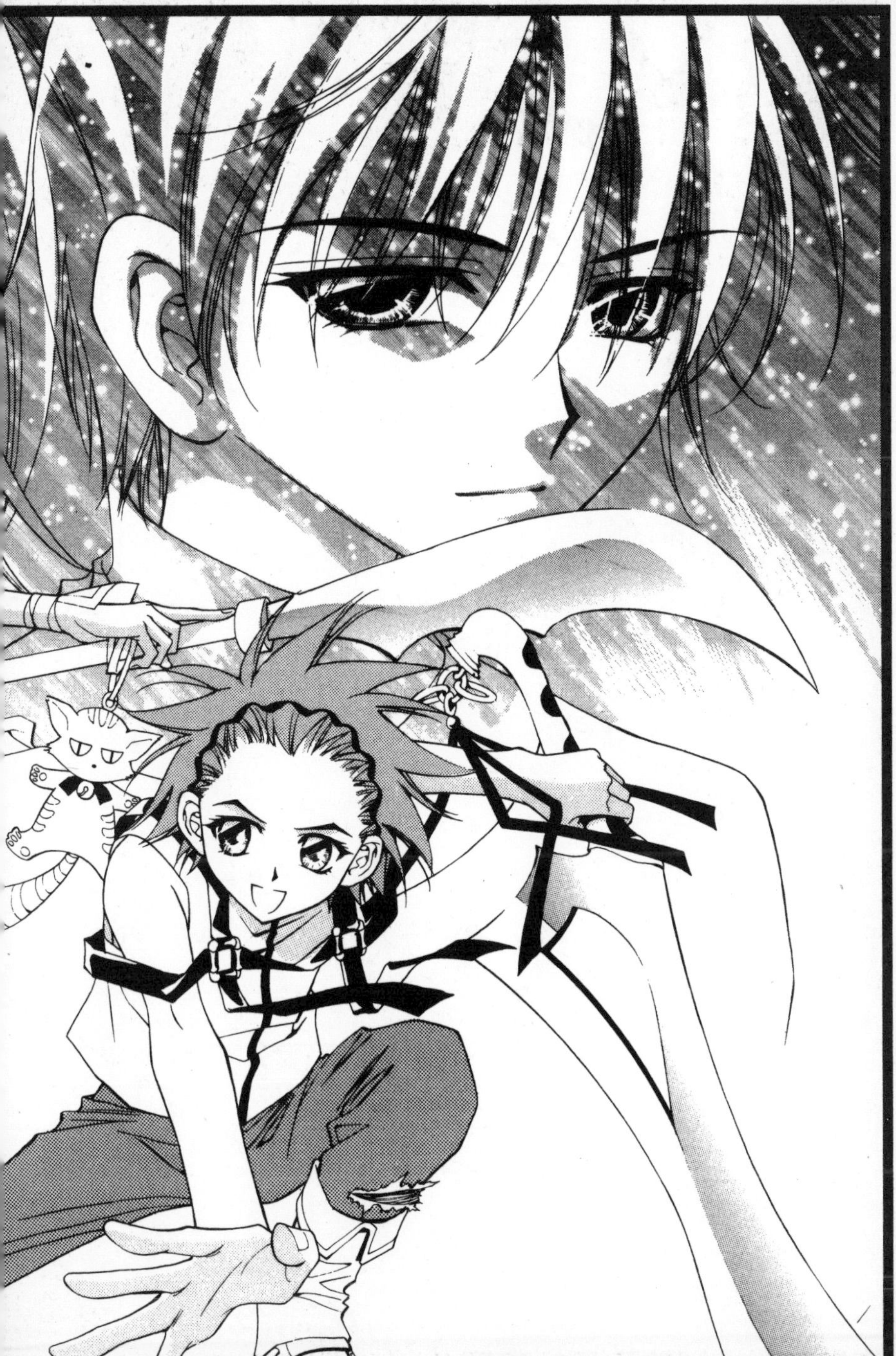

HISSING

vol.1

Kang EunYoung

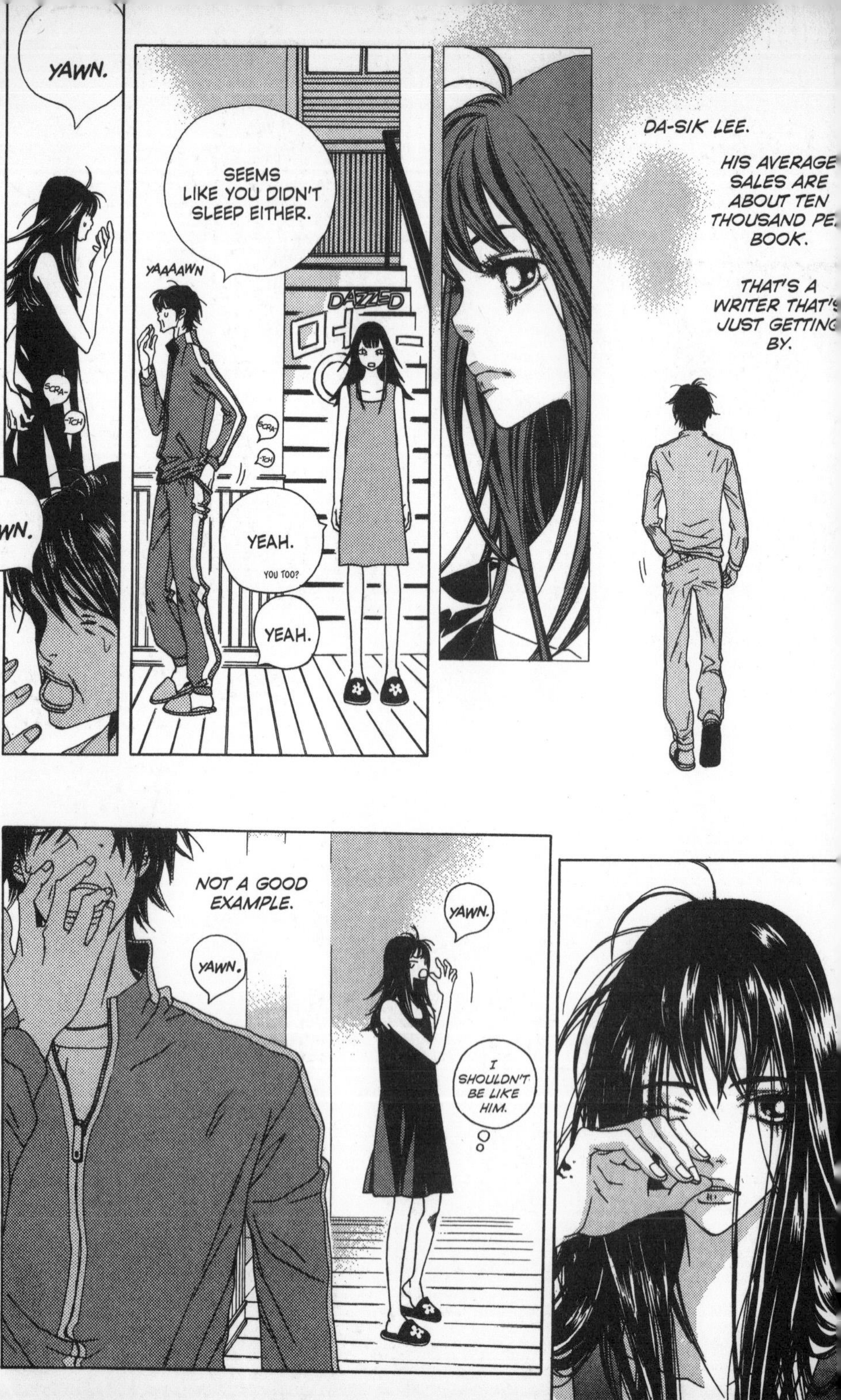
YAWN.
SCRA-TCH
YAWN.
SEEMS LIKE YOU DIDN'T SLEEP EITHER.
YAAAAWN
DAZZLED
SCRA-TCH
YEAH.
YOU TOO?
YEAH.
DA-SIK LEE.
HIS AVERAGE SALES ARE ABOUT TEN THOUSAND PE BOOK.
THAT'S A WRITER THAT'S JUST GETTING BY.
NOT A GOOD EXAMPLE.
YAWN.
YAWN.
I SHOULDN'T BE LIKE HIM.

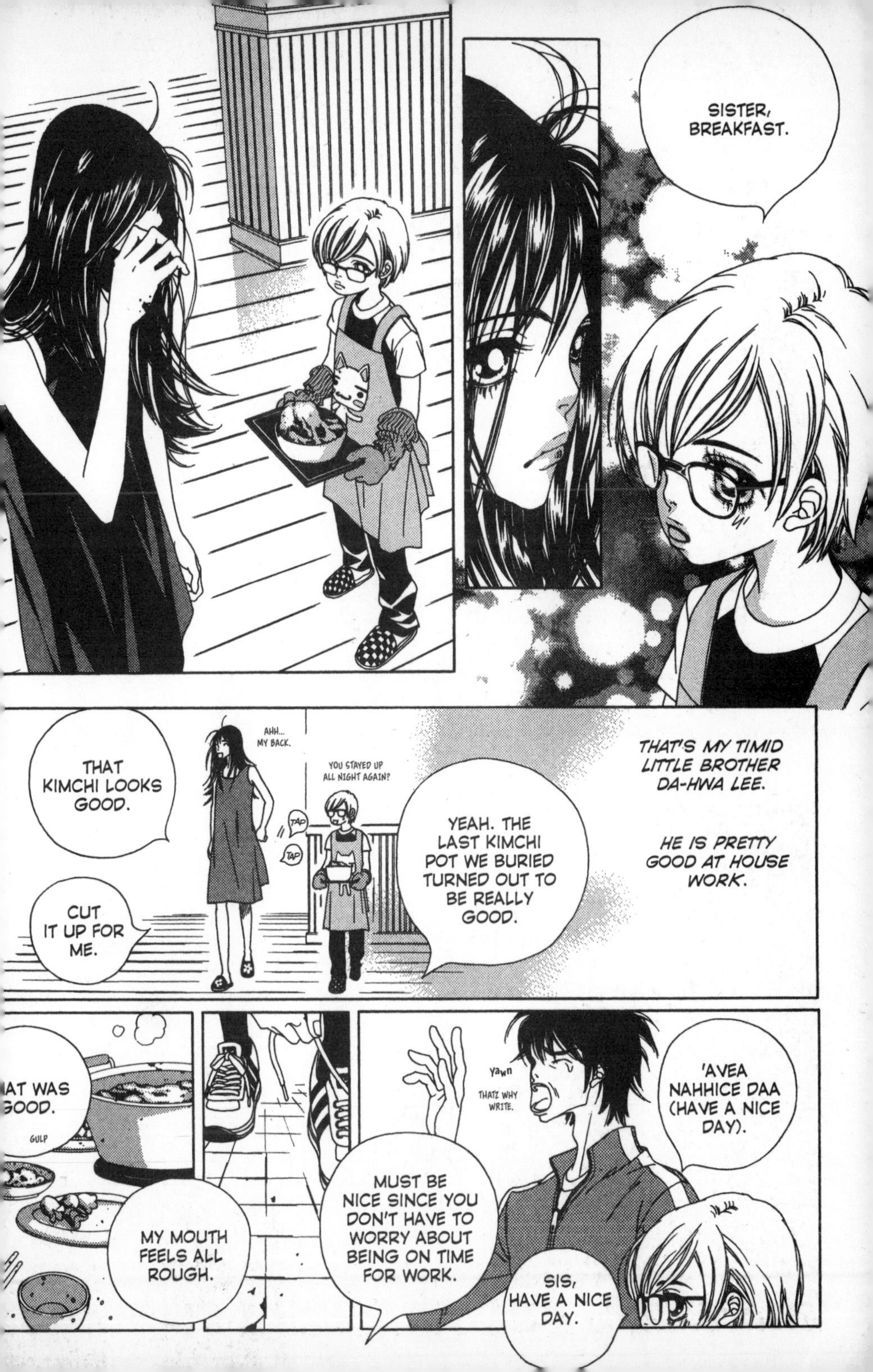
SISTER, BREAKFAST.
THAT KIMCHI LOOKS GOOD.
CUT IT UP FOR ME.
AHH... MY BACK.
YOU STAYED UP ALL NIGHT AGAIN?
TAP
TAP
YEAH. THE LAST KIMCHI POT WE BURIED TURNED OUT TO BE REALLY GOOD.
THAT'S MY TIMID LITTLE BROTHER DA-HWA LEE.
HE IS PRETTY GOOD AT HOUSE WORK.
AT WAS GOOD.
GULP
MY MOUTH FEELS ALL ROUGH.
MUST BE NICE SINCE YOU DON'T HAVE TO WORRY ABOUT BEING ON TIME FOR WORK.
Yawn
THATZ WHY WRITE.
'AVEA NAHHICE DAA (HAVE A NICE DAY).
SIS, HAVE A NICE DAY.

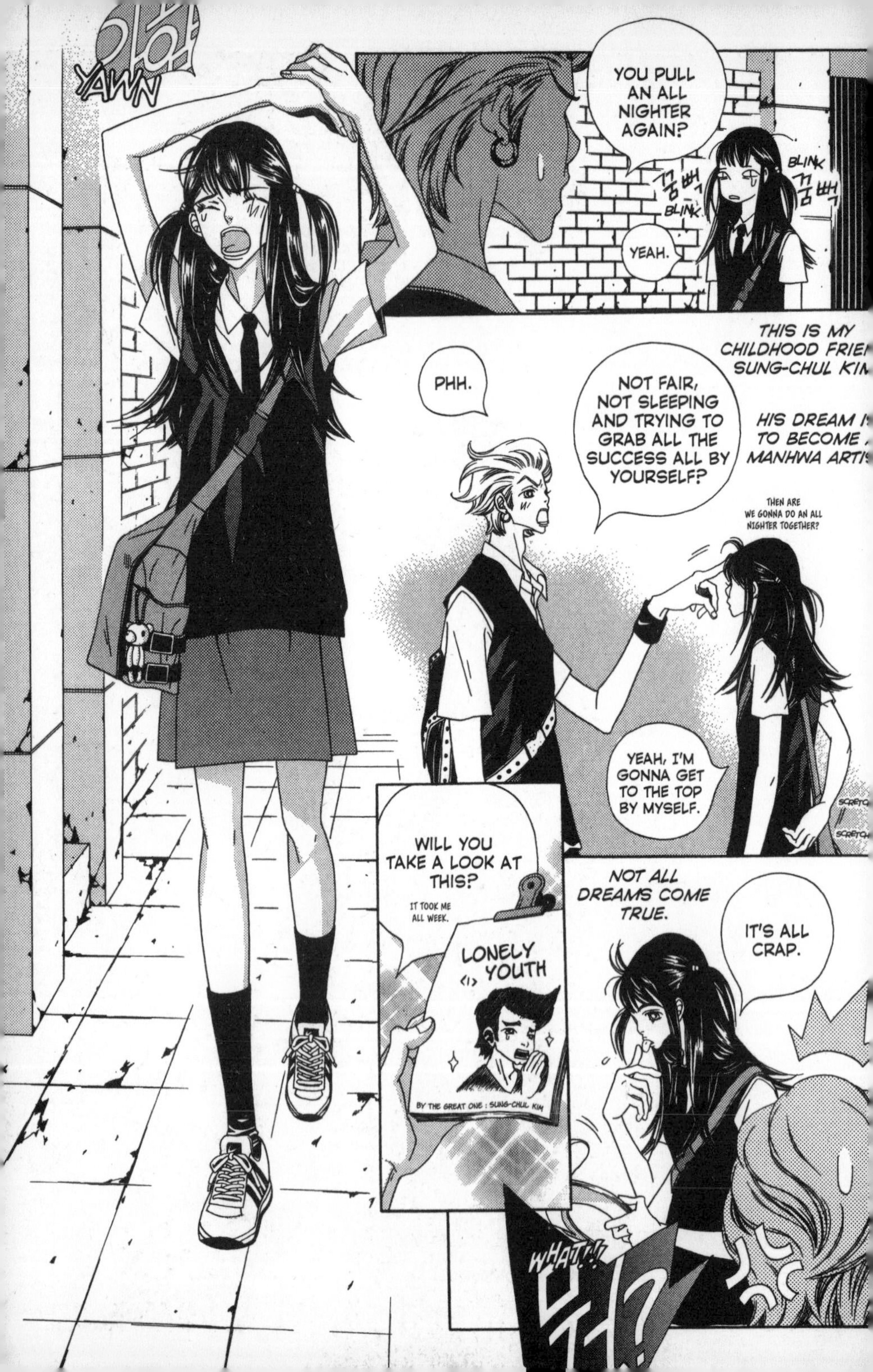

YAWN
YOU PULL AN ALL NIGHTER AGAIN?
BLINK
BLINK
YEAH.
THIS IS MY CHILDHOOD FRIE
SUNG-CHUL KIM
PHH.
NOT FAIR, NOT SLEEPING AND TRYING TO GRAB ALL THE SUCCESS ALL BY YOURSELF?
HIS DREAM I
TO BECOME
MANHWA ARTI
THEN ARE WE GONNA DO AN ALL NIGHTER TOGETHER?
YEAH, I'M GONNA GET TO THE TOP BY MYSELF.
SCRETCH
SCRETCH
WILL YOU TAKE A LOOK AT THIS?
IT TOOK ME ALL WEEK.
LONELY YOUTH
‹1›
BY THE GREAT ONE : SUNG-CHUL KIM
NOT ALL DREAMS COME TRUE.
IT'S ALL CRAP.
WHAT!?

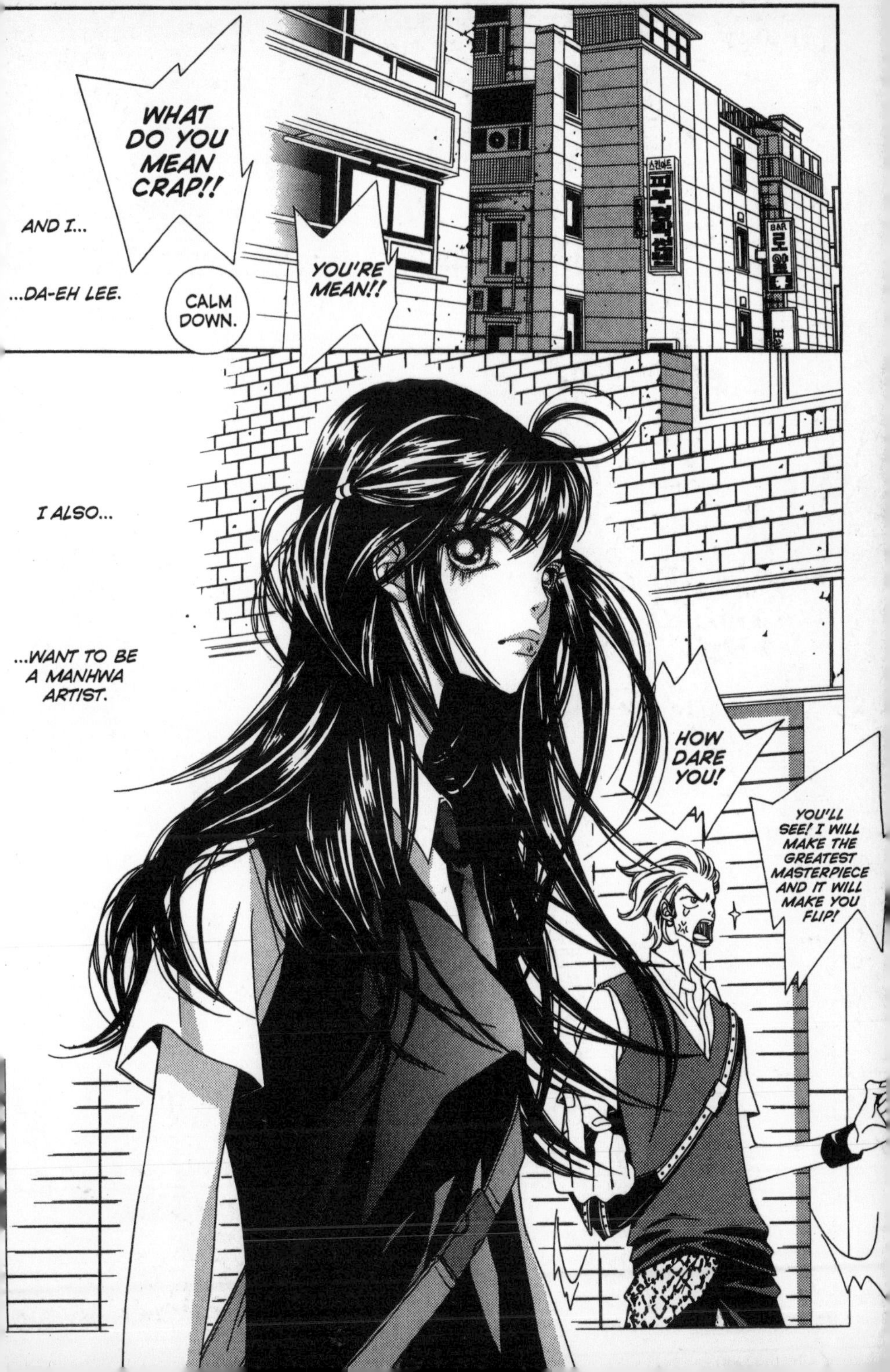
WHAT DO YOU MEAN CRAP!!
AND I...
...DA-EH LEE.
CALM DOWN.
YOU'RE MEAN!!
I ALSO...
...WANT TO BE A MANHWA ARTIST.
HOW DARE YOU!
YOU'LL SEE! I WILL MAKE THE GREATEST MASTERPIECE AND IT WILL MAKE YOU FLIP!

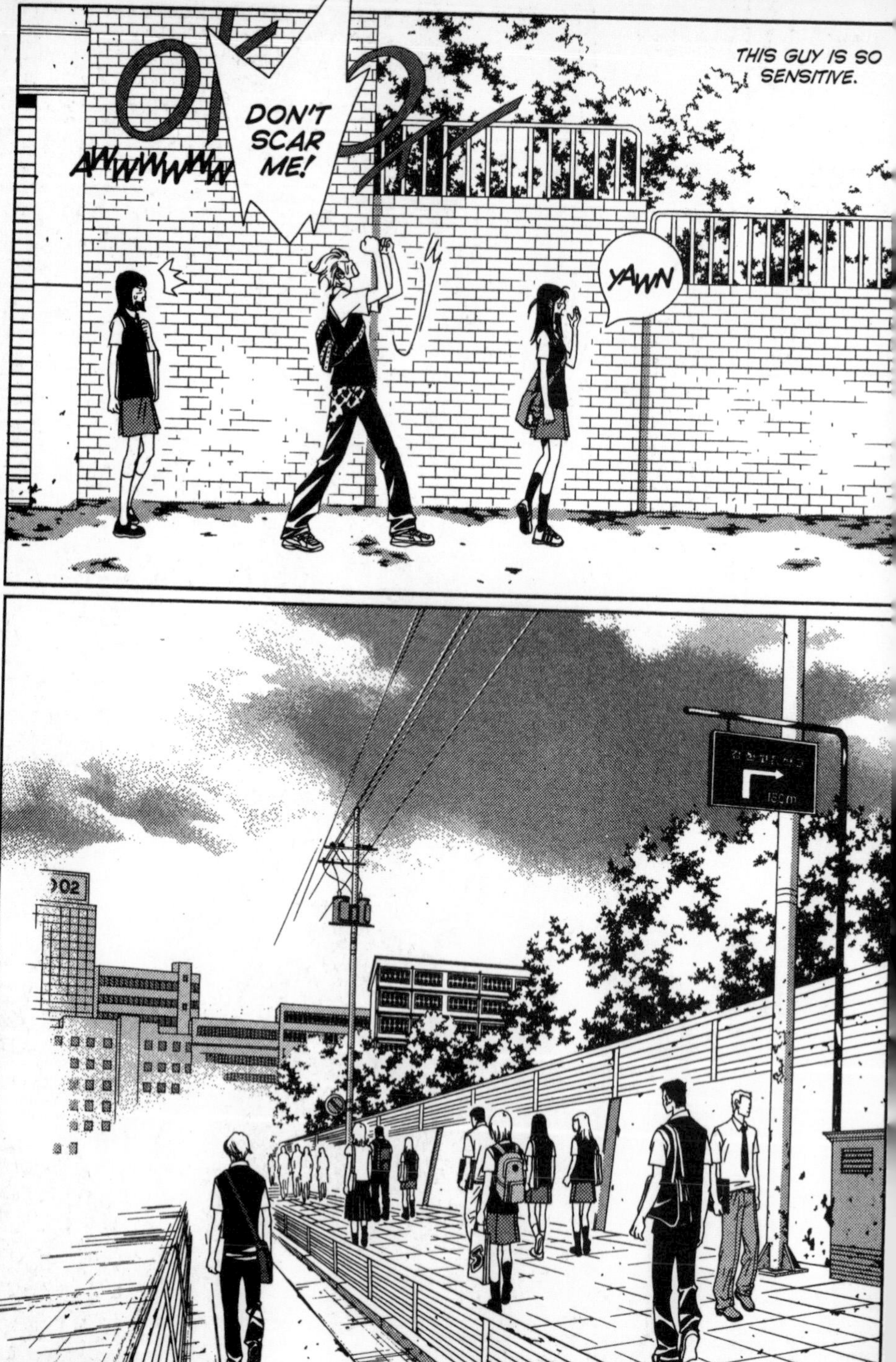
AWWWWWWW
DON'T SCAR ME!
YAWN
THIS GUY IS SO SENSITIVE.

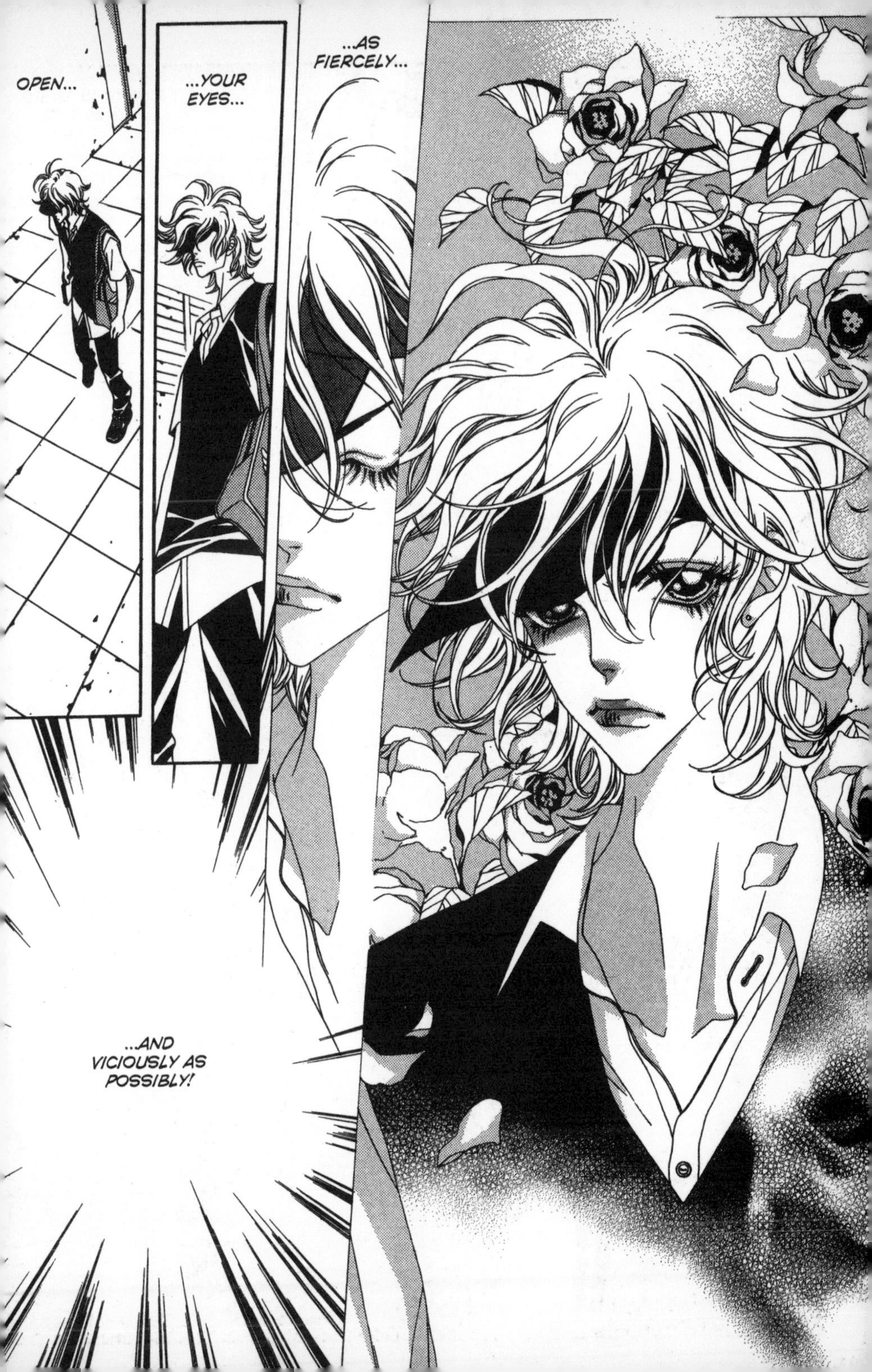
OPEN...
...YOUR EYES...
...AS FIERCELY...
...AND VICIOUSLY AS POSSIBLY!

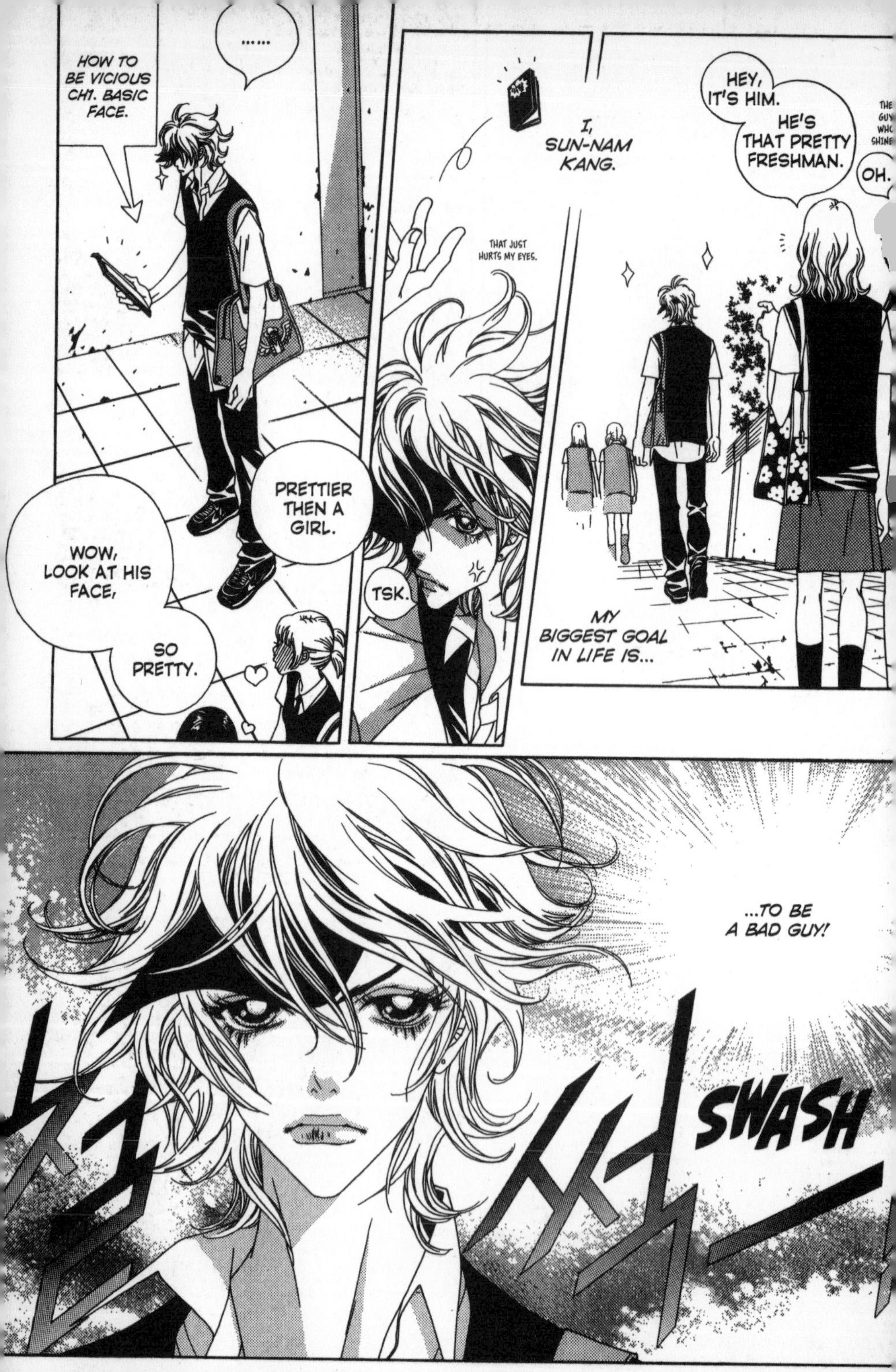
......
HOW TO BE VICIOUS CHI. BASIC FACE.
PRETTIER THEN A GIRL.
WOW, LOOK AT HIS FACE,
SO PRETTY.
THAT JUST HURTS MY EYES.
TSK.
I, SUN-NAM KANG.
HEY, IT'S HIM.
HE'S THAT PRETTY FRESHMAN.
OH.
MY BIGGEST GOAL IN LIFE IS...
...TO BE A BAD GUY!
SWASH

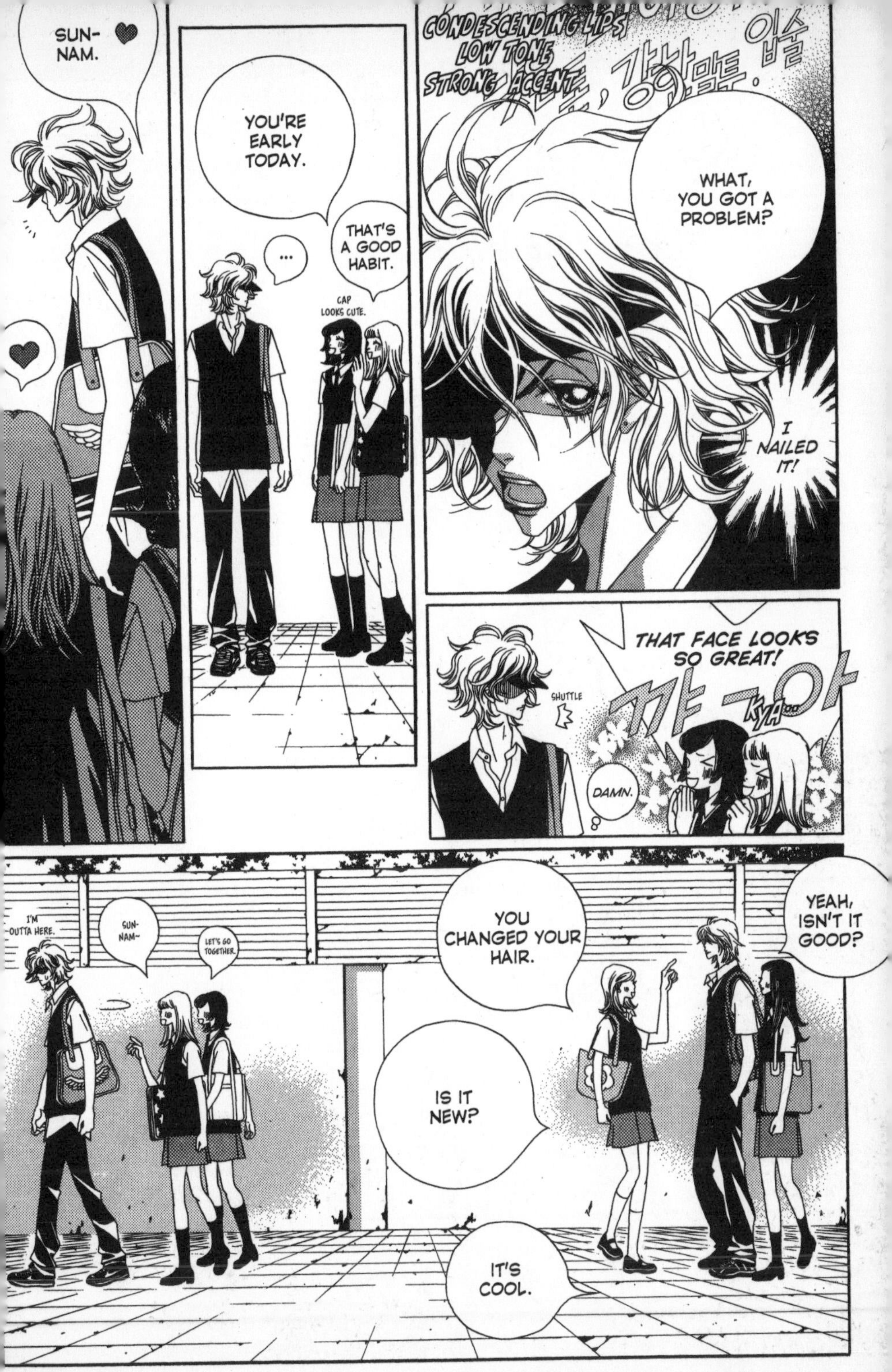

SUN-NAM. ♥
♥
YOU'RE EARLY TODAY.
...
THAT'S A GOOD HABIT.
CAP LOOKS CUTE.
CONDESCENDING LIPS
LOW TONE
STRONG ACCENT
WHAT, YOU GOT A PROBLEM?
I NAILED IT!
THAT FACE LOOKS SO GREAT!
SHUTTLE
KYA~
DAMN.
I'M OUTTA HERE.
SUN-NAM~
LET'S GO TOGETHER.
YOU CHANGED YOUR HAIR.
YEAH, ISN'T IT GOOD?
IS IT NEW?
IT'S COOL.

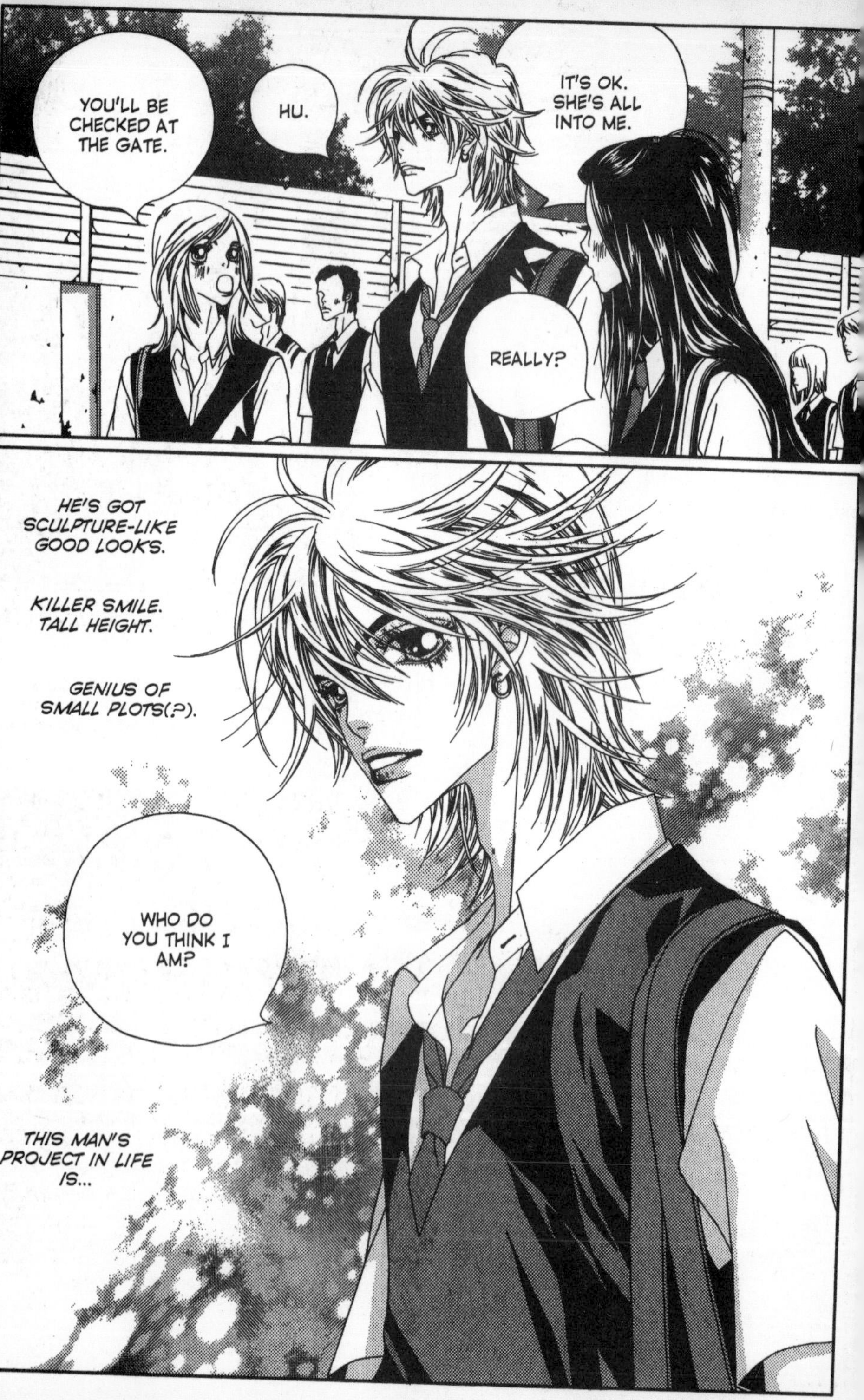
YOU'LL BE CHECKED AT THE GATE.
HU.
IT'S OK. SHE'S ALL INTO ME.
REALLY?
HE'S GOT SCULPTURE-LIKE GOOD LOOKS.
KILLER SMILE. TALL HEIGHT.
GENIUS OF SMALL PLOTS(?).
WHO DO YOU THINK I AM?
THIS MAN'S PROJECT IN LIFE IS...

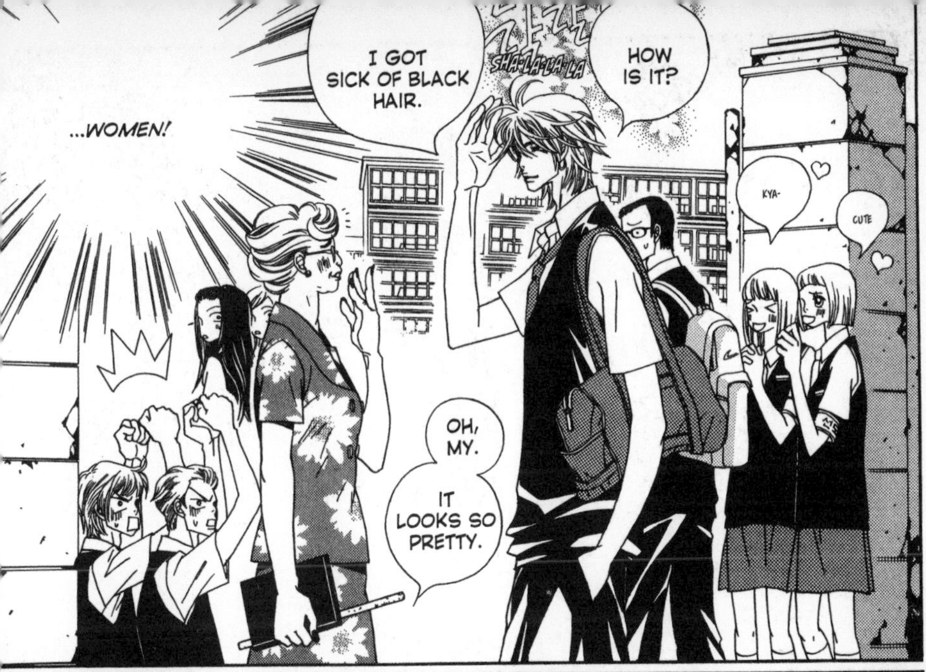
...WOMEN!
I GOT SICK OF BLACK HAIR.
SHA-LA-LA-LA
HOW IS IT?
KYA-
CUTE
OH, MY.
IT LOOKS SO PRETTY.

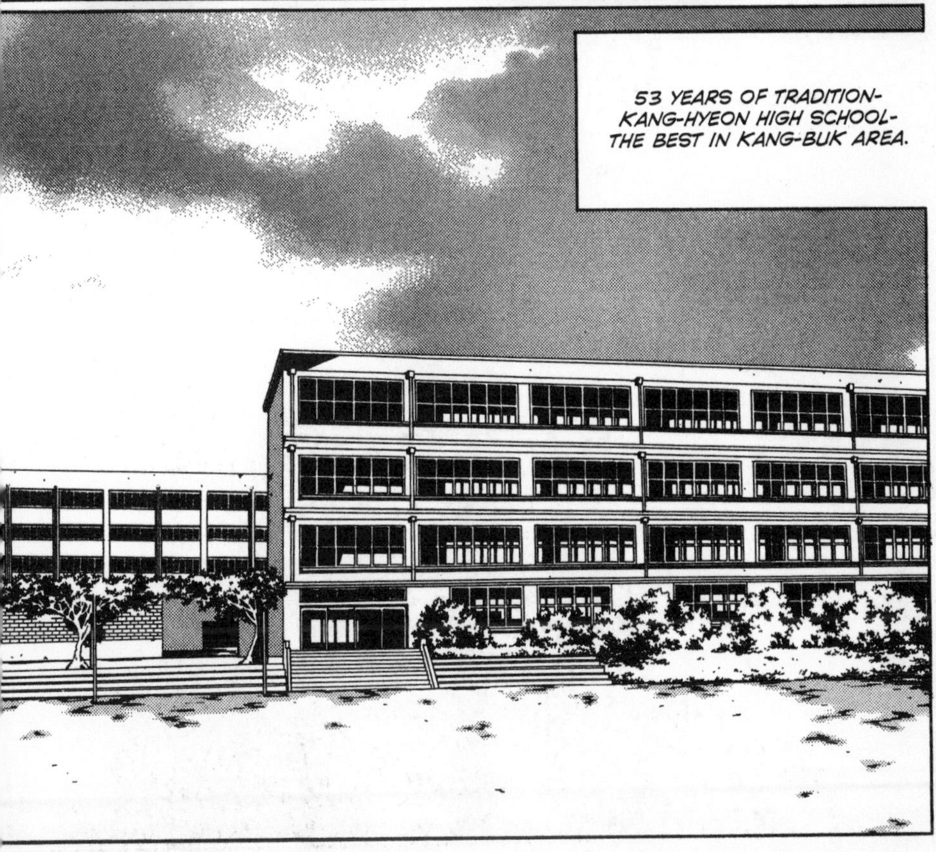
53 YEARS OF TRADITION-
KANG-HYEON HIGH SCHOOL-
THE BEST IN KANG-BUK AREA.

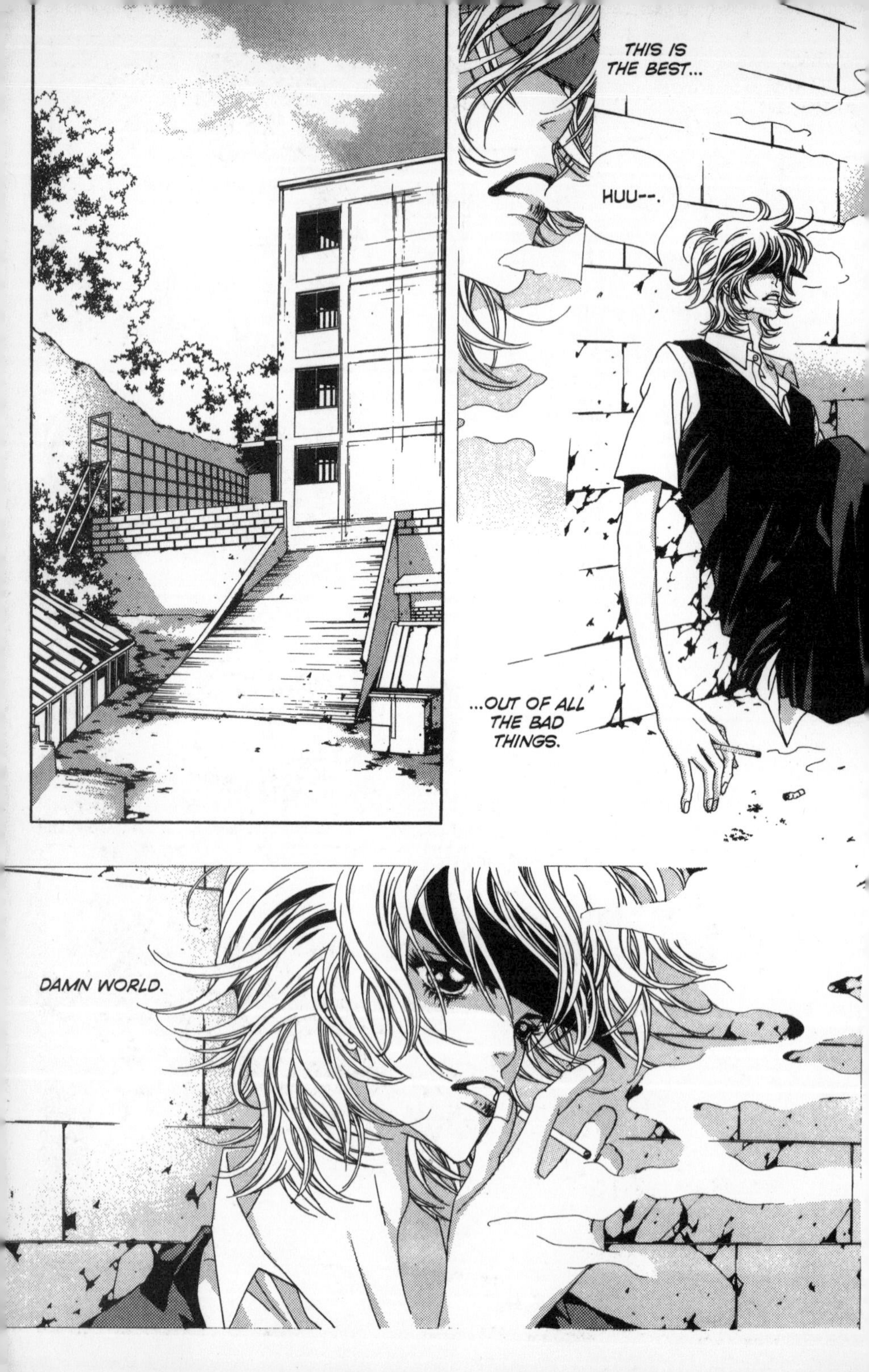
THIS IS THE BEST...
HUU--.
...OUT OF ALL THE BAD THINGS.
DAMN WORLD.

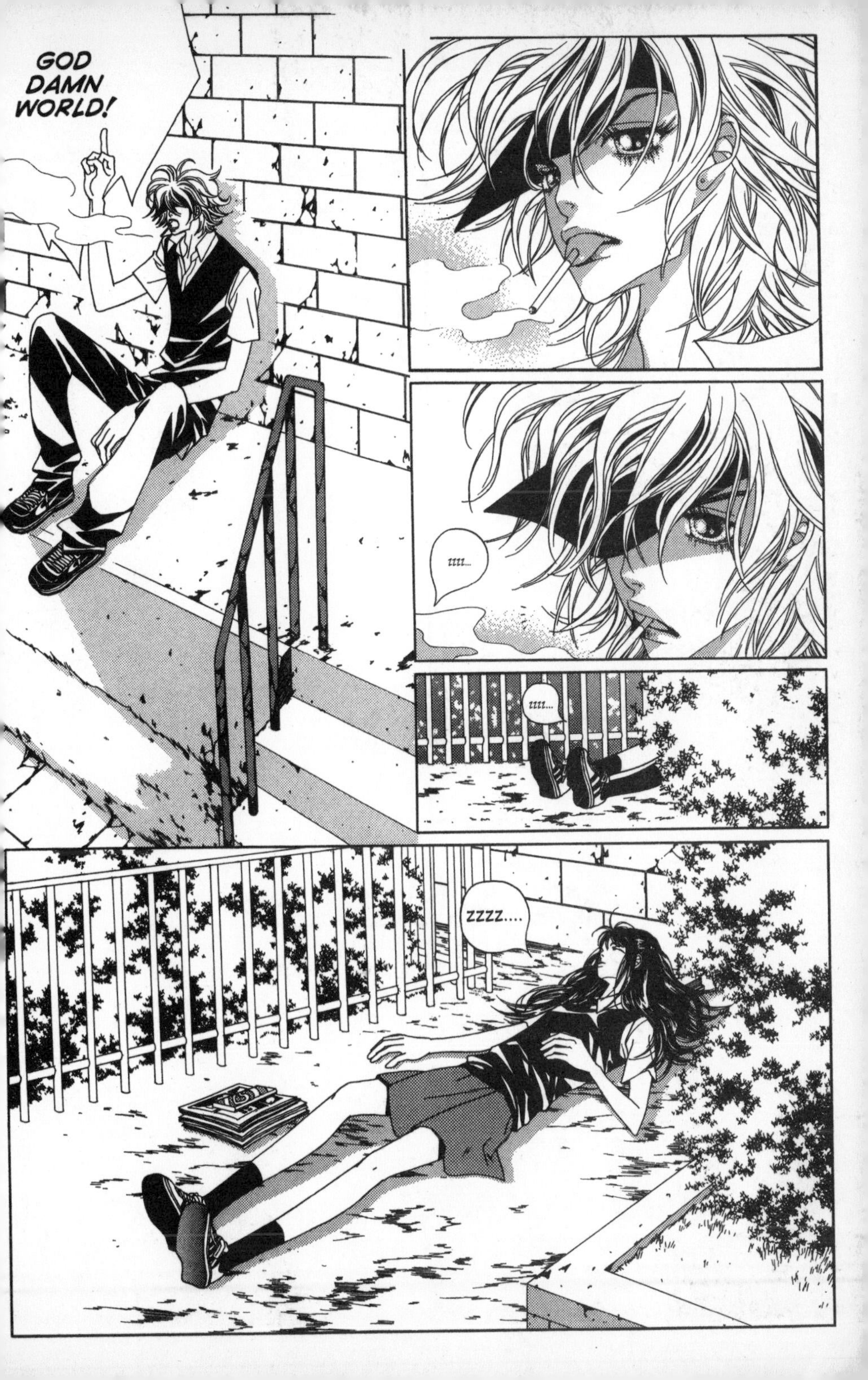
GOD DAMN WORLD!
zzzz...
zzzz...
ZZZZ....

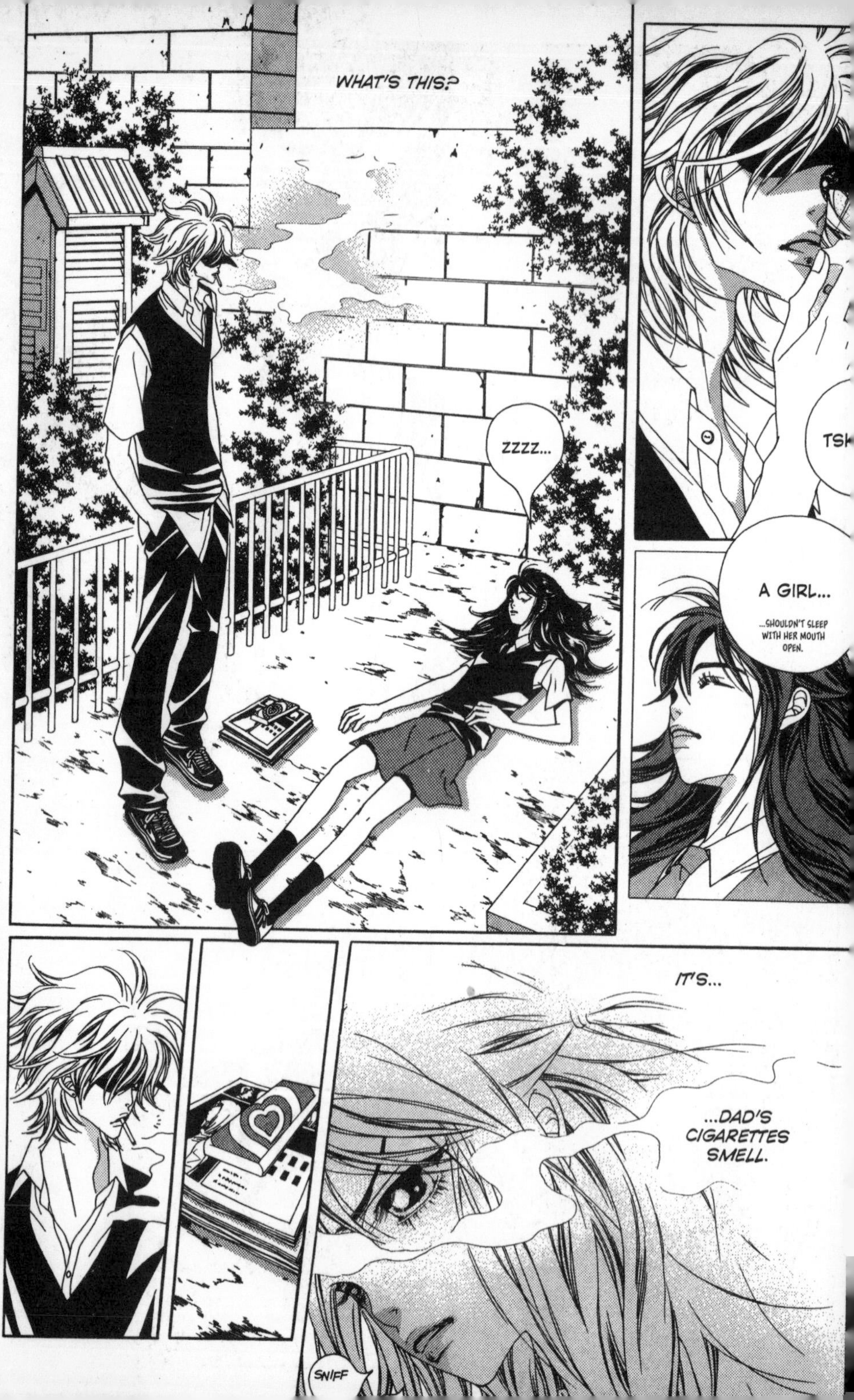
WHAT'S THIS?
ZZZZ...
TSK
A GIRL...
...SHOULDN'T SLEEP WITH HER MOUTH OPEN.
IT'S...
...DAD'S CIGARETTES SMELL.
SNIFF

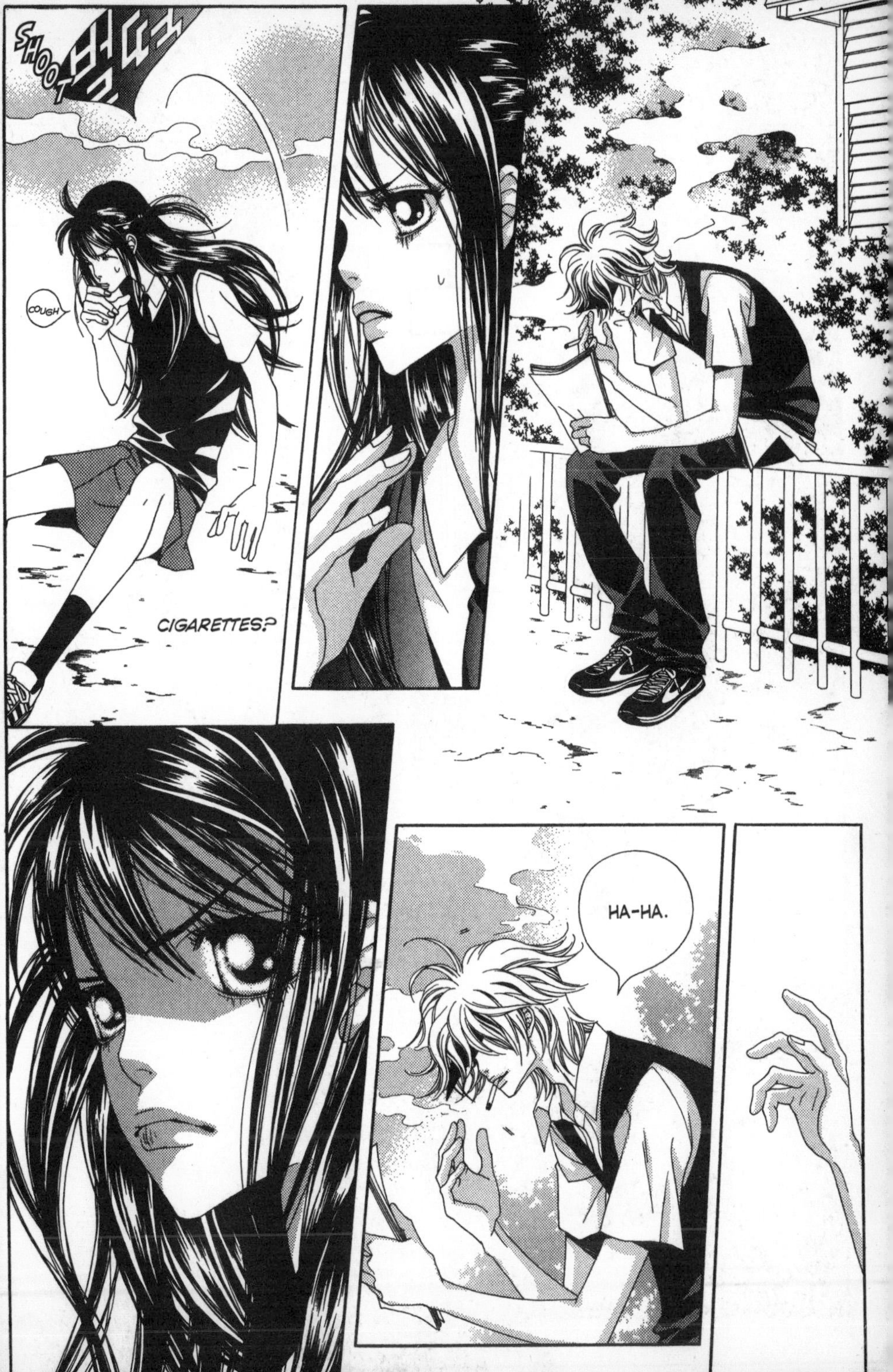
SHOOT
COUGH
CIGARETTES?
HA-HA.

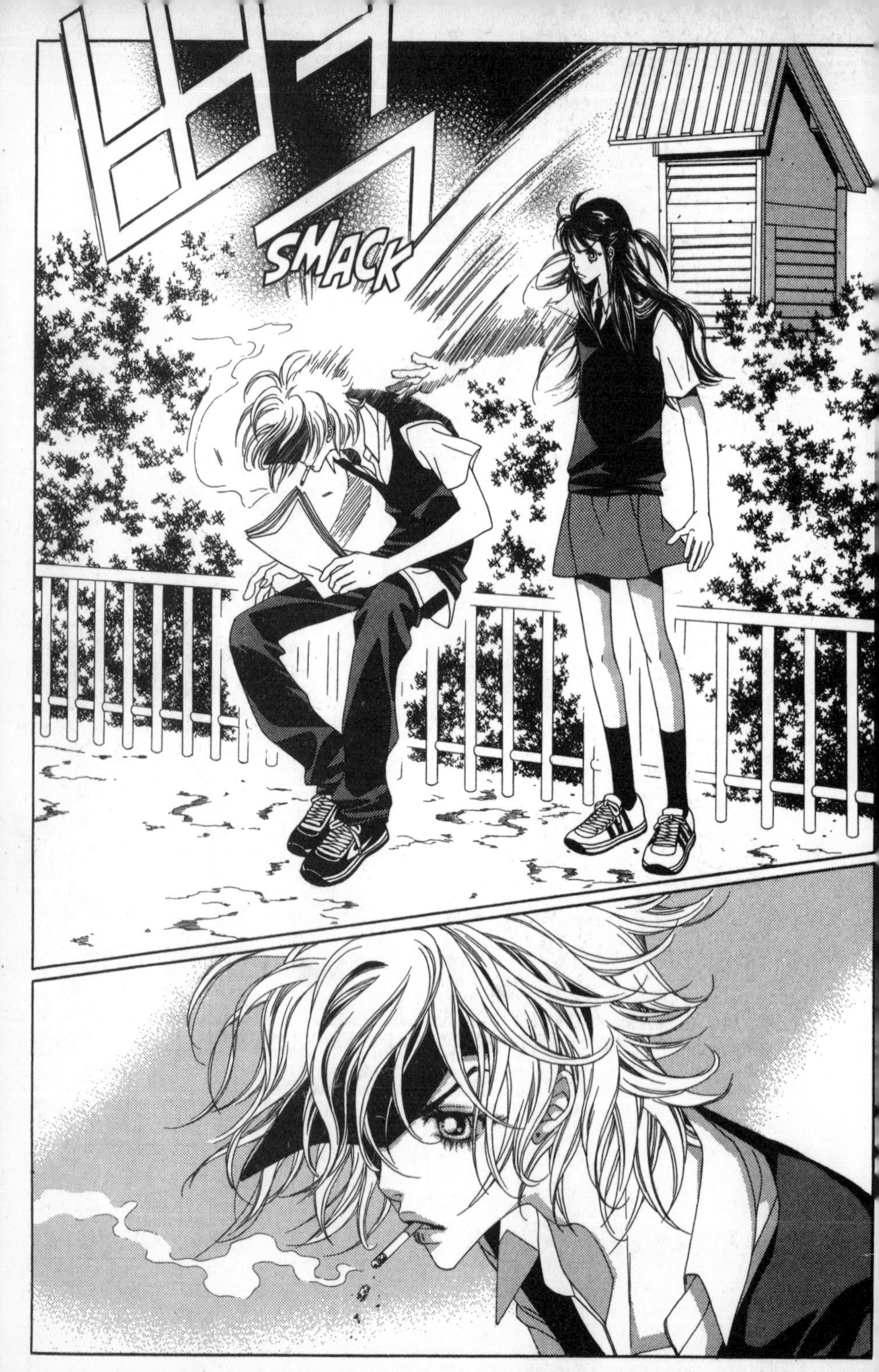
SMACK

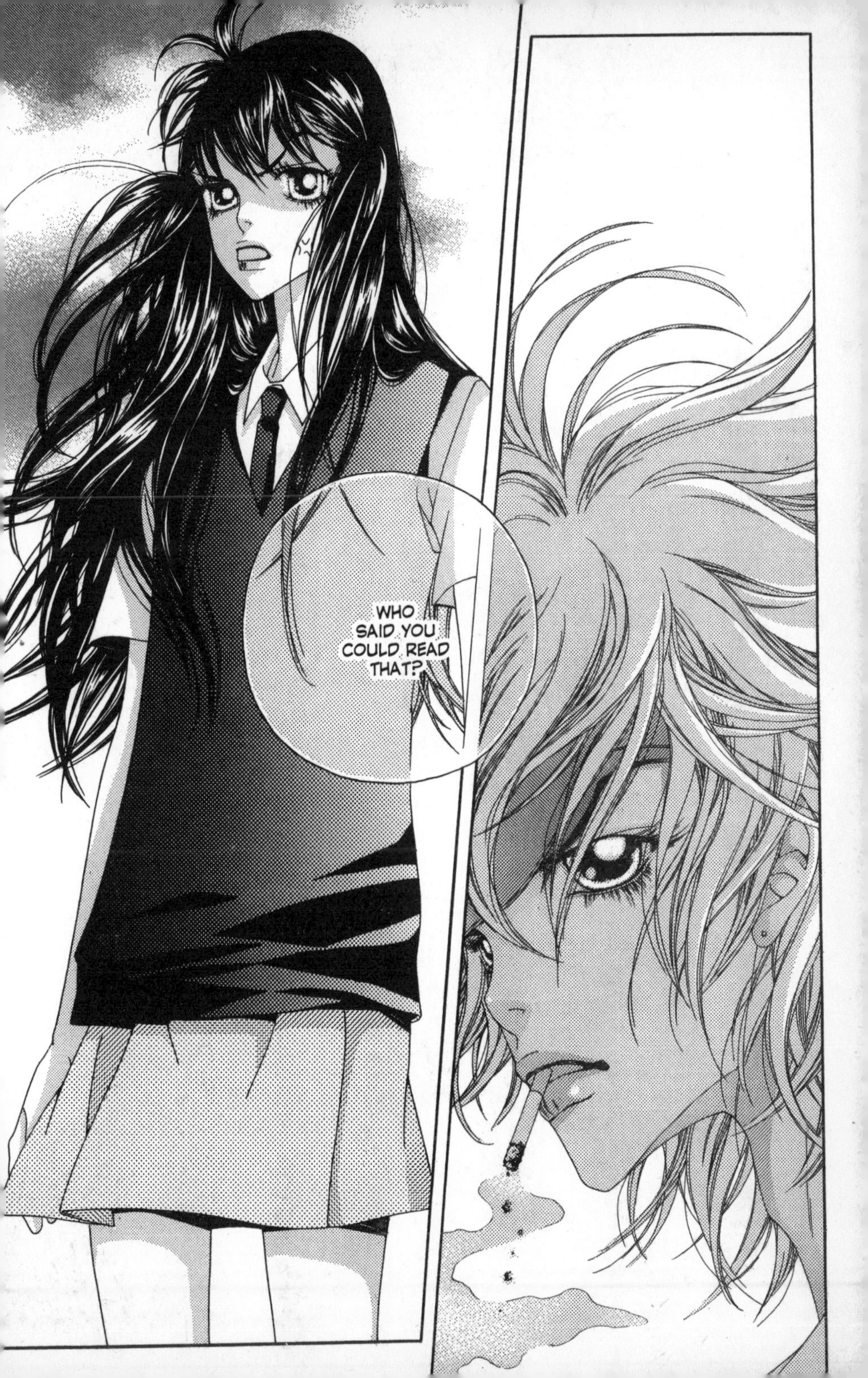
WHO SAID YOU COULD READ THAT?

Danbi Original

Angel Diary vol.3

Story by YunHee Lee
Art by KARA

Translation HyeYoung Im
English Adaptation J. Torres
Touch-up and Lettering Terri Delgado · Marshall Dillon
Graphic Design EunKyung Kim

ICE Kunion

English Adaptation Editor HyeYoung Im · J. Torres
Managing Editor Marshall Dillon
Marketing Manager Erik Ko
Senior Editor JuYoun Lee
Editorial Director MoonJung Kim
Managing Director Jackie Lee
Publisher and C.E.O. JaeKook Chun

Angel Diary © 2005 Kara · YunHee Lee
First published in Korea in 2003 by SIGONGSA Co., Ltd.
English text translation rights arranged by SIGONGSA Co., Ltd.
English text © 2005 ICE KUNION

Published by ICE Kunion.
SIGONGSA 2F Yeil Bldg. 1619-4, Seocho-dong, Seocho-gu, Seoul, 137-878, Korea

ISBN : 89-527-4482-9

First printing, June 2006
Second printing, August 2006
10 9 8 7 6 5 4 3 2 1
Printed in Canada